AFONSO I MVEMBA A NZINGA

King of Kongo

His Life and Correspondence

AFONSO I MVEMBA A NZINGA

King of Kongo

His Life and Correspondence

John K. Thornton

Translations by Luís Madureira

Hackett Publishing Company, Inc.

Indianapolis/Cambridge

Printed in the United States of America

26 25 24 23 1 2 3 4 5 6 7

For further information, please address
Hackett Publishing Company, Inc.
P.O. Box 44937
Indianapolis, Indiana 46244-0937

www.hackettpublishing.com

Cover design by E. L. Wilson
Interior design by Elana Rosenthal
Composition by Aptara, Inc.

Library of Congress Control Number: 2023936539

ISBN-13: 978-1-64792-139-2 (pbk.)
ISBN-13: 978-1-64792-141-5 (PDF ebook)

The paper used in this publication meets the minimum requirements of American National Standard for Information Sciences—Permanence of Paper for Printed Library Materials, ANSI Z39.48–1984.

∞

CONTENTS

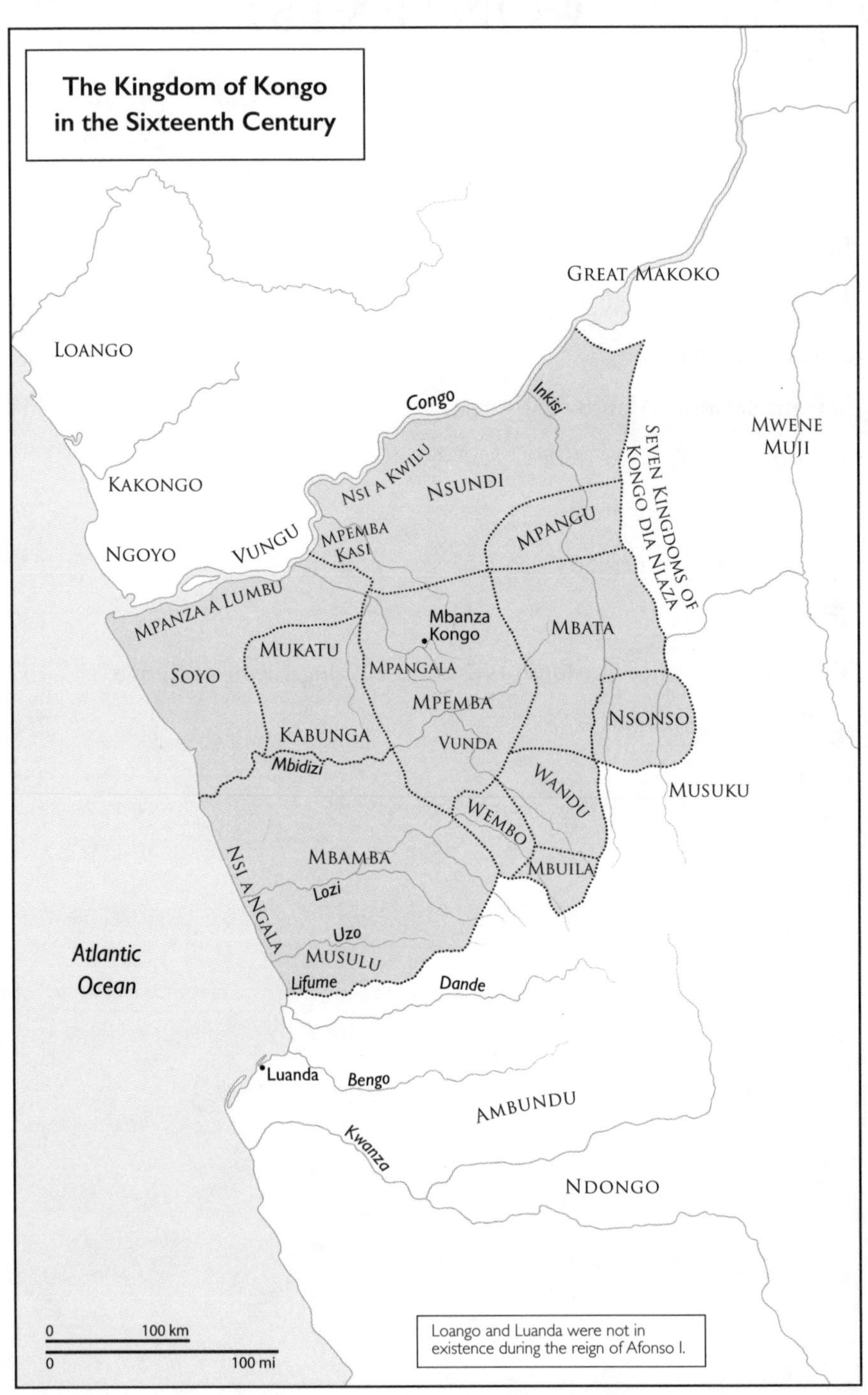
The Kingdom of Kongo in the Sixteenth Century
Great Makoko
Loango
Congo
Inkisi
Mwene Muji
Seven Kingdoms of Kongo dia Nlaza
Kakongo
Nsi a Kwilu
Nsundi
Ngoyo
Vungu
Mpemba Kasi
Mpangu
Mpanza a Lumbu
Mbanza Kongo
Mbata
Mukatu
Soyo
Mpangala
Mpemba
Nsonso
Kabunga
Vunda
Mbidizi
Wandu
Musuku
Wembo
Nsi a Ngala
Mbamba
Mbuila
Lozi
Uzo
Atlantic Ocean
Musulu
Lifume
Dande
Luanda
Bengo
Ambundu
Kwanza
Ndongo
0 100 km
0 100 mi
Loango and Luanda were not in existence during the reign of Afonso I.

INTRODUCTION

Afonso I Mvemba a Nzinga was the ruler of the Kingdom of Kongo—in today's northern Angola and the westernmost provinces of the Democratic Republic of Congo—from 1506 until 1542. The Kingdom of Kongo was one of the largest kingdoms in African history and the largest in sub-equatorial Africa until the Lunda empire developed in the later 1700s. In Afonso's day, it covered as much as 100,000 square kilometers and had more than 500,000 people.[1]

For most of the world outside Portugal and Kongo, King Afonso was best known as the "Apostle of Kongo," who converted his country to Christianity. His most famous single deed was the defeat of his pagan half-brother with the assistance of heavenly horsemen and the Virgin Mary. The account of this victory, first described by the Spanish geographer Martín Fernández de Enciso in 1519, was made more famous in João de Barros's historical accounts of Portuguese navigations in 1552, and even more so by Filippo Pigafetta's retelling of de Barros's story in 1591. Pigafetta's book, a perpetual bestseller, was frequently republished in its original Italian and eventually translated into all the major languages of Europe. His telling of the story appeared, in digested form, in many later works and the numerous collections of travel accounts published in the eighteenth century in Italy, England, and France.[2]

Stories about the Kingdom of Kongo were frequently included in seventeenth-century accounts of the Capuchin order's missionary work and thus popular for those with interests in religion—the Kingdom of Kongo became the subject of many books in the seventeenth century, just as Kongo reached the pinnacle of its success. Of these Capuchin-authored books, the most informative was probably Giovanni Antonio Cavazzi da Montecuccolo's, published in Italian in Bologna in

1. For estimates of the country's size and population in the early 1600s, see John Thornton, "Revising the Population History of the Kingdom of Kongo," *Journal of African History* 62 (2021): 1–12. This uses data from a larger kingdom and later population; my statements for Afonso's time are an educated guess of minimum population size and territorial extent.

2. On Pigafetta's legacy, see the French translation edited by Michele Chandaigne, *Le royaume de Congo & les contrées environnantes (1591)* (Paris: Chandeigne, 2002) pp. 7–22.

1687 and later translated into French and German.[3] The accounts of Cavazzi and other Capuchin writers became the source material for later works, such as the eighteenth-century collections.

While tales of Kongo's history were told and retold by travelers, only the story of Afonso's miracle had a lasting impact on Western lore. The account even made its way into a play based on Giovanni Pietro Maffei's 1585 Latin history of Portuguese voyages, performed at the Jesuit college in Landsburg, Bavaria, in 1670, the highlight of which was Afonso's victory.[4] However, the miracle story was Afonso's only real legacy. Although repeated frequently, stories of Kongolese history had less long-term impact and were far more concerned with the seventeenth-century reality than Kongo's distant history. Thus, Afonso and his miracle passed into Western lore, at least among the moderately well-educated.

However, the Western world's understanding of Afonso was dramatically revised when Afonso's extensive correspondence with the kings of Portugal and the papacy was revealed at the end of the nineteenth century. His letters were "discovered" in a rather unexpected way. Beginning in the 1840s, the British began suppressing the slave trade south of the Equator, particularly the brisk trade that Spanish, United States–based, and Brazilian slavers conducted along the coast of Kongo, from its southern border along the Lifune River up to the mouth of the Congo River. Britain pressed the Portuguese government to quell the slave trade but doing so would have been ruinous to Portugal's business interests in Angola, which were based almost entirely on revenues from the slave trade. Signing treaties with independent African rulers to abolish the slave trade was a common British tactic, one that often became the first step toward establishing colonial domination.[5]

Thus the Portuguese government needed to establish it was the sovereign ruler of the Kingdom of Kongo and therefore entitled to take charge of the slave trade question within its borders. In 1844, Joaquim Lopes de Lima published an extensive survey of the Portuguese empire, and in discussing the history of Angola, he

3. Giovanni Antonio Cavazzi da Montecuccolo, *Istorica descrizione de' tre regni Congo, Matamba ed Angola* (Bologna, 1678); for the further history of this text see the introduction by Graziano Saccardo da Leguzzano to the Portuguese translation *Descricão histórica dos três reinos Congo, Matamba e Angola*, 2 vols. (Lisbon: Agência Geral do Ultramar, 1965), 1:xi–xxiii.

4. *Alphonsus Rex Congi in Aethiopia di Mundo victor* (Augsburg, 1670) in Latin and German. The anonymous author's source was Giovanni Pietro Maffei, *Historiarum Indicarum libri XVI. Selectarum item ex India epistolarum libri IV* (Florence, 1585). The story, as revealed in the three pages of the libretto, is sufficiently divergent from any account that making a judgment on content is impossible.

5. João Pedro Marques, "A ocupação do Ambriz (1855): Geografia e diplomacia de uma derrota inglesa," *Africana Studia* 9 (2006): 145–58.

quoted, for the first time in print, from Afonso's unpublished correspondence held in the Portuguese archives. Lopes de Lima wished to establish that Portugal had "feudal" rights over the Kingdom of Kongo and quoted Afonso's letter of March 4, 1516, in which Álvaro Lopes's contentious relationship with other Portuguese was read to make it appear that Lopes was a sort of colonial administrator of a colonized country. Lopes de Lima developed this point more fully the following year in a pamphlet describing the "discovery and possession" of the Kingdom of Kongo.[6]

The end of the slave trade ultimately passed without Portugal relinquishing its claim to Kongo. Yet Portugal's claims to the country would be challenged again in the 1870s, at the start of the so-called European "Scramble for Africa," when controlling the mouth of the Congo River became a critical diplomatic concern. Levy Jordão de Paiva Manso, a lawyer with an interest in colonial questions, began working on a collection of documents related to Portugal's rights to Kongo. Having already completed extensive historical work to bolster, against outside challenges, Portuguese claims in Lourenço Marques (today's Maputo) in the Zambezi region, Paiva Manso brought his considerable historical skills to bear on the Kongo question.

Though he died before his work was finished, Paiva Manso's collection was published posthumously, without any introduction, in 1877 as "The History of Congo: Documents."[7] A large sample of Afonso's letters culled directly from the archives and carefully transcribed, formed a key part of the collection. This sample included the letters that have most interested scholars: Afonso's long letter of October 5, 1514 and his three letters from 1526 concerning the slave trade. This sample collection of Afonso's correspondence was augmented in 1892 when the Portuguese Academy, inspired by the country's wish to assert itself on the 400th anniversary of Columbus's voyages, worked to publish documents illustrating its role in the history of global exploration.[8]

Though originally published as Portuguese propaganda, early twentieth-century historians began to make real use of this corpus of letters. In his short 1901 history of Kongo, E. G. Ravenstein, an English geographer, drew on Afonso's letters to reconstruct Kongo's history beyond the miracle story, including Kongo's relations with Portugal and the slave trade.[9] Other serious work based on Afonso's letters

---

6. José Joaquim Lopes de Lima, *Ensayos sobre a statistica das possessões portuguezas . . .* , Book 3 (Lisbon, 1844), pp. 2–4; *idem*, *Descobrimento e posse do Reino do Congo* (Lisbon, 1845).

7. Levy Jordão de Paiva Manso, *História do Congo (Documentos)* (Lisbon, 1877).

8. *Alguns documentos do Arquivo Nacional da Torre do Tombo acerca das navigações e conquistas dos portugueses* (Lisbon, 1892).

9. E. G. Ravenstein, ed., *The Strange Adventures of Andrew Battel of Leigh in Angola and the Adjoining Regions* (London, 1901), pp. 102–16.

included Joseph Van Wing's anthropological study of 1920, which focused on missionary work, as well as Eugen Weber's study of the Portuguese missionaries in Africa in 1924. Weber's work added to the general knowledge of Afonso's specific role in promoting Christianity.[10] Perhaps the most important of these works was the historical-anthropological study of Kongo written by Alexander Ihle in 1929, although Ihle, like the other European historians, used Afonso's letters only to illustrate the spread of Christianity in Africa.[11]

Portuguese historians made more extensive use of the correspondence. In his 1933 history of Portuguese activity in Angola, which was based on a close reading of the letters (including a few new ones he'd discovered in the archive), Alfredo de Albuquerque Felner devoted considerable attention to Afonso.[12] Like the Portuguese historians before him, Felner used the letters to demonstrate that Portugal had conquered Kongo with Afonso's help and had both spread the Christian faith and organized the country.[13] Felner contended that the Portuguese could be thanked for most of Kongo's organization. In his 1948 history of Angola, Ralph Delgado, a Portuguese historian living in that country, traced Afonso's role further, painting a picture of a sort of tutelary relationship between Afonso and Manuel Pacheco; Delgado's account of this relationship was largely based on the statements Pacheco made in his letter of March 28, 1536.[14]

While Portuguese historians were using Afonso to support their framing of Portuguese colonialism in Angola—that is, that the relationship between the countries was a cooperative venture between an enlightened colonizer and eager subjects—the Belgian missionary Jean Cuvelier focused on Afonso as the great evangelizer of his people. Cuvelier was simultaneously deeply enmeshed in Kongolese culture (he spoke the Kongolese language, Kikongo, fluently and wrote in it) and committed to the idea that knowledge of their Christian past would serve future proselytizing efforts in the Belgian Congo. To this end, he published oral traditions in Kikongo and studied traditional Kongolese life and history. Cuvelier published his first history of Kongo in Kikongo in the missionary journal *Kukieke*

10. Eugen Weber, *Die Portugieische Reichsmission im Königreich Kongo* (Aachen, 1924).

11. Alexander Ihle, *Das Alte Königreich Kongo* (Leipzig, 1929).

12. Alfredo de Albuquerque Felner, *Angola; apontamentos sôbre a ocupacão e início do estabelecimento dos portugueses no Congo, Angola e Benguela* (Lisbon, 1933).

13. For a review of what less serious Portuguese colonial historians made of Afonso in promoting the colonial story for schools and the popular audience, see Bruno Maximo, "O Mbanza Kongo/São Salvador do Congo e o reino do Kongo na historiografia colonial portuguesa no século XX," *África[s]* (Salvador, Bahia) 7 (2020): 88–108.

14. Ralph Delgado, *História de Angola*, 4 vols. (Lobito [Angola], 1948).

in 1929–1931, linking events gleaned from documents to oral traditions. His style was free and elevated, deploying proverbs and praise names while adding a more traditional feel to the events.

Cuvelier also collected hundreds of documents from all the archives in Europe, editing and translating them into French. His book, *L'ancien royaume du Congo*, was initially published in 1944 in Dutch, the language favored by the German forces then occupying Belgium. In 1946, following the end of the Second World War, a French edition was published that reached a larger audience.[15] *L'ancien royaume* was essentially a biography of Afonso, the only one published at book length, and made full use of the documents then assembled on the king. Cuvelier was inclined to view Kongo's social structure, governance, and society as being static—aside from the introduction of Christianity—and so did not hesitate to use seventeenth- and even eighteenth-century documentation to illustrate and elaborate events during Afonso's life. *L'ancien royaume* made Cuvelier one of the premier interpreters of Kongo's culture and history and influenced subsequent generations of historians.

In the 1950s, the study of Afonso and his letters took another sharp turn. After studying Afonso's letters, a professional historian, James Duffy, considered Afonso not a triumphant promoter of the faith, as priests like Cuvelier had, nor a trusty neophyte led by the enlightened Portuguese colonizer. Instead, Duffy believed Afonso to be the victim of Portuguese brutality and the slave trade.[16] As the countries of Africa moved toward independence, fewer and fewer historians were prepared to accept the edifying ideas of the missionaries, let alone the colonial pact that Portugal was intent on maintaining even as other European countries were pulling out of their former colonies.

Adventurer, journalist, and activist Basil Davidson was probably the most successful writer promulgating this new vision of Afonso. In his careful reading of the correspondence, Davidson saw Afonso as a tragic figure, caught between his own idealism and Portuguese materialism. Davidson published English translations of excerpts from Afonso's 1526 letters, presenting them as examples of the king's struggle against the slave trade.[17] Davidson's work had a significant impact on public conceptions of Afonso. His approach to Afonso's reign became the principal narrative taught in schools, especially in the United States, with lesson plans built around Davidson's conception of Afonso and his relationship with the Portuguese.

15. Jean Cuvelier, *L'ancien royaume du Congo* (Bruges, 1946).

16. James Duffy, *Portuguese Africa* (Cambridge, MA: Harvard University Press, 1959), pp. 6–23.

17. Basil Davidson, *Black Mother* (London: Little, Brown and Company, 1961), pp. 116–50.

Professional historians had significant problems with Davidson's manipulation of the data on which he built his case. Particularly troublesome was Davidson's assertion that Afonso's passionate letters about the slave trade in 1526 foreshadowed the imminent collapse of Kongo, when it was clear that what might be regarded as Kongo's most glorious period actually lay in the late sixteenth century and the first two-thirds of the seventeenth century. Despite these hesitations on the part of professional historians, the story of Afonso's contentious relationship with Portugal and the slave trade based on Afonso's letters remains in popular circulation, the press, podcasts, educational supplements, and school curricula.

Literacy in Kongo

Only a small part of the written account scholars have of the history of the Atlantic coast of Africa was actually written by Africans. Africans living in the Islamic parts of the zone, Senegal, Gambia, and Mali, were literate; they wrote texts and kept documents. The libraries of Timbuktu contain material from as far back as the fifteenth century, and the historical chronicles generated in those regions cover the history of the Niger Bend region from the sixteenth century onward. Closer to the coast, in Senegal or Gambia, older written material is less common and less helpful for reconstruction history.

Outside of that area, most African countries were not literate and did not become literate until the late nineteenth century and even into the colonial period, when literacy was introduced. Given that some African leaders did write letters—such as some of the rulers in the Guinea region, the kings of Benin, rulers of Asante, and especially the kings of Dahomey—it is surprising that literacy there did not extend to the rest of society or generate archives. An early sixteenth-century king of Benin was educated as a child in São Tomé and was fully literate, yet as far as we know, he did not employ that literacy in government.

Because of this, an African perspective on its history has had to rely on oral traditions and the study of archaeology, material culture, and linguistics. For the immediacy of written texts, we must rely largely on European observations and perspectives. The Kingdom of Kongo, as we can see, is a notable exception to this trend. The members of the earliest embassy from Kongo to Europe in 1486 learned to read and write in Portuguese. Consequently, João I Nzinga a Nkuwu, the first Christian king of Kongo, had one of those returning from Portugal write letters for him. Afonso became literate in Portuguese during this period as well; he certainly could read it, and beyond that, in his letter of August 26, 1526, Afonso noted he was then learning Latin.

Afonso did not physically write his own letters. No monarch would sit and write letters, even in Europe; secretaries did such work. Afonso's first and most consistent secretary was João Teixeira, whom Afonso introduced in his letter of October 5, 1514, saying he wrote the letter "with the assistance of a schoolboy of ours." Afonso offered this as an explanation since "if anything in this letter is poorly written," it should be known that "we do not know Portugal's writing styles." He opted for someone whose writing would be inferior in style "because we do not dare do it with any of the learned men who are here; all the more learned ones are guilty of various sins."[18] The trust extended not just to this first letter, in which many in the Portuguese community of Kongo had been denounced. João Teixeira wrote seventeen of Afonso's letters, including all of the letters historians now consider most important. It was a long career for Teixeira; eventually, Dom João wrote Afonso's last extant letter on December 17, 1540.

If most pre-colonial African countries are documented by foreign visitors, Kongo in the first half of the sixteenth century is a striking exception. Afonso wrote most of what we know about Kongo's history in this period. His successor, Diogo I (1545–1561), himself the author of additional letters, investigated a treason plot against him, revealing a great deal about the inner workings of Kongo politics. Aside from a few letters by Portuguese residents or visitors, Kongolese created most of the extant writing on Kongo in the first half of the sixteenth century.

The earliest writing by Europeans that looks with any degree of systemization at Kongo's institutions or daily life comes to us from witnesses in the 1580s: Duarte Lopes, who came to Kongo in 1579 and left in 1583, and the Carmelite missionaries who arrived in 1584 and left in 1586. Their accounts set out explicit descriptions of the country's geography, flora and fauna, fiscal and judicial system, the pattern of royal succession, and some details on rural life and the economy.

This relatively comprehensive, if general account, of Kongo was overwhelmed by the amount of information generated by the renewed Jesuit mission following 1619 and then by the multiple book-length accounts created by the Capuchin missionaries starting in 1645 and running through the early eighteenth century. Most writers who have described Kongo in Afonso's day did not base their descriptions on evidence from Afonso's time but usually on works created a century or more after the events occurred.

Nevertheless, a steady stream of African-authored evidence about Kongo history continues throughout its history as an independent kingdom. Mostly, these are letters written by kings to authorities overseas; no archive from Kongo's independent period has survived to the present. That Kongo kept records in archives

18. See "Letter from the King of Kongo to D. Manuel I," October 5, 1514, in Correspondence.

is occasionally attested in the sources we have, though it's less clear what, exactly, they were recording.

A personal letter written by Afonso's son and short-lived successor Pedro Nkanga a Mvemba, intercepted in the late 1540s and added into the evidence in Diogo I's legal inquest, is the first known personal letter from a Kongolese to another Kongolese. In it, however, Pedro Nkanga a Mvemba mentions Diogo issuing orders to officials, establishing that at least at the end of Afonso's reign, the custom of giving written orders was established. Afonso was likely the king who began the practice, though when he did so is not known from the materials we currently have at hand.[19]

The best evidence of the sort of things that Kongo leaders documented is revealed in the personal papers of Antonio Manuel, Kongo's ambassador to Rome. Antonio Manuel's papers include documents dated as early as 1591 and up to his death in Rome in 1608. Because he had official documents in his collection of papers (of some seventy documents), we know that the kings in the late sixteenth century wrote out orders, made grants of income, appointed people to positions, and corresponded with officials. Antonio Manuel also had personal papers of his own, as well as documents he received from various bodies while living in Europe.[20]

While Antonio Manuel's papers show us something of the working of Kongo's chancellery in the late sixteenth century, we're unsure about when this system of written documentation of administration started. The mere fact of having a literate group living in the country is not enough to demonstrate the use of documentation for administration. However, it seems likely that the papers represented in Antonio Manuel's were the work of a mature institution.

Reading Afonso's letters

It is important to recognize that Afonso's letters are addressed to Portuguese officials (usually the king) and occasionally to others or the pope. They were not intended to offer a window into Kongo's life or politics but to address only those

19. The inquest was published by Paiva Manso originally; a new edition and English translation is in John Thornton and Linda Heywood, "The Treason of Dom Pedro Nkanga a Mvemba against Dom Diogo, King of Kongo, 1550," in *Afro-Latino Voices: Narratives from the Early Modern Ibero-Atlantic World, 1550–1812*, ed. Kathryn McKnight and Leo Garofalo (Indianapolis: Hackett Publishing Company, 2009), pp. 26–28.

20. His letters, left in the Vatican's possession when he died in 1608, are in Archivo Segreto Vaticano (Rome), Miscelanea, Armadio II, vol. 91, fols. 124–58.

topics relevant to the task at hand. Not surprisingly, therefore, the letters deal primarily with Portuguese living in Kongo or neighboring communities. Afonso took on a particular role with regard to his Portuguese residents, which was to monitor their activities using Portuguese law and to report them to Portugal. Afonso would extradite to Portugal for punishment any Portuguese he felt violated his laws or interests.

For this reason, Afonso's letters are often letters of complaint, either to support his discontent with the behavior of the Portuguese in his kingdom or in response to requests from Portugal for reports on them; his letter of 1514 is an example of this. At times, most notably in his letters of 1526, his complaints were about Portuguese illegal slave trading within his jurisdiction with the support of some Portuguese officials. While Afonso often referred to events in his kingdom—for example, wars or even administrative issues—they were secondary to his letters' primary purpose.

It is equally important to realize that we do not have anything like a complete set of Afonso's letters. The ones we have can seem like quite a lot, especially if we come to them with relatively low expectations of how much an African monarch would be writing to Portugal. Historians have found a few references—made in some of Afonso's extant correspondence—to letters written by Afonso that have not already been found in the archive; the most notable of these as-yet-undiscovered letters would be his of 1506, in which he first describes his miracle. Other letters we know were intercepted and not delivered, such as those seized by officials in São Tomé to cover their tracks or thwart his reporting; or those simply captured by French pirates on the high seas.

Aside from letters known only from a mention, there must be more, perhaps many more, that have simply been lost. The Portuguese archives for this period are far from complete; in fact, only a fraction of what was once held in the royal archives has survived to the present day. The letters we have from Afonso were found almost exclusively in what was called the Torre do Tombo. This collection is named for a tower in the Portuguese royal palace in which were archived important documents kept by the king and the various councils that served him. In 1755, a major earthquake struck Lisbon, followed by a massive fire. During the disaster, the tower holding the archives collapsed, and a very large part of it was destroyed.

Some of the archives survived in decent shape, including the section called Gavetas (drawers), in which were found special documents that had been pulled from the archives to serve one or another administrative purpose and then not returned to their normal place. Two of the extant Afonso documents, dated March 4 and March 5, 1516, were found in the Gavetas section. The rest come from another collection, called the Corpo Chronologico, or "Chronological body." These were documents salvaged from the wreckage of the collapsed tower. They were found in such disarray that their original organization (i.e., a classification of types, such as orders, requests, grants, general correspondence, and so on) could not be easily reconstructed. So they were simply collected and placed in strict chronological order without concern for their relationship to each other or their classification.

The Corpo has three large sections, each identical in basic composition: each section collects documents arranged chronologically from a specific period. Within each section, the documentation is then organized by *maços* (bundles), which are physically rather large but contain a manageable number of documentary pages. For example, Afonso's letter of May 17, 1517, is found in Part I, bundle 21, document 102. In the bundle, the letter falls after an order of May 11, 1517, in which the king requires a payment made to a nobleman in Portugal and precedes another fiscal document paying a salary of May 18, 1517. If a researcher goes to Part II, they can find a record of the equivalent date of May 18, 1517, in bundle 69, document 169, which is an order to support the saying of masses for a deceased person. The equivalent dated document from Part III is found in bundle 6, document 65, a mandate of the governor of Goa, a Portuguese colony in India, May 15, 1517.

Thus, the only order in all three parts is chronological, and even in this, the three bundles are all essentially the same chronology. So Afonso's letters are scattered randomly throughout the collection. Not long after the earthquake and recovery, archive staff members began writing descriptions of the surviving documents. This task took many years, and the descriptions have been transcribed into the digital catalog of the archive. Most descriptions are short, just a few lines, and often do not do justice to the overall tenor of the document. An extreme case is the archive's description of Afonso's letter of October 5, 1514, which says: "Letter of the king of Congo to Dom Manuel I, dealing with various subjects, and asking for the donation of S. Tomé, which was Fernão de Melo's, in payment for the difficulties he caused him, to found a college to educate boys and girls of Congo."[21]

The final section of remaining documents from the collapsed tower is called "Fragments." These documents, collected after the earthquake, were damaged to the point that their contents could not be sufficiently described for inclusion in the Corpo Chronologico. Most of the later discoveries, by Felner in the 1930s and then by António Brásio in the 1950s, were found in this section.

All of Afonso's known correspondence from these collections has been transcribed and published, starting with Paiva Manso's collection in 1877 and a few from Felner in his 1933 book. However, all the texts were published by António

21. ANTT CC I-16-28 cover sheet.

Brásio in a massive documentary collection concerning Angola, *Monumenta Missionaria Africana*, which began publication in 1953 and had issued fifteen volumes, mostly over 500 pages long, when the last volume was published in 1988. Many other documents aside from Afonso's records are contained in Brásio's collection, including material from Mina (São Jorge da Mina, in today's Ghana), São Tomé, and all of Angola as well as Kongo. António Luís Ferronha published an edition of Afonso's letters in modernized Portuguese in 1992, and Louis Jadin, a Belgian priest with great interest in the affairs of Kongo, produced an annotated French translation (with Mireille Dicorato) in 1975.

Afonso's correspondence has been well known since the earliest days of modern writing on African history. Almost all were published by 1877, and thus, even the earliest writing, such as E. G. Ravenstein's brief survey of Kongo's history in 1901 or Alexander Ihle's careful study in 1929, relied heavily on it for the earliest portions, and of course, Jean Cuvelier's pioneering book of 1946 also made extensive use of it. It has also been used in polemics, such as James Duffy's and Basil Davidson's denunciations of the slave trade and Portuguese colonialism. Above all, Davidson's use of Afonso's letters as a lightning rod to position an African response to the slave trade has given them a distinctive place in contemporary historiography.

CHAPTER 1

KONGO AND PORTUGAL: TWO WORLDS IN CONTACT

Kongo

The Kingdom of Kongo was situated on the western end of the great Central African savannah, lying just south of the tropical rainforest, including the northern provinces of today's Angola and the western ones of the Democratic Republic of Congo. Humans have lived in this area for perhaps 200,000 years, as long as our species has been on the planet. Contemporary Angola holds ancient fossil remains of these early humans, but the sixteenth-century inhabitants of the Kingdom of Kongo were not their direct descendants. Instead, branches of the human family that ended up in West Africa were the immediate progenitors of the kingdom's inhabitants who occupied the area in a slow-moving wave that headed south through the tropical rainforest band, following the coastline and the banks of the mighty Congo River to the savannah in the south. These ancient people, who replaced them in Angola and Democratic Republic of Congo around 1500 BC, spoke dialects of what was then probably a single language called Western Bantu by linguists. They practiced agriculture, cultivated trees, raised cattle, and only learned to work metals some centuries after crossing the rainforest.

The Bantu-speaking immigrants' numbers were small, but they displaced the ancient population that inhabited the region for hundreds of thousands of years, moving them southward—at the present time, there are no genetic traces of the ancient people found in known samples of current inhabitants' DNA. When the Bantu-speaking people first arrived, they lived in egalitarian societies and inhabited scattered small village communities. Even in the fifteenth century, when European ships first appeared on their coast, they were not numerous, although the population was growing.

Sometime around AD 1000, or even later, these village communities started to differentiate into stratified societies by a still poorly understood process. By force or agreement, leaders emerged and became the lords of the population, and then, probably through violence, still larger units formed. By 1200 or so, complex societies with multiple levels of authority, concentrations of population, and social inequality developed. The earliest of these that appeared around the Congo basin encircled the Malebo Pool near modern-day Kinshasa and east of it as far as Lake Mai Ndombe. Eventually, two groups located around the Malebo Pool and in the Central Highlands of Angola developed even larger and stratified societies, forming kingdoms. The process by which kingdoms formed is presently unknown; at this point, we can only say that there were several such kingdoms and can dare to give a few of them names.

The Kingdom of Kongo was not among the earliest kingdoms; it was born from a federation of three small polities, named Kakongo, Ngoyo, and Vungu, in a band some sixty miles inland from the Atlantic coast along the north bank of the Congo River. These little kingdoms, or mini-states, each scarcely occupying an area the size of a county in today's United States or perhaps a parish elsewhere, were founded at a point that cannot be established until archaeology in the region is better defined. In the late thirteenth century, perhaps 1275, the ruler of Vungu, the easternmost of the group, crossed the Congo River and conquered Mpemba Kasi.[1] Mpemba Kasi was valuable because it was a major producer of steel, and mining and smelting of iron had been going on there since at least the sixth century.[2]

Mpemba Kasi was not simply an independent mini-state like Vungu's neighbors in the federation, but the most northern district of a much larger kingdom called Mpemba, the capital of which lay some eighty miles farther south. Seventeenth-century tradition called Mpemba Kasi "the mother of Kongo." This may be a play on the mini-state's name, which means "spouse of Mpemba" or, since the Kikongo word *ngudi* can mean either "mother" or "origin," the moniker might refer to the act of conquest as the first step in the creation of the future kingdom.[3]

---

1. What follows is based on John Thornton, "The Origins of Kongo: A Revised Vision," in *The Kongo Kingdom: The Origins, Dynamics and Cosmopolitan Culture of an African Polity*, ed. Koen Bostoen and Inge Brinkman (Cambridge: Cambridge University Press, 2018), pp. 17–41; and Thornton, *A History of West Central Africa to 1850* (Cambridge: Cambridge University Press, 2020), pp. 24–33. It is quite possible that this first step was a mythical river crossing, important in tradition but not necessarily literally true.

2. Bernard Clist, "Our Iron Smelting 14 C Dates from Central Africa: From a Plain Appointment to a Full-Blown Relationship," in *Une archéologie des provinces septentrionales du royaume Kong*, ed. Bernard Clist, Pierre de Maret, and Koen Bostoen (Oxford: Archaeopress Publishing, 2018), pp. 231–41.

3. The conquest story was first recorded in 1624. Origin stories are often more ideological and constitutional documents than real history, and so conquest might be a metaphor for highly

Late sixteenth-century tradition recorded by Carmelite missionaries noted that Mpemba was one of several small kingdoms that covered the region: "Along the seacoast there were other kingdoms that were independent . . . and had their separate kings." In addition to Mpemba, it identified the kingdom of Soyo on the coast south of the Congo River and Mbamba to the southeast, centered in the valley of the Dande River. While they were once independent, by the sixteenth century (and likely in the fifteenth as well), the kingdoms were "subject and tributary to the King of Congo," with the exception of Mbata. The king selected rulers from his family or the kingdom's nobility and dismissed or continued according to their performance, particularly in paying tax and tribute.[4]

A tradition recorded in 1624 calls the leader of this occupation Ntinu Wene—more a title than a name as it means "king of the kingdom." He occupied not just Mpemba Kasi but also Nsi a Kwilu, or the "land of Kwilu," a stretch of the Kwilu River Valley that ran from the Kanda Mountains in northern Angola into the Congo River and was centered on the modern Congolese town of Kimpese. Nsi a Kwilu was strategically important since it was a narrow valley, its northern border defined by a spectacular range of cliffs several hundred feet high, marking the edge of a high plateau between the Kwilu and the Congo Rivers. The Lovo massif, which formed the southern border, were less impressive highlands but a barrier all the same. People passing south of the Congo River along this area, such as those carrying copper from the north or textiles from the northeast, would have to pass through the fifteen-mile-wide stretch between these two highlands.

The Lovo massif was also home to sacred places, for many of the rocks, caves, and grottos in the region are full of engravings, some dating as far back as the sixth and seventh centuries AD, others dating from around the time of the conquest by Vungu or the earlier years of Kongo in the late fourteenth or early fifteenth

---

centralized authority, see on this the reflections of Marshall Sahlins, "On the Atemporality Dimensions of History: In the Old Kongo Kingdom for Example," in *On Kings*, ed. David Graeber and Marshall Sahlins (Chicago: Hau Books, 2017), pp. 139–222.

4. Biblioteca Nazionale Centrale, Firenze, Panciatichiano 200, fol. 163v, anonymous untitled account. Internal evidence places its composition between 1586 and 1587. A likely author or source would be the Carmelite missionary Diego de la Encarnación, who had served there from 1584–1586. Its section on the former kingdoms being incorporated into Kongo is explicitly credited to de la Encarnación by the chronicler Francisco de Santa Maria, in *Reforma de los descalços de nuestra Senora del Carmen* . . . , 2 vols. (Madrid, 1655), 2:84. An analytical description of the manuscript with excerpts is in John K. Thornton, "The Florentine Relation: A Newly Discovered Sixteenth-Century Description of the Kingdom of Kongo," *History in Africa* 50 (2023).

centuries.[5] The kings of Mpemba Kasi, the line that would eventually come to rule Kongo, were buried in this massif, which seventeenth-century tradition considered so sacred that it was painful death even to look at their graves.

The western end of Nsi a Kwilu had been formed by the northern end of Mpemba, which was a substantial regional power, given the number of territories that it controlled. The eastern end of Nsi a Kwilu bordered Mbata, another substantial mini-state belonging to another sizable federation, the Seven Kingdoms of Kongo dia Nlaza.

Its northern and eastern end, including Kongo dia Nlaza, its capital area, was a part of the great Central African textile belt, where the raffia palm flourished.[6] In the later sixteenth century, the eastern provinces of Nsundi, Mpangu, and Mbata paid the king "the bulk of his income, because in them they make all the cloth and rich things for clothes and costumes in their fashion, they also come in as merchandise from the neighboring kingdoms."[7] Cloth made from raffia by skilled craftsmen was the most valuable cloth in the region, and could be woven to rival textiles produced elsewhere in the world, from silk to velvet.[8] The remarkable production quality and artistry created a widespread demand for the cloth, drawing trade through the Kwilu Valley.

For a few generations, perhaps until around 1350, the extension of Vungu in Nsi a Kwilu controlled the area between Mpemba and the Seven Kingdoms. It was probably this juncture of borders that caused the rulers of the still emerging Kingdom of Kongo to make an alliance with Mbata, one of the Seven Kingdoms. Afonso provided a partial description of the alliance in his letter of 1514, when his enemies were plotting against him by contacting Dom Jorge, then the Mwene Mbata, "who was the head of our kingdom, so that he would have us burned and destroyed." But Afonso asserted that he was the Mwene Mbata's uncle, so "that if he were to destroy us, his uncle, who else might become king who was a closer

5. Geoffrey Heimlich, *Le massif de Lovo, sur les traces du royaume de Kongo* (Oxford: Archaeopress Publishing, 2017).

6. On the significance and nature of raffia cloth production, see Jan Vansina, "Raffia Cloth in West Central Africa, 1500–1800," in *Textiles: Production, Trade and Demand*, ed. Maureen Fennell Mazzaoui (Farnham: Taylor & Francis, 1998), pp. 263–91.

7. Biblioteca Nazionale Centrale, Firenze, Panciatichiano 200, fol. 163v, untitled. See Thornton, "Florentine Relation." Filippo Pigafetta, following Lopes, held that Mbata paid twice as much income as Mpangu and Nsundi, in *Relatione del Reame de Congo e delle circonvince contrade* (Rome, 1591), p. 38.

8. For their extraordinary quality, see Cécile Fromont, "Getting to Know Early Modern Western Central African Textiles: New Evidence, Old Shadows, and the Puzzle of Pineapple Fibers," *Textile Museum Journal* 48 (2021): 138–51.

relation to him."[9] In proposing letters to be written to various provincial authorities, João III of Portugal noted in 1529 that Mbata's Dom Jorge "is the leading voice in Kongo and without whom, according to the custom of the land, no king may be elected."[10]

In the 1580s, Duarte Lopes, a Portuguese Jewish convert serving as ambassador to Rome, clarified the situation when interviewed by the Italian geographer Filippo Pigafetta. According to Lopes, Mbata submitted to Kongo voluntarily "without there being any war," but in his day, the king of Kongo chose the successors to the office from among Mbata's royal family to prevent usurpation and rebellion. In exchange, if Kongo's royal line should falter, Mbata would, in theory at least, take over the rule of Kongo.[11] A corollary comment by Carmelite missionaries in the kingdom at the same time noted that the ruler of Mbata could take over in the absence of a royal heir by being "closest to the trunk and lineage of the kings of Congo."[12] It was probably through intermarriage between the two allied families that Afonso came to be uncle to Dom Jorge, and asserted his own genealogical claim.[13]

Seventeenth-century traditions, recorded by Capuchin missionaries, provided a genealogical history of the relationship between the two countries. They described a dynastic marriage between Mbata's Nsaku Lau and a king of emerging Kongo named Nimi a Nzima.[14] The arrangement was to guarantee the succession of each of the two kings' families and to mark off claims that might be made against them by other families within or outside their domains. Nimi a Nzima married Nsaku Lau's daughter, Lukeni lua Nsanze, intending for the child of this union to become king in Nimi a Nzima's domain and for Nimi a Nzima's descendants to support the descendants of Nsaku Lau as rulers of Mbata against any usurpation.

The child of the union of Nimi a Nzima and Lukeni lua Nsanze was Lukeni lua Nimi, the founder of the Kingdom of Kongo. When he came of age, his father

---

9. See "Letter from the King of Kongo to D. Manuel I," October 5, 1514, in Correspondence.

10. See "Letter from Dom João III to the King of Kongo," end of 1529, in Correspondence.

11. Pigafetta, *Relatione*, p. 38.

12. Biblioteca Nazionale Centrale, Firenze, Panciatichiano 200, fol. 163. See Thornton, "Florentine Relation."

13. A history of Kongo written by Jesuit Mateus Cardoso in 1624 gave the ruler of Mbata the title "grandfather of the King of Congo," but this was what is called a perpetual relation of kinship marking relative status rather than actual kinship. See *História do Reino do Congo*, ed. António Brásio (Lisbon: Centro de estudos históricos Ultramarinos, 1969), fol. 16.

14. The tradition is recorded in Cavazzi, *Descrizione Istorica*, Book 2, no. 86. His probable source was Girolamo da Montesarchio, who traveled widely in Nsi a Kwilu in the 1650s.

allowed him to govern Mpemba Kasi, and he made his home in a fortress on the rocky cliffs south of the Kwilu Valley. His fortress allowed him to monitor the commercial traffic passing through the opening in the hills that separated the Nsi a Kwilu from places farther south. Mid-seventeenth-century tradition detailed Lukeni lua Nimi's various raids, sometimes winning and other times losing. His activities sent him farther and farther south into the territory of Mpemba.

In his excursions, he came upon a large flat-topped mountain with a shallow lake, the Mongo dia Kongo (Mountain of Kongo), which was mostly uninhabited and would make for a perfect fortress. At the base of the mountain was a trading town with the famous Mpangala-day market (markets were named after one of the four days of the Kikongo week). Lukeni lua Nimi arranged with the ruler of Mpangala to settle there, guaranteeing the ruler and his descendants' perpetual authority over their area in exchange for recognizing Lukeni lua Nimi. These arrangements were still being symbolically repeated 300 years later.[15]

Lukeni lua Nimi found the mountain so convenient that he moved there, draining the lake and bringing in people captured in his wars and his followers from Nsi a Kwilu. It became Mbanza Kongo, the capital of Kongo, the kingdom he would eventually inherit from his father.

Before Lukeni lua Nimi arrived, the Mpangala-day market was under the authority of Vunda, a complex combination of several smaller mini-states under the authority of Mpemba. To secure Mbanza Kongo and Mpangala, Lukeni lua Nimi also had to make an arrangement with the leader of Vunda. Lukeni lua Nimi granted Vunda the right to join Mbata as an elector of Kongo, perhaps as a proxy for Mpemba, so that Vunda would at least have a role in choosing its own ruler. Like Mbata, Vunda was also considered a symbolic grandfather of the king of Kongo.

Lukeni lua Nimi expanded westward and took over another independent region, Kabunga, the leader of which was said to control access to a powerful spirit (*nkita*), which was reputed to have supernatural authority over the whole area in which the mountain of Kongo was located. Lukeni lua Nimi married the leader's daughter, solidifying his hold on the capital both spiritually and materially. This authority continued to be recognized through the seventeenth century.

Between about 1275 and 1400, Kongo had grown from a relatively small entity to a substantial polity by skillfully playing off the relative decentralization of the great confederations of the Seven Kingdoms and Mpemba. Rather than directly taking them on, Kongo's founders had made alliances and concessions to territories

15. Cavazzi, *Descrizione Istorica*, Book 1, no. 86. Cavazzi may have recorded the story of Mpangala himself in 1664 when he resided in Kongo.

within them and then played those into support for increasing Kongo's domain. The traditions about the steps in this progression tell us little about how any of these entities were actually governed. Still, Kongo's subsequent growth suggests that the rulers were eventually able to parlay their collection of alliances into a much more centralized domain.

Around AD 1400, Kongo expanded more rapidly, conquering territory rather than making alliances and local concessions. It took in Nsundi, another province of the Seven Kingdoms that had become independent. Nsundi was situated along the south shore of the Congo River and controlled the highlands bordering Nsi a Kwilu in the north. The territory was conquered, its previous leadership ignored, and its governance granted to whomever the king of Kongo chose. Then Mpangu, lying south of Nsundi and sharing the valley of the Inkisi River with Mbata, fell and was also put under the control of the king's choice. In this way, an eastern border was secured, and Kongo continued expansion to the south. The remaining lands of Mpemba were incorporated, again as a royal province, under the leadership of whomever the king chose.

A move westward from Kongo's capital region brought in Soyo, also a previously independent kingdom, which controlled the mouth of the Congo River, important salt works, and the first contact with the sea. Another drive south, perhaps from Kabunga, took in Mbamba and, south of that, the valuable island of Luanda. Conquering Luanda was in many ways the longest expansion that Kongo took, and for good reason, as it was the center of production of *nzimbu* shells, unique shellfish only found in the area around the island of Luanda that served as money in a much wider area.

In these later thrusts, Kongo bypassed some areas, perhaps because they were less interesting or valuable or because they were harder to conquer. The islands that lay in the broad mouth of the Congo River and the swampy shores on the southern bank resisted Kongo's attempts at conquest and were still independent as Soyo was taken in hand. Likewise, Kongo's armies also bypassed the coast south of the Mbidizi River as they advanced from Mbamba, focusing their advance on taking the island of Luanda.

The area along the coast north of Luanda, a fairly arid region, was called Nsi a Ngala, and its core was a petty kingdom of Musulu, which paid tribute and recognized Kongo's authority but was not integrated into the emerging kingdom.[16] Already in the late fifteenth century, Soyo was expanding southward with the

16. Musulu was named as an area over which Afonso declared himself "lord" in his 1535 letter to the pope, rather than the central provinces grouped as the region where he was "king." For Nsi a Ngala, see Thornton, *West Central Africa*, p. 67.

permission of the kings, since when Soyo's ruler was baptized, Nzinga a Nkuwu granted him an extension of Soyo's territory that probably reached to the mouth of the Mbidizi River.[17]

In securing Luanda, Kongo also confronted the rugged terrain of the mountains that separated Mpemba from lands south of it. These mountains formed a linguistic frontier; to the north and all the areas where Lukeni lua Nimi ruled, the people spoke a common language, Kikongo. But in the mountains and the highlands south of Mpemba, they spoke a similar but distinct language, Kimbundu.

Because of the language barrier and the fact that the mountains were the home to a large number of fiercely independent lords who held out against attempts to conquer them, the Kongolese called them "the Ambundus" from their language name and the fact they were politically divided. The highlands that made up the core of Ambundu were attractive to Kongo's rulers as they were ideal for raising cattle, which could barely survive in Kongo. As in the region north of Luanda, many leaders paid tribute or recognized Kongo as a leader without allowing the king of Kongo to choose their leadership or govern them directly.

The scant written tradition and the limited oral traditions recorded later about this early period do not allow us to say exactly in what order these conquests came or how many could be credited to Lukeni lua Nimi and how many to his successors. Lukeni lua Nimi may not have lived very long, for a tradition recorded in the seventeenth century says that when he died, his own children were deemed too young to succeed him. The electors, who we can imagine were primarily the leaders of Mbata, Vunda, and perhaps other nobles who had some influence, opted to choose two of his nephews to take over in order, the first named Kinanga and the other Nlaza. Only after their reigns did Lukeni lua Nimi's son, Nkuwu a Lukeni, finally take up his position as king. He was then followed, probably in the late 1470s, by his own son named Nzinga a Nkuwu, who was ruling when Portuguese vessels reached the coast in 1482, the first firmly fixed date in Kongo's history.[18]

The history of Kongo up to 1482 can only be reconstructed using oral traditions, and even those were only recorded in the sixteenth and seventeenth

---

17. Garcia de Resende, *Chronica de el-rei D. João II*, cap. 155, in António Brásio, *Monumenta Missionaria Africana*, 15 vols. (Lisbon: Agência Geral do Ultramar, 1952–1988), 1:74 (this source will henceforward be cited as *MMA*).

18. The date is often given as 1483, which was an official contact. However, Diogo Cão's exploratory voyage of 1482, as reconstructed by Carmen Radulet, visited Kongo and took in hostages to serve as translators. See Carmen Radulet, "As viagens de Diogo Cão: um problema ainda em aberto," *Revista da Universidade de Coimbra* 24 (1988): 105–19, see summary chart at p. 119.

centuries.[19] These traditions give little detail about how the territories of the country were assembled and the rights that some territories had by virtue of this history that continued to be recognized in later periods. The actual administration and government of the country were not recorded in tradition or remembered, but by 1482 literate witnesses started to leave an eyewitness record of Kongo.

The Portuguese in the South Atlantic

The Portuguese began their expansion into the Atlantic in the fourteenth century, when they participated in the earliest voyages and attempted the conquest of the Canary Islands. It was from their adventures in the Canaries that they made a crucial navigational discovery, that is, learning to use the "Little Wheel."[20] The Little Wheel is the convergence of winds and currents in the Atlantic, in which the southward-flowing Canary Current and the northward-flowing Gulf Stream pass near each other. The Canary Current runs along Africa's Saharan coast and gives ready access to the Senegal River and lands beyond it for sailors from Europe. But it is a one-way street: there is no immediate way to sail back, as the current never reverses. However, for those sailors brave enough to sail out into the Atlantic, there is an opposing current, the Gulf Stream, which allows a return voyage. These currents converge around the islands of the Atlantic: the Canaries, Madeira, and the Azores. It was thus possible, once a sailor knew of the Little Wheel, to sail down to West Africa and then tack out to sea from there, knowing that the Gulf Stream's southern edge would carry the ship back to Europe for a round trip.

Drawn by the prospect that round-trip maritime travel to Senegal would allow them to tap into the sub-Saharan gold trade without dealing with the middlemen in the Sahara Desert, Portuguese mariners sailed down the coast and reached the mouth of the Senegal River in 1441. They soon realized that they could divert the trade in both gold and slaves who crossed the Sahara through their early African

---

19. Oral traditions collected in the twentieth century were recorded by officials and missionaries, especially Karl Laman (but not, for the most part, within the borders of the kingdom) and particularly Jean Cuvelier. Cuvelier claimed that these traditions related to the earliest periods following the establishment of the country. For a challenge to it, see John Thornton, "Modern Oral Traditions and the History of Kongo," *International Journal of African Historical Studies* 55 (2022): 1–20.

20. This section follows John Thornton, *Africa and Africans in the Making of the Atlantic World, 1400–1800*, 2nd ed. (Cambridge: Cambridge University Press, 1998), pp. 13–82; and Thornton, *A Cultural History of the Atlantic World, 1250–1820* (Cambridge: Cambridge University Press, 2012), pp. 7–28.

base at Arguim (in modern-day Mauritania) and then through the Senegal River, and thus altered the competition between the Saharan and Atlantic trade routes—known as being between what Portuguese historian Vitorino Magalhães Godinho called "the caravel versus the caravan," respectively—to their advantage.[21]

The risks, both financial and personal, of these early ventures were largely taken on by young squires of the Order of Christ, with financing provided by private and often foreign merchants. However, once the route to Senegal was opened and gold was in the offing, the Portuguese crown stepped in and demanded to share in and regulate the commerce, giving grants to favored elites. As a result, the entrepreneurial groups that had made the first commercial arrangements, being shouldered out by the crown, moved on, looking southward for other places to trade. Soon the traders reached Sierra Leone and, beyond that, the pepper-producing lands along the Ivory Coast (then called the Malagueta Coast from the peppers they produced).

The mechanism for the crown's control of commerce was the *feitoria* (literally, factory) or a royally controlled trading post. Merchants visiting the area controlled by the factory were expected to trade through it, or at least pass through it, to ensure they had properly paid dues and taxes. The factory at Arguim, established in 1445, was the first such post on the coast of Africa; then, in 1461, a fortified post was built on a nearby offshore island. Further discoveries, with equally promising prospects, called for further regulation.

The crown sought to regularize exploration by granting the right to explore the African coast to Fernão Gomes in 1469, giving him extensive powers and privileges in exchange for his systematically investigating the lands beyond Sierra Leone. In 1471, Portuguese navigators entered into relations with merchants in the small state of Sama to buy gold on what was soon to be called the "Mina Coast" to the Portuguese and the "Gold Coast" to other Europeans, and is today's Ghana. The gold trade from here was more substantial than elsewhere, and it soon attracted a wide range of competitors, including English, French, and Spanish ships. The gold trade's African side was not controlled by a single powerful state but by a dozen or more small independent polities, so it was impossible to make some sort of diplomatic deal to monopolize the trade on the landward side.

Furthermore, the merchants selling gold to the Portuguese demanded to be paid in slaves as well as other merchandise. This forced the Mina-based ships to move farther east along the coast to the mouth of the Niger Delta, where slaves could be procured. The trade on this section of the coast, in full swing at the end

21. Vitorino Magalhães Godinho, *Os descobrimentos e a economia mundial*, 2nd corrected ed., 3 vols. (Lisbon: Editorial Presença, 1991), pp. 139 et seq.

of the 1470s, eventually led Europeans to learn of the powerful kingdom of Benin, an important naval power in parts of the "Rivers of Slaves," as the area was called by Portuguese sailors.[22]

João II, who became the king of Portugal in 1481, decided to consolidate his country's position against foreign competitors, centralize trade in the Gulf of Guinea, and continue explorations along the coast of Africa. Consequently, to create a permanent naval presence in the Gulf of Guinea, in 1482, the Portuguese crown dispatched Diogo d'Azambuja to build a fort, dubbed São Jorge da Mina, on land that lay between the small kingdoms of Fetu and Komenda.[23] The fort would be the base for the factory established there and would apply the same sort of control over the gold trade that Arguim had done for the earliest trade. It was fortified early to store gold as traders from the interior brought it to the coast and as a base for a local fleet whose job would be to seize and hold all competing vessels from rival European nations.

João II looked to Diogo Cão, a sailor already operating in the Gulf of Guinea, to handle the continuing exploration. Cão started his first voyage in 1482, even as d'Azambuja departed for Mina. Initially, the land south of the great bend on the African coastline was a sparsely settled rainforest. But Cão's ships eventually met what they called the "Powerful River": the Congo River, which turned the seawater fresh for "twenty leagues" off the coast. The lands along the shore and river were cultivated and inhabited by many people. Cão anchored there and planted a temporary wooden cross (*padrão*) as a marker and claim.

Cão did what European explorers often did when encountering new lands: he captured someone, or some people, from the shore and carried them off, sailing farther before eventually returning to Portugal at the end of 1482. There the captive person or people were treated well, and a Third Order Franciscan named João da Costa, a talented linguist who had already learned Arabic, taught the captives enough Portuguese to serve as translators and learned the language of Kongo himself.[24]

---

22. A. F. C. Ryder, *Benin and the Europeans, 1485–1897* (New York: Longmans, 1969), pp. 25–27.

23. For detailed descriptions and documents, see P. E. H. Hair, *The Founding of the Castle of São Jorge da Mina: An Analysis of the Sources* (Madison: University of Wisconsin Press, 1994).

24. Vicente Salgado, *Origem e Progresso das Linguas Orientaes na Congregação da Terceira Ordem de Portugal* (Lisbon, 1790), p. 10. Salgado claimed to have learned this detail from archival research done in 1777 among church records that are probably now lost, written by the bishop of Beja, Manuel do Cenáculo, whose "Compendio histórico" is at the Biblioteca Pública e Arquivo Distrial de Évora, CXXVIII/2–6.

Soon after arriving in Portugal, Cão headed a second mission to the Gulf of Guinea to follow up on the contact with Kongo and to see how far south the coast went. He anchored again off the coast south of the Congo River and replaced the wooden marker he had left earlier with an inscribed stone one. Thanks to having a linguist with him, he was able to learn that the river flowed through a large kingdom, the Kingdom of Kongo. The king, Nzinga a Nkuwu, lived far in the interior, and Cão dispatched some of his own crew, as well as João da Costa and some other priests, to go to the king and establish diplomatic relationships.[25]

The captain then sailed farther down the coast, nearly to South Africa, and returned to Kongo. Disappointed that the Portuguese he had left on shore as ambassadors had not returned, he invited several high-ranking people, including Kala ka Mfusu, to come and inspect the ship. Then, without warning, Cão sailed off with his visitors, promising to return within "15 moons." His idea was that these high-ranking hostages could serve to redeem the Portuguese group if they had been imprisoned or avenge them if they had been killed. Once again, he returned to Lisbon where, on April 8, 1484, the king granted Cão and his first heir an annual income of 10,000 silver reals as thanks for his service.

Sometime in 1485, Cão was back in the Gulf of Guinea to settle the diplomatic mission. He sailed as far as the end of the continent, but did not go around the Cape of Good Hope, and then doubled back up the coast to Kongo. Nzinga a Nkuwu had received the Portuguese mission and wanted to continue contact with Portugal. He designated Kala ka Mfusu to lead his embassy, as the latter man had already been to Portugal and learned Portuguese.[26] Nzinga a Nkuwu's decision to continue contact with the Portuguese was certainly based on what the returned hostages told him of Portugal. Wishing to impress the Portuguese, he sent presents for the king of Portugal: "Ivory tusks, worked ivory, which shone with the hand of the master, and many pieces of palm cloth, expensive among them, well made and of fine colors."[27] In so doing, he revealed what he considered the most interesting

25. Salgado, *Origem*, pp. 10–11.

26. Rui de Pina, "Chronica del Rei D. Joham Segundo" (MS of 1515), chap. 58, and untitled Italian MS, fols. 87ra–87rb; both texts in Carmen Radulet, *O Cronista Rui de Pina e a "Relação do Reino do Congo": Manuscrito inédito do "Códice Riccardiano 1910"* (Lisbon: Comissão Nacional para as Comemorações dos Descobrimentos Portugueses, 1992). I have merged information from the two variants.

27. De Pina, "Chronica," Book 3, chap. 58. In this finalized text, de Pina calls the Kongolese ambassador Caçuta; in the earlier untitled text by de Pina, known only in an Italian translation (fol. 87ra) based on testimony taken upon the arrival of the Portuguese fleet, he was named "Chranchafusus" (my respelling is an attempt to render it into Kikongo). Jean Cuvelier, in his classic text *L'ancien royaume de Congo* (Bruges, 1946), p. 43, gave his name as Nsaku, from the

and important items in the Kongolese cultural inventory: the fine textiles that were indeed widely praised in Europe, and its most durable art in the form of worked ivory, with a good many tusks of unworked ivory.

Nzinga a Nkuwu also asked that, in return, he be sent items and that his people be taught skills he thought would be the most interesting to him and the Kongolese elite in general. He asked foremost that he receive full instruction in the Christian religion and, therefore, to receive priests who would teach Christianity. Written language was also among the components of Portuguese culture that he considered valuable since he also sent young people to learn "to speak Latin and write in the Latin alphabet" so that they "know each other's language" to teach the new religion.[28]

The first Kongolese visitors to Portugal had seen the European propensity to build in stone. We can imagine that their description of Lisbon's churches and elite houses sparked Nzinga a Nkuwu's imagination. To that end, he wanted to transfer that technology to Kongo and asked to have carpenters and masons who could construct houses and churches after the European pattern. It might also be that he thought stone buildings were a fundamental part of Christianity since he linked the masons and carpenters to the construction of churches. But the idea of palaces was surely not far behind.

Finally, it seems that the Kongolese had been impressed with bread and realized that making bread would require seeds and techniques to grow the grain and make the bread itself. And so Nzinga a Nkuwu asked for European farmers to demonstrate Portuguese cultivation techniques for crops like wheat, along with European women to teach the art of baking bread. While this might simply have been because bread was a new and interesting food, it was also fundamentally connected to Communion, and thus he thought to have that made in his own lands. Doing this, he concluded, would then make "one and the other kingdom" equal, and support a good relationship.[29]

During his stay in Kongo, Cão sailed up the Congo River as far as one could sail to the falls at Yelala, where his men carved their names on the rock and engraved on it the brand new (1485) coat of arms that João II had designed for Portugal. Then he returned to Portugal to deliver the Kongolese diplomatic mission to

---

spelling Zacuta in later chronicles. Anne Hilton, *Kingdom of Kongo* (London: Oxford University Press, 1985), pp. 50–51, following Cuvelier, links him to her own theory of the importance of the Nsaku ne Vunda clan.

28. De Pina, "Chronica," Book 3, chap. 58.

29. De Pina, "Chronica," chap. 58, and untitled Italian MS, fols. 87va and 87vb, again merging information from the two.

Lisbon, arriving late in 1486. A visiting Italian noted that the mission's head, a "great lord," was very tall, "beyond human stature and very large."[30]

João II, who was in Beja at the time, received the Kongo mission joyfully, understanding them to be representatives of a very powerful king who also wanted to become a Christian. For the mission to proceed successfully, the king decided to send the members of the mission to the monastery of São João Evangelista, commonly called Lóios, to live and study. Much of the teaching part of the mission was in the hands of one of the priests, a choirmaster named Vicente dos Anjos.

It was dos Anjos who took on the task of teaching them Portuguese and learned Kikongo himself in the process. As the Lóios' seventeenth-century chronicler noted (citing dos Anjos's obituary in the archive), "He had great trouble with them at first because he could not understand them; but by persisting and frequenting them, he came quickly to understand their language to such a degree that the Ethiopians [here meaning Kongolese] themselves admired the facility and fluency with which he spoke." In fact, it earned him the nickname "Vicente de Manicongo."

Dos Anjos served as an interpreter for both the king when he interviewed them and for the ambassadors while he taught them Portuguese. He also served in the role of catechist, a task that required a knowledge of Kikongo. According to his obituary, he used "the science of language" to teach "the truths of the Faith and the prayers of the Church."[31] Naturally, in order to teach even the fundamentals of religion, one must enter into the philosophy of the language of both the teacher and the learner; we can imagine that they needed to develop a shared spiritual vocabulary to describe basic concepts. That spiritual vocabulary had to come from his Kongolese students, and, in the interchange of ideas and vocabularies, the Kongolese interpretation of Christianity was born.

João's interest in Kongo went along with a number of other African initiatives with similar objectives to reinforce fiscal control of rich resources that would benefit the crown and to block out foreign competition. Even as Cão was initiating

30. Lorenzo di Giovanni Turnobouni to Benedetto Dei, November 4, 1486, published in Kate Lowe, "Africa in the News in Renaissance Italy: News Extracts from Portugal about Western Africa Circulating in Northern and Central Italy in the 1480s and 1490s," *Italian Studies* 65 (2013): 326. Turnobouni heard the news from Zanobio de Nero in Florence, who read out a letter from a friend in Lisbon; Turnobouni reported that the baptism of the king and the dispatch of a mission to Rome had already taken place, but in fact, it was at this point only in the planning state. Although Kongo is not mentioned by name, the circumstances and date can refer to no other kingdom in "Ghinea."

31. Vicente dos Anjos's biography, assembled from his obituary in the order's archives, formed the basis for these statements by the order's chronicler, Francisco de Santa Maria, *O Céu aberto na terra* (Lisbon, 1697), p. 895.

contact with Kongo, João Afonso d'Aveiro approached the kingdom of Benin in 1486, following up on an earlier contact by Fernão Po in 1485. Discovering that Benin could export valuable pepper, d'Aveiro arranged with King Ozolua to construct a second factory at Ughoton, an important town accessible by sea but now connected to a second powerful king. As in Kongo, the idea of forming an alliance was joined to the possibility of Christianizing Benin, especially as the king himself had queried them about Christianity and asked for missionaries to come to his land.[32]

Ozolua also sent an ambassador to Portugal who, confirming what d'Aveiro had learned, told the Portuguese that his country was ultimately subject to another powerful lord called Ogané, whose lands lay thirty moons' distance inland. Ogané, he said, sent newly enthroned Benin kings their regalia, which included a brass cross similar to "that worn by the Order of Saint John." By studying a map of Ptolemy, the Portuguese concluded that this Ogané must be none other than Prester John, a mysterious Christian king legendary in Europe since the twelfth century.[33]

To further add to his fiscal and security efforts, in 1488, João also entertained Jelen, an overthrown king of Jolof, situated along the Senegal River, and sought to restore him so that he could allow the Portuguese to build a fort at the mouth of the Senegal. The Portuguese hoped that the fort at the river would allow them to control the coast's gold trade. Furthermore, rumors had reached them of a land beyond Timbuktu with customs resembling those of the supposedly extensive Christian kingdom of Prester John, and they hoped to establish relations. The mysterious country they thought was Prester John's Ethiopia was probably the Mossi Kingdom, located in today's Burkina Faso, and a long way from Ethiopia. This mission to return Jelen to Jolof and establish a factory failed when the captain tasked with delivering the renegade king and materials for the fort killed him in an argument.[34]

Reaching Prester John's lands had been one of the goals of João II's son, Prince Henrique (known as "the Navigator"), among more prosaic endeavors, and in fact, Ethiopia was by then universally regarded in Europe as the land of this Christian ruler in "India." Ethiopian monks had visited Rome, and an Aragonese prince with family connections to Portugal had been involved in a proposed double marriage

---

32. Full details on the Benin mission are found in Ryder, *Benin and the Europeans*, pp. 30–41.

33. João de Barros, *Décadas da Ásia* (Lisbon, 1552), Decade 1, book 3, chap. 4, fol. 28.

34. Avelino Teixeira da Mota, "D. João Bemoim e a expedição portuguesa ao Senegal em 1489," *Boletim Cultural da Guiné Portuguesa* 36 (1971): 63–111. Bemoim arrived in Lisbon around November 1488, according to an Italian letter of November 20, 1488 published in Lowe, "Africa in the News," p. 326.

to seal an alliance between Aragon and Ethiopia. A new route to that land was an interesting possibility. In fact, in 1487, as missions from Kongo and Benin were visiting, João II dispatched Pero de Corvalhão to go to the court of Ethiopia/Prester John through the eastern Mediterranean. To complement this outreach, a second Ethiopian monk named Lucas Marqos arrived in Lisbon in 1488 as an ambassador and translated a return letter to be sent to the Prester.[35]

All of João II's strategic initiatives were coming together in the late 1480s. When Kala ka Mfusu and his mission arrived in Lisbon, they surely met their analogous African visitors, Jelen, Benin's ambassador, and Lucas Marqos. While there is no record of their interacting with each other, it is likely, given their high status, freedom of movement, and relations with the highest authorities in Portugal, that they met each other and probably interacted. If they did meet, it was likely to have been at the Lóios' church, which would become the place where foreign dignitaries and students came to study the Portuguese language and culture.[36]

To ensure his knowledge of Kongo was not confined to what the embassies had told him or what he might learn from an official mission, João II also commissioned an additional fund for independent information. By a royal order of August 9, 1490, a counterfeiter named Manuel de Vila Maior of Porto was ordered to have his prison sentence commuted to exile on São Tomé. From there, he was to make his way to Kongo by the first ship passing to "discover the things that he heard in the said county and to notify us of all matters in our service."[37] Nor was he the only such person, for Vasco da Gama, beginning his voyage to India in 1497, included in his crew a certain Martim Affonso, who had been "long in Manicongo" and who "knew many languages of the Blacks."[38]

Late in 1490, the mission prepared to return to Kongo. Heading it was a knight of King João II's household named Gonçalo de Sousa. The mission included Kala ka Mfusu, the Kongolese ambassador, now baptized as João da Silva, and a number of missionaries, including both secular priests and friars of various orders, notably the Franciscan contingent that included the linguist, João da Costa. Beyond the

35. Matteo Salvadore, *The African Prester John and the Birth of Ethiopian-European Relations, 1402–1555* (London: Routledge, 2017), pp. 88–96.

36. Manoel Severim de Faria, *Discorsos varios politicos* (Lisbon, 1624), fols. 32v–33. While this source relates to 1538, it suggests a longer standing role for the Lóios.

37. Royal order to Manuel de Vila Maior, August 9, 1490, in Luís de Albuquerque and Maria Emília Madeira Santos, eds., *Portugaliae Monumenta Africana*, 4 vols. (Lisbon: Imprensa Nacional, 1993–2002), 2:56.

38. References to Martim Affonso in original sources are cited in E. G. Ravenstein, *A Journal of the First Voyage of Vasco da Gama, 1497–1499* (London, 1898), pp. 12 and 17.

strictly ecclesiastical element, it also included the whole panoply of Portuguese workers that Nzinga a Nkuwu had requested: masons and carpenters to teach Portuguese building techniques and some peasant families to teach the art of making bread.[39] The expedition also carried a considerable number of weapons, including muskets and crossbows, as well as artillery. Along with deploying the weapons, the Portuguese soldiers were expected to teach the Kongolese something of European warfare.

Both ambassadors died on the return trip, victims of the plague that had struck Lisbon. The Portuguese ambassador was replaced by a relative named Rui de Sousa. On April 29, 1491, the ships arrived with great fanfare at the port of Chela in Kongo's province of Soyo. They were received by the ruler of Soyo, a fifty-year-old man who was the uncle of King Nzinga a Nkuwu (the brother of the king's mother).[40] After some discussion, it was decided that he and his followers could be baptized first, before the king, as he was older than the king was. The Mwene Soyo was baptized as Manuel, and his first-born son became Antonio.

The group then moved on to Mbanza Kongo, where Nzinga a Nkuwu was duly baptized as João, his first-born son as Afonso, and his wife Nzinga a Nlaza as Leonor, taking the Christian names of the king, presumptive heir, and queen of Portugal. Finally, within days of the baptisms—even as the first church, eventually dedicated to the Virgin Mary, was being built—the heavily armed Portuguese and the Kongo army headed off to war, bearing Christian standards, taking on rebels, "certain of his subjects who he held under his jurisdiction, on certain islands near the River of the Padrão."[41] After assembling what was described (with no small exaggeration) to be 80,000 troops as well as deploying the Portuguese naval force, the king reported a victory.

---

39. De Pina, "Chronica," Book 3, cap. 58, in cap. 63 (in the untitled manuscript, fol. 88rb, he said "friars of various orders" and not just Franciscans). He noted the head of the mission who died in Kongo as Friar João and was replaced by Friar António; in Academia das Ciências de Lisboa, MS Vermelho 804, p. 4, Salgado gave the names of four Franciscans who went to Kongo: João da Costa, António de Porto, João de Conceição, and António Sepúlveda.

40. The kinship is given in de Pina, untitled Italian MS, fol. 90va, "fratello della Madre," in Radulet, *O Cronista*.

41. De Pina, untitled Italian MS, fol. 98ra, "isole appresso lo fiume do Padrone," in Radulet, *O Cronista*. João de Barros placed the rebels in "certain islands near a great lake" and called them Mundequetos, which would mean the Teke of the kingdom of great Makoko, rather than the islands near the mouth of the river. Jean Cuvelier, *L'ancien royaume de Congo*, pp. 277–79 supported this interpretation, with a modification using later traditions from 1624, that it was a region near Teke, Nsanga, that revolted. I am inclined to support the original document in this case.

Sometime later, the Portuguese departed, carrying Dom Pedro, a new Kongolese ambassador to Portugal, along with a party of others. One of the Kongolese students, who recently returned from Portugal, penned instructions for the ambassador as well as a formal letter of introduction to the king of Portugal. He noted that the farmers sent from Portugal were growing wheat (an experiment that would not succeed) but that the women who had come to demonstrate baking bread had mostly died. He hoped that his ambassador would be able to pay homage at the Holy See in Rome, as Christian kingdoms do.[42] These were the first extant documents written by a Kongolese author and the start of Kongo's own written documentation.

The arrival of this mission created a major stir in Lisbon, as reported in an Italian letter contemporary with the event. João II, the letter noted, was sending experts to Kongo to teach the Portuguese language and customs.[43] Shortly after arriving, Pedro learned of the recent death of João II's son Afonso (whose name Nzinga a Nkuwu's son Afonso Mvemba a Nzinga had taken) the victim of an unfortunate equestrian accident. Pedro, who had dressed in European clothing that João II gave him, exchanged those clothes for mourning clothes "as if he were a native of the kingdom [of Portugal]."[44] Pedro remained in Portugal for about a year but was not able to continue to Rome to make obedience to the Holy See, and was on his way back to Kongo in December 1493.[45]

The first meeting of Portugal and Kongo was as much that of unexpected strangers as Columbus's meeting the Tainos in Hispaniola would be a decade later. Neither group expected to encounter the other, and the Kongolese, at least, had no idea of Europe, unlike the West Africans, who had been in contact with Europeans or North Africans directly or indirectly for centuries before the Portuguese voyages. European maps since the fourteenth century had depicted the geography of sub-Saharan West Africa quite accurately. They were able, with some degree of clumsiness, to match those maps with the reality they encountered along the coast. But no map showed the whole mass of sub-equatorial Africa, even as a speculation.

The Portuguese were, of course, aware that they were meeting people who were previously unknown to them. Indeed, the acclaimed sixteenth-century Portuguese

---

42. De Pina, untitled Italian MS, fols. 99rb–100rb, in Radulet, *O Cronista*.

43. Anonymous Italian letter, November 6, 1491, published in Lowe, "Africa in the News," p. 327 (retranscribing an earlier publication of Adriano Capelli, "A proposito di conqueste Africane," *Archivio Storico Lombardo* [1896], pp. 416–17).

44. Anonymous Italian letter, November 6, 1491, p. 326.

45. See various orders concerning his travel, the latest dating December 10, 1493, *MMA* 1: 150–51; 154–56.

poet Luís de Camões noted that "here, the very great kingdom is of Congo / converted by us to the faith of Christ" on a river "by the ancients never seen."[46] If they were unaware of the new region, however, it was not so different from what they had already been dealing with in Africa for the past half-century. Thus the early accounts have little of the awe factor that early Spanish accounts of the Aztec Empire had.

But if Kongo was, to the Portuguese, merely an extension of what they already knew of the rest of Africa, it was probably not the same for the Kongolese. Certainly, they had never seen people with the physical appearance of Portuguese, although the ships probably had Africans among their crews. No doubt the size of their vessels was impressive, even if Portuguese observers claimed Central Africans had "many great canoes" as Pacheco Pereira observed around 1506, which others maintained could carry a ton of merchandise and as many as 150 people. Yet these vessels were definitely not for sailing on the sea but for the Congo River and the adjacent coast.[47] If the Kongolese formed odd notions about these foreigners at that time, we cannot know from the documents we have of the encounter. In fact, their reaction appears to have been more or less unsurprised, though eventually, it did become the stuff of legend.

A hundred years after the Portuguese reached Kongo, the story of the countries' meeting had taken on legendary form in Kongo. According to a report circulating at the time, before the Portuguese came, there was a powerful "wizard" who lived on the coast and predicted that one day people with no toes and white faces would come. They should not be allowed to remain, the wizard warned, because they would put an end to the religion he represented. When the Portuguese did come, held back by contrary winds on a return voyage from India and thus forced to stop at the Congo River, the people mistook their ship for a floating house, and reported that the sailors had no toes (because they wore boots), had white faces and bodies of many colors (because they wore fitted and colorful clothes).[48]

---

46. Luís de Camões, *Lusíadas* (many editions, originally published Lisbon, 1572), canto 5, number 13.

47. Duarte Pacheco Pereira, *Esmeraldo de Situ Orbis*, ed. Epiphânia da Silva Dias (Lisbon, 1905), p. 133; Martín Fernández de Enciso, *Suma de geographia* (Seville, 1519), n.p.; Jean Alphonse de Saintonge, *Voyages adventureux* (Paris, 1559), fol. 55.

48. The story is recorded by the Spanish Carmelite Diego de Santissimo Sacramento, on the authority of a royal family member around 1585, Biblioteca Nacional de España, MS 2711, "Relacion de viaje . . ." fol. 99/118.

The Encounter of Two Worlds

It is easy to imagine that the meeting of these two societies would be that of unequal partners since so often, modern Africa's relationship to the West has been seen as one of inequality, with Europe possessing superiority in technology and economic development and using that superiority as a tool of exploitation. However true this might be in today's world, the situation was different in the pre-Industrial period. This view simultaneously credits early modern Europe with more progress than is warranted while not recognizing Africa's level of development in the same period.

If we use demography as a tool to explore performance, both regions possessed the same basic capacity to sustain human life. Kongo is the only African society for which we have some of the statistical possibility of studying demography because statistics of baptisms left by a later generation of priests allow us to measure it. Using late seventeenth- and early eighteenth-century data, scholars have been able to reconstruct a broad outline of the regime of life and death in Kongo; much more detailed work in ecclesiastical records in Europe has allowed a highly refined vision of early modern Europe. What these data show are broad similarities in the basic regime of life and death: Kongo had a higher birth rate than seventeenth-century Europe and a somewhat lower infant mortality rate. Both regions had very similar rates of survival of children to adulthood and thus similar overall average life expectancy of some thirty to thirty-five years.[49] Certainly, the stark disparity between today's Africa and Europe or North America was absent in the sixteenth century.[50]

The demography suggests that the fundamental base economy of the two regions was similar in its results, if not in their strategies toward achieving them. Portuguese peasants farmed, often using plows and yoked animals; grew wheat and other grain crops; raised cattle and small stock like chickens; and fished and hunted. According to an anonymous Italian letter of 1491, Kongolese peasants did much the same. Though they practiced hand cultivation with the hoe, they had a "great harvest of millet."[51] In 1517, Venetian geographer Alessandro Zorzi,

---

49. Basic information on demography comes from John Thornton, "Demography and History in the Kingdom of Kongo, 1550–1750," *Journal of African History* 18 (1977): 507–30, as amended in Thornton, "Revising the Population of the Kingdom of Kongo," *Journal of African History* 62 (2021): 201–12.

50. For comparisons, Thornton, *Cultural History of the Atlantic World*, pp. 30–32.

51. Anonymous Italian letter, November 6, 1491, p. 327. The anonymous author's ultimate source was the group that had just returned from Kongo and perhaps also their Kongolese compatriots, led by Dom Pedro.

relying on Portuguese informants, noted that in Kongo, they took in two harvests a year on a single field.[52] While the question of plow versus hoe in agriculture has been discussed in the history of economic development, descriptions of Kongolese farming and its output have tended to suggest it was as efficient as that of Europe, and the demography supports the idea that it delivered adequate results.[53]

A fuller account of peasant life in Kongo does not appear until the 1580s. Around that time, one Carmelite missionary wrote, "there are no poor people among them, because all are equal, and no one lacks sustenance, because they are content with little." In the eyes of the missionaries, their houses were well made, of wood with palm and grass walls and roof, and "artistically painted inside, quite good looking, in which they live well." Inside, one could find beds made on short posts with wickerwork tops, a couple of calabashes to keep palm wine, an earthenware cooking pot, and an earthenware pitcher decorated with many designs. Outside, they had some domestic animals, and the fields in which they grew their crops spread out around the houses; with this, "they live as contented and carefree as if they had all the gold in the world."[54]

Kongo and its neighbors were also industrially advanced when compared to sixteenth-century western Europe. If one considers metallurgy an industry, we can see a certain parity between the two regions. We have no direct data about the volume of ferrous metals that Kongo produced, but Spanish geographer Martín Fernández de Enciso, writing in 1519 from Portuguese sources available in Spain, claimed that the country had many smiths and ironworkers, smelting "iron and steel," who made "everything that we make" including excellent weapons. Later, in a letter of October 5, 1514, Afonso noted that he had sent a very good sword to Portugal to have a scabbard made. Making a fine sword was the ultimate mark of ferrous virtuosity, for the quality of steel was a critical part of making an excellent sword, and no piece of equipment had to meet such exacting standards. That

52. Alessandro Zorzi, "Informatiõ," fol. 134v.

53. On this debate, see John Thornton, "Precolonial African Industry and the Atlantic Trade," *African Economic History* 19 (1990–1991): 1–54, including Thornton's article and critiques of Ralph Austen, Jan Hogendorn and H. A. Gemery, E. Ann McDougall, and Patrick Manning with a response by Thornton.

54. This assessment is drawn from Carmelite accounts, of which several exist with varying degrees of detail, quoted here from a summary document in Biblioteca Apostolica Vaticana, Vatican Latina, MS 12516, fols. 109v and 117v, untitled report on Kongo, c. 1608, but based on Carmelite reports as well as Pigafetta. The author may have been Diego de la Encarnación, as it is written in a mixture of Italian and Spanish. Another anonymous untitled Carmelite account, attributed to him in *MMA* 4:399, has similar details as does the anonymous report in Biblioteca Nazionale Centrale Firenze, Panciatichiano 200, fol. 171; see Thornton, "Florentine Relation."

such a gift would be deemed appropriate—and Afonso's complaint that a servant's substitute sword was "wasn't worth two cents [*ceitis*]"—is a statement of the recognized quality of a Kongolese sword.[55]

In the past twenty years, archaeological research has radically altered our ideas of the antiquity and quality of African iron production, now placing it as early as in other parts of the world and with comparable quality. There were several important iron and steel-producing regions within Kongo. One of them has been investigated archaeologically and shows production in this period. However, the archaeological work cannot testify to the total volume of production.

Most of the early sources also establish that Kongo and its neighbors produced fine copper, sold as *manilhas* or horseshoe-shaped ingots.[56] In his 1514 letter, Afonso regularly refers to sending these *manilhas* along with slaves as payments or gifts. As in the case of ferrous metals, archaeology has explored the production of copper in this corner of West Central Africa and confirms what the written sources say.

Finally, West Central Africa, including Kongo, was a world-class producer of textiles. The Italian letter of 1491 mentions palm cloth as the normal form of clothing.[57] However, beyond this unusual (to Europeans) material, Portuguese observers still lauded the high quality of cloth made of raffia trees from the tropical rainforest belt that stretched into eastern Kongo. Pacheco Pereira praised the cloth produced in Kongo in his 1506 report, comparing it to the finest cloth in Italy.[58] Studies of existing samples of these early productions show very high levels of technical skill in producing cloth of the highest quality.[59] Early seventeenth-century statistics from Luanda, Angola, showed that the Portuguese then established in that port imported over 100,000 meters of this cloth annually from several regions, some in Kongo and others farther east or north. This statistic, which might be higher than the level produced a hundred years earlier, still indicates that these regions probably had a very high volume when compared to regions in Europe of equivalent size.[60]

Quite apart from questions of essential productivity and efficiency, however, societies are often judged based on what might be called their level of civilization,

55. See "Letter from the King of Kongo to D. Manuel I," October 5, 1514, in Correspondence.

56. Anonymous Italian letter, November 6, 1491, p. 327; Pereira, *Esmeraldo*, p. 134; Alphonse, *Voyages adventureux*, fol. 55v.

57. Anonymous Italian letter, November 6, 1491, p. 327.

58. Pereira, *Esmeraldo*, p. 134.

59. Fromont, "Getting to Know Early Modern Western Central African Textiles," pp. 138–51.

60. See as a foundational text, Jan Vansina, "Raffia Cloth in West Central Africa," pp. 263–81.

which typically focuses on a perceived quality of elite consumption: artwork, size and complexity of buildings, clothing styles, and ultimately concentrated income. "High" civilizations tend to have highly concentrated wealth, and the patronage that wealth supplies, which allows the elite consumers to have the material culture associated with wealth. Sixteenth-century assessments of wealth typically focused on these elements. However, modern economists are more likely to consider economic strength in terms of income equality as gauged by measures such as the Gini coefficient or GDP per capita. For example, most economists would not consider a society like modern Angola, which derives much of its GDP per capita from oil revenues but also has vast slums, as a healthy or wealthy society.

Viewed from the sixteenth-century perspective, Kongo was less developed than Portugal. Although Mbanza Kongo was a large city, even by European standards (the anonymous Italian letter compared it to Portugal's second city of Évora), its architecture was of wood and wood products like palm leaves; houses were modest, even if "of wood and well made" and among the best in Guinea, according to the anonymous Italian letter and anticipating the more detailed Carmelite reports.[61] Although the description of Nzinga a Nkuwu's appearance at the time of the arrival of the missionaries in 1491 was generally admiring, it was probably perceived by the Europeans as less substantial than what a king would wear in Portugal, seated on a rich throne, if for no other reason than he left his upper body bare.[62]

Exactly how one might measure the basic strength of the economies of Europe and Africa in this period is not easy. It is difficult to compare the values of what we might consider luxury sectors. Certainly, performance in daily life for the bulk of the population was equal, but perhaps Nzinga a Nkuwu's assessment of what he wanted from Portugal included stone buildings and some military technology, but with that, he thought the two countries would become equal. He offered in exchange material from the luxury sector of his own economy worked ivory, copper, and, above all, textiles.

61. Anonymous Italian letter, November 6, 1491, p. 327.

62. De Pina, "Chronica," Book 3, chap. 58, and untitled Italian MS, fols. 93va–93vb. A less detailed image of the Mwene Soyo is at 89rb.

CHAPTER 2

TAKING POWER

Though historians do not know much about the last years of João I Nzinga a Nkuwu's reign, we do know that sometime around 1506, he sent a letter to Portugal to ask for military aid against "rebels in the islands"; these were probably the same rebels who had given him trouble in 1491. King Manuel dispatched a war fleet, under the command of Gonçalo Rodrigues Ribeiro, to conduct marine operations against the islands on João's behalf.[1] But when Rodrigues reached Kongo in early 1507, he discovered that João had died, and there was a new king on the throne: João's eldest son, Afonso.[2]

In his letter of October 5, 1514, after his father's death, Afonso mentions a miraculous victory against his brother, who had challenged his right to rule. Afonso had the priest Francisco Fernandez write an official description of this victory for Manuel. But this letter never reached its intended recipient as Fernandez died on the way back to Portugal. A second letter, sent by Afonso via his nephew Gonçalo, was delivered, and Manuel replied to Afonso. Later, in 1508, when Afonso sent his cousin Dom Pedro de Sousa to Lisbon as an ambassador to Portugal (and eventually to the pope in Rome), he also sent another man named Pedro, who had personally witnessed the miracle, to vouch for its authenticity. Thus, Afonso's letter, the testimony of Pedro regarding the miracle, and no doubt additional information supplied by Pedro de Sousa likely created a small body of documentation

1. Instructions to Gonçalo Rodrigues, undated, António Brásio, *Monumenta Missionaria Africana*, 15 vols. (Lisbon: Agência Geral do Ultramar, 1952–1988), 4:60–62 (this source will henceforward be cited as *MMA*). Rodrigues made two visits to São Tomé: in 1506 and again in 1509, according to an inquest conducted into his behavior in 1511 (*MMA* 1:215). Brásio dated these instructions to 1509 in the belief that Rodrigues had only visited Kongo in 1509. Documents establish that he came to Kongo in 1506, and as the instructions were for a military mission against the islands that had revolted, it seems likely that it should be dated 1506.

2. An account of Rodrigues's activities is found in an inquest into various atrocities he was alleged to have performed, taken in December 1511 and January 1512. The prologue says that Rodrigues came to São Tomé some five years earlier, or in early 1507, *MMA* 1:215.

on the event, perhaps including a formal inquiry. There are no surviving original copies of any of these letters or documents: the whole body of evidence was probably lost in the Lisbon earthquake and fire of 1755, along with so many other early Portuguese documents from the period.

The earliest account of the miracle now extant is found in some letters from 1512, regarding a proposed coat of arms to be circulated among Kongo's nobility; it was prefaced with a brief description of the battle and miracle.[3] However, the lost accounts clearly had much more detail. We can gain a reasonably good idea about the contents of the whole testimony by seeing how other writers, who probably saw much longer original accounts, made use of them in their later works.

A near-contemporary account published in 1519 by the Spanish geographer Martín Fernández de Enciso provides an overview with a few details (and variants) not found in the 1512 letters.[4] But a much more detailed account was put together by the Portuguese chronicler João de Barros. Although it was only published in 1552, de Barros's version was certainly based on the documents and whatever testimony came from Pedro de Sousa's mission.[5] Another historian, the Italian Jesuit priest Giovanni Pietro Maffei, who had been commissioned to write an account of Portuguese discoveries, may also have seen the same documents. He spent four years in Lisbon with privileged access to the Portuguese royal archives and published his version in 1588.[6] His account is very similar to that of de Barros but also includes other details that might have come from other parts of the same collection he saw in Lisbon.

According to de Barros's version, Afonso became a fervent Christian.[7] But his brother Panso Aquitimo (probably Mpanzu a Kitemu) refused to be baptized along

3. This letter was quoted by the Portuguese chronicler Damião de Góis, *Chronica delRey Dom Manuel*, Part III, chap. 38, *MMA* 1:194–95. There is another copy of this letter in the Biblioteca Nacional of Lisbon, with a few minor variations, probably a draft of the final version in de Góis. Another letter, addressed to the "People," also similar in content, is found in the Public Library and Archives in Évora; all versions published in *MMA* 1:256–69.

4. Martín Fernández de Enciso, *Suma de geographia* (Seville, 1519), fols.109–10. This is the earliest printed account. Enciso spent much of his time in the Americas but did visit Europe at various times before *Suma* was published, although he does not appear to have been to Portugal.

5. See "The Reign of D. Afonso I of Kongo," 1493?–1543, in Correspondence. De Barros served as head of the Casa de Mina e India, the central repository for all overseas business at the time, with some breaks, from 1524 to 1568.

6. Giovanni Pietro Maffei, *Historiarum Indicarum libri XVI* (Florence, 1588), p. 12.

7. In the account that follows, I will use primarily de Barros, augmenting or emending where other accounts provide other details or contradictions.

with the king and other nobles and distanced himself from the court.[8] Like other nobles, Mpanzu a Kitemu was troubled by the Christian conception of monogamous marriage. Becoming a Christian would require that the converted nobles repudiate all but one wife, with considerable political consequences. The problem of Christianity's demand for monogamy was also mentioned in other early sources as a significant problem, one by the Italian visitor to Lisbon written in 1491; another by Pacheco Pereira, a Portuguese official serving as a royal factor in the fort of Mina, writing in 1506. De Barros explained the problem in more detail, probably from Afonso's perspective, contending that the repudiated wives of the court nobles pleaded with their husbands to reject the new religion and restore their status. Faced with these difficulties, João cooled to the faith and returned to the old rites and customs. Chagrined by João's change of heart, Afonso denounced his father's decision.

Upset by Afonso's insistent criticism, the councilors persuaded the elderly king to demote Afonso from his favor. In his letter of October 5, 1514, Afonso described the effects of this disfavor, directed both at him and his cousin Pedro. The king threatened to kill Pedro "to see if God would deliver him." As for Afonso, the king threatened to take away his *renda*, a Portuguese term referring to an income-producing asset; in Kongo, this term usually referred to a noble's right to collect a share of tax income from a territory. Afonso's *renda* was the "Commander of the Kingdom," another name for the province of Nsundi, located in the country's northeast corner and traditionally held by the heir apparent. Removed from his *renda*—and lacking any private property—Afonso, with his brother Pedro, would, in Afonso's words, "wander about like a wayward man" until the king might simply decide to kill them.[9]

The anti-Christian nobles conspired to advance Afonso's rival brother, Mpanzu a Kitemu, to be next in line for succession when João Nzinga a Nkuwu died. This would allow them to return to the "customs of the past," specifically the taking of multiple wives. To poison the king's mind against Afonso, the anti-Christian councilors accused Afonso of witchcraft. They claimed that he was using his Christian powers to dry up rivers and spoil crops to ruin the productivity of the

8. No contemporary source translates this name, but in the Kikongo dictionary of 1648 [Biblioteca Nazionale da Roma, MS Fundo Minori 1896, MS Varia 274, fol. 106v], the stem *-tema* appears in the Latin entry *taúritas* reglossed in Spanish as *taúri ferocia* or "ferocious bull," and in Kikongo as *utéma üangonbe* (actually, "the fury of a bull"). In this definition, the stem is in a noun class appropriate to abstract principles, defined by *ki-*, here it becomes specific to names. I have chosen to respell de Barros's term with an "e" rather than an "i." Formal name: Mpanzu a Nzinga.

9. See "Letter from the King of Kongo to D. Manuel I," October 5, 1514, in Correspondence.

rendas from which the nobles drew their tax-based income and provoking the inhabitants of those *rendas* to revolt. They also claimed that the Christians had "taught him [Afonso] to fly" and that he used these powers to fly from Nsundi, "some eighty leagues away" from the court, to sleep with the wives that the king had repudiated and return on the same night.[10]

Outraged, the king took the governorship of Nsundi away from Afonso. Afonso's supporters swore that he had done no wrong, saying they had stayed by his side and knew that he never left on any nocturnal journeys. To test whether his son possessed any secret powers, João Nzinga a Nkuwu announced that he would kill his former wives for betraying him. He then had a "fetish" wrapped in cloth and secretly delivered to "Cufua Coanfulo," the wife he suspected of receiving Afonso. Though de Barros does not explain more about this woman, Cufua Coanfulo would not be a personal name, but a nickname or byname—Kufwa kwa Mfulu—meaning "the death [or destruction] of a place," and so one likely to able to use occult powers herself to wreak havoc or deploy them for protection.[11]

The servant who delivered the fetish was to tell Cufua Coanfulo that it was a gift from Afonso, intended to protect her from the king's plan to slaughter his wives who were sleeping with Afonso. However, since she knew she was "innocent of the crime that would have earned her the death sentence from which the gift was meant to protect her" she took the object to the king to ask him about it, and the king was satisfied that Afonso was innocent. Secretly, he restored Afonso to his favor, and not only returned Nsundi to him but also expanded his revenue. He then called together the councilors who had advised him of Afonso's plot, told them of the gambit, and had them killed.

But other anti-Christians soon spread the word that Afonso, who was fervently proselytizing in Nsundi, had ordered the death penalty for anyone still worshipping idols. The anti-Christian councilors told João that residents in Nsundi were so upset by this (false) decree that the province was ready to "rise up against his Royal Person if he did not deal with this matter." João once again summoned his son to the court. But Pedro, one of the few remaining Christians in the court, defended Afonso and used his own reputation for wisdom and caution to support

---

10. A massive exaggeration: 80 leagues would be some 450 kilometers, the actual distance would be about 200 or 250 kilometers if one followed the normal route due east to the Inkisi River and then north along the river to Mbanza Nsundi, identified as the archaeological site of Kindoki.

11. In the sixteenth century, Kikongo still used the prefix *ku-* for the infinitive form of verbs (it was lost in the eighteenth century); the verb *-fwa* means to die or to be destroyed. The dictionary of 1648, for example has *kufwa kwa ulongo* (death of a ship) to describe a shipwreck.

him.[12] Citing various issues regarding governance, revenues, and the like, Pedro stalled for time, making it possible for Afonso to delay his return to court. Meanwhile, Pedro let Afonso know that he had heard that João was close to death and that Afonso might want to arrive in the city before his father died. Other nobles, who would pass judgment on Afonso, were also probably moving toward the city in anticipation of João's demise.

When the announcement of João's impending death reached Afonso, he ignored it at first, thinking it was a trick being played on him by his enemies. But when his supporters confirmed that Mpanzu a Kitemu was advancing on the capital to claim the crown for himself, Afonso moved as fast as possible to arrive at the capital. As he approached Mbanza Kongo, Afonso's mother, Leonor Nzinga a Nlaza, sent him a message advising that he arrive secretly, at night, with only a few followers in small groups; she told Afonso that his men should hide their weapons in baskets, disguised as food deliveries for the queen.[13]

The morning after he arrived in Mbanza Kongo, Afonso summoned the nobles to the *mbazi*, the great central square, and announced that he was claiming the kingdom. He delivered "a well-reasoned speech," which began by praising Christianity and its benefits. Afonso explained that, as the faith was now widely accepted in Kongo (contrary to his assertions that he was practically the only Christian in the kingdom), he had an obligation to defend it. He then pointed out that Mpanzu a Kitemu and his partisans had lied to and cheated him, causing him to lose his positions and income. Afonso contended that he was the legitimate successor according to the country's ancient laws, perhaps by citing his control of Nsundi. After hearing this speech, "the [nobles] proclaimed him king according to their custom, with a great celebration, loud cheers, and music."[14] But Afonso's brother Mpanzu a Kitemu was also arriving at the city with his army and heard the music and fanfare.

De Barros gives a brief account of the ensuing battle, and Maffei augmented it with a few other details. But it might be useful here to refer to another version of the battle, one relayed to the Italian humanist Filippo Pigafetta in 1587–1588 by Duarte Lopes, a Portuguese converted Jew (New Christian), then representing Kongo in Rome. Lopes had lived in Kongo from 1579 to 1584 and had certainly

12. De Barros named him Gonçalo, but Afonso's own correspondence names him Pedro. See "Letter from the King of Kongo to D. Manuel I," October 5, 1514, in Correspondence.

13. There are variations in the accounts of these events that would modify the battle; for example, in his letter to his lords in 1512, Afonso said that Mpanzu had occupied the city.

14. The quotation is from de Barros. Afonso's speech to the nobles is in Maffei, *Historiarum,* pp. 11–12.

heard local stories of these events.[15] Although Pigafetta drew heavily on Maffei and de Barros's books for many portions of his account of the miracles, he also drew on "the writings and discourses" supplied by Lopes.[16] It is likely that what Lopes heard in Kongo was a secondhand account since an eyewitness at age fifteen would have been in his nineties in 1579, but no doubt descriptions of the battle were widespread and linked to landmarks around the city, when he lived there.[17] Lopes also had intimate knowledge of the geography of Mbanza Kongo, unlike de Barros and Maffei.

Pigafetta wrote that a good number of the troops who had come to support Afonso deserted when Mpanzu a Kitemu issued an ultimatum demanding that he be named king and that Afonso renounce his claim and Christianity, or he and his followers would be killed. This desertion made Mpanzu a Kitemu think that Afonso was so weakened he had given up all hope. Pigafetta also added, from Lopes, a story of a heavenly vision that came to Afonso and his followers as they prayed on the eve of the battle; this vision, not found in any other accounts, revealed to Afonso the five swords he subsequently placed on his coat of arms.[18]

When Mpanzu a Kitemu issued his challenge, Afonso claimed he had only thirty-seven supporters with which to face his brother's army. But this may be misleading, for if later practice is a guide, Kongolese armies were usually composed of two components: heavy infantry (typically nobles who fought with a sword or assegai, protected by a shield) and light infantry (usually men of lower status primarily armed with bows). The use of the shield among the heavy infantry was notable: the Portuguese sources called them *adargueiros*, or "shield men." They were highly skilled in hand-to-hand combat and formed the core of an army. But Kongolese armies usually included ten times as many light infantry, made up

15. On the adventure of Duarte Lopes and his connections to Pigafetta, see Teobaldo Filesi, "Duarte Lopez ambasciatore del re del Congo presso Sisto V nel 1588," *Africa* (Rome) 23 (1968): 44–84.

16. The title of Pigafetta's book, *Relatione del Regno di Congo e cinconvince contrade, Tratta dalli scritti e ragionamenti di Oudardo Lopez, Portughese* (Rome, 1591), suggests writing and reasonings (Margarite Hutchinson's 1881 *A Report on the Kingdom of Congo* translation has "discourse").

17. I heard several stories of battles of the Angolan civil war, linked to places and even pointed out, when traveling in northern Angola in 2011. The people describing them were of course eyewitnesses to events just ten or fifteen years earlier, but they were surrounded by crowds of interested children who might retell it to their own children.

18. The letter, however, does not describe the vision in detailing the meaning of the swords, only saying they represented the armed horsemen who were in fact angels coming to his aid.

of the commoners who fought as archers and whose volleys began each battle.[19] Maffei, in his account of the battle, noted that Afonso appealed to his heavy infantry but also to the "now panic-stricken crowd of civilians which had gathered at the palace, to be of good courage," that God would help them if they fought on his side, "and so it came to pass."[20] These civilians likely made up the light infantry. Also, Mpanzu a Kitemu's heavy infantry may not have been an advantage, as it was difficult for large numbers to travel the narrow passages into the city.

In his 1512 letter to his nobles, Afonso wrote that his brother was already inside the city when he arrived and that, upon entering, "my brother came against us with a mighty army of people from within the city, which was large, as well as from the outskirts."[21] This seems unlikely, however, given de Barros's and Maffei's accounts that Afonso arrived secretly, met the nobles, made his speech, and was named king while Mpanzu a Kitemu remained outside the city. Only if his small force was inside the city, defending it, would Afonso have stood a chance against his brother's larger army; they would not have succeeded in attacking the entrenched larger force from outside the city.

Mbanza Kongo is situated on a plateau at the top of a sheer-sided mountain; the only approach on the east side was through a steep incline north of the city and up a narrow road. At the top of this road was a fort that controlled the entry to the city.[22] Afonso would have deployed his heavy infantry at this narrow passage to stop his brother's advance. What seems most likely is that Mpanzu a Kitemu drew up his army on the northern side of the great plateau of Mbanza Kongo and prepared to advance up the road, placing sharpened stakes in a shallow marsh, which covered the space between the end of the road and the river; this would force would-be counter-attackers to narrow their front.[23]

---

19. John Thornton, "The Art of War in Angola, 1575–1680," *Comparative Studies in Society and History* 30 (1988): 360–78.

20. Maffei, *Historiarum*, p. 12.

21. See "Letter from the King of Kongo to the Lords of the Kingdom," 1512, in Correspondence.

22. Only Enciso mentions a fortress (*fortaleza*) over which the two armies fought, but his account, although early, varies more than the others. There certainly was a tower there later, as it is shown in the engraving of Mbanza Kongo/São Salvador in Olfert Dapper's *Naukeurige Bescrhijvinge der Africa gewesten* (Amsterdam, 1668). No other visitor described a tower, except Adolph Bastian, visiting in 1857, *Ein Besuch in San Salvador, der Hauptstadt des Königreichs Congo* (Bremen, 1859), p. 124. There is no tower at that point now, though there is a small cement cone in the present-day royal cemetery, perhaps to recognize the old tower.

23. Pigafetta, *Relatione*, pp. 51–52 (for the battle). This geography is reinforced by my own visits to Mbanza Kongo in 2002, 2007, 2011, and 2014, as well as my discussions with members of

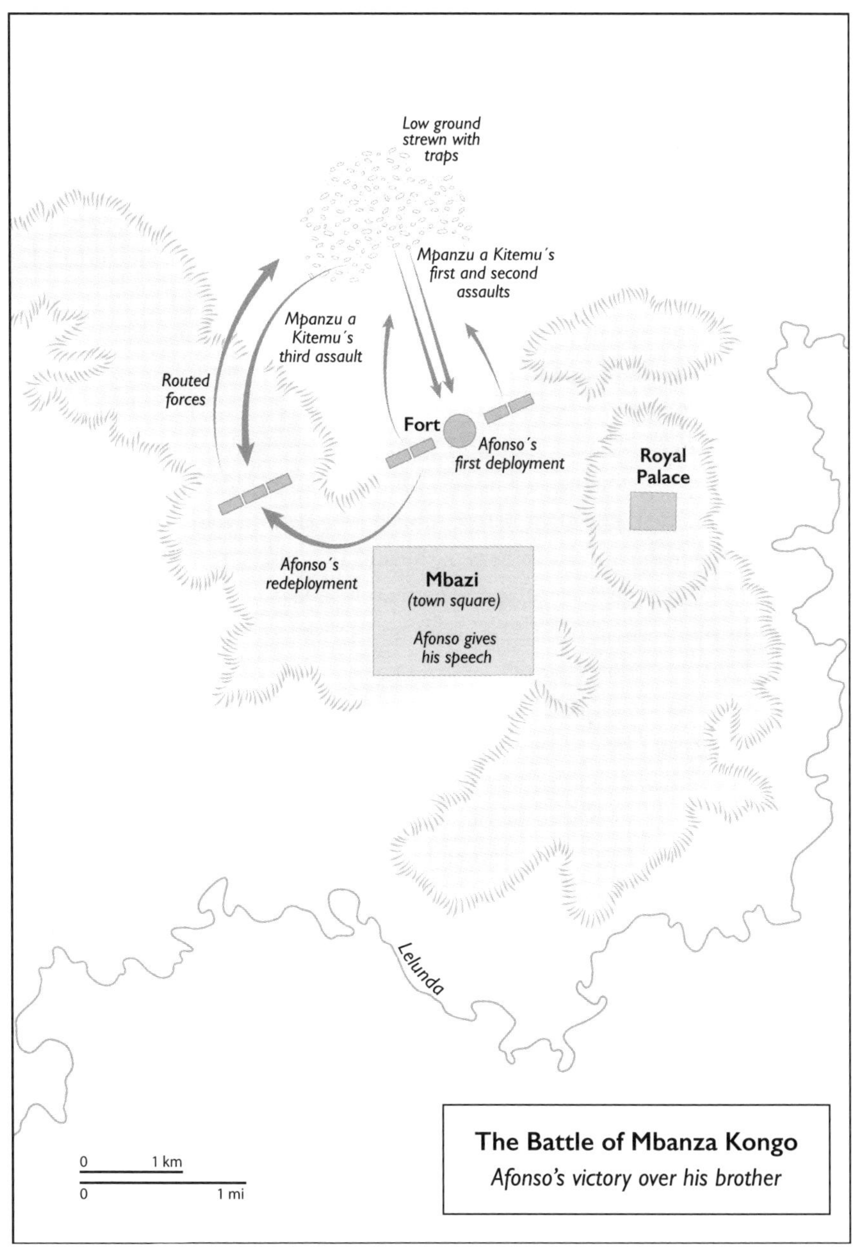

The Battle of Mbanza Kongo
Afonso's victory over his brother

From that base, Mpanzu a Kitemu led two consecutive assaults up the road to the summit of the mountain; he was repelled both times. For the third assault, he split his forces. One diversionary detachment went up the main road and was again repelled. But the second force—under Mpanzu a Kitemu himself—took a more northern route up a second, narrower valley to appear, unexpectedly, on Afonso's left flank. When Afonso's troops redeployed to face them, Mpanzu a Kitemu's men rained arrows on them in preparation for a final attack with sword and assegai. Afonso's soldiers, fearing this would be their end, called out to Santiago (Saint James the Greater), the Portuguese military saint, while Afonso appealed to Jesus. To their surprise, Mpanzu a Kitemu's troops suddenly fled in panic and rushed back through their own ranks, completely disorganizing them, resulting in a headlong retreat of all the men down the valley.[24] In the sudden retreat, Mpanzu a Kitemu was impaled on one of the stakes he himself had set in the marsh at the foot of the mountain.

Bewildered by this sudden turn of events, Afonso and his supporters interviewed the survivors. Mpanzu a Kitemu's captain, who fled alongside the would-be king, was captured and brought before Afonso. The captain told Afonso that when Afonso and his men shouted to heaven, he and the others in Mpanzu a Kitemu's party beheld "a great number of armed men on horseback following a sign just like one the Christians worshipped."[25] This vision frightened Mpanzu a Kitemu's men so much that they fled in disorder.

The captain was convinced by this miracle that Christianity was true and asked only to be baptized before he was executed. Moved by his conviction, Afonso spared his life, ordered that he be delivered to Pedro (the Christian councilor who had supported Afonso before his father), granted an income, and tasked with sweeping and cleaning the churches and fetching water for baptisms.[26] The captain was then baptized, taking the name of Pedro after his sponsor. Afonso eventually sent him to Portugal to testify as a witness to the miracle along with the ambassador Pedro de Sousa.

As matter-of-fact as these accounts are (allowing for the miracle), however, there is reason to doubt elements of their presentation of the events. Afonso's victory

---

the archaeology team excavating Mbanza Kongo in 2014. Daniel Pinto of that team had located the springs, buildings, and other landmarks that are consistent with this description.

24. The split force is only noted by Enciso, *Suma*; Maffei, *Historiarum*, p. 12, has them advancing in a double line; this could be with the heavy infantry in front and the light infantry behind.

25. See "The Reign of D. Afonso I of Kongo," 1493?–1543, in Correspondence.

26. De Barros called this councilor Gonçalo, but Afonso, in his letter of October 5, 1514, names him Pedro, specifically associating him with this event.

could have been the result of skillful tactics taking advantage of fortifications and terrain on Afonso's part and the luck of the battle. Some scholars claim that Afonso had help from Portuguese forces, but this is unlikely as João had asked for forces to come to attack the islands on the eve of his death, a request that would not have been necessary if there was already a body of Portuguese there. Afonso's letter makes it clear that Rodrigues's forces did not arrive until the battle was already firmly won.[27] Furthermore, the Portuguese contributing to the victory would surely have made this known back in Lisbon; no documentation supports this, even though both de Barros and Maffei had access to the archives and would have been delighted to claim it.

What little outside evidence there is of the Christian versus anti-Christian showdown that Afonso describes does not entirely support the idea of a religious conflict. First of all, it seems unlikely that Mpanzu a Kitemu refused to be baptized: the contemporary account notes that all the great nobles were baptized. Dissention at that point, especially from a high-placed noble, would certainly have been noted.

If there had been any dissension, it certainly did not emerge until much later. Damião de Góis, whose chronicle is based largely on the early sources (he reproduces the final version of the 1512 letters), describes the well-received arrival of a mission of new priests in 1504—thirteen years after João's conversion and just over two years before his death. This party included scholars and teachers, musicians and their instruments, and a large number of books to render the Christian message and teach the elite.

The mission was gladly received by the multitude, and "they converted many of the inhabitants to the faith of our Lord Jesus Christ." Nobles and lords of this "vast province" sent their children to be educated by them, and some Kongolese students even traveled to Portugal for further study.[28] All this suggested that, so far as the chronicler was aware, this Christian mission was successful for some time in Kongo without any signs of trouble. However, Duarte Pacheco Pereira's account of the coast of Africa, written in 1506, as the events Afonso described were unfolding, indicated that there were some problems with Christianity in the country. Pereira notes that the elites were reluctant to allow non-elites full participation in Christian

---

27. Suggested by W. G. L. Randles, *L'ancien royaume du Congo* (Paris: Mouton & Co., 1965), pp. 97–98; and Anne Hilton, *Kingdom of Kongo* (London: Oxford University Press, 1985), pp. 53–54. Hilton's influential book has shaped a number of accounts, for example, tentatively, Howard French, *Born in Blackness: Africa, Africans and the Making of the Modern World, 1471 to the Second World War* (New York: Liveright Publishing, 2021), p. 285.

28. De Góis, *Chronica*, Part I, chap. 76, *MMA* 1:194–95.

rituals, and they were unwilling to give up their many wives. In summary, Pereira observed that "through our little engagement with these people, [Christian] doctrine amongst them has lost as much as it could."[29]

In any case, Afonso had based his entire account on the idea of his conversion and firm adherence to Christianity in the face of his brother's challenge. In both his 1512 and 1514 letters, Afonso spoke of denouncing his old religion. What would that entail?

Religion in Kongo

We have only a vague understanding of Kongolese religious beliefs when the first Portuguese arrived or when João was baptized in 1491. No one wrote a treatise on the religion of the country at that time, or at least no such treatise survived. To learn about the Central African traditions of which Kongo was surely a part, we must read the treatises written in the late sixteenth and particularly in the seventeenth century about the religion of unconverted neighboring countries. For example, in 1668, Dutch geographer Olfert Dapper published a lengthy description, based on Dutch accounts written in the 1640s, of the religion of the Kingdom of Loango, a country that spoke a dialect of the same Kikongo spoken in Kongo itself.[30] At about the same time, Giovanni Antonio Cavazzi, an Italian missionary, wrote a lengthy treatise on the religion of Ndongo, a country that bordered Kongo on the south. Though Ndongo did not speak Kikongo, the country's language was similar to Kongo's, as close as Italian is to Portuguese.[31]

These comparable cultures likely possessed many of the same features as Kongo a century and a half earlier, but of course, all religious traditions change over time,

---

29. Duarte Pacheco Pereira, *Esmeraldo de Situ Orbis*, variorum ed. Augusto Epiphânia da Silva Dias (Lisbon, 1905), Book 2, chap. 2, pp. 133–34. I am departing slightly from George Kimball's translation of 1937.

30. Dapper's source for this was probably Abraham Willaerts, a fine artist who was sent to Angola in 1641 with the specific task of documenting the customs of the people (see Cornelis de Blie, *Het Gulden Cabinet vande Edele Vry Schilder-Const* [Antwerp, 1662] p. 247). He is probably also responsible for the artwork that became the engravings in Dapper's book, including the panorama of Mbanza Kongo.

31. This, and the section that follows, is largely based on John Thornton, "Religious and Ceremonial Life in the Kongo and Mbundu Areas," in *Central Africans and Transformations in the American Diaspora*, ed. Linda Heywood (Cambridge: Cambridge University Press, 2002), pp. 71–90. As for the language similarity, my statements are based only on experience in both languages and not formal linguistic analysis.

and no two cultural traditions are completely identical. To these accounts, we can also add complaints by missionaries to Kongo, especially those from Capuchin missionaries (like Cavazzi) who denounced many customs practiced by Christian Kongolese they considered remnants of the old religion. Finally, since they are often more systematic (although greatly removed in time and function), we can also use more recent ethnographic accounts of religion in the same areas both during and after the intense missionary activity that took place in the region during the colonial period.

It is important to note that Central African religions were not dogmatic. That is, they did not have a fixed body of beliefs that one could recite, nor did they have what might be considered a priesthood responsible for educating people on these beliefs. People freely disagreed on such subjects as the residence of the ancestors or even on life after death. Indeed, early witnesses even reported people who did not believe another supernatural world existed. There does not appear to have been conflict over differing ideas of the cosmos, but religious differences might have arisen over perceived misuse of spiritual entities.[32]

The variations in religious ideas existed partly because of the dominant role of continuous revelation in Central African religion. Continuous revelation means that the activities and intentions of whatever beings live in the Other World are constantly revealed as a result of supplication. For example, if supplicating a particular deity results in a successful outcome, the existence of the being is confirmed; but if the outcomes are consistently less satisfactory, the being might be held to not exist or to have lost its power. By the same token, some believers might have continued to supplicate the less-effective entity, thinking that their approach or other aspects of the supplication were erroneous. Thus, relative success, and not a fixed and established cosmology, determined belief.

Abrahamic religions like Christianity, Judaism, and Islam rely on discontinuous revelation, typically a very extensive message from the Other World revealing a complex cosmology. Such revelations are only rarely transmitted (hence "discontinuous") but are preserved either in memorized texts or written documents. Much of the strife of the early Christian church, revealed in records from, for example, the councils at Nicaea and Chalcedon, involved cosmological issues like the nature of Christ, the relative positions of the three figures of the Trinity, the nature of Creation, and so on. Central Africans did have general cosmological ideas, but the specifics were much less important or fixed, as a more experimental approach would reveal.

---

32. Some of these remarkable contradictions can be found in the seventeenth-century descriptions, for examples, see Thornton, "Religious and Ceremonial Life," pp. 74–75.

Thus, we can draw on our limited sources to sketch out the outlines of a general framing cosmology for Kongo at the start of the sixteenth century. Although missionaries and modern researchers alike usually start by defining the Supreme Being or high god—and though there is reason to believe that Kongolese did recognize such a deity, probably called Nzambi a Mpungu—most Kongolese might not begin a discussion of their religion with an examination of this Supreme Being. Rather, they would more likely start with their deceased ancestors, the supplication of whom formed the core of Kongo's everyday religious beliefs.[33]

Like their neighbors and successors, the Kongolese of the 1500s probably believed that the dead lived on in an ill-defined location and that the dead could and did intervene in the lives of their descendants with the additional supernatural power of spirits. If a person fell sick or was hoping to have success in farming, commerce, or hunting, an ancestor might be able to assist. Ancestors could also make demands of the living, and those who ignored them might be plagued with bad luck or illness.

Everyone had ancestors, but not all ancestors were equal. Powerful nobles' or kings' ancestors could intervene in their lives in such a way that the whole community was affected. For that reason, people might also seek assistance from those souls or be directed to do so by the descendants of these powerful ancestors.

There were, in addition to ancestors, more powerful spiritual beings who controlled the fate of whole territories. In the non-dogmatic religion of Central Africa, these beings were sometimes held to be ancient ancestors, such as the first person to live in a place; other times, they were considered eternal spirits. These were called various names, *nkita* (plural *zinkita*) being the one most common in the texts relating to Kongo, while *simbi* (plural *isimbi*) is a common term in modern anthropological literature. Often *nkitas* inhabited a particular spot, and a shrine to them might be constructed there.

Finally, there was a host of lesser spirits, which might have been ancestral in origin but had since lost their moorings and were free, though with limited power. They could be a nuisance or a threat. Some of these lesser spirits might be captured and put to use if one could create a portable vehicle (a *kiteke*, plural *iteke*) in which to entrap them.

A force called *nkisi* (plural *zinkisi* or *minkisi*)—the essence of spirit that inhabited all living and otherworldly beings—held the whole spiritual world together.

33. For continuous and discontinuous revelation, see John Thornton, *Africa and Africans in the Making of the Atlantic World, 1400–1800*, 2nd ed. (Cambridge: Cambridge University Press, 1998), pp. 235–53; Thornton, *Cultural History of the Atlantic World, 1350–1820* (Cambridge: Cambridge University Press, 2012), pp. 398–418.

It could divide and become specialized spiritual forces, often with specific names. *Nkisi* could inhabit particular objects or shrines, in which case the object itself would become *nkisi*. Because of this idea that an inhabited *kiteke* became the inhabiting *nkisi*, the term *nkisi* is widely used today to describe these spiritual vessels (especially in northern dialects such as those spoken in Loango).

Finally, Central Africans believed that while spiritual forces would normally be used in beneficial ways, they could also be used selfishly to cause harm to others. Whatever the source of the damaging power was—be it an ancestor, a *nkita*, or one of the lesser spiritual beings—using it to harm others was considered witchcraft. The Kikongo word *kindoki* was used to refer to persons who used spiritual power in harmful ways. Derived from the term for "cursing" (*-loka*), the word *kindoki* is frequently translated as "witchcraft." While some spiritual entities (most often lesser spirits) were evil in their own right, it was also possible to use ancestral spirits for wicked purposes as well. The *nkita* would not allow themselves to be used for harmful purposes though they were capable of doing harm on their own.

Afonso gave a certain amount of verification to these ideas in his lost letters, the contents of which we believe were preserved in de Barros's and Maffei's account of Afonso's miracle. At one point, Afonso claims he was denounced by his influential enemies because he had used the powers of Christianity to dry up rivers and spoil crops, thereby inciting rebellions. Clearly, such acts were beyond the abilities of the ancestors; Afonso must have called upon *nkitas*, the higher spirits who could control the weather and the flow of rivers. This reference suggests that Afonso believed, or his enemies believed, that Christianity, with its emphasis on the very highest powers in the cosmos, could thus provoke the *nkita*. However, this provocation, which caused serious harm to many people, was also a profound act of witchcraft.

The second reference Afonso makes to the Kongolese spirits concerned the test his father put to his wives. Afonso's alleged ability to travel in a spiritual form to visit his father's wives and sleep with them would have required spiritual help and given its intent, would also be considered witchcraft. While a *nkita* could grant such powers, other, lesser spiritual entities (including ancestors) could do it as well.

Afonso alleged that his father had tested his defenders, giving "a common fetish," probably a *kiteke*, to the wife the king suspected of conducting nocturnal trysts with his son. Since the woman in question was not sleeping with Afonso, she asked the king about the *kiteke*, proving his innocence; the statement supports the idea that lesser spirits inhabited spiritual receptacles.

As noted earlier in this chapter, the wife under suspicion had a strange name—Kufwa kwa Mfulu, or "the death [or destruction] of a place," one that suggests some sort of mystical destructive power. It is the sort of name that might be given to a person with unusual spiritual power, which in Kikongo is *-gangu*, often glossed as knowledge or wisdom—either of the natural world or the supernatural world. Such a person could have the capacity to ruin places but also to protect them from supernatural attacks. It would make sense that such a woman might be found in the midst of a spiritual battle.

A person possessing *-gangu* was called a *nganga* (plural *zinganga* in the central dialect of Kikongo), a term often defined as "priest." *Ngangas* were believed to have special talents, which allowed them to be in touch with various beings in the Other World. They could then advise people how to proceed in addressing problems, making requests, and the like, to the inhabitants of that Other World. They sometimes did this through divination, interpreting dreams, going into trances, or even being physically possessed by spiritual entities.

When there were communal problems that required a communal solution, *ngangas* would seek a remedy and might direct a response. Similarly, if political authorities faced a problem or wanted to determine the outcome of their actions, they might also seek the advice of the *ngangas*, who in turn might offer suggestions to be recommended to the community.

Some of these supplications might be delivered in ritual form. There were rituals for spiritual intervention at both the community and individual levels. Though communal activity was important, Kongolese spiritual belief at the time did not involve what we might call liturgies or any formal church services.

This limited body of information on the religion in Afonso's day, when supplemented by indirect information from elsewhere and later, gives us a sense of the Kongolese religious universe. Now, what kind of Christianity did Afonso propose as the new religion for Kongo? When the first Kongolese emissaries traveled to Lisbon in 1486, they began conversations about religion with João da Costa and Vicente dos Anjos, who had learned Kikongo. Not surprisingly, these conversations would be about linguistic issues and how to translate concepts from one cosmology to another.

We know these conversations developed in what Cécile Fromont calls the "space of correlation": the theoretical space in which two religious systems can converge and agree. While we have no direct information of what was shared in these discussions, we do know that the emissaries and the Jesuits who came to Kongo in 1548 found at least one linguistic convergence, deciding that the Christian God was the same person named "Zambem-apongo" (Nzambi a Mpungu), a Kikongo term referring to the highest spiritual entity.[34]

---

34. The term was used when the embassy returned to Kongo in 1491, Rui de Pina, "Chronica delRei D. Joham Segundo," cap. 58, in mod. ed. Carmen Radulet, *O Cronista Rui de Pina e a "Relação do Reino do Congo": Manuscrito inédito do "Códice Riccardiano 1910"* (Lisbon: Comissão

It was the first linguistic and conceptual juncture between Kongo's religion and Christianity. There were probably others; we know that by the time the first extant catechism was published in 1624, Kongo had a tradition of linguistic correlation. The editor of this catechism, a Jesuit named Mateus Cardoso, alluded to what was already traditional terminology in criticizing some terms he found then in use. While these terms, as well as those he did not criticize, might have existed as early as Afonso's day (there was a printed catechism in 1557, but no copies of it can be found today), we cannot know for sure.

The medieval form of Western Christianity was substantially different from the post-Reformation version of the religion now observed by most modern Western Christians, whether Protestant or Catholic. Thus conversations between Portuguese priests and Kongo nobles were predicated on a medieval understanding of the supernatural and not the post-Reformation beliefs we associate most closely with the missionary activity of the early modern period.[35] Medieval Christianity offered plenty of room for correlations with other faiths; after all, much of northern Europe had been won to Christianity via the latter faith's absorption and adaptation of local religious beliefs, and their world was full of a wide range of supernatural forces which had no roots in Christianity. The church was hostile to any supplication to these forces, but they could not and did not end it.[36]

One of the central features of medieval Christianity was the cult of the saints. Saints were people who, after their death, continued to help the living from the Other World. Christians could consult saints at such fixed locations as their gravesites but also through relics, physical items, or body parts the saints had left behind. Saints often patronized specific locations, towns, provinces, and so on. In fact, they were remarkably like the Kongolese *nkitas*, especially since an original

---

Nacional para as Comemorações dos Descobrimentos Portugueses, 1992), p. 140. "Lord of the World" in Kikongo would probably be *Mfumu a nza*. This text, only found in the 1515 version, says, "king of Portugal who they call *Zambem apongo* which is to say among them Lord of the World." I expect that de Pina, not knowing Kikongo simply confused what he had been told, as elsewhere (cap. 60), he refers to the Kongolese saying of the king of Portugal that he was "the Lord of the World and [may] God increase him." De Pina must then have confused the "lord of the world" part with the "God increase him" part.

35. On the sharp theological break that took place in the Counter Reformation, see Jean Delumeau's classic *Catholicism between Luther and Voltaire: A New View of the Counter-Reformation* (London: Burns & Oats, 1977 [original French, 1971]). On the idea of "re-Christianization" in the Reformation-Counter Reformation, see Scott Hendrix, "Re-routing the Faith: The Reformation as Re-Christianization," *Church History* 69 (2000): 558–77.

36. Euan Cameron, *Enchanted Europe: Superstition, Reason, and Religion, 1250–1750* (Oxford: Oxford University Press, 2010).

nkita might be the soul of an ancient ancestor. Whether or not dos Anjos taught his Kongolese students about saints, no visitor to fifteenth-century Portugal could fail to observe the daily practice of the cult of the saints or miss that these saints were often called upon at specific sites called "churches."

Observant Christians wore (and many still wear) medals and other small blessed items designed to recall the saints and channel some small measure of the saint's power. In form and function, these medals closely resembled the Konolgese *kitekes*, or spiritual fetishes, such as the one given by king João to Kufwa kwa Mfulu. Though the reformers and intellectuals of the Christian church were careful not to make these smaller items of devotion into literal homes for some aspect of a saint's power—that would be like idolatry, a cardinal sin—surely many ordinary followers, whether peasant or noble, believed the objects themselves possessed spiritual efficacy.

In addition, medieval popular Christianity had recourse to a good many remedies, prediction techniques, and protections not connected to the saints.[37] The intellectual elite of the medieval church denounced these practices as superstition or magic and were on the verge of declaring them all of diabolic origin. But the Kongolese who lived in Lisbon for four years had plenty of time to learn all the intimate aspects of Portuguese religious life and to incorporate them into their developing understanding of their religion. They surely found familiar elements of the Christian practices of predicting the future, seeking protection, and finding cures—some of which were at times denounced by the church as magical or superstitious.

Medieval Christians' history of their religion began with the story of Creation and continued through the life of Jesus. This story was codified in catechisms (though catechisms only became widely popular in the mid-sixteenth century, when they were circulated by the church to combat the dangerous Protestant ideas of the Reformation). Most of these catechisms were created with the Christian community of Europe—or anyone practicing other Abrahamic religions like Islam or Judaism—in mind, not non-Christians on the receiving end of an evangelizing mission.

European expansion into the non-Christian world through Atlantic navigation had only begun in 1486, and Kongo was among the very first of these non-Christian regions to be contacted and converted to Christianity. Only the Canary Islands converted earlier, in 1405. An account of the conversion of the Canaries,

---

37. Some of these popular beliefs were denounced in Pedro Cirelo's *Tratado en el cual se repruevan todas las supersticiones y hechizerias*, first published in 1530 and reflecting the kinds of practices that the church disapproved of but were clearly still being done.

found in a chronicle of the islands' conquest, describes a sort of catechism for non-Christians. It begins with a summary of the Old Testament, including descriptions of Creation, the Garden of Eden, and original sin, as well as a history of the Jews' wanderings and a description of the Promised Land. Other sections explained punishment for idolatry, the prophets' revelations, and the prophecy of Jesus. This basic catechism ended with Jesus's birth, his crucifixion and resurrection, and the story of the disciples carrying his message out into the world.[38]

In his letter of 1514, Afonso describes a speech he delivered in which he presented his own version of a catechism. The occasion of the speech, which was delivered to his people, was the arrival of the Lóios mission in 1509. Since the Lóios were the first to provide religious instruction to the Kongolese delegation to Lisbon in 1486–1490, the arrival of the new mission seemed an appropriate occasion to review their original teachings. Though Afonso's letter describes his history of the Christian faith as more of a summary than the kind of fuller explication offered in the account of the conquest of the Canaries, it covered roughly the same key points. He began with God's creation of the world, and Adam and Eve in the Garden of Eden. Although God had forbidden them to eat the fruit of the tree, the Devil persuaded Eve to do so, thus establishing original sin. Afonso used the example of Eve to remind his listeners that violating even one commandment would doom them to hell—and that they were now obliged to obey all ten. While it was through a woman that sin was introduced, through a woman we were also redeemed. Thus, the Virgin Mary gave birth to Jesus Christ, who died to redeem our sins, and left the twelve apostles "to preach the Gospel throughout the whole world and teach his holy faith."[39]

While this history would be completely new to the Kongolese who assembled to hear Afonso's speech, it presented no particular challenge to their beliefs; to them, it was just the history of another place. The speech did not call for the rejection of any specific religious belief and only affirmed the need to obey God's laws (without being specific) and accept the story of Jesus.

A series of events following João's baptism helped to establish Christianity within a context that Kongolese could understand from a religious perspective. As the nobles were gathering, one named Dom José announced that the previous

---

38. There are two distinct versions of this chronicle, which, however, do not vary much in this section. For a full critical edition of all manuscripts, see Elias Serra Rafols and Alexandre Cioranescu, eds., *Le Canarien*, 3 vols. (Las Palmas: La Laguna, 1959–1965). For a later and manipulated manuscript in a bilingual French-English edition, see Henry Majors, *The Canarian* (London, 1872); the crucial elements are found in chap. 47–52.

39. See "Letter from the King of Kongo to D. Manuel I," October 5, 1514, in Correspondence.

night he had seen a beautiful woman who "shone like the light of the sun and the moon, with the glow of a star of heaven." She stayed with him, asking him to "tell your Majesty that there would be peace in your kingdom" as long as he was firm in his faith and that Afonso should have all his nobles and people baptized. If Afonso did this, he would "overcome his enemies with the image of the Holy Cross and his strength would double." This remarkable dream was confirmed by Dom Diogo, the brother of the late ambassador Kala ka Mfusu, who not only had the same dream but also reported finding a remarkable stone wrapped in a cloth which, when opened, revealed a perfectly shaped image of the cross. He maintained that it was a miracle for two people to have the same dream at the same time.[40]

Both the priests who were present and many, if not all, of the Kongolese accepted these dreams and the stone cross as miracles—that is, events occurring in the natural world that are actually messages or revelations from the Other World. These statements confirmed—to both the Kongolese, who also accepted the idea of revelations of the Other World, and to the Christian priests—that the Virgin Mary (the beautiful woman) and Jesus (represented symbolically by the cross) were real and could appear to Kongolese. This would thus be a co-revelation, a miraculous event accepted as valid within two different religious traditions.

Co-revelations would take place in a space of correlation, that is, in the theoretical overlap between the two religious traditions. The determination, in 1486–1490, that the Christian God and Nzambi a Mpungu, the Kongolese high divinity, were one and the same, with the only difference between them being linguistic, was the first correlation. These new miracles, or co-revelations, introduced to the Kongolese a new, crucial element of the Christian spiritual community: the existence of the Virgin Mary and Jesus.

Afonso then presented a third co-revelation: the appearance of Saint James the Greater and his heavenly horsemen in the battle with Mpanzu a Kitemu. This vision established that at least some of the European Christian saints were also prepared to work on behalf of the Kongolese. The rest of the saints, by implication, could be accepted as legitimate and worth petitioning. Indeed, over the course of the years, some of those saints did intervene in Kongo, at least to the satisfaction of the people there.

The message delivered by the Virgin Mary during her visit to Dom José also undercut João Nzinga a Nkuwu's initial assertion that only a small part of the community was worthy of baptism and that women, in particular, could not be baptized. After all, the Virgin had told the king to baptize everyone, noble and common. With this in mind, Queen Leonor pressed the king to allow her and

40. Rui de Pina, "Chronica," chap. 62; and untitled Italian MS, fols. 97rb–97va in Radulet, *O Cronista.*

other women (and ultimately everyone) to be baptized. To João Nzinga a Nkuwu, she "presented many reasons for this proposition" that women should be baptized. After stalling at first on the grounds that the church was not completed, João Nzinga a Nkuwu relented a few days later and asked the priests to baptize her, which they did on June 5.

When the priests subsequently visited her, she asked them for additional details regarding the faith, specifically about the articles of the faith, the Trinity, and other "ministries necessary for her salvation." They were delighted by her attention and answered her questions in detail. To help her remember these things, she took pebbles from the street and arranged them as "her memory art." Even today, people in Kongo use pebbles of different shapes and colors to visualize interpretations and relationships, and some also elicit proverbs.[41]

Not content with only religious matters, Queen Leonor also asked the priests about the king of Portugal and other issues. Finally, she made them a grant of money from her own income and gave them cows, chickens, star apples, and flour.[42] The initial meeting and meshing of the two religious traditions, in Lisbon and then in Mbanza Kongo, enabled the missionaries to present Christianity in a positive light and even as a tradition not so different from—maybe even identical to—the local ones. The theoretical and theological overlap between the two traditions could gradually be extended so that ultimately—through an ongoing process of renaming and co-revelation—the two could merge completely. But some issues would arise during this process, and from the early stages, Kongolese religion was identified as having unacceptable elements, called either idolatry or fetishism, or both.

Kongolese Christians understood that idolatry would need to be ended before the country's conversion to the faith would be complete. Afonso made this clear in his October 5, 1514 description of his father's apostasy and his response to it. When he broke with his father and pagan councilors, Afonso stated that he and Pedro were "Christians and believed in God, not in his [the king's] idols."[43] Both Portuguese and Kongolese had agreed that the entity called Nzambi a Mpungu was the same one the Portuguese called Deus or God. Stating a belief in God was, in effect,

41. My thanks to Adrien Ngudiankama for sharing this information from his experiences living in the former Kingdom of Kongo and discussing religious matters with others in the region.

42. Rui de Pina's account, combined from the untitled Italian MS, fols. 97rb and 97vb, and "Chronica," chap. 63. The text has her giving them *mele* (in Italian) or apples. Apples are not native to Africa, but the star apple (*Chrysophyllum africanum*) is found in Angola, National Research Council, *Lost Crops of Africa*, 3 vols. (Washington, DC: National Academies Press, 2008), 3:321.

43. See "Letter from the King of Kongo to D. Manuel I," October 5, 1514, in Correspondence.

claiming that this particular spiritual being existed, had effective power, and would respond when supplicated. Testing the efficacy of a spiritual supplication would fit well into Central African religious ideas about the strength and efficacy of spiritual entities, which were tested whenever they were appealed to. As noted above, an entity was understood to exist if it delivered help, healing, or luck when supplicated. If it did not, either the supplicant had bungled their petition in some way, was deemed unworthy, or the deity in question had lost power or perhaps did not exist.

Thus, when Afonso's father abandoned Christianity (as Afonso claimed he did), he ordered Pedro's execution as a test to see if God/Nzambi a Mpungu would save him. Likewise, the king took away Afonso's *renda*. Detached from his income-generating land, Afonso would either be impoverished and at João's mercy, or God would give Afonso new subjects. João conducted this test to see whether Afonso or other Christians could get Nzambi a Mpungu to protect them and favor their supplications. No one doubted the existence of Nzambi a Mpungu or his capacity to do things like dry up rivers or spoil crops; the question was whether he would readily respond to pleas from Afonso or Pedro.

In any case, believing in God (or not) was not as big an obstacle to the conversion to Christianity as was the idea of belief in idols, a practice strictly forbidden by the ten commandments. The seventeenth-century Kongo catechism—surely one of the first religious texts to be translated and the translation of which was probably already traditional in 1624—used the verb *-kwila* to mean "believe" in the opening of the Apostle's Creed (I believe in God . . .). We can assume that when thinking in Kikongo, Afonso meant this word. Its semantic field in Kikongo (according to the dictionary of 1648) was more to "accept the existence of" than to "adhere to," as the verb meant in a Portuguese and Christian conception. Afonso probably meant he did not plan to have spiritual recourse to "idols" because he actually did believe they worked.

Afonso's rejection of idols must be understood in the context of how contemporary European Christians understood idols. The great witch hunt, which would eventually envelop most of Europe, was just beginning at the time, and the church was eager to cleanse itself of what it considered non-Christian elements. Forbidden practices might have included astrology, palm reading, or various kinds of divination, among others. Though such occult practices were common in medieval Europe and church leaders had long regarded them as diabolic, the reforms took them on more formally and aggressively. Generally speaking, the Iberian countries of Spain and Portugal were not as witch-crazed as the rest of Europe.[44] But one has

---

44. On Portuguese ideas in this period, and the one immediately following it, see José Pedro Paiva, *Bruxaria e superstição num país sem "caça às bruxas," 1600–1774*, 2nd ed. (Lisbon: Editorial Notícias, 2012).

only to look at the records of the Spanish and Portuguese Inquisition to know that Iberia had its own share of sorcery-related trials.

At least as it was understood in Portugal at the time, the concept of diabolic agency included any action directed to the supernatural that was not linked specifically to a saint, Jesus, Mary, or God. Such petitions to the Other World—including those made via a fetish (the word evokes witchcraft) or another kind of idol—were considered "vain." Christians believed that God would reject such petitions, regardless of the intentions of the petitioner, and the Devil would almost certainly intercept them. The Devil might fool an otherwise pious person into following him by answering supplications made to the stars, for example, or by providing demonic responses to requests for knowledge made via divination or auguries. Whether or not the person calling on supernatural forces was intentionally asking the Devil, participation in any occult activities was considered engaging in witchcraft or making an implicit pact with the Devil.

This theory was applied to non-Christian religions as well. In order to judge extra-European religions by the same logic, the church set aside a long history of engagement with other Abrahamic religions like Islam and Judaism. Since the religious life of non-Christians necessarily involved supplications to some sort of otherworldly powers not included in the Christian roster of divine beings, the church decided that the power who received, and presumably answered, any such supplications must be the Devil. Since these religions' prayers, rituals, and practices had never been addressed to Christian figures, in the eyes of the church they amounted to nothing more than witchcraft.[45]

The Kongolese considered witchcraft, in practical terms, as a method for using spiritual entities for selfish or harmful ends. Thus asking a deity to dry up rivers in order to harm others would be an act of witchcraft; asking the same deity to provide rain to benefit all would not be. Even a positive action—such as seeking divine protection—could be placed in this category. Thus, when João sent Kufwa ka Mfulu the fetish intended to protect her, he was not engaging in witchcraft in the Kongolese sense. The fact that his wife's name implied the power to do great harm, to destroy an area, indicates that using the supernatural could be used either to protect or harm.

One further hint of Afonso's understanding of fetishism as witchcraft is found in his design for a coat of arms for his kingdom, described in his letters of 1512. It was to include two broken idols at the base of the shield. In a near-contemporary

---

45. Ideas developed more fully for the whole expansion of Europe in Thornton, *Cultural History*, pp. 397–419, and specifically for Kongo in Thornton, "Afro-Christian Synthesis in the Kingdom of Kongo," *Journal of African History* 54 (2013): 53–77.

illustration of that coat of arms, these broken idols each appear with one arm raised and the other down. Such imagery, as Cécile Fromont has shown in her analysis of the coat of arms, depicts a specific type of *kiteke*, called Nkondi (meaning hunter) which, at least in more recent times, is considered a particularly aggressive figure that can be used to attack others, either in legitimate defense or as an act of witchcraft.[46]

Even if João Nzinga a Nkuwu accepted Christianity personally and decided to convert his people as well, there was still the question of what the content of Christianity actually *was* and how he would get his people to accept it. While he received a catechism, it was likely in the form presented in the Canaries or in Afonso's speech, which supplied a formal but superficial introduction to Christian history and its basic tenets without much deeper penetration.[47] In outlining these beliefs, priests and intellectuals used correlation to find common ground.

In 1624, a group of Kongolese Christians working for generations as teachers prepared a translation of Marcos Jorge's *Doutrina Christãa*, a popular Portuguese catechism. Mateus Cardoso, a Jesuit priest, revised the translation, noting in places that the traditional language was, in his opinion, inaccurate or misleading. His statement suggests that there was already an established Christian vocabulary in Kikongo, the roots of which might go back as far as Afonso's day. Sadly, the printed catechism published in 1557—the author of which was likely a bilingual Portuguese named Cornelio Gomes born in Kongo c. 1520—is no longer extant.

The church considered many Kikongo spiritual terms valid. For example, priests in Kongo were simply called *nganga*, a term also used by traditional religious practitioners. The 1624 catechism was also notable for using the term *-kisi* to mean "holy," in much the same way Kikongo used it to refer to the all-encompassing spiritual force that could also fill up the very items that Afonso called idols. Indeed, in some instances, the idols were called *nkisi* (though in missionary complaints about idols or fetishes, European priests used the Kikongo term *kiteke*).

The Bible was called "mucanda auquissi" (*nkanda* [book] *a ukisi* in modern spelling), and churches were called "nzoauquissi" (*nzo* [house] *a ukisi*). If this were not enough, the Trinity was called "Antu atatu" or "the three people," a usage which Cardoso specifically criticized, as it implied that all three members were simply humans now living in the Other World. Such a concept would be wholly comprehensible as an extension of the idea that the oldest and most powerful ancestors were the functional equivalent of gods and would be the case for *nkitas*.

46. Cécile Fromont, "Dance, Image, Myth and Conversion in the Kingdom of Kongo, 1500–1800," *African Arts* 44 (2011): 60–61.

47. See "Letter from the King of Kongo to D. Manuel 1," October 5, 1514, in Correspondence.

It seems that Kongolese Christianity—as it was developed by Afonso and the various Kongolese who had studied in Portugal—was a particular form of their indigenous religion, one that took particular aim at witchcraft. If we accept Afonso at his word, he might have considered any use of *kiteke* to be a form of witchcraft, even if he was prepared to accept new Christian *iteke* in the form of religious medals and similar items of Christian devotion. In short, even in its most extreme form, the new religion simply offered a new type of *kiteke* while denouncing the older types as "witchcraft." History shows that most Kongolese were content with the Christian *kitekes*, but were not prepared to systematically reject all other *kitekes*.

CHAPTER 3

CONSOLIDATION: AFONSO'S EARLY YEARS

The triumphant tone Afonso took in his letter to Manuel I could lead us to believe that, with the defeat of Mpanzu a Kitemu, he had won full control of the country. But in fact, this victory did not secure his succession. Though Afonso was quick to claim it was his devotion to Christianity—and his desire to stamp out their idolatry—that drove him to take action against his enemies and rivals, we have reason to believe his election was not contested on purely religious grounds, and that his claim to the throne was not as straightforward, in Kongolese law, as he contended.

We cannot be sure exactly what measures were required for a person to become king of Kongo in 1506. Later in the country's history, a candidate was required to have a mixture of qualifications: to claim descent from a former king; be favored by his predecessor; hold governorship of Nsundi; and be elected by one or another group of nobles, of which the semi-independent ruler of Mbata was one. In seventeenth-century elections, kings claimed the office for themselves through various combinations of descent and election or simply by seizing power.[1] While in his letters of 1512 Afonso claims he was entitled to the throne by virtue of the fact he was the eldest son and that Mpanzu a Kitemu—the illegitimate younger brother—was ineligible, neither monogamous legitimacy nor being the firstborn son were decisive qualifications, though birth order and the mother's status might count significantly. Afonso admitted that his father's favor was also critical. According to traditions recorded in the seventeenth century, two of Afonso's predecessors were older siblings chosen by electors to take the throne

1. For the remarkably dissonant constitutional claims of the seventeenth-century kings, see John Thornton, "The Correspondence of the Kongo Kings, 1613–1635: Problems of Internal Written Evidence on a Central African Kingdom," *Paideuma* 33 (1987): 407–21, see 414–18.

ahead of younger sons.[2] Afonso's claim to the throne was probably directed at European audiences as much as the lords of his land.

In his account (as reported by João de Barros and Giovanni Pietro Maffei) of his elevation to the throne, Afonso noted that he summoned "the country's principal nobles" to the square. These nobles must have journeyed to the city precisely to elect a new king, and they "proclaimed him king according to their custom." The nobles would have traveled to the capital when word reached them that the king would be soon to die. Afonso also received this notice but did not initially believe it. While election might have been the custom of the country, being elected was no guarantee of final success in becoming king.

Subsequent Kongolese history indicates that mere election to the throne was scarcely enough to make a king's would-be rivals bow down and forget their ambitions. Mpanzu a Kitemu was probably only one of several rivals to Afonso's crown. De Barros, perhaps using later correspondence, notes that, subsequent to his victory, Afonso "maintained peace in his kingdom, despite several rebellious noblemen in several regions who fought for their idolatry."[3] But, de Barros maintains, Afonso was always victorious against these rivals.[4] These nobles may have had their own reasons to rebel, but they were also perhaps hoping to dethrone and replace him. Since his older uncle, the Mwene Soyo, was in his fifties in 1491, we can guess that João would have been in his mid to late sixties when he died.[5] At that age, his place on the throne would likely have been contested by both others of his generation as well as a good number of his children's generation; Afonso himself was nearly fifty. This is exactly what happened when Afonso died: his son and grandson both contended for the throne.

Afonso must have been delighted to see Gonçalo Rodrigues arrive with his fleet and military force so soon after the battle, probably early in 1507.[6] Rodrigues's

---

2. This tradition was noted in an account of the deliberations on the election of Pedro II in 1622 as a justification for not choosing children of his predecessor, as recorded by Mateus Cardoso in "Relação da morte de Alvaro III, rei de Congo . . . 1622," António Brásio, *Monumenta Missionaria Africana*, 15 vols. (Lisbon: Agência Geral do Ultramar, 1952–1988), 15:494 (this source will henceforward be cited as *MMA*). Pedro was chosen from a branch of the royal family that had not claimed a king since Afonso, so the evocation of a principle of election might have been politically devised.

3. See "The Reign of D. Afonso I of Kongo," 1493?–1543, in Correspondence.

4. João de Barros, *Décadas da Ásia* (Lisbon, 1552), Decade I, book 3, chap. 10.

5. Rui de Pina, "Chronica delRei D. Joham Segundo" (MS of 1515), chap. 58; and untitled Italian MS, fol. 90va.

6. In the inquest into Rodrigues's service (*MMA* 1:215–21), he was described as coming about five years before early 1512, or early 1507.

instructions were not dated but were probably issued in 1506 and specified that he would fight on "the islands" or elsewhere at the king of Kongo's direction.[7] In his summary of the events in the letter of 1514, Afonso does not mention Rodrigues taking any military action; he says only that Rodrigues traveled through Mina (specifically not through São Tomé) and that he took with him two of Afonso's most loyal priests, Antonio Fernandes and Rodrigo Eanes. These priests had served Afonso for a long time and presumably wanted to return to Portugal.

When Rodrigues left, he also took Afonso's son Henrique and his nephew Rodrigo de Santa Maria with him. These young men were to study for the priesthood in Portugal and deliver Afonso's own introduction of himself as the new king of Kongo. Afonso's introduction to the Portuguese court included his account of his miraculous succession to the throne and a payment of 1,500 copper *manilhas* (ingots shaped like horseshoes) and fifty slaves for Rodrigues. But, as he later learned, his introduction did not reach Portugal; the messengers died on the way there. Afonso also wrote a letter to Fernão de Melo, the captain of São Tomé, asking him to send him some priests to replace the ones returning to Portugal.

Fernão de Melo did send a ship, captained by Gonçalo Pires, with one priest and a small collection of gifts for Afonso, which Afonso considered miserly.[8] Pires found Afonso greatly concerned about continuing opposition in the country, which he described as being religiously motivated. Afonso was planning to break with the existing religious tradition by burning "the great house of idols" in Mbanza Kongo.[9] As he told Pires, Afonso feared this action would bring a great rebellion against him, and so he asked if de Melo could send him cannons and small arms to assist him in the anticipated war.

Pires told Afonso that he did not have the means to bring military supplies with him. However, if Afonso would send a suitable amount of money in the form of copper *manilhas* and slaves, he could acquire war material for him. So Afonso sent Pires back with a cargo of slaves to be sold off in 1508 to raise the necessary

---

7. Instructions to Gonçalo Rodrigues, n.d., *MMA* 4:60–62 (Brásio dated it 1509 on the theory that it represented Rodrigues's second trip to Kongo; I have redated it as being the first one).

8. Valentim Fernandes mentioned receiving information for his report on São Tomé of 1506 from Gonçalo Pires, who was perhaps his primary informant ("Descriptio Africanae," *MMA* 4:42).

9. See "Letter from the King of Kongo to D. Manuel I," October 5, 1514, in Correspondence. This section of the letter was the inspiration for Pepetela [Artur Carlos Mauricio Pestana dos Santos], a well-known Angolan novelist, to write the play *A revolta da casa dos ídolos* (Luanda: União dos Escritores Angolanos, 1988), or "The Revolt in the House of Idols." One might add that a common word for a church in Kikongo in 1624 was *nzo a nkisi*, which could be translated as "house of idols."

funds.[10] But help was not to come, and after waiting "a whole year," in 1509, Afonso decided to go ahead and secretly burn the house of idols.[11]

Given Afonso's penchant for explaining all his actions—and the motivations of his opponents—in religious terms, it is hard to assess whether the burning of the house of idols was the cause for a sharp turn against him or whether his rivals had already been gathering their forces for a showdown. If the subsequent history of Kongo is any indication, kings often had to handle various rivals—each of whom might have their own motivations for opposing the crown's rule—before they could safely claim the full powers that a Kongo king theoretically possessed.

Judging from his letter of 1514, only the "Christians from Sundy" [Nsundi] helped Afonso win his battle against Mpanzu a Kitemu. But Afonso probably also had the support of Soyo, the coastal province, even though he does not mention it as much. Filippo Pigafetta, however, does include Soyo in his account of the battle and gives a significant role to Afonso's great uncle Manuel, the Mwene Soyo, who first received the mission of 1491. In Pigafetta's telling, Manuel was a longtime supporter of Afonso who had spoken on his behalf when João Nzinga Nkuwu challenged Afonso. The Mwene Soyo was also there when Mpanzu a Kitemu's army arrived. The Mwene Soyo reconnoitered Mpanzu a Kitemu's position and gave a rousing speech to encourage a group of deserters planning to defect to the rebel's side.

Afonso does not mention Soyo in his accounts, nor do the other writers or documents of the time. Duarte Lopes, Pigafetta's informant, may have also played up Soyo's role in the story as Soyo was later an important player in Kongo's politics.[12] Yet indirect evidence does support the idea of Soyo playing an important role in the conflict with Mpanzu a Kitemu, mostly because Mpanzu a Kitemu

---

10. Antonio Carneiro to Antam Soarez, November 10, 1508, in Luís de Albuquerque and Maria Emília Madeira Santos, eds., *Portugaliae Monumenta Africana*, 4 vols. (Lisbon: Imprensa Nacional, 1993–2002), 5:334–35. Pires's cargo of slaves was being sold in Lagos, Portugal in November 1508, which suggests that it was loaded early in 1508 at the latest.

11. This evidence forces a revision of François Bontinck's contention that Afonso took the throne in 1509, basing it on the idea that Rodrigues's visit to Kongo in 1509, as calculated from the dates in the inquest, was his only visit to Kongo; see François Bontinck, "Ndoadidiki Ne-Kinu a Mubemba, premier évêque kongo (c. 1495–1531)," *Revue africaine de Théologie* 3 (1979): 154–55. Bontinck's ideas contradicted the long-standing consensus established by Jean Cuvelier in 1946 (in *L'ancien royaume du Congo* [Bruges, 1946], n. 39, pp. 286–87) that Afonso became king in 1506, which must now be considered accurate.

12. In *A History of West Central Africa to 1850* (Cambridge, 2020), p. 91, I allege that this whole story was proposed by Álvaro's partisans to enhance Soyo's recognized status in the late sixteenth century.

chose to attack Mbanza Kongo from its difficult north and eastern site, when the city is more easily approached from the west. In Lopes's day, a twisting, five-mile road led through hills to the city, a point easily noted on topographical maps.[13] If Manuel brought forces with him, they would likely have been deployed to the west of the city, thus cutting off that route. In any case, evidence that Soyo was on Afonso's side is also provided by the fact that when Gonçalo Rodrigues landed in Soyo immediately after Afonso's victory, he did so without difficulty and found that shipping was proceeding regularly; the incident-free arrivals in Soyo, of at least two other subsequent missions (in 1508 and 1512), also suggest that Soyo was a friendly neighbor to Afonso.

Pigafetta also provides evidence from Lopes that when Afonso defeated Mpanzu a Kitemu, he also won his province, Mpangu. On this matter, Pigafetta again departs from de Barros's account, referring to Mpanzu a Kitemu not by his name but by his title, calling him "Pango," which, Pigafetta goes on to say, refers to Mpanzu a Kitemu's position as "Governor of the region of Pango."[14] In his 1514 letter, Afonso encouraged Manuel to write to the Mwene Mpangu ("Moeni pango"), one of the "principal lords" of the country, using the provincial title rather than his name. It is reasonable to assume that when he defeated Mpanzu a Kitemu, Afonso would also take over his province and give it to one of his supporters.

Mpangu appears to be an unusual province; Pigafetta noted that it had been an independent kingdom and was conquered from Nsundi as the kingdom formed. In the 1514 letter, Afonso asked Manuel to write to the rulers of Mpangu and Mbata but not any other provincial leader, suggesting these two had some special relationship. In his letter of March 18, 1526, Afonso notes that his son Henrique, now a bishop, held the province. It seems that after Henrique's death in 1531, Afonso vested it in a man named Francisco, who held it, according to Lopes's account in Pigafetta, "more than fifty years" (up to 1583) and "faithfully governed this region, without quarrels, nor has the king taken it away from him."[15] Although documentation never makes it clear, this province seemed to have a special relationship to the crown, so that at least four kings allowed him to keep it.

Lopes also supplied Pigafetta with important information related to the province of Mpemba, the southern province that once controlled Mbanza Kongo. In his account, Pigafetta notes that Mpanzu a Kitemu's second in command—whose life was spared when captured because he requested baptism, taking the

13. Filippo Pigafetta, *Relatione del Regno di Congo e cinconvince contrade* (Rome, 1591), p. 39.

14. Pigafetta, *Relatione*, p. 47.

15. Pigafetta, *Relatione*, p. 36.

name Pedro—held the title "Manibunda."[16] Vunda was a small province, part of Mpemba. Thanks to an arrangement made during Kongo's takeover of the region during the formation of Kongo, the Manibunda became known as one of Kongo's "grandfathers" and was made a royal elector. As an elector, his presence in Mpanzu a Kitemu's army was an important legitimating force, and his surrender to Afonso was thus crucial. This province would subsequently be loyal to Afonso.[17]

In 1508 and 1509, Afonso moved another step closer to control when he decided to burn the house of idols without Portugal's support. In his 1514 account, Afonso said that his enemies, enraged by the burning, began to appeal to "Jorge Moeni bata" to get him to support them against him.[18] The Mwene Mbata was, as we have seen, something of a co-regent in Kongo with a particularly important role in guaranteeing succession. He was held to be the "leading voice" in Kongo and his assent was crucial as without it "no king may be elected."[19] It is possible that the Mwene Mbata had not participated in the election that Afonso hastily arranged in Mbanza Kongo before his battle with Mpanzu a Kitemu; or that he had not made up his mind and Afonso's rivals hoped he could be persuaded to support them. But Afonso prevailed here, Jorge supported him as king, and another piece of his legitimacy was established.

In his 1514 letter, Afonso also noted that the province of Mbamba, the large southwestern territory that bordered the Atlantic and included the island of Luanda with its precious *nzimbu* shellfishery, was governed by one of his sons when a Mbundu lord named Munza revolted unsuccessfully against Afonso's son sometime before 1512.[20] When the province came into Afonso's hands is not known, but all of Kongo's major provinces were in Afonso's hands by the time he wrote his letter of 1514.

---

16. Pigafetta, *Relatione*, p. 53.

17. Thornton, *History of West Central Africa*, pp. 28–29.

18. The name of the person was transcribed by Paiva Manso, *História do Congo* (Lisbon, 1877), p. 16, as *moxuebata*, a reading which Brásio followed in *MMA* 1:298. In the original MS, ANTT CC I-16-28 fol. 2, it clearly reads as *moeni bata*. The name occurs later on fol. 8v, where the reading is more ambiguous, but could be *moyne* as read by Paiva Manso and Brásio, but might also be *moene*. The related title for Mpangu is read immediately after as *moeni*. It is clearly the Kikongo word *mwene*, meaning ruler. Later, the term *Mani* was used, not just by Portuguese who might not know Kikongo but also by Afonso and other Kongolese.

19. See "Letter from Dom João III to the King of Kongo," end of 1529, in Correspondence.

20. The province is not mentioned by name and was only neighboring "Ambundo." It is possible that this province was Mpemba, which also bordered on "Ambundo," though it seems that most of the military action was focused on Mbamba.

But his control was not yet complete. Afonso also complained about rebellions originating in Mpanzu a Lumbu (a likely reading of the term), a region located on the banks of the Congo River near its mouth, including the large islands in the river. These were most likely the rebels that had given João trouble in 1491 and against whom the Portuguese crown had sent Gonçalo Rodrigues in 1506 to assist the king of Kongo in his fight against "rebels in the islands" even before Afonso became king.[21]

Though it's possible Mpanzu a Lumbu was a place name, it is unusual in its form. Moreover, such a name does not occur in the seventeenth-century geography of the area. Congolese archaeologist Igor Matonda has proposed it might mean "fortress of Mpanzu," as the term *lumbu* means "walls" in Kikongo and could, by extension, be applied to a fortified place. It might refer to the fortified position of would-be king Mpanzu a Kitemu, perhaps a fortress belonging to him or even a location where he ruled for a time.[22] What seems likely, if this idea bears weight, is that his followers, who might be called the party of Mpanzu, took refuge there. They might have allied with the defiantly independent people of the area who proved a long-standing thorn in Afonso's side.

Afonso mentions that Portuguese clients of Fernão de Melo, the governor of São Tomé, were trading with Mpanzu a Lumbu. He was unhappy that the Portuguese were trading with his enemy and probably providing militarily useful commodities as part of the trade. Afonso asserted that de Melo's trade with Mpanzu a Lumbu was leading some of his nobles to believe that Mpanzu a Lumbu was the whites' real friend, that Mpanzu a Lumbu had the "true" religion, and that the Christianity Afonso advocated was lies. As a result, these nobles were suggesting they might rise against Afonso and restore their idols. This language certainly suggests that Afonso regarded Mpanzu a Lumbu as a particularly pagan place, one of active resistance and thus perhaps indeed associated with his former rival. It also seems that Mpanzu a Lumbu presented a challenge to Afonso's rule, not just because they could break Afonso's monopoly on trade but also because there was a chance their hostility to his rule might spread beyond their borders.

Given that Afonso perceived Mpanzu a Lumbu as a serious threat, it is not so surprising that he had "waged many wars against them, in which they have killed many of our nobles, relatives, and white men."[23] When he finally prevailed over

21. Instruction to Gonçalo Roiz [Rodrigues], n.d., *MMA* 4:60–62.

22. Igor Matonda, "L'identité des Pamzoallumbu ou Pangelungus du royaume kongo: essai d'interprétation du sens et du context d'un terme au XVIème siècle," *Cahiers d'études africaines* 60 (2020): 371–401.

23. See "Letter from the King of Kongo to D. Manuel I," October 5, 1514, in Correspondence.

the rebels in the region, he proudly added the "conquered territory of Mpanza Lumbu" to the titles he granted himself in his letter of March 18, 1526.[24] Yet even that victory was not so final: in the 1580s, at least some of the islands of the Congo River were still in a long-lasting period of rebellion, and moreover, they were given to the worship of a great snake.[25]

Governing Kongo

It is probably true that Afonso gained control of his whole kingdom, save for Mpanzu a Lumbu, by about 1510. How did he then govern his kingdom? Most of the earliest documentation, including that from the period of Afonso's rule, does not explicitly describe Kongo's government. But it does provide some hints. Though we have some fuller descriptions of Kongolese systems of government starting in the 1580s, some writers have argued that the Portuguese in Kongo, or Afonso himself, introduced the most centralized aspects of the later Kongolese government.[26] So it might be best to see what information we can glean from the hints provided by the earliest texts—and those hints seem to indicate that the governmental institutions of Afonso's day greatly resembled those more explicitly described in the 1580s.[27]

The earliest written evidence for Kongolese systems of government is found in two documents based on the testimony from the mission of 1491. The longest of these testimonies is found in Rui de Pina's account of Kongo's conversion, written

24. See "Letter from the King of Kongo to King João III," March 18, 1526, in Correspondence.

25. Biblioteca Nazionale Centrale, Firenze, MS Panciatichiani 200, fol. 166.

26. The idea of a weak monarchy in which powerful noble forces situated in the countryside limited royal power is especially prominent in W. G. L. Randles, *L'ancien royaume du Congo* (Paris: Mouton & Co., 1965), an early writer; and Anne Hilton's highly influential, *The Kingdom of Kongo* (London, 1985), pp. 32–49.

27. In addition to Pigafetta, *Relatione* (from Lopes, in Kongo 1579–1583), these sources include two reports from the Carmelite mission of 1584–1586, by Diego de Santissimo Sacramento and Diego de la Encarnación, *MMA* 4:355–415. In addition to these two, a lengthy draft of a description, written after 1608, which draws on all of these sources but includes additional information (written in a mixture of Spanish and Italian) supplied, I propose, by a Spanish Carmelite, probably Diego de la Encarnación, who was also part of this mission, at Biblioteca Apostolica Vaticana, Vaticana Latina, MS 12516 (now online at the BAV's website), especially fols. 116v–118 (this severely lacerated MS was partially published in French translation in Cuvelier and Jadin, *Ancien Congo*, pp. 133–36 (including the first explicit description of Kongo's governmental, taxation, and judicial system).

in about 1492. De Pina's testimony is based on his reading of the ship's log and interviews with six unnamed witnesses. (De Pina subsequently revised his testimony, rendering it more "literary" for inclusion in his 1515 chronicle of King João II's reign).[28] The main purpose of de Pina's text was to give a detailed description of the arrival of the Portuguese and their reception in Kongo; it makes only passing references to Kongolese institutions or political systems.

But we can assume that some of these passing references from de Pina's six witnesses are not just based on the testimony of Portuguese visitors but also by members of the Kongolese embassy, some of whom had already been in Portugal from the 1486–1490 mission. After four years of residence in Portugal, the leader, "Dom Pedro de Manicongo," could speak and write in Portuguese and remained in Lisbon for a time.[29] So de Pina may have interviewed them himself.

A second independent account comes from an anonymous letter written on November 6, 1491, from Lisbon to someone in Milan. It is a brief report written on a single sheet of paper, probably based on testimony provided by the same group de Pina interviewed.[30] The author of this letter, however, asked his witnesses more explicit questions about the nature of Kongo.

From these limited references, we can see that in Nzinga a Nkuwu's time, Kongo's kings were widely obeyed.[31] The king's country was divided into several provinces, of which only one, Soyo, was named in these accounts. Soyo itself had sub-provinces, and its ruler, baptized as Manuel, summoned his own subordinate nobles to come to him. Manuel was attentive to the wishes of the king, however, who was a relative of his—though, interestingly enough, a junior relative, the son

28. More details on the nature of the two chronicles and their relationship to each other are found in Radulet's lengthy introduction in *Cronista Rui de Pina e a "Relação do Reino do Congo": Manuscrito inédito do "Códice Riccardiano 1910"* (Lisbon: Comissão Nacional para as Comemorações dos Descobrimentos Portugueses, 1992).

29. Several items of clothing were given to them when they were returning to Kongo in December 1493, *MMA* 1:150–51, 154–55, 157–58.

30. Anonymous Italian letter, November 6, 1491, Capelli (in "Alcune conquiste") read the name of the country as "Monigorgo" (followed also by Kate Lowe, in "Africa in the News in Renaissance Italy: News Extracts from Portugal about Western Africa Circulating in Northern and Central Italy in the 1480s and 1490s," *Italian Studies* 65 [2013]: 327). I read the original MS (now at Archivio di Stato, Milan, Carteggio viceconteo Sforzesco, Potenze Estere, Spagna-Portogallo, Miscellanea, cart. 649), as "Monigongo." (My thanks to Maria Barbara Bertini for a photocopy of the MS.)

31. I have drawn this information from both versions of the chronicle, the Italian 1492 and Portuguese 1515, as published in Radulet, *O Cronista Rui de Pina*, and from the Anonymous Italian letter, November 6, 1491 report.

of his mother's brother. He used his age as a justification for being baptized sooner than the king, who he was otherwise afraid of offending.

The king himself controlled at least seven major provinces. According to the Kongolese witnesses, the rulers of six of these each commanded 100,000 people.[32] Afonso, the king's son, controlled another major province, which was far away and equally large. Some twenty nobles serving the king at court assisted in clearing ground for early religious services. Another, more important noble, the Mwene Kubala (*mbala* meant "court" in Kikongo), the king's relative, brought the Portuguese embassy from Soyo to the court. The king had sufficient authority over the provincial structure to grant the Soyo's ruler a large stretch of coastal territory—thirty leagues long and ten leagues inland—with "all of the vassals and income from it."[33]

Provincial rulers drew income from their provinces, and Manuel of Soyo granted a share of his income to the church. The king could also demand extraordinary income; we know this because the king commanded that the party escorting the Portuguese to the royal court be freely supplied and continued that policy after they reached the capital. The officials in charge of supplying the Portuguese often abused their authority by forcibly seizing people's goods, at least in the opinion of the Portuguese. However, the people suffered it patiently because "it was the king's command."[34] In his letter to Afonso of 1529, João III remarks upon this arbitrary and common levying of demands on people to support official travel.[35]

The king also provided the Portuguese mission with money in the form of *nzimbu* shells. These shells were used as legal tender in exactly the same way the Europeans used their currency. Pacheco Pereira, another early witness (1506), notes that Kongo's kings made grants of money to their nobles and others.[36]

The anonymous Italian letter remarked, as de Pina did, on the strict obedience paid to the king but also added that the king "did very great justice, especially for

---

32. While it is unlikely indeed that they could raise so many soldiers, it could represent all people. If so, a total population for Kongo's provinces of some 600,000 is not at all unlikely. Based on baptismal data from 1623, Kongo had some 790,000 inhabitants that year and would only require a growth rate of less than one per thousand to reach that level. On potential growth rates of about two per thousand, see Thornton, "Demography and History in the Kingdom of Kongo, 1550–1750," *Journal of African History* 62 (2021): 526–27.

33. Garcia de Resende, *Crónica de el-rei D. João II* [1554], cap. 155, in *MMA* 1:74. De Resende was secretary to João II in 1490 and so heard this account firsthand.

34. Rui de Pina, untitled Italian MS, 1492, fol. 93rb, in Radulet, *O Cronista*.

35. See "Letter from Dom João III to the King of Kongo," end of 1529, in Correspondence.

36. Duarte Pacheco Pereira, *Esmeraldo de Situ Orbis*, ed. Epiphânia da Silva Dias (Lisbon, 1905), p. 134.

those who use another's wife, who rob, and who did treachery."[37] From this, we can infer that the king had supreme judicial authority, and perhaps that there were royal laws as well. Rui de Aguiar, a priest who came to Kongo in 1516, noted that Afonso had judicial officials in the country and that they were helping fight against idolatry.[38]

Afonso's correspondence adds a few more details. In his 1514 letter, he adds the names of two more provinces, Nsundi and Mbata, to the list of territories under his command, and in his March 18, 1526 letter, he adds Mbamba, Mpangu, and Wembo to a partial list of the areas to which he would send clergy to create a diocese of Kongo. In a 1529 reply to Afonso's letters of 1526, João III added the names of two more regions under Afonso's control: Wandu and Swana.

Most powerful offices were not hereditary possessions and could be taken away at the royal will. In his 1514 letter, Afonso notes that his father took away his province in Nsundi and that without it, he had no income. This letter marks the first time a Kongolese writer uses the term *renda* to refer to an income-bearing asset in the context of a province. In his 1529 letter, João proposed that Afonso end this system of holding office according to royal will. João suggested Afonso instead enter into written contracts with the nobles and agree to the payment of set taxes and duties; in return, Afonso should guarantee he would not strip a noble of his lands without good reason. João wrote he was "astounded" at the system in use in Kongo, certainly supporting the idea that it was not Portuguese assistance that led to Kongo's revenue system.

In Afonso's day, taxes were paid only once in three years; João thought an annual tax would better serve Afonso's income. Despite João's admonitions, a highly centralized tax collection system was very much like the one that was in place in 1580, although at that point, the king collected his taxes twice a year.[39]

In his letter of October 18, 1526, Afonso reveals he had assigned the royal revenues of Mpangu to his son, the bishop Henrique; if this was a source of income and not actual rule, then the unnamed ruler of Mpangu would have continued to enjoy the portion allotted to him. These documents, taken together, suggest that the nobility owed their primary income to their *rendas*, which were temporary grants of the right to collect income from their lands. But they were also required to pay the king a certain percentage of this income, and the king, in turn, could grant to others of his choosing any income he received from this system of taxation.

37. Anonymous Italian letter, November 6, 1491, p. 327.

38. Rui de Aguiar to Manuel I, May 25, 1516 in de Góis, "Chronica," Pt 4, chap. 3 *MMA* 1:362.

39. Biblioteca Apostolica Vaticana, Vaticana Latina, MS 12516, fols. 117–117v.

In his 1529 letter, João III—probably acting on the advice of both his own officials and Kongolese nobles residing in Lisbon—suggests that to secure his claim to the throne, Afonso should undertake a letter-writing campaign, targeting prominent key officials, including most of the provincial nobles. Among those important figures to be included in this campaign was a woman—both the mother and daughter of a king—who João says is "ruler of the entire Kongo," and the Captain Major responsible for Afonso's security.[40] Afonso also had the power to name other officials on an as-needed basis. For example, he appointed three at-large officials who would supervise the slave trade, as noted in his letter of October 18, 1526.

Finally, a great deal about administration is revealed in the documentation from the legal inquest into a plot led by Pedro, Afonso's son, to overthrow King Diogo I in 1550. King Diogo I was Afonso's grandson and had previously knocked Pedro off the throne; Pedro was alleged to have plotted a rebellion to return to power. The inquest took sworn testimony from Kongolese witnesses. It clarifies many of the hints found in the earlier documentation: that officials were appointed by the king and removable at his will, and that local officials were royal appointees all the way down to the sub-provincial level. The witnesses regularly described holding provinces or other administrative units as *rendas*, just as Afonso had in 1514. The significance of their use of the term *rendas* also indicates that such holdings were the primary source of income for those lucky enough to have them. *Renda* holders were very anxious about their position, but since Pedro believed his official appointees were still loyal to him, they could also mobilize local resources and raise armies in his support.[41]

This system of collecting income from *rendas* is more fully described in a document created by missionaries in the 1580s, outlining the way in which the income of a *renda* was generated. The document outlines the country's structure, with the king being served by "viceroys." (Since the Kongolese had only one word—*mwene*—to describe someone with political authority, the missionaries created their own terminology.) The viceroys, in turn, were served by "governors," who ranked above village heads (*cabeças de pueblos*), mirroring the structure revealed in the inquest of 1550.[42] The account of the 1580s then describes taxation as a system

40. See "Letter from Dom João III to the King of Kongo," end of 1529, in Correspondence.

41. A modern edition and translation is John Thornton and Linda Heywood, "The Treason of Dom Pedro Nkanga a Mvemba against Dom Diogo, King of Kongo, 1550," in *Afro-Latino Voices: Narratives from the Early Modern Ibero-Atlantic World, 1550–1812*, ed. Kathryn Joy McKnight and Leo J. Garofalo (Indianapolis: Hackett Publishing Company, 2009), pp. 2–29.

42. Biblioteca Apostolica Vaticana, Vaticana Latina, MS 12516, fol. 116v. About one-half of the left hand side of the page is missing, so part of this reading is supposed by context (and informed by the Inquest of 1550 as well). Not all of this section was translated by Cuvelier in his edition.

in which the "governors" take "tributes that they owe to the king" from their "inferiors" and transmit them to the "viceroy of their province." The viceroys then go twice a year to deliver the income to the king, who expected no determined or fixed amount but would signal his approval to the official by saying "*uote*" (*mbote,* "good" in Kikongo), meaning "you have done well."

If, however, the amount did not please, the official delivering it tried to return, bringing "as much as he can" to the king. If subsequent offerings still failed to please the king, the income-delivering official was relieved of his office and became "as poor as the most disgraced black" of the country. As the king did with the governors, the governors, in turn, did to those lower down the scale, all the way down to the villagers who "pay by the head," a capitation tax.[43]

In describing the Kongolese government, most modern scholars have relied solely on the detailed accounts of the Kongo administration written between 1580 and 1665. But the pre-1550 documentation reveals that most, if not all, of this administrative system was likely already in place by 1491 and certainly so by 1550. There is nothing in Afonso's correspondence or other documentation that would lead us to believe that he had made any fundamental changes in the administration of Kongo, and it seems clear that Afonso's power probably derived from his complete takeover of the government of Kongo and his recruitment, or replacement, of the old administration. Later Kongolese history confirms that the machinery and process of succession both worked more or less according to this model.

São Tomé

As Afonso was consolidating his hold on power, he also asked the Portuguese to assist him in any way possible. He hoped for the kind of military aid Rodrigues had provided in 1506 in Afonso's efforts against the rebels in the islands of Mpanzu a Lumbu. Afonso undoubtedly hoped they might also help him establish a trading relationship that would benefit him personally and the broader Kingdom of Kongo. To some degree, Afonso believed the ideal commercial relationship to be some form of partnership in which the kings of Kongo and Portugal would jointly

43. Biblioteca Apostolica Vaticana, Vaticana Latina, MS 12516, fol. 117. In translating this section, Cuvelier inserted the Kikongo word *baleke* for the text's Italian term *creati* (servants), misleadingly suggesting that this Kikongo word, describing a particular type of slave/servant, was the equivalent.

monopolize the lucrative trade in the Gulf of Guinea and the South Atlantic and split the revenue between them.

At least initially, an alliance with Kongo fit into Portugal's king João II's (1481–1495) larger strategy of controlling trade in the Gulf of Guinea; this strategy involved the fort at Mina and possible cooperation with—and the foundation of a factory in—Benin. Given the failure of other Portuguese initiatives on the African mainland, the Kongo alliance must have seemed a blessing to João II. The Portuguese had also received Jelen, the ousted king of Great Jolof in Lisbon, but that mission ended in 1489 with his murder, and the factory in Benin was abandoned (during Manuel I's reign, 1495–1522) in 1506 when that country proved resistant to a longer-term alliance. Even the fort in Mina had significant problems. It was not particularly secure—local authorities resisted Portuguese control to the point that the Portuguese responded with force. Any commercial opportunities still available to the Portuguese in either Benin or Kongo required a delicate negotiation with sovereign powers who seemed uninterested in restricting other European countries' interference in Portugal's plans to monopolize trade in the region. Furthermore, the region around the fort at Mina was clustered with independent sovereign countries that had nothing to do with the fort or factory and were content to allow other Europeans to trade there at will.

To address the relative insecurity of Mina, and the uncertainty surrounding their trade status in Benin and Kongo, João II decided, in 1485, to support colonization of the otherwise uninhabited islands of São Tomé and Príncipe; they would not, however, take concrete steps toward colonization at that time.[44] As an uninhabited island, São Tomé was the perfect place to establish a secure base free of land-based interference. Arguim—also an island uninhabited at the time of the Portuguese arrival—was such a location and was proving to be an effective base from which to regularize trade and support the Portuguese crown's aims in Upper Guinea. Similarly, the Cape Verde Islands were already serving as a hub for trade with the lands south of Senegambia. Seeking to secure another such commercial base, João II granted João de Paiva the right to claim São Tomé as a donation, with the understanding that de Paiva would populate the island.[45]

Conditions on the island were difficult and the mortality rate high, and de Paiva did relatively little to populate it. In 1493, João II granted Álvaro de Caminha the captaincy of the island, with more explicit instructions to encourage population

---

44. The following section is based largely on Arlindo Caldeira, "Learning the Ropes in the Tropics: Slavery and the Plantation System on the Island of São Tomé," *African Economic History* 39 (2011): 35–71.

45. Privileges of the settlers of São Tomé, September 24, 1485, *MMA* 1:50–51.

growth. De Caminha moved there, taking with him a good number of semi-free people, such as criminals pardoned on condition that they settle on the island or the children of Jewish parents expelled from Portugal. They did the initial heavy clearing of this thickly forested island to create the farmland necessary to feed the population.

João II died in 1495, just as the São Tomé colonization was getting started. His successor, Manuel I, did not make any significant changes in the strategy for the Gulf of Guinea. Álvaro de Caminha had substantial privileges, and the island was successfully colonized. But, as they often did when pioneer ventures proved promising, the crown decided not to renew their grant to de Caminha when he died in 1499. Instead, the crown decided to lease the island to a new donatory: a royal favorite named Fernão de Melo, who also had substantial privileges to grant land, supply financial support to the church, and especially control justice.

While the Portuguese originally occupied São Tomé to create a safe base from which to operate shipping in the Gulf of Guinea, the colony there did not generate its own profits and became expensive to maintain. Ultimately, the crown wanted the population of São Tomé to start growing sugar cane, a crop that had proven immensely profitable elsewhere in the Atlantic, especially on Madeira. Since São Tomé's rainy climate did not require extensive irrigation and its soil was ideal for growing sugar cane, it had significant advantages over Madeira. Still, it took considerable time to get the subsistence crops started and producing at least some sugar, while the technology for larger-scale production was still lacking. Sugar production for export only began around 1515, but it soon caught on, and São Tomé became, if only briefly, the Atlantic world's foremost sugar-producing center.

De Melo himself took on the task of expanding sugar production to fulfill the goal of creating a self-sustaining and revenue-producing colony. He also considered sugar production to be a means to rapid personal enrichment. His grant gave him broad powers to do as he liked; he was almost a local king. Like many privileged Portuguese grantees, de Melo exceeded his authority and abused his position and thus left himself vulnerable to legal complaints. In 1505, a number of people on São Tomé complained to the crown about de Melo's behavior. They accused him of having undertaken such offensive and illegal acts as the theft of their goods, the misuse of power, and many adulterous relationships with their wives. They claimed he also regularly beat and insulted people and generally behaved in a high-handed way.[46]

---

46. António Carneiro to Antam Soarez, November 10, 1508, in *Portugaliae Monumenta Africana*, 5 vols., ed. Luís de Albuquerque, Maria Amília Madeira Santos, and Maria Luísa Esteves (Lisbon: Imprensa Nacional-Casa da Moeda, 1993–2000), 5:334–35.

It was difficult for residents of São Tomé to do business without de Melo's support. So, although he taxed them legally and illegally and stole as much as possible from the traders, most decided to continue to act as his clients and hope he would allow them to keep as much revenue as he would. De Melo did not appoint priests; they technically answered to the bishop of Tomar in Portugal. But his charter gave him control over clerical salaries, which gave him ample leverage to control them as well. To obtain any goods—including basic theological supplies—not made on the island, priests were forced to trade slaves, and in this trade, they also subjected themselves to de Melo's power.

Slave Labor on São Tomé

As São Tomé developed into a sugar-producing colony, it was clear that it would need an enslaved labor force to make it work. The earlier sugar-producing islands in the Atlantic, notably Madeira, had demonstrated that enslaved labor produced better profits than earlier experiments in the labor of serfs or free workers from Europe; in São Tomé, an enslaved labor force was taken for granted. Slaves purchased in the Gulf of Guinea rather than Kongo formed a substantial part of the initial labor force on São Tomé. These slaves came from the "Rivers of Slaves," the many streams flowing from the mouth of the Niger River and nearby Benin; many were also sold to African buyers near Mina. A 1506 description of São Tomé noted that the island had some 2,000 slaves working in agriculture and 5,000 to 6,000 others awaiting shipment elsewhere.[47] A 1509 audit of de Melo's holdings says all of his slaves came from Benin.[48] But the Portuguese hoped Kongo would also become a major source of slaves, and in 1500 the residents of São Tomé were given the right to trade in slaves "from the Rio Real (in the Niger Delta) and the island of Fernardo Po, up to all the land of Manicongo." The only exception was that no slaves could be traded in gold-producing lands (should any be found) without royal permission.[49]

Kongo's earliest participation in the slave trade was noted on the famous Cantino Planisphere made in 1502, where a legend next to Kongo's label reads, "this king deals with those of the Island of Santo Tome and gives slaves for low-priced

47. Valentim Fernandes, "Descriptio Africae," fol. 198, *MMA* 4:34 (earlier editions corrected by António Brásio).

48. Carta da Quitação de Fernão de Melo, December 9, 1509, *MMA* 4:58.

49. Privileges of the settlers of São Tomé, March 26, 1500, *MMA* 1:183.

things."[50] São Tomé was opening up with slaves drawn from the "Rivers," and Kongo's participation was limited. In 1506 Duarte Pacheco Pereira observed that "in this country one rescues [buys] a small quantity of slaves."[51] Of course, at this early date, when the sugar industry in São Tomé was still in its infancy, the slave trade was generally fairly limited. But in the 1510s, as sugar sales escalated on the island, so did sales of slaves, and exports from Kongo became more critical.

The initial successes of sugar production revealed that the island had great promise as a source not just of naval security but wealth. So, in the early 1510s, the crown began a series of maneuvers to place the island under stricter control and push the pioneers of sugar production out. There was a two-pronged strategy: first, as sugar became important, it was necessary to take control of the supply of slaves and maximize profit on that end; and second, to rearrange government from a free-wheeling and uncontrolled developer to crown control and administration.[52] The quickest way to obtain effective monopoly powers was to work with an African state that was supplying slaves and propose a joint monopoly over the trade. No single power controlled the "Rivers." Benin had potential but did not have control over the tiny polities that regulated the Niger Delta. However, Kongo was a large and centralized kingdom and offered greater promise for managing the African supply.

Thus, the first step, in 1512, was to establish a factory in Kongo to cooperate with Afonso and ensure that he would be the only seller to Portuguese colonies. Recognizing the role of Kongo's unified administration, Manuel decided to establish the new factory in Mbanza Kongo, its inland capital and administrative center, instead of on the coast. He chose Simão da Silva to lead the mission and to serve as captain, giving da Silva the power to lead the Portuguese community in Kongo.

If there was any formal understanding that Kongo would have a monopoly of trade from Kongo, no extant document proves it, but da Silva's instructions certainly suggest it. To determine if Afonso had the power to enforce his end of the monopoly, Manuel instructed da Silva to investigate trade routes and sources in Kongo and to learn exactly how much control Afonso had over trade in his country. If Afonso did not appear to be in a position to help, the information provided by da Silva could enable Manuel to implement a different strategy. Da Silva was

---

50. Armando Cortesão, *Cartografia e Cartógrafos portugueses dos séculos XV e XVI*, 2 vols. (Lisbon, 1935), 2:142.

51. Pereira, *Esmeraldo*, Part 2, chap. 2, p. 134.

52. For an overview of these tactics in general, see John Thornton, "Early Kongo-Portuguese Relations: A New Interpretation," *History in Africa* 8 (1981): 183–204.

even ordered to undertake extensive reconnaissance to possibly locate a route to Prester John through the "great lake" of the interior.[53]

Certainly, da Silva's instructions that specified that Kongo's seaport of Mpinda would be the only place where Europeans could trade make sense as a measure to assist Kongo in guaranteeing its monopoly. To prevent the Portuguese already operating in Kongo from using alternate routes to circumvent this measure, da Silva was ordered to evict all Portuguese merchants and priests then residing in Kongo and ship them back to Portugal. Da Silva was then to effectively replace these banished merchants and priests with Portuguese traders handpicked for their loyalty and service to the crown. As they left Kongo, the expelled Portuguese were not allowed to export any slaves, even those they owned outright; their slaves were to be sold by the crown and carried off on royal ships. Given this arrangement, it's hard to imagine the owners received any income at all from the sale of their slaves.

Although de Melo's control over São Tomé would not be directly affected by the royal factory in Kongo, it would inevitably curtail de Melo's capacity to profit from the slave trade by using the factory to route slaving profits to the crown. Seeing this as a fundamental threat to his wealth, de Melo would do everything he could think of to prevent the establishment of the factory. This is probably why the royal instructions advised da Silva to avoid stopping in São Tomé unless forced to by emergencies.

The next step in asserting crown control, however, was to develop a legal case against de Melo to revoke his charter, a project that began two years later in 1514. Since he could not legally be removed from the terms of his original charter, the crown would have to do this by finding a legal, and criminal, way to end his control of the island. Such ploys were typical of the way the crown in Spain and Portugal operated in new colonies in this period. The crown would give great power to the pioneering founder of a settlement, then claw the power back when the colony proved profitable. Often these schemes were couched in high-minded claims of justice for one or another injured party. Such policies contributed to Iberian colonialism's reputation for violence and cruelty: charges of atrocity enabled the crown to strip a landowner of his holdings in the name of "justice."

De Melo had made many enemies among the settlers of São Tomé, and while the crown had not acted on their complaints in 1505, the king was now prepared to enlist de Melo's enemies in an effort to unseat him. However, these earlier complaints were not followed up, and now in 1514, Manuel began organizing criminal investigations, dispatching a *corregedor* (representative of royal justice) named Álvaro Frade to oversee and inspect the functioning of the government in

53. Regimento to Simão da Silva, 1512, *MMA* 1:228–46.

São Tomé. Frade's letter of appointment was dated February 7, 1514, and he was probably on the island by July or August.[54] Although the exact terms of Frade's task have not been revealed in existing documentation, his appointment was undoubtedly made in light of the complaints, like those of 1505, Lisbon was receiving about de Melo.

Afonso and the Removal of de Melo

It seems quite likely that Afonso's letter of October 5, 1514 was written in the light of the Portuguese plans to terminate de Melo's contract. De Melo's misdeeds and those of his partisans form the majority of topics in the long and somewhat rambling letter. It is not impossible that Manuel asked Afonso to outline his complaints against de Melo to strengthen whatever scandalous behavior Frade might dig up on São Tomé itself. Whether requested or not, it was a good time to put in his own complaints, which Afonso certainly did. However, he also devoted a considerable amount of space in the last half of the letter describing in detail the extreme lengths that de Melo's friends and clients in Kongo took to upend the establishment of the royal factory in 1512.

Afonso was probably quite aware of the way the Portuguese crown operated since noble Kongolese had been visiting Portugal, and could and did circulate among high-placed Portuguese nobles. Lawsuits and investigations were the stock and trade of the Portuguese government, and the many Kongolese with experience in Portugal were more than able to advise Afonso of the situation. Thus, it is probably best to see the letter of 1514 as Afonso presenting evidence against de Melo and his clients while simultaneously putting in complaints of his own.

Afonso began with the various ways in which de Melo's men had cheated him in the sale of slaves in São Tomé since the beginning of his reign. In 1507, Gonçalo Pires, one of de Melo's agents, came to Kongo to negotiate the purchase of munitions but, anticipating a better exchange rate, brought few goods to pay for them. Around 1509, de Melo himself came to Kongo on a ship captained by his cousin Estevão Jusarte, bringing Afonso a shoddy gift of cloth, "which was not fit to dress small mice."[55] In return, Afonso supplied de Melo and Jusarte with slaves, copper, local cloth, honey, and civet cats to carry to King Manuel. Upon arriving in São Tomé, de Melo helped himself to a large share of the goods intended for Manuel, a point that Manuel would surely like to know. Carefully noting that Jusarte had

54. ANTT Chancelaria de D. Manuel I, livro 15, fol. 23, Letter of Introduction, February 7, 1514.

55. See "Letter from the King of Kongo to D. Manuel I," October 5, 1514, in Correspondence.

appropriated Manuel's gifts, Afonso related that those few gifts remaining were sent on to Portugal by João Fernandes, who negotiated a substantial return from Manuel. However, de Melo seized them in São Tomé and sent an empty chest to Kongo, thus cheating both kings of Portugal and Kongo.

In late 1509 or early 1510, Gonçalo Rodrigues returned to Kongo, bringing some stonemasons and carpenters to assist in building churches.[56] When he left, Afonso dispatched his nephew Pedro Afonso to Portugal with him to purchase goods directly and to deliver letters to the king (and to address other matters not discussed in the letters). De Melo seized both Pedro Afonso and his cargo, holding Afonso's nephew for an entire year, insulting him, and even putting him in irons while selling his goods on the cheap.

Afonso's 1514 letter also reveals a corollary problem for Kongo: it relied on Portuguese shipping for its external connections. Afonso complained on several occasions of letters being seized, destroyed, or delayed; letters containing information that reflected badly on de Melo or that reported illegal activities were especially prone to disappearing. Estevão da Rocha, sent to arrest Gonçalo Rodrigues in 1510 or 1511, was charged with taking an embassy, led by Afonso's cousin Pedro de Sousa, to Lisbon with a report on Afonso's miracle and other affairs. Afraid of what the members of the embassy might tell King Manuel about his misdeeds, da Rocha threw Pedro de Sousa and other important Kongo officials—including Afonso's brother Manuel and another Pedro who had once been Mwene Vunda under Mpanzu a Kitemu, and who was a witness to Afonso's miracle—off the ship. When Pedro de Castro, one of Afonso's nephews, tried to resist his expulsion, da Rocha's sailors broke his arm while wrestling with him.

All these complaints were lodged by Afonso for actions that directly affected him, his capacity to profit from trade, his contacts with Europe, and his diplomacy. But complaints after this preamble concern the establishment of the factory, commissioned in 1512, but only arriving early in 1513. Although the da Silva mission was not officially charged with conducting a formal investigation into de Melo or his clients, it had instructions to report on all persons hindering Afonso's work and named Gonçalo Rodrigues as a person of particular interest.[57] It seems that Rodrigues, commissioned originally to assist Afonso against rebels in the islands, was being charged with a variety of thefts and murders.[58]

56. Having established that Rodrigues arrived on his first venture in 1506 or perhaps 1507, this represents his second voyage in 1509 or 1510. See n. 10 and 11 above.

57. Regimento to Simão de Silva, 1512, *MMA* 1:243.

58. Inquest into Gonçalo Rodrigues, December 11, 1511 to January 15, 1512, *MMA* 1:215–21.

These affairs did not affect Afonso so much since it was primarily among the Portuguese in Kongo, but his attention to them was more useful to Manuel. However, it would be wrong to believe that his complaints were just about Portuguese misbehavior among themselves, for he undoubtedly perceived that the royal factory would benefit him and its failure would be a loss for Kongo.

Thus Afonso began the last part of his 1514 letter by describing in detail the problems faced by the establishment of the royal factory in Kongo, which again provided strong evidence against de Melo and his many clients in Kongo seeking to thwart Portuguese policy. When the ship carrying da Silva and Kongo's ambassador Pedro de Sousa arrived in 1513, landing at Mpinda, de Sousa went directly to Mbanza Kongo, while da Silva remained at Mpinda. Immediately de Melo's clients began interfering. Rui do Rêgo, a teacher Afonso was expelling for publicly refusing to teach and breaking the Lenten fast by eating meat, approached da Silva with such negative stories about Afonso and Kongo that da Silva decided to delay departing for the capital. Instead, he sent his personal physician ahead to learn more.

When the doctor arrived in Mbanza Kongo, a vicar from São Tomé loyal to de Melo, probably named Father Nuno, asked to host him. De Melo had written to Nuno specifically, Afonso claimed, "to look after his things in Kongo, though he owned nothing here. However, he was referring to Your Highness's factory." The priest told the doctor still more damning stories about Afonso, and the doctor eventually wrote a letter (intercepted by Afonso) to advise da Silva not to come to Kongo because the king was a "Mr. Nobody" undeserving of respect.[59]

Afonso was sending a large group of Kongolese to represent him and study, as well as carry letters that would surely be damaging. Rui do Rêgo and other Portuguese priests and laypeople loyal to de Melo did everything they could to prevent the embassy from departing. The captain that had arrived in Soyo with da Silva's mission departed with a cargo of slaves for São Tomé before the Kongolese nobles arrived at the port because, Afonso believed, they did not wish his ambassador Pedro de Sousa to tell Manuel that they were stealing slaves belonging to Manuel.

Now concerned that de Melo's agents were working to undo the mission, Afonso sent his cousin João and some other nobles to Soyo to urge da Silva to come to Mbanza Kongo. Though da Silva agreed to make the trip, he died of a fever before he could arrive at the capital. His death triggered a bitter scramble for power among the members of da Silva's party, with several claiming to be the next in command.

59. See "Letter from the King of Kongo to D. Manuel I," October 5, 1514, in Correspondence.

Afonso was now reporting matters that had relatively little to do with his own interests since it was a contest over who would lead the factory, not whether it would be established. Indeed, it only makes sense as outlining for the Portuguese crown damaging evidence about de Melo's attempts to hinder the establishment of the factory. To resolve the question of leadership, Afonso convened a commission of all the "white men" to decide who should replace the late da Silva as director. They decided that command should be given to Álvaro Lopes, who had been appointed royal factor and seemed the logical next in line. But Lopes's ship, the *Gaio*, had not yet arrived at Soyo, and so the immediate question of leadership was left unresolved.

When the long-delayed Lopes finally arrived in Soyo, he discovered that one of de Melo's pilots had come there and threatened to undermine the mission. De Melo had written several fervent letters to his clients in Kongo, who "stirred up great discord and greed among the priests as well as the salaried men." Afonso wrote that these letters, presented by Father Nuno, succeeded in "convincing them that Fernão de Melo ordered them to turn back to stop the factory he had here from being destroyed."

Nuno had even gone so far as to withhold, for three days, the king's instructions to da Silva before ultimately turning them over to Afonso. Thinking that the instructions were not valid, some merchants, presumably de Melo's clients, continued to buy their slaves and other commodities outside the control of the royal factory, perhaps to avoid or stave off the consequences of their imminent deportation and impoverishment.

When Afonso accepted Lopes as captain, some members of the diplomatic mission who accompanied him tried to undermine him and found a common cause with de Melo's clients. One of these disillusioned men was Diogo Fernandes, a bachelor of law who was assisting Afonso in the interpretation of a new legal system established by the Portuguese crown for the trading agent. Under this new system, a Portuguese resident in Kongo would be governed according to Portuguese law, and a local Portuguese official holding the investigating office of *corregedor*—Fernandes himself—would enforce this law. Though he agreed that Portuguese citizens living in Kongo would be judged according to Portuguese law, Afonso was to retain ultimate authority over the Portuguese living in his country, and Fernandes was to ensure that Afonso fully understood all of the nuances of this new system.

Manuel even suggested that Afonso adopt Portuguese law for his own country as well. But here, Afonso did not care to be advised. Afonso, reading the text, playfully asked Baltasar de Castro, who also tried to explain Portuguese law to Afonso, "What punishment is given in Portugal to those who place their feet on the ground?" According to de Castro's recollection shared with the chronicler

Damião de Góis, he found Portuguese law, which he was expected to enforce on the Portuguese in his country, so convoluted with laws, rules, and exceptions "that it was impossible for anyone to live in full compliance with them and not to do something that would incur a criminal sentence, civil infraction, convict exile, or fines to the crown and officers of the law."[60]

Apart from interpreting the law, Fernandes told Afonso that Lopes was incompetent to be captain and asked that Afonso appoint him, Fernandes, captain instead. Afonso denied the request, noting that Fernandes already held a position and could not hold both. Disappointed, Fernandes asked to return to Portugal. Afonso granted him permission to do so—but, when no ship arrived in Mpinda to take him back to Portugal, Fernandes returned to the capital.

There, Fernandes took up his role as *corregedor* and joined with some of de Melo's clients to persecute Lopes. A group of priests, led by Father Nuno, threatened Afonso with excommunication if he did not grant them formal permission to investigate Lopes's alleged crimes. Using his power as *corregedor*, Fernandes brought charge after charge against Lopes and made him the subject of numerous investigations.

When Afonso mentioned, in a casual conversation with Fernandes, that the Portuguese who came with da Silva should live together in the palace with Afonso and not with the lower-ranking Portuguese, Fernandes responded with a racist insult: that he "would not live with us for all Your Highness's treasure, nor for all the wealth of Portugal, and that it would be an ill-fated day when he would live with a Black man."[61] In Portugal, such a statement would amount to lèse-majesté, a criminal offense that Manuel would surely recognize.

Matters came to a head, however, when Fernandes accused Lopes of cheating both him and Afonso and physically beat his rival in front of the king. Subsequently, Lopes killed Fernandes and took refuge in a church. Fernandes's followers demanded that Afonso seize him from the church and cut off his head. Though Afonso refused to do this, he could not let the murder go unpunished. In his letter of March 4, 1516, he wrote something of an exculpatory account of the event and returned Lopes to São Tomé (and presumably on to Portugal) to receive whatever justice the king would mete out, assuming he made it past de Melo.

Afonso reported these incidents in detail to King Manuel. Judging by Afonso's tone, he was genuinely scandalized by the deportment of de Melo, who was, of course, blatantly cheating Afonso out of profits generated by the sale of slaves. But, since Afonso had read, understood, and agreed (in general) to the new legal

60. See "Letter from the Vicar Rui de Aguiar to King Manuel I," May 25, 1516, in Correspondence.

61. See "Letter from the King of Kongo to D. Manuel I," October 5, 1514, in Correspondence.

system set in place by the Portuguese crown, he did not consider the Portuguese to be under his jurisdiction and did not intervene in the quarrel. When Frade arrived in 1514—and Afonso almost certainly knew of Frade's arrival—Afonso was surely aware that de Melo was doomed, and his own additions to the pile of accusations from São Tomé could allow him a chance to make claims of his own.

But the situation with Lopes and the establishment of a royal factory in Kongo was another matter. Afonso clearly favored concentrating trade since sharing tax income with the king of Portugal benefitted both men. But that did not mean he was prepared to support blindly all plans proposed by the Portuguese court. After all, it was King Manuel who sent the unethical de Melo to São Tomé, and while de Melo was the worst example of venality on the part of the Portuguese, Lopes and others were not above cheating Afonso outright with regard to business dealings in external trade. And while Manuel wanted Lopes to attend to Afonso's wishes and hear his complaints, he also charged Lopes with maximizing the commercial power of the factory. To that end, when a large contingent of slaves was brought in by a war Afonso waged, Lopes sent the choice ones to Portugal, leaving only the weaker and less desirable ones in Afonso's hands and cheating him of some of the profit.

Eventually, the criminal charges Manuel leveled against de Melo enabled the crown to begin the process of voiding de Melo's contract and reclaiming São Tomé. This was initiated in 1514 when Manuel sent Frade to São Tomé to start the legal reclamation process. Since no report from Frade is extant, we don't know much about his actions. We do, however, have a report from a second *corregedor* named Rui Segura, sent to São Tomé by Manuel in 1516. Segura's damning report enumerates a variety of abuses against both the king's interests and those of the local people, including some in Kongo.[62]

De Melo died during Segura's investigation, and according to his contract from 1499, his rights devolved to his son João de Melo. In 1520, João de Melo, true to family form, subsequently arrested Frade on charges of mishandling gold shipments from Mina.[63] But the Portuguese court was not about to repeat its drama with the elder de Melo, and João was soon charged with the same variety of claims as had been brought against his father. João was arrested in 1522. The grant returned to royal hands and then was vested in an appointed and salaried captain until such time as the title became governor.[64]

62. Bernardo de Segura to Manuel I, March 15, 1517, *MMA* 3:377–92. The report does mention elements of Frade's ongoing investigations, however.

63. ANTT CC I-26-14 João de Melo to Manuel I, May 9, 1520.

64. Sentence against João de Melo, December 19, 1522, *Gavetas* 3:9–13.

Although Manuel was quite satisfied with taking royal control of São Tomé, Afonso had his own ideas. When he saw that Fernão de Melo was doomed, Afonso proposed in his 1514 letter that he be given the grant for São Tomé instead. Rather than present the idea as a fiscal matter, he justified it by telling King Manuel that São Tomé would be a wonderful place to educate Kongo's children. They could not run away from school there, as he claimed they were doing in Kongo, and the proximity of the island to the mainland would spare them a long and dangerous trip to Lisbon. One can hardly imagine that Afonso actually believed Manuel would agree to this plan, but it was a clever way of shrouding, in pious notions, Afonso's clearly financial interest in the island.

If he did not expect to be granted control of São Tomé by royal grant, Afonso did propose a way to benefit from the change of command while solving the problem of independent communication. In his letter of May 26, 1516, Afonso notes that he had already written to ask that he be allowed his own ship with which to conduct slave trading with São Tomé, or barring that, be given an exemption from the taxes levied on ships returning to the island from Kongo. He had just reason to seek such an exemption. Pedro de Sousa, his former ambassador to Portugal and now appointed to lead an embassy to Rome, complained, in an undated letter of about 1515, that he'd been forced to pay a tax of eight slaves on the cargo he'd sold in São Tome to cover the expenses of his trip. In this letter, de Sousa pointedly notes that Portuguese royal ships did not pay such taxes in Kongo.

Either way, it seems Afonso was looking for ways to hold on to money being paid to Portugal, and it was a reasonable request. There is no indication that Manuel responded to Afonso's request, and it was only in his long letter to Afonso in 1529 that João III (who became king in 1522) addressed the question, which apparently had been coming up regularly. In this message, João III remarked that Fernão de Melo had cheated Afonso of some 2,000 *escudos* in an attempt to buy his own ship.[65]

While fiscal questions might have been important, Afonso must also have wanted to have a ship of his own with which to conduct business in Europe without having to depend on the goodwill of the king of Portugal or his agents in São Tomé. The fact that no king of Portugal—neither Manuel, to whom Afonso addressed his first requests, nor João III ever granted Afonso a ship suggests that they were unwilling to give up the benefits of controlling Afonso's contacts with Europe.

In his 1529 letter, João III focuses on fiscal matters, insisting that Afonso had free use of Portuguese ships and thus did not need one of his own. The answer was

65. See "Letter from Dom João III to the King of Kongo," end of 1529, in Correspondence.

either evasive or supportive: if he meant that Afonso already had tax exemption on royal ships, then he was saying the point was moot, and Afonso did not need to own the ship; if he was claiming that Afonso wanted a ship because he lacked shipping capacity, then he was simply stonewalling Afonso. Either way, it seems reasonable to believe that João did not want to give up this convenient method of controlling Kongo's communication with the broader world.

As savvy as Afonso was in European politics, thanks to his band of students and other visitors going back and forth, he was not in a position to benefit fully from this knowledge or connections if his ambassadors could not travel freely or his letters be delivered. It would be the most difficult problem that Afonso faced in his external politics.

CHAPTER 4

BATTLE OVER THE SLAVE TRADE

With the voiding of the de Melo contract and establishing the royal factory in Kongo, Afonso and the new Portuguese king João III (crowned in 1522) created a commercial arrangement that would benefit both parties. While the merchants and planters of São Tome had been legally shut out of commerce in Kongo by royal interests, their local connections would mean that they still possessed a considerable capacity to subvert and undermine attempts to control them. The slave trade was a critical part of the development of São Tomé, and both Afonso and his Portuguese royal counterparts would come to clash over its control.

The sugar industry in São Tomé had grown remarkably in the decade following the establishment of the royal factory in Kongo. Sugar production had reached a point of profitability that the crown had started investing directly in São Tomé's sugar production and was planning to grow substantially, with plans for a dozen new royally owned "engines."[1] And above all else, this new industry demanded slaves and more slaves, and Kongo was rapidly becoming the primary source for slaves. How was Kongo able to organize a slave trade of this magnitude over the period?

Although some historians claim that Kongo did not have an institution of slavery in the early sixteenth century, we have no reason to believe that slavery or slave dealing was something new to Kongo or that Afonso had, at least initially, used slaves as a means to pay for expenses in the overseas sphere.[2] In his October 5, 1514 letter, Afonso includes slaves as payments for various exchanges, beginning

1. Arlindo Caldeira, "Learning the Ropes in the Tropics: Slavery and the Plantation System on the Island of São Tomé," *African Economic History* 39 (2011): 44–47.

2. On claims of the absence of slaves, see Anne Hilton, *The Kingdom of Kongo* (London: Oxford University Press, 1985), p. 21, supported by vocabulary in n. 86. A vigorous restatement, based largely on linguistic work by Vansina and an assessment by Joseph Inikori, is found in Paola Vargas Arana, "O Reino de Congo frente ao escravismo europeu (1483–1549): Considerações prelimares," *Anais de X Jornada de Estudos Históricos Professor Manoel Salgado* 1 (2015): pp. 1–24.

with the fifty slaves he gave Gonçalo Rodrigues in 1507 and another fifty to Gonçalo Pires in 1508 with which to buy munitions. Pedro de Sousa, Afonso's ambassador, complained in 1513 that, out of the fifty or so slaves he planned to sell in Portugal to fund his trip to that country, he had to pay eight as taxes in São Tomé.

In early seventeenth-century Kikongo, the word for "slave" was *múbhica* (modern *mvika*). This term derives from an older Bantu root referring to a dependent who supports others from a socially degraded position.[3] Writing in Portuguese, Afonso used both *peça*, a Portuguese accounting term describing a healthy adult male slave, and *escravo*, a more generic word, to refer to slaves. However, he probably considered the terms equivalent to *mvika*. Such *mvika* were probably captured as prisoners of war. Though it is possible that *mvika* could also be enslaved through legal processes, we have no documentation to prove as much.

Central Africans did not enslave people specifically for use as carefully supervised forced labor in plantations or mines as Europeans would. That is, unlike Europeans, who would actively seek to capture or acquire people to serve as forced laborers, Central Africans intended to capture people to increase and concentrate the productive population in a particular place.[4] As far as we can tell, these involuntary migrants did not face any new or harsh demands for their labor in the provinces where they were settled; they were generally treated like the rest of the citizens in a given province. Many of these involuntary migrants probably just established new lives in new villages, where they were subjected to taxation and perhaps some forced labor. However, non-slaves seem to have been subject to forced labor demands as well.

Rulers in West Central Africa found forced relocation a useful tool in maximizing their taxation profits. The population density of Kongo was very low; in the early seventeenth century (when population was probably greater than in Afonso's day), the country had around 790,000 residents, spread out over about 130,000 square kilometers. Thus, the population density in Afonso's time was likely about 3–8 people per square kilometer, with the density lower along the coast and higher

3. Its Kikongo plural is *avika*. The *bh* probably represents a bilabial "v" as opposed to the sound equivalent to "v" in English, also found in Kikongo (the difference is between the "v" in *vutuka* and the "v" in *vova*). The word is first found in the Kikongo catechism of 1624, fol. 2v, to mean "slaves of the Devil." In the dictionary of 1648, it occurs to define *captiuos* (Latin) *escalvo* (Spanish regloss). For etymology and origin, see Marcos Leitão de Almeida, "Speaking of Slavery: Slaving Strategies and Moral Imaginations in the Lower Congo (Early Times to the Late Nineteenth Century)," (PhD diss., Northwestern University, 2020), pp. 141–46.

4. Leitão de Almeida, "Speaking of Slavery," pp. 196–236.

in the interior.[5] Most people lived in small villages, widely spread apart. In 1518, Lóio missionaries João de Santa Maria and Luis de São Miguel traveled across "vast meadows (*campanhas*) . . . only inhabited at great distances." (De Santa Maria ultimately died after he and his companion were abandoned by their porters and left to wander for several days in completely empty country.) In the 1580s, the Carmelite missionaries reported that "the towns and populated places are commonly very small" and "the houses or huts are far from each other, as here [in Europe] in the mountains" but built away from roads so that the royal servants would not rob them, as the Portuguese witnessed in 1491.[6]

Such a scattered population made it difficult for the political elite to collect tax revenue. It was easier simply to resettle the commoners together around the settlements where the elites lived and tax them there. Afonso's 1514 letter (concerning the war in Ambudu) suggests he adopted this strategy of resettlement for purposes of taxation and goes a long way to explaining how. In a 1491 letter, an anonymous Italian estimated the population of Mbanza Kongo at 60,000 and compared the city to the thriving Portuguese urban center of Évora.[7] Records of baptisms performed in 1548 in the area around Mbanza Kongo point to an average density of 50 per square kilometer in the region, over ten times the density of the rural areas. Baptismal returns also suggest that the Mbanza Kongo parish contained 100,000 people in 1623, supporting the earlier and smaller estimate of the 1491 author.[8] Since we have no decisive documentary evidence to prove otherwise, it is possible that people voluntarily immigrated to the region, thereby increasing its population density. But it is more likely that the dense mass of people living in Mbanza Kongo parish was created primarily through forced relocation for taxation purposes.

Sources from Afonso's period say very little about how slaves were employed, but what evidence there is comes from Carmelite witnesses in the 1580s who

5. For a recent estimate of the population of Kongo in 1623, based on baptismal statistics, see John Thornton, "Revising the Population History of the Kingdom of Kongo," *Journal of African History* 62 (2021): 1–12. The slave trade is sometimes held to have depopulated Kongo, based largely on Afonso's claims that it was in 1526. But the numbers exported and the likely origin of the slaves in question (in Angola) do not point to Kongo itself suffering depopulation.

6. Biblioteca Apostolica Vaticana, Vaticana Latina, MS, 12516, fol. 109.

7. Anonymous Italian, November 6, 1491, published in Kate Lowe, "Africa in the News in Renaissance Italy: News Extracts from Portugal about Western Africa Circulating in Northern and Central Italy in the 1480s and 1490s," *Italian Studies* 65 (2013): 416.

8. For fuller documentation, see John Thornton, *A History of West Central Africa to 1850* (Cambridge: Cambridge University Press, 2020), pp. 5–7. Note that the Italian may have interviewed the Kongolese and Portuguese returning to Lisbon and so may have had a more precise basis (for example, number of households) than what might appear as an unfounded guess.

noted: "There are no agricultural laborers, no day workers, no one wants to serve for a salary. The slaves are the only ones who toil and serve, those who are powerful have a great number, those they have made in war or purchased."[9] This suggests that slaves would be employed for personal service and for special purposes, though this certainly overlooks their permanent settlement in villages.

Capuchin missionaries who came to Kongo in 1645 did describe local slavery. While they had a good deal to say about the exporting of slaves, they added that "those who remain in Congo have only the name of slaves, the rest are no different from their masters, they are not beaten, some slaves have others under them."[10] Internal slavery at that time was so great that one missionary claimed, with some exaggeration, no doubt that "the number of slaves surpasses the number of free people."[11] While it is certainly possible that this large number of locally held slaves was an outgrowth of the external trade, the conditions of their servitude had probably not changed.

In the 1514 letter, Afonso reveals how he acquired slaves and how he disposed of them. This letter includes an account of Afonso's war, probably waged in 1513, against Munza, the rebel ruler from Ambundu. At the war's conclusion, Afonso sent 410 of Ambundu's captives to the capital as slaves; one of the Portuguese who went to war with Afonso brought as slaves 190 more of the captured enemy. Álvaro Lopes, who was at the time handling affairs in the capital, took 320 of these slaves Afonso sent from the front, leaving just 90, the "thin and old," for Afonso.[12] Though not all captured fighters—perhaps not even the majority of captives—became slaves, these numbers give us some idea of how many people might be captured in a war. Afonso was not capturing slaves just to sell them to Portugal. He would have planned to keep some for himself in the capital and was probably not entirely satisfied with receiving only 90 of the total 410, even if the 90 were healthy.

That slaves or war captives were kept in Kongo for local purposes, and were not solely intended for sale abroad, explains the existence of a slave market in Kongo. In his 1514 letter, Afonso notes that Estevão Jusarte, a ship's captain who came to Kongo in about 1510, asked to be paid in slaves for goods he sold to Afonso; he said he'd accept either the slaves themselves or money with which to buy slaves. Afonso

9. Biblioteca Apostolica Vaticana, Vaticana Latina, MS 12516, fol. 117v.

10. Archivo Propaganda Fide [APF]: Scritture Originali delle Congratione Generale [SOCG] 250, fol. 28, "Delle schiavi che se cõprano e vendono nel Regno di Congo."

11. APF: SOCG 250, fol. 198v–199, Giacinto Brugiotti da Vetralla "Alcune accontamenti notabile . . . ," c. 1658.

12. See "Letter from the King of Kongo to D. Manuel I," October 5, 1514, in Correspondence.

paid Jusarte in money, which he then used to buy 27 slaves. In his March 4, 1516 letter, Afonso relates the details of a fight over some slaves: in 1514, Afonso gave Álvaro Lopes, then the factor, some money with which to buy slaves. Later, having successfully purchased 25 slaves and received orders to buy more, Lopes was giving an account of the exchange when Diogo Fernandes, his bitter enemy, accused him of cheating the king. In defending his honor, Lopes ultimately killed Fernandes.

All of this information gleaned from Afonso's correspondence points to the existence of a slave market in Mbanza Kongo as well as the sale and purchase of slaves throughout the kingdom. We cannot, however, get from these letters a sense of the overall scale of the Kongolese slave trade. But it is unlikely that Kongo would have supplied the Portuguese with slaves so early in the two countries' relationship had the institution not already been well established in Kongo.

Kongo's sales of slaves to São Tomé grew steadily in 1512–1516, even as Afonso was working to hammer out trade agreements with Portugal. While Kongo started selling slaves to the Portuguese very early in the countries' relationship—certainly as soon as 1502 and probably earlier—the numbers were still quite small when Afonso came to the throne. They must have been considerable by 1512, or Manuel would not have considered the royal factory necessary.

There are a few guideposts to determine how many slaves were being exported at this moment in Kongo's history. In 1516, Bernardo de Segura did an inspection of São Tomé's customs records and discovered that a total of 4,072 slaves had been delivered on fifteen ships.[13] But the region "Rivers of Slaves" around Benin was actively exporting slaves at this point; as recently as 1509, the majority were from there, so it is difficult to figure the proportion of slaves coming from each source. If we assume that Kongo was exporting about half of all slaves coming out of the region, they would have been selling about 2,000 per year. Presumably, the captives of the war with Munza would have made up a considerable proportion of that number in 1512, given the partial statistics of Afonso's report. Another report by Manuel Pacheco, the Portuguese judge residing in Kongo, indicates the steepness of the trade's growth. Pacheco wrote, in his letter of March 28, 1536, that in the five years (1531–1536) he held the post, "never have fewer than four to five thousand slaves been shipped per year," aside from the "countless number" who died before embarking for lack of shipping.[14]

13. Inquest of Bernardo de Segura, March 15, 1517, António Brásio, *Monumenta Missionaria Africana*, 15 vols. (Lisbon: Agência Geral do Ultramar, 1952–1988), 1:378 (this source will henceforward be cited as *MMA*).

14. See "Letter from Manuel Pacheco to King Dom João III," March 28, 1536, in Correspondence. For Pacheco's activities in Kongo, see Jadin and Dicorato, *Correspondance*, p. 135, n. 1.

In Afonso's time, most of these slaves were captured during war. Though being taken as a captive soldier was not necessarily the only way a person became a slave, it was surely the most common and important way. The 1648 Latin to Kikongo dictionary also defines *mvika* as "captive" when defining Latin words relating to servitude and slavery. Even before Afonso became king, Pacheco Pereira describes regular outbreaks of war between Kongo and the Kingdom of Makoko (or Anziko).[15] Afonso's 1513 war against Munza resulted in the capture of slaves. Afonso claimed he fought to defend Kongo after Munza launched an attack on Afonso's son, who was probably ruling Mbamba at the time. Afonso was at war again there in 1516 and then in 1517, when it was noted that captives were again taken. He fought Mpanzu a Lumbu earlier in 1506 or 1507 and probably continued to fight that district regularly before he claimed to conquer it around 1526, crowning himself lord of the "conquest of Pamzelumgo." Writing in 1517, the Italian geographer Alessandro Zorzi speaks of Afonso fighting "continual war with his neighbors"; in 1519, the Spanish geographer Martín Fernández de Enciso describes naval warfare on the Congo River, with only African watercraft involved.[16]

A more general summary of warfare in Afonso's reign comes from the Lóios, who worked in Kongo from 1509 until the 1530s. In 1697, chronicler Francisco de Santa Maria wrote in his biographies of the Lóios missionaries, drawn from archival documents, that "King Afonso had great wars which lasted many years with some rebel vassals, the principal motive of these being their rebellion against the Faith." In his letter of 1529, João III suggests that, as he's now elderly, Afonso should stop leading his troops into battle. The Lóio biographies also reveal that Afonso sometimes asked generals to lead his armies on his behalf. De Santa Maria's biographies note how, around 1525, Lóios João de São Vicente and Antonio de Cristo accompanied an army as chaplains; as a result of some treachery by the commander, the two missionaries were handed over to the enemy, who killed and ate them.[17] The allegation of cannibalism suggests an eastern campaign, perhaps against the Kingdom of Makoko, or "Anzico," as Afonso usually called it, since the people of that kingdom were alleged to eat their enemies.[18]

---

15. Duarte Pacheco Pereira, *Esmeraldo de Situ Orbis*, ed. Epiphânia da Silva Dias (Lisbon, 1905), p. 134.

16. Alessandro Zorzi, "Informatiõ hauuto jo Alexandro da Portuguesi, 1517 . . .," fol. 131v, in Avelino Texeira da Mota, "Novidades naúticas e ultramarinas numa informação dada em Venezia em 1517," *Memórias da Academia das Ciência de Lisboa* 20 (1977): 7–75. Martín Fernández de Enciso, *Suma de geographia* (Seville, 1519), n.p.

17. Francisco de Santa Maria, *O Céu aberto na terra* (Lisbon, 1697), p. 897.

18. Made quite explicitly in Pereira, *Esmeraldo*, Book 3, cap 2.

While Afonso typically claimed to go to war to subdue rebels in the area over which he claimed rule and not just to take captives, we know that he also anticipated the capture and removal of people in battle. When he left for the war in 1513 against Munza, fully expecting to capture people, he gave Álvaro Lopes instructions on how to dispose of the slaves he would be sending back.

European Soldiers and Weapons in Kongo

It is unclear what role European soldiers or weapons might have played in these wars or if supplying or withholding weapons played a role in Kongo's participation in the trade. Certainly, there are no explicit records of this in the extant documentation. Early Kongolese visitors to Europe must have been impressed with European military culture. Right from the beginning of their relationship with Portugal, João Nzinga a Nkuwu and Afonso both requested military assistance in their battles against rebels as well as training in the use of European arms. The Portuguese crown ordered Simão da Silva to assist in such training when he came to Kongo in 1512.

Historians of early European expansion have focused on horses and firearms as critical to their victories, especially in the Americas. In discussing the slave trade, the role of munitions is described as the famous "gun-slave" cycle and "horse-slave" cycle, whereby European sellers were able to force African rulers to sell slaves by threatening to withhold guns or horses or providing enemies with them. The situation in Kongo was somewhat different, however. Though by the 1510s, horses were starting to arrive in West Central Africa, the region was inimical to a horse's survival, and the animals never counted for much in combat.

European firearms, on the other hand, both infantry small arms and artillery, were the most interesting part of the array of European weapons for Central Africans. As Afonso was considering European weaponry, Portuguese mercenaries were also serving the king of Benin; their guns were a prominent part of Benin's depiction of them in its famous sixteenth-century art.[19] We know Afonso ordered European guns for his army: a receipt authenticated by Antonio, the Mwene Soyo, on December 1, 1520, notes a box of muskets among the items received. Since these guns were earmarked for Afonso, they were probably ordered specifically for his soldiers and not requested for general resale by one or another of the Portuguese merchants.

---

19. A. F. C. Ryder, *Benin and the Europeans, 1485–1897* (New York: Longmans, 1969), pp. 45–50.

In 1491 and again in 1506, Portuguese soldiers—and probably ships equipped with artillery—participated in attacks on the Congo River islands. The islands, a common site for Portuguese forces, were perhaps the best targets for them because of their capacity to deploy seaborne artillery. One hundred eighty Portuguese soldiers carried muskets and crossbows in these engagements and, in the case of the 1506 war, forty of them were musketeers according to Gonçalo Rodrigues's inventory of supplies. It is possible that Portugal regularly sent equipment. Damião de Góis writes in his chronicle that Portugal sent ships bearing messages to Kongo every year. Of the vessels for which we have arrival records—those sent to Kongo in 1504, 1506, 1508, 1509, and 1512—we unfortunately do not have inventories that would allow us to determine whether they carried weapons or soldiers. Unlike Rodrigues's 1506 mission, which carried twelve quintals (about 1,700 pounds) of gunpowder, the 1512 expedition carried only a single quintal even though it also delivered equipment for horsemen and infantry, which indeed suggests that most ships carried one or another type of military equipment, but perhaps fewer carried firearms.

All of this data suggests that some number of Portuguese soldiers were brought to Kongo. What is unclear, however, is whether they remained in the country or returned to Portugal with the ships that brought them. In his 1514 letter, Afonso notes he had frequent wars with Mpanzu a Lumbu in which both his men and "white men" died, suggesting that some may have remained longer. When Afonso went to war against Munza in 1513, he took with him nine Portuguese residents, of which only three arrived with the mission of 1512. The other six (that he named) were already resident, along with a mason who asked to come along but, after begging Afonso for meat, returned to Kongo. Afonso did not say if they were armed or simply coming to buy slaves.

How vital, to Afonso, was Portuguese military support? He certainly welcomed the soldiers who assisted him in his attacks on the islands, just as his father had previously done. Gonçalo Rodrigues was dispatched to Kongo in 1506 in response to João Nzinga a Nkuwu's request for military aid. Although Afonso mentions, in his 1514 letter, Rodrigues's arrival (and a few of Rodrigues's misdeeds), he does not mention any war. Afonso also requested, in that letter, Portuguese weapons (though not soldiers) to help fight against potential rebellions when he burned the forest of idols. Yet a year later, Afonso wrote that he had destroyed the forest, and if there were a rebellion, he managed to put it down with his own resources. Whether he needed or wanted Portuguese soldiers, his 1520 request for muskets indicates his continued interest in European military technology.

Taken overall, Afonso's correspondence doesn't seem to indicate that he depended on Europeans for soldiers or weapons; but he was still deeply interested in European military technology. We should recall here that the role European firearms had in European expansion has often been overestimated. The once-dominant theory that muskets were key to Spain's conquest of the large empires of the Americas has been replaced in recent years with a growing focus on the role played by Spanish alliances with, and reliance on, indigenous polities and military groups who used their own weapons and tactics to overthrow the indigenous ruling governments.[20]

The musket and crossbow—weapons that impressed the first Kongolese visitors to Portugal—might be called "special purpose" weapons, used only by a minority of European soldiers in fifteenth- and sixteenth-century armies. Soldiers bearing such weapons tended to be few, whereas whole battalions of infantry were equipped with pikes and swords. Muskets and crossbows, with their tremendous penetrating power, were largely used to neutralize the heavily armored knights of European warfare. Reloading these weapons was a difficult and time-consuming process, however, and while reloading, they had to be protected by pike men and cavalry in the thick of battle.[21]

Kongo did adopt firearms technology, perhaps as early as 1520, for its soldiers. In the 1580s, Duarte Lopes noted that most of the musketeers in Kongo were Portuguese (that is, locally born people of Portuguese or mixed ancestry); only in Mbata were the local authorities allowed to use their "own natural vassals" as musketeers.[22] Exactly how and when the ultimate deployment of European military technology took place in Kongo remains a mystery. However, it was significant enough to become an element in Kongo's army.

The Rise of Ndongo and the Struggle for Ambundu and the Slave Trade

Perhaps the most important documents that expressed Afonso's views on the slave trade were a series of letters he wrote to João III in 1526, in which he appeared to claim that the trade was out of control and destroying the country. It is often seen as an early and poignant cry of an African leader against the trade. But Afonso's

20. See, for example, the work of Matthew Restall, *Seven Myths of the Spanish Conquest* (Oxford: Oxford University Press, 2003); and Laura E. Matthew and Michel R. Oudijk, eds., *Indian Conquistadores: Indigenous Allies in the Conquest of Mesoamerica* (Norman: University of Oklahoma Press, 2007).

21. For a broader statement and evidence, see John Thornton, *A Cultural History of the Atlantic World, 1250–1820* (Cambridge: Cambridge University Press, 2012), pp. 40–42 and 159–61.

22. Pigafetta, *Relatione*, p. 37.

statements need to be placed in their proper context to be fully understood, not as a general cry against the slave trade, but in a complaint concerning the trade of São Tomé based merchants operating illegally in Angola, a particularly poorly controlled part of Kongo's larger domains. It is more a desire to keep the shared monopoly of the trade between Kongo and Portugal intact than to stop the trade.

The settlement of the royal factory in 1512 had dislocated São Tomé merchants from participating in the trade of Kongo—their goods were seized, and they were expelled from Kongo by the royal order that established the factory. It would hardly be surprising that they would look for new places to acquire slaves outside the reach of Portugal and Kongo in the Kimbundu-speaking world called "Ambundo" in Afonso's correspondence. He claimed it in his titles from the very beginning but in the areas over which he was "lord" rather than in Kongo, where he was "king." Ambundu was separated from Kongo by rugged terrain and traversed from east to west by the Kwanza River, one of the few that could be navigated for some distance into the interior.

Since João II had explicitly banned São Tomé residents from trading south of Kongo's border in 1504, the traders' operations were illegal under Portuguese law and left no documentation.[23] Early maps and descriptions of the area do not mention any important polities or kingdoms south of Kongo. The most notable of these maps, the Cantino Planisphere, made about 1502, shows the mouths of the major Central African rivers and identifies a number of locations; it also provides a brief description of the Kingdom of Kongo, but none of the region to its south.[24] Duarte Pacheco Pereira, who served as factor of Mina in the early sixteenth century, composed a geography in c. 1506. This geography includes a description of Kongo and a brief account of the Island of Luanda—which he refers to as the "Islas de Cabra"—but offers no description of the interior.[25]

Late sixteenth-century oral traditions claimed Ambundu was composed of 736 independent territories called *murindas*, which made war on each other and occasionally developed into larger formations called *kandas*.[26] The area may well have

23. Alvará of Manuel I, November 13, 1504, *MMA* 1:203–4.

24. A detailed description and illustration of the map are found in Armando Cortesão, Avelino Teixeira da Mota, and Alfredo Pinheiro Marques, eds., *Portugaliae Monumenta Cartographica*, 6 vols. (Lisbon: Imprensa Nacional, 1960), plates 4–5, pp. 7–12.

25. Pereira, *Esmeraldo*, pp. 134–35.

26. This account is based primarily on Francisco Rodrigues, "Historia da residência dos Padres da Companhia de Jesus em Angola . . . ," 1594, *MMA* 4:551 and Pierre du Jarric, *Seconde partie de l'Histoire des choses les plus memorables* . . . , 3 vols. (Boudeaux, 1608–1614), pp. 76–78. The number of *sobas* supposes a village group of perhaps 1,000 people with a *mbanza* of 500 and five villages of 100 people. Jesuits might well have had an exact number by 1594.

witnessed the rise and fall of still larger groupings, the names of which are now lost to history over the years.[27] But in the early sixteenth century, one of those *murindas*, Ndongo, rose powerfully and steadily within Ambundu.

Afonso was clearly alarmed by this development. In 1517, Alessandro Zorzi, a well-informed Italian geographer, published a description based on accounts he received about Central Africa. Zorzi notes that, of wars being waged by Kongo "in all directions," the largest were fought in the south, where there were "wild and very cruel" men. He also called these southern neighbors "Ambundos," who lived near a certain lake and were people "the king of Manicongo was never able to subdue."[28] Zorzi probably heard about one of several unsuccessful campaigns against Ambundus, perhaps including one in 1516, the year before he wrote.[29]

In 1520, Portugal received an embassy from a kingdom in this area called Angola (or "e Ngola"),[30] the title of the ruler of Ndongo. The core territory of Ndongo was located in the highlands some 120 miles inland, not far from today's town of N'dalatando.[31] It was only starting to become prominent as it expanded westward toward the coast; traditional genealogies of the rulers date the start of the founding king's reign to around 1515, a date which corresponds tellingly with Zorzi's descriptions of Kongo's military activities.[32] In 1535, Afonso would claim Angola among the titles he held in his first detailed listing of lands he ruled as lord.

---

27. A fascinating attempt to map some earlier large polities using the naming pattern of the rulers is found in Joseph C. Miller, *Kings and Kinsmen: Early Mbundu States in Angola* (Oxford: Clarendon Press, 1976), pp. 80–111. The presentation was marred by occasional speculative working and reworking of names and genealogies.

28. Zorzi, "Informatiõ," fols. 139–139v. In the notes to the edition of this text, Avelino Teixeira da Mota proposed that the lake and river section seemed to suggest the Malebo Pool and the Congo River and thus war against Makoko. However, the region around the lower Kwanza also has numerous lakes, some quite large, and Portuguese vessels could not sail up the Congo River to reach Malebo Pool.

29. Damião de Góis, *Chronica delRey Dom Manuel*, Part IV, chap. 3, *MMA* 1:373; also mentioned by several witnesses to an inquest Afonso made concerning the ship that brought them, April 28, 1517, *MMA* 1:398–403.

30. For the early history of Ndongo, see Thornton, *History of West Central Africa*, pp. 56–58. The "e" in "e Ngola" is a definite article, so properly translated would be "the Ngola."

31. The exact location has not been discovered. In 2004, Linda Heywood and I interviewed people in N'dalatando about the site and were pointed somewhat vaguely to the southeast, but they agreed that no one knew for sure.

32. For a fuller investigation of the evidence, see Linda Heywood and John Thornton, *Central Africans, Atlantic Creoles and the Foundation of the Americas, 1585–1660* (Cambridge: Cambridge University Press, 2007), pp. 72–79; Thornton, *History of West Central Africa*, pp. 56–58.

However, it is quite likely that traders from São Tomé started visiting Angola and purchasing the slaves generated there by Ndongo's rapid expansion soon after the Kongo factory opened. They may also have been involved in the military activity that Zorzi recorded. Perhaps royal knowledge of their activities caused Manuel to issue a regulation in 1519 requiring that all the trade of Central Africa to São Tomé take place on royal ships and exclusively from Kongo sellers.[33] However much Afonso or Manuel wished to centralize trade, it was not at all unusual, as the history of São Tomé shows (and Afonso's complaints reveal), that residents of that island flaunted regulations and traded all along the coast.

In the first years of the seventeenth century, Pierre du Jarric, a French Jesuit, wrote a history of early Portuguese activities based on documentary sources supplied by Portuguese members of the order, which are now lost to us. Du Jarric claims in his history that some Portuguese, having traded with Kongo's island of Luanda, discovered the Kwanza and began exploration, trading with the people along its banks.[34]

In these ventures, São Tomé traders first encountered subjects of Angola and began to assist him in his wars. The Portuguese assistance helped him expand his borders. When these forces withdrew, he hoped to continue receiving Portuguese help and thought of becoming Christian to encourage them to stay. He sent an embassy to Afonso in 1518 requesting contact with Portugal. Afonso sent the mission on to Portugal, and in response, Manuel sent a mission in 1520 led by Baltasar de Castro and Manuel Pacheco, which included a Cistercian priest, to Angola.[35]

Their instructions were vague and revealed Manuel's limited knowledge of the area. De Castro and Pacheco were to ascend the "River of Angola" (the Kwanza) and, upon arriving in Ndongo's domain, announce the arrival of Manuel's emissaries. These instructions were impossible to carry out as described: reaching Ndongo from the nearest accessible anchorage point on the Kwanza required an overland journey of several days.

---

33. Alvará of Manuel I, November 18, 1519, *MMA* 1:429.

34. Du Jarric, *Histoire*, 2:82. Du Jarric was a Jesuit whose work was compiled from other texts, especially Filippo Pigafetta's *Relatione del Regno di Congo e cinconvince contrade* (Rome, 1591), pp. 19–20, but also otherwise unpublished material of the Jesuit missions to Angola in 1560 and 1575. He probably had access to materials on the earlier mission from them.

35. Regimento to Baltasar de Castro and Manuel Pacheco, February 16, 1520, *MMA* 1:431–32. In these instructions, Manuel does not say an ambassador reached Portugal. However, in his own account of the events later, de Castro notes that the king of Angola killed the ambassador "who went there" [to Portgual] when de Castro came to Angola in 1520, *MMA* 1:485.

The river route to Ndongo had the benefit of skirting the southern edge of Kongo's effective domain. (Afonso's more significant claims included lands as far south as the mouth of the Kwanza. He certainly had strong control over the island of Luanda and its vital *nzimbu* shellfisheries, but was not very near the Kwanza.) Afonso probably thought the mission to Angola would pass through his domains first, as he claimed sovereign control over the area. João III mentioned that he had one in his 1529 reply to Afonso's letters of 1526, in which Afonso had complained to him about this mission; we do not know the exact nature of his complaint.

Whatever Afonso thought about the Portuguese mission to Angola, the São Tomé based traders clearly saw it as another attempt to monopolize trade and shut them out, just as the royal factory in Kongo of 1512 had. They took strong action against it, and João III's 1529 letter to Afonso reveals that his mission to Ndongo was a failure. Though he claimed the king of Ndongo was baptized, du Jarric's account maintained that he only wanted the missionaries to assure Portuguese military support but never converted.

According to João's 1529 letter, the whole embassy was spoiled when local Portuguese, surely from São Tomé, clashed with de Castro and Pacheco, and a sword fight ensued in the newly built church. The whole episode corresponds with the period between the establishment of the factory in Kongo and the revocation of Fernão de Melo and then João de Melo's contract. As a result, the king of Ndongo, Ngola Kiluanje, destroyed the church, arrested Baltasar de Castro (who wrote his account of events in his letter of October 15, 1526), and held him for six years.

Happy to begin recovering control of the mission to Angola, Afonso intervened and rescued de Castro in late 1525 or early 1526, leaving one of his own priests, Alvaro Anes, to continue mission work in the court of Ndongo, thus reasserting his claim to a dominant role in Ndongo's external relations. In the meantime, various interested parties—presumably ones with connections to São Tomé—denounced de Castro in Lisbon, and he'd lost all his material goods by the time he reached Mbanza Kongo.

Thus, São Tomé interests, established since the period of the de Melos, interfered with the forming of a high-level link between Ndongo and the Portuguese crown, and they tried again to stop the mission of 1520—much as they tried to do with Simão da Silva's mission in Kongo in 1512. And as in the earlier imbroglio, Afonso complained, in his letter of August 25, 1526, that captains and merchants connected to the island intercepted, destroyed, or refused to carry to Lisbon Afonso's correspondence denouncing their "unregulated" trade. When Afonso complained to João in 1526, the king's reply in 1529 was supportive but evasive, saying that Angola's conversion benefitted and honored Afonso. Larger issues were surely at stake.

Afonso's Denunciation of the Slave Trade

In the same year of 1526, Afonso wrote three letters to João III complaining about the disastrous effects of the slave trade. Given his apparently ready acceptance of the slave trade earlier, Afonso's famous and remarkable 1526 denunciations of the trade are perplexing. While many commentators on Afonso's letters assume that he was referring to devastation within Kongo, the general observation of the Lóios—that his wars were against "rebel vassals"[36] who refused to accept Christianity—it seems more likely these were from the areas that Afonso claimed to rule as lord rather than king, of which Angola was one.

Much of Afonso's 1526 correspondence has survived (but not all, as we can see from João III's references), and most of his letters from this year tackle more than one subject. In three of these letters—those dated July 6, August 25, and October 18—Afonso directly addresses the regulation of the slave trade. While they reflect the negative effects of the slave trade, the 1526 letters revolve around the implicit arrangement Afonso had with Portugal to a joint monopoly of the slave trade, this time Afonso complaining that João had not kept up his end by failing to control the traders of São Tomé.

The problem, as Afonso describes it in his letter of July 6, was that Portuguese royal "trading agents and officials allow the men who come to this kingdom to establish shops and sell merchandise," including items "we strictly forbid" (presumably weapons). These merchants were selling goods to "our vassals," who then renounced their obedience to Afonso because they had "greater abundance of goods available to them than we do." Afonso goes on to note that his people had previously been satisfied with the "goods we provided them" and thus remained "subject to our laws and their vassalage to us." Always pious, Afonso observed that this illicit trade not only damaged the church but also undermined the "security and peace of our state and our kingdoms."[37] The corruption, he supposed, was the work of the Devil, perverting Christians as well as heathens, and was undermining the Christianity that Portugal had worked so hard to establish.

If this were not enough, Afonso contended, "thieves and unscrupulous men, driven by their greed for goods from your kingdom, snatch them," including all manner of people, free commoners, and nobles—from both the ordinary to the highest classes—sons of nobles and vassals, even "relatives of ours." In his letter of August 25, he notes that those who were to blame included sailors from Cape Verde

36. De Santa Maria, *Céu aberto*, p. 897.

37. See "Letter from the King of Kongo to King João III," July 6, 1526, in Correspondence.

and Guinea (*grumetes*) and also people from Benin. It seems Afonso decided not to name specifically the Portuguese in São Tomé. But the two groups he did name were probably resident in and conducted their business through São Tomé and may have indicated that the lower ranks of the mercantile community on the island were the most willing to take the risks of illegal trade. In the final letter of the series, on October 18, Afonso does name "white men" as the principal culprits without, however, mentioning their origins.

The letter contends that the culprits, those "thieves and unscrupulous men" he noted in July, were not only Portuguese, people from Benin, or Cape Verde, but also "our countrymen." This must also include the "vassals" he noted on July 6, as greed for foreign goods drove them in both cases. And their victims were "native-born countrymen and the children of our nobles and vassals as well as relatives of ours," who were sold as captives. The only remedy would seem to be a massive military crackdown, which on August 25, Afonso thought he was not strong enough to do: "Short of executing our people in great numbers. In this way, the just will suffer with the unjust."[38] Recall, too, that this same year, Afonso had pulled the de Castro mission from Angola, thanks to a sword fight in the church. This action may well have resulted in much more extensive violence on both sides.

Therefore, Afonso delivered a dire threat in the July 6 letter. He presented the possibility that he would simply stop all commerce with Portugal rather than have the land so corrupted—to the point of being "completely depopulated"—by this illegal trade in slaves. So long as priests would continue to visit Kongo to say mass and teach, Afonso would gladly prevent the Portuguese from sending more than one ship a year and limiting the cargo of that one ship to materials used in the celebration of mass or for the decoration of churches.

The warfare, which resulted in the capture of a wide range of Afonso's subjects—including his countrymen and even nobles—suggests that armed encounters, including perhaps those that had precipitated Afonso's removal of the Portuguese mission from Ndongo, had taken a serious turn. This might have included armed encounters between elements of the royal army (stationed in particular at the valuable and vulnerable island of Luanda) and Ndongo forces and their allies from São Tomé, now active in the regions just to the south of Luanda. Given the significance of Luanda island to Kongo, noble shield-bearing heavy infantry and officers, and potentially members of the Afonso's extended royal family, might have been captured.

Afonso's proposed total ban on the slave trade, ostensibly to halt the damage done by the traders, was also a reminder to João III that he had a stake in

38. See "Letter from the King of Kongo to King João III," August 25, 1526, in Correspondence.

maintaining control over the São Tomé–based merchants who were undermining Portuguese royal trade as well as Kongo's. Afonso surely knew that trade had grown rapidly and that the island was taking off as a sugar producer, becoming an increasingly valuable asset for the Portuguese crown, which had just begun heavily investing in the island.

After his dire threat, Afonso announced his own potentially workable solution to the problem in his letter of October 18 by creating a central clearing body that would consist of three judges—Pedro Mwene Mpunzu, Manuel Mwene Saba, and Gonçalo Pires—who would determine if a person had been stolen or enslaved legally. Two judges would be Kongolese officials, and Pires, an experienced trader, would represent Portuguese interests.

Afonso's intentions and the nature of the implied threat he gave João III, was that he presented creating this panel, weighed in his favor, as a special favor, writing that we "grant the favor of continuing the slave trade to Your Highness because of your stake in this trade and because you earn a lot of profit from the slaves shipped from our Kingdom." Fully aware of Portugal's dependency, Afonso proposed his solution, which was probably his plan from the beginning of the letters. He undoubtedly knew that João would favor a plan to place some sort of regulation over the rapidly developing Angolan leak in their joint project to monopolize the trade and control São Tome's renegade trade effectively.

Misinterpreting the complex political game Afonso was playing ever since these letters were first published in 1877, commentators have wondered exactly what was happening in Kongo in 1526. Afonso's letters appear to describe a situation of stark anarchy in which Portuguese merchants seemed to be literally traveling all over Kongo to persuade nobles and even common people to kidnap and sell all and sundry people, including nobles of the highest rank, who were then surreptitiously snuck out of the country.

Historians have seized upon this description to contend, on the one hand, that Afonso had effectively lost control of the country and hoped to restore his grip on power via his proposed board of inspectors.[39] Others have suggested that Afonso's power over his subjects in Kongo itself rested in part on his capacity to supply them with goods as a sort of return on the tribute they paid him, and the Portuguese had usurped this strange sort of mutual patronage between Kongo and its vassals, mistaking the weak obedience of Ndongo to the steel-clad

39. Basil Davidson, *Black Mother* (London: Little, Brown and Company, 1961), was among the first to do so; more recently, this analysis has been repeated by Toby Green, *Fistful of Shells* (Chicago: University of Chicago Press, 2019), pp. 214–19.

subjection that Kongolese officials had to the Kongolese throne.[40] What seems more likely is that Afonso maintained he was supplying goods to Angola, his vassal, through his monopoly on Portuguese trade, and Angola was seeking direct access to them, than that forces within Kongo were challenging an alleged system of redistribution.

We have no independent eyewitness descriptions of the state of Kongo in this period; everything we know about the situation within the country comes from Afonso's correspondence. Judging from his letters, Afonso appeared to have control over the country in 1526. In his letter of March 18 from that year, he identifies his own loyal officials, most of them his family members, as rulers of his major provinces.[41] In his letter of 1529, João acknowledged this when he proposed that Afonso stop arbitrarily deposing his nobles, a suggestion that assumes a high degree of local control by the Kongo crown.[42]

João III's response to Afonso was undated, but internal evidence suggests 1528 or 1529, two or three years after Afonso had sent his flurry of letters to the Portuguese crown. This long delay has sometimes been seen as a sort of snub, implying that Afonso's complaints were not a high priority in Portugal. But there is little doubt that the credible threat that Afonso might stop the slave trade to São Tomé, emerging as it became more and more dependent on Kongo, needed to be taken seriously. São Tomé was valuable enough to the crown that it was in the process of making large-scale investments there, a fact Afonso was surely aware of. It is better, perhaps, to view the delay as a tactic to see how affairs would develop in Angola and São Tomé and consider a counteroffer that would satisfy Afonso while benefitting Portugal as much as possible.

In his letter, João casts doubt on the seriousness of the damage the illegal trade had on Kongo, questioning whether the country was really being depopulated. He noted that Afonso could, if he wanted to, order slaves to be imported from outside the country, perhaps from the northeastern regions of Mpumbu, as he knew well that the Kingdom of Makoko, Kongo's rival, was a large source of slaves.

However, in what appears to be an offhand comment not related to Afonso's complaints about the slave trade but about the management of Portuguese residents in Kongo, João noted, "I am told that the number of disturbances and unpleasant encounters they [Portuguese travelers] have had along the roads of

40. A clear early statement was in W. G. L. Randles, *L'ancien royaume du Congo* (Paris: Mouton & Co., 1965), pp. 75–77. The idea was taken up more fully in Hilton, *Kingdom of Kongo*, pp. 35–36, 58.

41. See "Letter from the King of Kongo to João III," March 18, 1526, in Correspondence.

42. See "Letter from Dom João III to the King of Kongo," end of 1529, in Correspondence.

your kingdom has greatly increased." It is possible that there had indeed been an increase in lawlessness that affected Portuguese, although he also notes that the Portuguese travelers themselves may be responsible. Nevertheless, he adds that "at other times, the people's lawlessness could be the cause."[43]

Depopulation seems unlikely just judging the trade volume: in 1516, as we have noted, the slave trade could not have exceeded 4,000 per annum and was probably closer to half that. Pacheco's report of 1536 noted the number was 4,000–5,000 between 1531 and 1536. He was in a position to know formal exports and was in the country earlier, in 1525, when he participated in the capture of the French traders. Thus, Pacheco could comment on the very period Afonso was referring to. These numbers were not likely to lead to literal depopulation in a country of well over half a million inhabitants.[44] Considering that annual exports in the eighteenth century numbered in the tens of thousands when depopulation was probably taking place, this relatively small number was unlikely to result in literal depopulation.

João accepted Afonso's judgment and acknowledged that, as sovereign, Afonso could decide whether or not to continue trading with the Portuguese. Then João countered that if Afonso carried out his threat, it would deprive Kongo of the profits of the slave trade, as well as in other commodities. In this way, he reminded Afonso that both sides benefitted from a regulated trade. This left two options: they could cooperate to control the Angola trade, or João could see what he might do in Angola on his own, given he had already had some contact there.

None of Afonso's extant letters from this period mention the Angola situation, but João's letter suggests that more correspondence had transpired. João acknowledged, for example, that Afonso was displeased with Portugal's contacts with Angola, though that is not in Afonso's extant letters. João also answered some discussion Afonso had presented about the mission, noting his appreciation of Afonso's influence in the baptism of Angola's king but regretted the resulting swordplay that led Ngola Kiluanje to demolish the small church built by priests, again information not found in Afonso's known correspondence, but showing how critical the developments of 1526 had been.

The question of a renewed mission to Ndongo had also been discussed, for João proposed how a new priest might go to Angola, suggesting that it would be easier to send one via sea than land—a method of travel that would, in effect, make it

---

43. See "Letter from Dom João III to the King of Kongo," end of 1529, in Correspondence.

44. Our first reasonable estimate of Kongo's population relates to 1623 when it had some 780,000 inhabitants; this guess assumes a growth of population in the intervening century.

harder for Afonso to control a traveling priest's movements.[45] Perhaps too, this was a signal that Portugal could establish its own relationship with Ndongo, more or less as it had with Kongo earlier.

Afonso had also apparently considered a military attack on Ndongo, implied in his letter on July 6, though he clearly did not think that feasible, but João took the question up again, suggesting a joint military venture against Ndongo.[46] Since Kongo and Portugal were partners in trade, with an ongoing understanding regarding the control of external trade, a joint military expedition using ships and ground troops against Ndongo (probably the ultimate supporter of the illegal enslavement) was quite reasonable. Indeed, when Portugal decided to colonize Angola in 1575, its first stages were accomplished through a joint military venture with Kongo.[47]

The Portuguese were most effective when operating from river stations and using their ships and artillery—the history of their later conquest in Angola shows this. However, João was perhaps too confident that such a solution would work in the case of Ndongo. Afonso was also aware, moreover, that Ndongo was a powerful country, that his troops would do the majority of the fighting, and he was not prepared to attempt its conquest. In fact, as the seventeenth century shows, Portugal was unable to conquer all of Ndongo, even with considerable effort and local support.[48]

Afonso's solution to the problem of Ndongo was to regulate the slave trade through his team of Portuguese and Kongolese inspectors, who were probably officials based in Luanda. In his 1529 letter, João seems to have accepted Afonso's idea of establishing a review board but proposed that it would meet in Mbanza Kongo, which would not have addressed the problem of the slave trade in Angola. In the end, João decided to take the Angola trade into his own hands.

João's solution to the problem of the Angola trade was to establish his own new trading factor on the Angola coast, sidestepping Afonso's claims to control Ndongo and creating a separate and competitive avenue for the slave trade. In

45. João III to Afonso, n.d., *MMA* 1:525–36; 531–32. Brásio proposed a date of late 1529, nearly three years after the letters they clearly address, based on a passage concerning the "sack of Rome" in 1527 in which rioting German troops forced Clement VII to abandon Rome temporarily, and he subsequently called for a church council to resolve issues involving Luther's challenges. The event could be dated as early as February 1528, when Clement returned to Rome (as noted in the letter); the idea of a council had been discussed for some time.

46. See "Letter from the King of Kongo to King João III," July 6, 1526, in Correspondence.

47. Thornton, *History of West Central Africa*, pp. 82–85.

48. Thornton, *History of West Central Africa*, pp. 89–216 passim.

1532, noting that Portuguese trade with Angola had troubled the king of Kongo, João forbade São Tomé from shipping any further goods to Angola.[49] Documents written that same year show that João had established a royal factory in Angola; the factor there, João Rodrigues de Vasconcelos, was receiving goods and handling business.[50]

None of Afonso's extant letters reveal how he responded to the establishment of this new Portuguese factory in Angola, but we can guess he was not pleased. However, in his letter of March 28, 1536, Manuel Pacheco, serving in the royal factory in Kongo, reported that many slaves were dying awaiting shipping, as the number of ships arriving had declined.[51] In later documents, a legal inquiry directed by Diogo I, Afonso's successor in Kongo, in 1548, would reveal that more and more shipping was going to Angola and bypassing Kongo, resulting in increased mortality among those awaiting export in Kongo.[52] The Angola factory was thus a first small step to the eventual Portuguese colonization of Angola in 1575.

49. Regimento de São Tomé, August 2, 1532, *MMA* 2:14–15.

50. Two acknowledgment documents by Rodrigues of the receipt of goods in Angola on September 20 and 22, 1532, are found in ANTT CC II-179-7 and ANTT CC II-179-12.

51. See "Letter from Manuel Pacheco to King Dom João III," March 28, 1536, in Correspondence.

52. An inquest conducted in Kongo in 1548 to ascertain how much Kongo shipping suffered at the hands of Angola merchants produced a somber report, November 12, 1548, *MMA* 2:197–206.

CHAPTER 5

ESTABLISHING THE CHURCH

Developing a Kongo Church

While much of Afonso's correspondence and all of his best-known letters are about the commercial relations between Kongo and Portugal, his correspondence also develops another great theme of his rule: the development of Christianity in Kongo. Afonso, having established Christianity as Kongo's official religion, undertook an ambitious program to both expand the religion in Kongo and use the faith to make international connections. While he failed to achieve his highest goals for the church, he did establish a permanent place for Christianity within Kongo's culture.

When the Portuguese mission departed Kongo in 1491, some priests stayed behind; the departing priests took with them a letter from King João Nzinga a Nkuwu requesting that more missionaries be sent, as his land was "great and full of people."[1] João also sent some young people to Lisbon to study; at least fifteen arrived in Portugal.[2] In sending them abroad, João must have intended that these students become the future priests of the country. After all, simple catechists could have completed their studies in Kongo.

In 1504, a second Portuguese mission arrived in Kongo. Among the passengers were "men with degrees in sacred theology," teachers of reading and writing, and even music instructors. The presence of so many theologians in the party supports the idea that the kings of both countries intended to found a rapidly self-sustaining

1. Instructions of João I, 1491, Rui de Pina, untitled Italian MS, fols. 99rb–99va, in Carmen Radulet, *O Cronista Rui de Pina e a "Relação do Reino do Congo": Manuscrito inédito do "Códice Riccardiano 1910"* (Lisbon: Comissão Nacional para as Comemorações dos Descobrimentos Portugueses, 1992).

2. De Pina, untitled Italian MS, fol. 87ra and "Chronica del Rei D. Joham Segundo" (MS of 1515), cap. 58, in Radulet, *O Cronista*. Records of clothing distributions (normal for noble guests) from 1493 and assignment to schoolmasters confirm the arrivals, António Brásio, *Monumenta Missionaria Africana*, 15 vols. (Lisbon: Agência Geral do Ultramar, 1952–1988), 1:148–58 (this source will henceforward be cited as *MMA*).

church. Moreover, these "men with degrees" brought "many books of Christian doctrine," suggesting they would impart Christian knowledge to Kongolese elites. João also encouraged his noble subjects to send more young people to study in Portugal so that "many would become literate." He wanted the youth to study "philosophy, fine arts and [Christian] customs" so that, upon returning to Kongo, they would work to gain "much fruit in their country, preaching the Catholic Faith."[3] In Lisbon, the students became literate and fluent in Portuguese and would eventually introduce it to Kongo. It is likely that João Teixeira, who eventually became Afonso's long-term secretary, was among this initial group of students. While in Portugal, Teixeira became both literate and a near-native, if not native, speaker of Portuguese.

The dramatic tale Afonso told in his lost letter of 1506 and subsequent correspondence of his father's apostasy and the nobility's abandonment of Christianity has greatly influenced how modern historians understand this period. Judging by the reports of the 1504 mission, João's faith was not cooling, and his apostasy, if it happened at all, was short-lived. The contradictions in these accounts of the strength of the king's faith suggest that Afonso promoted an agenda in his description of the last years of his father's reign: he wanted to recast the struggle over his ascension to the throne as an apocalyptic battle between Christianity and paganism. While it is true that his succession faced opposition, it might not have been quite so religiously oriented as he presented it.

João clearly had a plan to develop the church in Kongo. Even if he abandoned this plan in the last year of his life, he set the foundation for Afonso to build his church. Both the Portuguese king Manuel and Afonso wanted to develop, as soon as possible, a locally trained cadre ready for higher studies. The crucial first step would be to develop an educational system capable of training the Kongolese with the language skills (Latin) and theological background to become priests. As a Catholic country, Kongo needed ordained priests to perform the sacraments, an absolutely essential aspect of the salvation of the country and its people. Training these priests locally would prevent Kongo from having to send candidates to Europe for their education.

Problems with Clergy

While Afonso and his government supported European priests working in his country, they were themselves often given over to scandalous behavior in their private lives. The canons of São João Evangelista (Lóios) played an important role

3. Damião de Góis, *Chronica delRey Dom Manuel*, Part I, cap. 76, in *MMA* 1:194–95; Pacheco Pereira, *Esmeraldo de Situ Orbis*, ed. Epiphânia da Silva Dias (Lisbon, 1905), Book 3, cap. 2.

in teaching and supporting Kongo's initial mission to Portugal in 1486–1490. Vicente dos Anjos, one of the canons that the original mission encountered in Lisbon, was reputed to be such an excellent speaker of Kikongo that he was often called, even in official documents, "Vicente de Manicongo."[4] Afonso specifically asked that they come to Kongo to teach, as they indeed did, around the spring of 1509, if not earlier.[5]

While in Kongo, the Lóios did missionary work, teaching and baptizing. In prefect João de Santa Maria's obituary, he was said to have sent the priests into the provinces two by two to teach and baptize, even though the king pressed him to restrict their activities to the capital.[6] Though Afonso continued to rely on Portuguese priests for higher-level education and the administration of the sacraments, he simultaneously began to send young Kongolese teachers into the provinces to teach the Christian gospel while preparing to obtain ordinations for Kongolese to follow.

In his 1514 letter, Afonso notes that he has founded a school in the capital for use by the Lóios along with 400 of his family and nobles; he also notes that he felt obliged to build thorny walls around the school to prevent the students from running away. This school, probably constructed in 1509, included housing for the priests as well as space for classes and related activities. The royal instructions called for João de Santa Maria to be the superior and to keep the priests living in a community.

If the Lóios were respected for their teaching, they were not well disciplined. De Santa Maria ignored his instructions and broke up the community, an action considered so scandalous that it prompted two of the Lóios to return to Portugal. The priests, for their part, asked that Afonso elect a non-Lóio priest named Pero Fernandes to be their superior, but Afonso claimed he lacked the authority to make this appointment. The remaining priests then established classes, taught

---

4. De Góis, *Chronica*, Part II, chap. 30. Additional information on the missionaries is also found in their biographies, Francisco de Santa Maria, *O Céu aberto na terra* (Lisbon, 1697), pp. 886–97.

5. The Lóios' seventeenth-century chronicler, Francisco de Santa Maria (*Céu aberto*, pp. 263–64), contended that the Lóios had come in 1491, citing unpublished archival material. António Brásio searched the archives in Portugal to prove de Santa Maria's claim and found compelling evidence that the Lóios had not left Portugal before 1500 and that likely they did not until 1508. However, Brásio did confirm that they helped to educate Kongolese students who came to study in Lisbon as early as 1486. See Pedro Vilas Boas Tavares, "Participação das Lóios nas primeiras 'missões' africanas," in *Actas, Congresso Internacional Bartolomeu Días e sua época*, 5 vols. (Porto: Universidade de Porto, 1989), 1:555–63.

6. De Santa Maria, *Céu aberto*, pp. 888–91.

not in a cloister (as the royal instructions envisioned) but around their own houses.

Afonso was concerned about the Lóios' behavior and complained in his 1514 letter that they constantly begged him for money, which they then used to buy and sell slaves. Afonso asked them "for the love of our Lord Jesus Christ" to buy only male slaves. But the priests ignored him and "began filling their houses with whores." According to Afonso, one of the enslaved women even gave birth to Pero Fernandes's mixed-race child, the same priest the Lóios asked to be their superior, which Afonso regarded as a scandal and a bad example.[7]

The Lóios' interest in the slave trade for their support led to a larger scandal. In his 1529 letter, João III issued a royal order forbidding priests to engage in private commerce. Despite the prohibition, at least two Lóio priests, Fernão de São João and António de São João, were discovered to be so thoroughly engaged in commerce they had established a "trading post in São Tomé and hired a commercial agent in Lisbon."[8] When the priors of the order commanded them to end this business, António de São João desisted and turned his profits over to the order, which then used the money to support the education of Kongolese students. But Fernão de São João continued to trade and directly defied not one but two royal orders—issued in 1532 and 1535—to cease. Ecclesiastical leaders eventually caught up with him, however, even going so far as to alert the pope to Fernão de São João's misdeeds, just in case he tried to appeal to the Vatican against them. Ultimately his fortune was seized, and Afonso was said to be shocked by the whole business. The two Lóios were eventually returned to Portugal and from there, sent to Rome, and Portuguese authorities seized their commercial fortune.[9]

In addition to the Lóios, the 1504 mission brought some lay teachers to Kongo. In his 1514 letter, Afonso complains about Rui do Rêgo, one of these lay teachers who, Afonso claims, "made himself out as a noble." Not only is do Rêgo lazy, Afonso says, but he also has not taught a single boy. Do Rêgo also demanded meat during Lent, scandalizing Afonso and his nobles, who were diligently fasting. He subsequently played a role in promoting the side of the São Tomé traders in the founding of the royal factory.

For all Afonso's complaining, however, the Lóios and other priests continued teaching. The students who graduated from these early classes were sent to the

7. See "Letter from the King of Kongo to D. Manuel I," October 5, 1514, in Correspondence.

8. See *Epílogo e Compêndio da Origem da Congregação de São João Evangelista*, Chapter 8, in Additional Translations.

9. Arquivo Distrial de Braga, MS 924, pp. 228–30; Jorge de São Paulo, *Epílogo e Compêndio*, Chapter 8, in Additional Translations.

provinces to start their own schools. Afonso remarks in his 1514 letter that he has sent "schoolboys" to "teach" residents in the provinces of Mbata and Mpangu. In his 1516 report to Lisbon, vicar Rui de Aguiar—sent to Kongo to be the head of the whole ecclesiastical community—notes that the school founded in 1509 had grown to enroll over a thousand students. More to the point, according to de Aguiar, Afonso "has already distributed many kingdom-born Christians throughout his kingdoms, who run schools and teach the people our holy faith." De Aguiar also notes that Afonso has also opened a school for girls. This school was overseen by one of Afonso's sisters, a woman who was at least sixty years old but who could "read very well, which she learned to do in her old age."[10]

The creation of this local educational establishment, which was still producing teachers, *mestres de escola* in Portuguese and *alongi a aleke* in Kikongo for a network of schools over 300 years later, became one of Afonso's most enduring achievements.[11] But Afonso was not only interested in providing a basic religious education to the ordinary people of Kongo; he also wanted, from the earliest stages of his contact with Portugal, to create a church in Kongo resembling European churches, led by bishops effectively chosen by their respective kings. Afonso would select a bishop from among his subjects, and this bishop would subsequently have the power to ordain those schoolteachers as priests and to make his school a seminary.

All of this was clearly on Afonso's mind when, in 1512, he sent 22 young nobles, in a party led by his son Francisco and including many of his own extended family members, to study in Portugal. This advance party would serve as a sort of nascent priesthood until Afonso could develop higher religious studies in Kongo. He also sent 500 slaves to accompany these young theological students. The sale of these slaves—including an extra 30 additional slaves to replace any that might die during the trip, thereby ensuring that no income would be lost—was probably intended to fund the students' lives in Portugal so that they would not be entirely

10. De Góis, *Chronica*, Book 4, cap. 3, including Rui de Aguiar to Manuel I, May 25, 1516, in Correspondence.

11. Documents regularly use the term *mestres de escola*; the Kikongo name is found in the catechism of 1624, edited by Mateus Cardoso, *Doutrina cristãa* (Lisbon, 1624) fol. 1, written as *dungi* to translate the *mestre* who is teaching the lessons. In the dictionary of 1648, it is more carefully used to define *paedagogus* translated as *ndongui a aleque* (literally, "teacher of children"), plural *alongui a aleque*. Biblioteca Nazionale Vittorio Emanuele (Rome), Fundo Minori 1896, MS Varia 274, fol. 70v, "Vocabularium latinum, hispanicum e congense." For the performance of the schoolmasters in the nineteenth century, see John Thornton, "The Kingdom of Kongo and Palo Mayombe: Reflections on an African Religion," *Slavery and Abolition* 37 (2016): 4–8.

dependent on Portuguese royal pleasure. By 1513, the Kongolese students were living—and some of their slaves serving—at the Lóios' school in Lisbon.[12]

Afonso was attentive to the progress of these and the other students he had sent. In his letter of May 27, 1517, he responds to a letter, the contents of which have been lost, from Manuel. Apparently, the students had either not been studying well or had perhaps been in trouble with the authorities for rowdy behavior typical of students of those days. In any case, Manuel asks whether the students ought to be expelled from Lisbon. Afonso was clearly concerned about this prospect and suggested other remedies: perhaps punishing them or breaking them into smaller groups sent to several different schools.

Looking for a Bishop

The end goal of Afonso's educational project was a Kongolese bishop. The rules of the Catholic church required that only bishops could ordain priests; having a Kongolese bishop would allow Afonso to appoint his own clergy. With this goal in mind, he sent his son Henrique to study in Lisbon soon after taking the throne.[13] When, in 1512, he sent Simão da Silva to Kongo, Manuel proposed that Afonso make formal obeisance to the pope, thereby securing some important recognition within Christendom. Manuel also suggested that Afonso present a case for Henrique's promotion to bishop of Kongo.[14]

Afonso immediately sent Pedro de Sousa—the cousin who had traveled with Henrique to Europe and served as Kongo's ambassador there—to lead the mission back to Portugal. But, as Afonso wrote in his 1514 letter, priests loyal to Fernão de Melo did what they could to thwart this mission. Beating his messengers to the ship, they ordered it to "depart with all the haste in the world without Dom Pedro [de Sousa] and without our message." De Sousa, "crying out for them to

12. They were noted in records in Portugal following September 1513, *MMA* 1:279–80. Also, on January 4, 1514, there is provision for students at Saint Eloi, *MMA* 1:281–83. Francisco, who either led or was one of them, is specified in a document of August 1514, *MMA* 1:287–88.

13. De Santa Maria, *Céu aberto*, p. 263, *MMA* 1:96 says that he stayed in the convent of S Eloy for ten years before going to Rome, which would put his departure from Kongo in 1503. This is unlikely, especially as it also says he was sent by Afonso, and so post 1506.

14. There was a long scholarly debate over whether this mission took place or not; the last word was probably that of Sébastien Meno Kikokula, "Autour de l'ambassade de Mbanza Kongo de 1514," *Annales Aequatoria* 18 (1997): 471–88). The version presented here, in turn, uses documentation that Meno did not know of to tell a different story.

wait," unsuccessfully tried to pursue the ship in a canoe and ultimately returned to Mbanza Kongo.

After locating a new ship, de Sousa was off again to Portugal, but he didn't complete his mission. Upon his arrival in São Tomé, he was taxed on the slaves he was planning to sell to fund the embassy's passage to Rome. In an undated letter from that time, he complains to the Portuguese officials about this unfair treatment, contending that if Portuguese royal ships did not have to pay taxes in Kongo, the reverse—that Kongolese ships be exempt from taxes in a Portuguese port—ought also to be true.

De Sousa eventually reached Portugal, probably in mid-1515, where he faced more travails.[15] The fine mule given to him by the king was taken away and substituted with a wild one that kicked and bit, then with a broken-down nag. In another undated document, he again protests his treatment to Portuguese officials, arguing that Portuguese nobles would never be so mistreated in Kongo.

But cranky mules proved to be the least of de Sousa's problems. He soon discovered that the carefully drafted letter and credentials he was to present to the pope were invalid: they were addressed to Pope Julius II, who had since died in 1513, and the new pope, Leo X, required credentials addressed specifically to him. Not only that, but Italy was engulfed in the War of the League of Cambrai (1508–1516), and the fighting in 1515 and 1516 was intense when de Sousa was waiting in Portugal to continue to Rome for his audience with the pope. The mission was scrapped, and Kongo was unable to make its formal presentation to the Vatican.

In 1514, during a yearlong lull in the war and before de Sousa reached Europe, Portugal made obeisance to the pope on Kongo's behalf. But their communique to the pope did not mention anything about a Kongolese bishop; it only notified him of the conversion of "the king of Manicongui and his numberless people," who was "the greatest and most powerful king of Ethiopia," and presented "tokens of its obeisance."[16] Henrique, who was originally to travel to the Vatican as part of de Sousa's mission, was therefore not elevated to the episcopate.

Partly in response to Portugal's dramatic mission of 1514, which presented the pope with an elephant and a rhinoceros (later illustrated by Albrecht Dürer), Leo X issued a papal bull—a sort of public decree—granting Portugal the right of patronage over all the churches it might establish in any part of the world stretching from the island of Funchal (in the Azores) all the way to India.[17] He also granted

15. Pedro de Sousa was issued clothing in Portugal on December 28, 1515, *MMA* 1:334–35.

16. See Kikokula, "Ambassade de Mbanza Kongo," pp. 479–81.

17. Bull *Dudum pro parte*, March 31, 1516, in *Bullarium Patronatus Portugalliae Regnum*, ed. Levy Maria Jordão (Lisbon, 1868), 1:113–14.

Portugal the right to choose bishops for any churches in the emerging Portuguese empire. While the bull did not immediately impact Kongo, it would become a crucial barrier to Afonso's plans for a Kongolese bishop. It is impossible to know how the matter might have turned out had de Sousa's mission been able to have its audience with the pope in 1515 or 1516.

Something about the failed mission caused Afonso to be upset with de Sousa. When in 1517, King Manuel sent António Vieira to replace Álvaro Lopes as the Portuguese royal representative in Kongo, he instructed Vieira (in an undated memorandum) to ask Afonso whether Pedro ought to be returned to Kongo or remain in Portugal.[18] Afonso's anger with de Sousa may well have stemmed from the latter man's failed mission to Rome, and Manuel took pains to explain to Afonso the many reasons the mission could never have succeeded.[19] Whatever problems there may have been, Manuel himself then pressed Henrique's case to be promoted to bishop even though church standards dictated that at twenty-three, Henrique was too young to be promoted. Opposition to his youth was eventually swept away, and on May 7, 1518, Leo X appointed Henrique bishop.[20]

Because Kongo was not an episcopal see (or diocese), he was not named bishop of Kongo. Instead, he was named an auxiliary bishop for Utica, a North African town then under Muslim control. The papacy retained these "phantom" dioceses (that is, containing no bishops, priests, or even Christians) to support bishops who were not in charge of a specific diocese. This Utica posting helped Henrique as it entitled him to a salary of 200 ducats. Given his youth, however, he was forced to wait until 1521 to claim his full episcopal powers.[21] The appointment also did not address the problem as to which country, Portugal or Kongo, would be allowed to nominate further episcopal candidates should a diocese be created.

When in 1521, Henrique was fully ordained as bishop and returned to Kongo (with four additional Lóio priests), he was well situated to wield a bishop's powers. We have no records to tell us whether Henrique started ordaining schoolmasters as priests or even how many of those schoolmasters might have been fully qualified

18. See "Letter from D. Manuel I to the Mwene Kongo," c. 1517, in Correspondence.

19. For an accounting of the legal measures and understandings that Portuguese kings made to establish ecclesiastical dominion over Kongo, see Jaime Ricardo Teixeira Gouveia, "The Creation of a Portuguese Diocese in the Kingdoms of Kongo and Angola in 1596: Imperial Strategies and Religious Implications," *Hispania Sacra* 74 (2022): 495–509.

20. Bull of Leo X, May 3, 1518, *MMA* 1:414–15.

21. For a detailed account and explanation of each step in the process, see François Bontinck, "Ndoadiki Ne-Kinu a Mubemba, premier evèque Kongo," *Revue africaine de théologie* 3 (1979): 149–69.

to become priests. In any case, Henrique does not appear to have ordained many priests at all in his five years as bishop.

With Henrique as his bishop, Afonso now laid out a plan in his letter of March 18, 1526, for what he plainly envisioned as the diocese of Kongo. He was clearly short of his own priests, as the plan relied heavily on Portugal to supply them. Afonso requested fifty priests from Portugal able to provide continuous sacramental services to a large and rather spread-out rural population. Presumably, Kongolese priests would replace or relieve the Portuguese as soon as Henrique could ordain some. Afonso outlined his plan to deploy thirty-seven of the requested fifty priests—of which five would be vicars—assigning six priests and a vicar to each province. His description of the plan ends before he provides details on how the remaining thirteen priests were to be deployed, but we can guess that they were to be sent to the provinces he had not yet named (Soyo and Mpemba, for example). (Indeed, adding another group of six and a group of seven to his list of assigned priests would make use of all fifty.)

We have to assume that Afonso had a good idea of how large his provinces were and what effort would be required to provide the sacraments on an adequate basis; he probably drew on his schoolmasters' experiences to inform his thinking on the matter. In his letter of August 26, 1526, Afonso offers a short description of how the priests would work, following the Lóios' long-standing practice of traveling in pairs through the provinces to perform the sacraments.[22]

In the same letter, Afonso also expressed concern that a single bishop would not suffice for the spiritual needs of his country. Though he begged to travel the country, Henrique was sickly, and Afonso kept him close in the capital, thus preventing him from carrying out his pastoral duties as bishop. Referring again to Henrique's health problems in his August 25, 1526 letter, Afonso proposes that a third nephew, also named Afonso, who was then studying in Lisbon, be returned to Kongo to serve as a second bishop. In an undated fragmentary letter of c. 1526 to João III, Afonso is more explicit and proposes ordaining two of his nephews as bishops since one bishop will not be enough to see to the needs of a kingdom as large as Kongo.

Afonso was also intent on having the capacity to train priests in Kongo; he wanted to avoid exposing candidates to the expense, risk, and hardship of studying in Portugal. In his August 25, 1526 letter, Afonso notes that he has enough teachers for reading and writing but asks for three or four good grammarians to instruct future priests in Latin and more philosophical subjects. He even notes, in

22. On the Lóio practice, de Santa Maria, *Céu aberto*, p. 888, the biography of João de Santa Maria, referring perhaps to the mission of 1508–1509, and connected to his death in May 1518.

an August 26, 1526 letter, that he is retaining one of the French prisoners he had taken at Soyo because the Frenchman was an excellent grammarian and was, in fact, teaching Latin to Afonso's family.

Responding to João's questions regarding Afonso's letter of August 25, 1526, Afonso points out that he is dependent upon Portugal for religious support and maintains that "it is not the place of the king of Castille or France, and we will not request any other Christian king to do it [support him] because of the high respect we have for you." Afonso writes that he relies on Portugal for religious support not just because other kingdoms had little contact or were far away but because Kongo "is as loyal and willing to serve you as Portugal."[23]

Aware that supporting the growth of the Catholic church in Kongo would give them a certain amount of leverage in that country's future, Portuguese kings generally supported Afonso's religious goals, including the investiture of a Kongolese bishop. Yet even Portugal's rulers were probably surprised by the speed with which Christianity took off in Kongo under Afonso's guidance. Afonso's efforts to have the Kongo church recognized internationally and his fervent adherence to the central components of Catholicism certainly suggested the possibility that the investiture of a Kongolese bishop could simultaneously bring Afonso the international recognition he sought and present the Portuguese crown with a bishop they could control. In 1514 the Vatican had already granted Portugal patronage over all churches founded in that country's "conquests"; with a bishop in place, João III would have near-total control over the church there.

To further encourage Afonso's efforts to establish the Catholic church in Kongo, João III, in his long letter to Afonso of 1529, addresses some of Afonso's complaints about the clergy and, since "all Christian kings" had recently been "ordered to send their prelates to Rome for a Vatican Council," proposed that Afonso should send Henrique to participate in the council.[24]

While the wording of João's letter makes it sound as if he still supported the idea of Afonso getting his bishop, João also appears to have believed that he, or Portugal, in some ways *owned* the Kongo church. Thus the bishop that Afonso wanted was likely to be Portuguese. João believed and wished for Rome to believe that Kongo was at least an ecclesiastical colony of Portugal and that its priests and bishops (if Kongo were to have its own bishop) answered to the crown of Portugal just as its own priests and bishops did.

This belief in the Portuguese "ownership" of Kongo's church was made clear when, in 1531, Henrique died, and João III laid claim to Henrique's personal

---

23. See "Letter from the King of Kongo to King João III," August 25, 1526, in Correspondence.

24. See "Letter from Dom João III to the King of Kongo," end of 1529, in Correspondence.

goods and wealth. Asserting that Kongo was "territory subject to King João III of Portugal and Algarve,"[25] João III stated that he, not Afonso, was the true head of its church and thus the legal inheritor of Henrique's estate. Though the church theoretically controlled ecclesiastical goods—and though the pope, Clement VII, could have granted their administration to whatever authority he chose—Clement's acceptance of Portugal's, not Kongo's, claim to Henrique's estate revealed that Portugal had the papacy on their side.

Pope Clement clearly anticipated some resistance from Afonso to his ruling on the legal ownership of Henrique's personal property. Clement instructed several Portuguese officials to draw up an inventory and ordered "the king of Congo or his great men or all others who might hold them" to remit those goods to Portugal. He forbade anyone in Kongo from objecting to or resisting his decision and even authorized the king of Portugal to use the "secular arm" to force submission to it. The order even forbade the right to appeal.[26] Portugal had influence in Rome, using it to ignore Afonso and take control of Kongo's church even as Afonso was consolidating it.

Afonso must have been stunned by the letter he received, dated March 17, 1535, from the newly installed Pope Paul III. In that letter, Paul informed Afonso that he, the pope, had established a new diocese, to include Kongo, on the island of São Tomé. Further, the seat of the Kongolese bishop's power would now be a cathedral on that island.[27] All of this meant that Afonso's church would now be dependent on a Portuguese-appointed bishop residing on an island that had, at the very best, a strained relationship with his kingdom.

There is some evidence that Afonso had proceeded with his plan for his own bishop following Henrique's death in 1531. The fragmentary note on his proposed expansive diocese seemed quite certain that he expected another bishop when he wrote, "if you permit our two nephews to travel from Rome after being ordained as bishops." While no Vatican documents mention a second bishop, the historian João de Barros, who wrote extensively about Afonso's reign, claimed in 1552, "there have already been two bishops in his Kingdom, who served God by exercising their office."[28] Many in Kongo apparently believed it, as King Garcia II, writing around 1651, also claimed in a letter addressed to the pope that "if

25. Brief of Clement VII to Diogo Ortiz de Vilhegas, November 17, 1531, *MMA* 15:75.

26. This statement is quoted in the papal bull issued to Diogo Ortiz de Vilhegas, November 17, 1535; an original letter from João III or Ortiz de Vilhegas is lacking, but the intent is clear from the disposition of the property, *MMA* 15:175.

27. See "Pope Paul III's Brief to the King of Kongo," March 17, 1535, in Additional Translations.

28. See "The Reign of D. Afonso I of Kongo," 1493?–1543, in Correspondence.

you read in the history of the bishops, you will see they are of various nations, and two from the royal house of Congo."[29] Francisco de Santa Maria's history of the Lóios claimed that Pedro de Sousa, Afonso's ambassador, had been ordained as bishop of São Tomé, but died on the way back from Rome in 1538.[30] Given the papacy's position on Portugal's right of patronage and the ruthless way João III pursued it, it seems quite unlikely that there was another bishop. It's possible Afonso had expectantly sent to Rome to have one of his descendants elevated to bishop, perhaps named Pedro, who died on the way back and was believed to be returning to Kongo.

Not long after the delivery of the papal letter, the Portuguese crown used the authority vested in the new bishop to consolidate what it could in the spiritual world. Although it would be several years before a fully functioning bishop occupied the new see, Manuel Pacheco, acting on behalf of the bishop's authority and as the informal head of the Portuguese community in Kongo, quickly demanded the removal of all existing priests from Kongo.

In his letter to the crown dated March 28, 1536, Pacheco asserted that Portugal's new bishop needed to move quickly to appoint priests of firmer morals than those working in Kongo at the time. His statement was made in light of and given weight by the slave-trade scandal involving the Lóios, previously the most admired priests working in Kongo. Most of the priests left Kongo willingly. But one, known only as "Master Gil," resisted and relented only when Afonso, having carefully read the orders Pacheco carried, commanded him to go.

In his letter, Pacheco took the opportunity to defame Master Gil's character, suggesting that Gil was a man of low morals who would probably attempt to denounce Pacheco. As Gil was supposed to teach advanced theological studies in Kongo, his removal was likely a key part of the Portuguese plan to undermine Afonso's attempts to establish his own episcopate.

When Master Gil was about to return to Portugal, Afonso sent with him two letters, both dated December 28, 1535, to be delivered to João III. One of these letters announced Gil's departure from Kongo and recommended him to the Portuguese crown for his good service; in it, Afonso asks that he, Afonso, "may hear the word of God from his lips" and requests his rapid return to

---

29. Garcia II to Pope, c. 1652, *MMA* 11:140.

30. Except in *MMA* 1:96, 100. De Santa Maria was often confused and attempted to link what he read in chronicles and the archives. Clearly, Pedro de Sousa was never bishop of São Tomé, and perhaps the Pedro from Kongo who died in 1538, which de Santa Maria probably did read in the archival record, was indeed a relative of Afonso, but could not have been bishop of São Tomé or Kongo in that year.

Kongo.[31] In the other letter, Afonso asks that João "include . . . among the Portuguese students . . . sent to pursue their studies in Paris" Master Gil's nephew António, who had arrived with Gil in Kongo when he was nine years old and learned to speak Kikongo while serving as a valet in Afonso's court. If António were to complete his studies in Paris, he could return to Kongo to preach "Christian doctrine to our peoples in their native language and ensuring the salvation of their souls."[32]

This request indicates that Afonso was not giving up easily on his dreams of establishing a Kongolese church independent of the Portuguese bishop. Educating one of his subjects (albeit one of Portuguese ancestry) in Paris would be another step in improving the quality of the church Afonso aspired to build in Kongo. The University of Paris was the epitome of European education, lay and clerical. A degree from the school would put the young António on the same intellectual rank as other high-ranking church members in Europe, including some of Portugal's best intellectuals. Manuel had purchased the University's College of Saint Barbara to educate Portuguese youth in 1523, and in 1526, João III endowed fifty scholarships for students attending the college.[33] Unfortunately, we do not know if António managed to get a seat in Paris or if he returned to Kongo later. But given Portuguese plans for the church in Kongo, it seems unlikely that João would have wanted to sponsor António's education. In any case, we know that Master Gil never returned to Kongo; even a decade later, Afonso's successor Diogo was still asking for Gil's return.[34]

While Afonso worked to get António admitted to the loftiest educational institution in Europe, numerous Kongolese students continued their studies at various colleges in Portugal. The community of Kongolese students in Portugal was self-sustaining in many ways, in effect creating its own school within Lisbon. Arriving in Lisbon in 1526, Afonso's "third nephew," also named Afonso, had by 1533 established a "public school of the humanities in the Paço do Castello." The school subsequently moved to the Dominicans' territory, and by 1538 João III was paying "third nephew" Afonso a salary.[35] At the same time, the Lóios, longtime

31. See "Letter from the King of Kongo to King Dom João III," December 28, 1535, in Correspondence.

32. See "Letter from the King of Kongo to King Dom João III," December 28, 1535, in Correspondence.

33. Jules Étienne Joseph Quicherat, *Histoire de Sainte-Barbe: Collège, communauté et institution*, 3 vols. (Paris, 1860–1864), 1:124–27.

34. Diogo I to Diogo Gomes, December 12, 1546, *MMA* 2:151–52.

35. Luís de Sousa, *História de São Domingos*, quoted in *MMA* 15:90. See other documents quoted on 89–90; and António Brásio, "D. Afonso, sobrinho de rei do Congo, Mestre-Escola em Lisboa."

supporters of Kongolese students, were drawing on the "money of Congo" to pay some of the students' expenses. This college fund may have originated from the fortune generated by the disgraced Lóios in 1535.[36]

A Route to Ethiopia?

In 1532, João III received an embassy from Lebna Dengel, the king of Ethiopia. When he sent this embassy on to Rome to pay obeisance to the pope, João III was planning to gain control over Ethiopia's church just as he had done in Kongo. In the letter he wrote to Clement VII regarding the Ethiopian embassy, he reminded the pope that he had already converted the Kingdom of "Manicongo," and noted that country's proximity to Ethiopia (on maps and in the European imagination).[37] João III and (perhaps) Clement were prepared to bring Christian Ethiopia under papal obedience and Portuguese patronage, and nearly did in the seventeenth century.[38]

Afonso's interest in developing his church may well have dovetailed with a desire to know of other African Christians, including Ethiopia. It is likely that the initial Kongolese mission to Portugal in 1486 had encountered the Ethiopian Lucas, and from there, an interest would develop. Portugal also had an interest in Ethiopia as a potential ally in the endless war against Islam, and both Afonso and João believed that the two African countries were near each other.

Since the early sixteenth century, European cartographers had been drawing maps of Africa that showed a great central lake from which the Nile and the Congo Rivers flowed. As they learned more about Ethiopia in the early sixteenth century, cartographers came to identify Lake Tana, on the western side of Ethiopia, as this lake. They began to assume that the rumored lake east of Kongo might be Lake Tana and that the Congo River flowed from it. (In fact, the lake in question was probably Lake Mai Ndombe, whose waters derive through a flow northward from

---

36. For a thorough investigation of the financial and educational aspects of this relationship, see Nuno Fernando de Pino e Silva de Almeida Falcão, "A reforma em carisma e ação: A congregação de S. João Evangelista (Lóios) (Italia, Portugal e África)—c. 1420/1580" (PhD diss., Universidade de Porto, 2016), pp. 323–46.

37. Damião de Góis, *L'Ambasciaria di David Re dell' Etiopia all' Santissimo S. N. Clemente Papa VII* (Bologne, 1535), p. 8, n.p. For details, see Matteo Salvadore, *The African Prester John and the Birth of Ethiopian-European Relations, 1402–1555* (London: Routledge, 2017), pp. 153–67.

38. Merid Wolde Aregay and Girma Beshah, *The Question of the Union of the Churches in Luso-Ethiopian Relations, 1500–1632* (Lisbon: Junta de Investigações do Ultramar and Centro de Estudos Históricos Ultramarinos, 1964).

a branch of the Congo River). The Portuguese crown took an early interest in finding a way to reach Ethiopia via Kongo; the royal instructions given to Simão da Silva in 1512 asked him to find out more about the lake that lay east of Kongo and whether it could be reached.

In 1520, Gregório da Quadra, a Portuguese navigator who had served in the Indian Ocean, went to Kongo to pursue the same plan. However, Afonso did not support the idea at the time.[39] Afonso did have a strategic interest in the whole region around Lake Mai Ndombe that may have led to his disinterest in da Quadra's plan. Mai Ndombe was part of the textile belt of Central Africa, an area Afonso wanted very much to control. His eastern province, Mbata, and the Seven Kingdoms of Kongo dia Nlaza, the distant "Empire" of Mwene Muji, as well as the rival Kingdom of Great Makoko, all controlled other parts of the textile-producing region, and more and richer textiles were produced still farther east.[40]

But Afonso changed his mind not long after. The failed 1520 Portuguese mission to convert Angola resulted in Baltasar de Castro, one of its members, returning to Kongo in 1526. It was perhaps to fulfill a project to reach Ethiopia or just to learn more about the textile belt that Afonso now tasked de Castro with building ships to explore the region; in an undated memo from about 1526, he requested supplies from Portugal for the task. Though de Castro did not manage to carry out the plan, we learn from his letter of 1536 that Manuel Pacheco, then the representative of the Portuguese crown in Kongo, was, in fact, building small ships to explore the area. Expectations were that he could complete it within a year.[41] None of the contemporary records mention the completion of this task.

Curiously, though, when Carmelite missionaries came to Kongo in 1584, they heard of an earlier king, one they did not name, who had actually succeeded in sending an expedition up the river. The mission had failed, they were told, because the crews spotted monsters along the banks of the river and returned with tall tales of the dangers of the region.[42] This strange story points to another feature of Central Africa in the European imagination: that the headwaters of the Nile not only

39. De Góis, *Chronica*, Part IV, chap. 54, *MMA* 15:59.

40. John Thornton, *A History of West Central Africa to 1850* (Cambridge: Cambridge University Press, 2020), pp. viii, 12–14. Mwene Muji is only attested in 1587 but likely existed earlier.

41. Manuel Pacheco to João III, March 28, 1536, *MMA* 2:58.

42. Biblioteca Nacional de Madrid, MS 2711, fol. 101, Diego de Santissimo Sacramento, "Relacion del viage a Guine que hiço el Padre . . . ."

contained lakes, but the mysterious Mountains of the Moon, and the Garden of Eden, now believed to be a Terrestrial Paradise.[43]

The Carmelites were told that the Congo River flowed from this paradise, and as the European legend had it that monsters and angels guarded the paradise, the failure was one more piece of evidence that Kongo bordered on it.[44] In a casual interview with Kongo's king Álvaro I around 1585, the Carmelite missionaries learned that he believed that the fig leaves Adam and Eve used to cover their nakedness were in fact, leaves of the Central African *misafu* tree.[45] Álvaro's conviction of the connection between the Garden and Kongo may well have led to the idea, reported in seventeenth-century sources, that the Kongolese believed that when God created the earth, he sent his angels to create other countries so as to devote himself to Africa, and particularly to Kongo.[46]

The Portuguese Community in Kongo

Afonso had accepted the idea that the Portuguese in his country would have some extra-territorial status and generally left them alone. However, he was still forced to ensure they stayed within the limits of the law—even if expulsion from Kongo was the only punishment he could bring to bear against offenders—and to do this, he carefully studied Portuguese law in 1516. João III alluded to this state of affairs in his letter of 1529, essentially saying Afonso could do whatever he wanted with Portuguese living in Kongo and should not complain to Portugal about their behavior.

The Portuguese community in Kongo was in a sort of limbo, ruled by officials appointed in Portugal, but still partially under Kongo's jurisdiction. As we have seen, Álvaro Lopes lost his position as captain of Kongo's Portuguese community after killing Diogo Fernandes, and in 1516 was sent back to Portugal. Manuel Pacheco, who accompanied the embassy to Angola, was eventually appointed head of the Portuguese community around 1525 and, in 1531, was formally named a judge. Though João invited Afonso to enforce Kongolese laws in his country, there

43. Alessandro Scafi, "The African Paradise of Cardinal Carvajal: New Light on the Kunstmann II Map (1502–1506)," *Renaissance and Reformantion* 31 (2008): 7–28; Francesc Relaño, "Paradise in Africa: The History of a Geographical Myth in Medieval Thought to its Gradual Demise in Early Modern Europe," *Terra Incognita* 36 (2004): 1–11.

44. Biblioteca Nacional de Madrid, MS 2711, fol. 101, De Santissimo Sacramento, "Relacion."

45. Biblioteca Nazionale di Firenze, Pancitichiani 200, fol. 165, untitled account.

46. Cavazzi, *Istorica Descrizione*, Book 1, no. 156.

is little evidence that Afonso did more than translate into Portuguese the titles of some of his officials.[47]

Resident Portuguese in Kongo had also come as part of the larger scheme, conceived as early as the reign of João Nzinga a Nkuwu, of importing or reproducing in the country those components of European culture that would augment Kongo's existing structure. In 1486, when João sent his first embassy to Portugal, he asked to be sent, among other things, artisans capable of building European-style stone buildings. Some masons arrived when the mission returned to Kongo in 1491; another group arrived with Gonçalo Rodrigues in 1507; still more arrived with Simão da Silva in 1513. But those masons, like many of the other European tradesmen who followed them, did not always perform as Afonso hoped.

His descriptions of the artisans' behavior are extreme to the point of being strange and require some explanation. In his 1514 letter, Afonso claimed that he paid the European masons a *lufuku* of *nzimbu* shells for each stone they laid, and despite that, they kept asking for more pay. Given the value of a *lufuku* (one *lufuku* could buy seventeen slaves), the statement has to be a sort of exaggeration for effect, like saying, "I paid him a million bucks for a haircut, and my hair is uneven."[48] Afonso might also have been applying this rhetorical device when he described the pace of their work: "They [perhaps the group of masons that traveled to Kongo in 1509 with Gonçalo Rodrigues] have been working on this house for five years, and they have not yet completed it, nor will they complete it in ten years."[49] This would certainly be an extraordinarily slow pace of work; the 1491 mission to Kongo built a stone church in roughly three and a half weeks. In his letter of June 13, 1517, Afonso notes that work on the "house" (presumably a palace) was as yet unfinished and that he needed more carpenters to complete both the "house" and a church.

Beyond the glacial pace of their work, the builders refused to train local people, spat on them, abused them, and when called upon to use their slaves, complained that the slaves had run away. For all this flagrant insubordination, Afonso seemed unwilling to discipline them. When threatened with punishment, they told Afonso they did not work for him or the king of Portugal and did not owe

47. The renaming of Kongo's provinces using European titles—like count, marquis, or duke—was not Afonso's doing; this was done by Alvaro I (1568–1587).

48. In his letter of December 17, 1540, Afonso gives an account of Álvaro Lopes, describing the expenditure of 4 *kofus* of money which he purchased twenty-five slaves with and had six and a half *lufukus* of change, so that 1.5 *lufukus* could buy seventeen slaves. In his letter of December 4, 1540, Afonso sets an exchange rate of 40 *kofus* of *nzimbu* against 5000 cruzados, or 16.8 cruzados per *lufuku*.

49. See "Letter from the King of Kongo to D. Manuel I," October 5, 1514, in Correspondence.

anyone anything. Afonso ruefully acknowledged that he did not have the heart to punish them and let them continue their bad behavior.

Perhaps these workers realized that they possessed a rare skill, one difficult to replace, and hoped to milk that skill for as much and as long as possible. They must also have realized that as soon as they trained local tradesmen, they would be out of a job or competing with their students for work. Therefore, they made life as difficult as possible for their students so they would not complete their training. While Afonso may well have exaggerated the degree of the European workers' laziness or greed, he needed them and was prepared to get them to work simply by browbeating them.

It seems clear, too, that for whatever reason, Afonso was unable to have enough local people trained in either carpentry or masonry to have a self-sustaining class of such workers. As late as 1526, he was still claiming not to have enough artisans to complete work on existing churches or start new ones.[50] In his letter of August 26, 1526, Afonso says that after capturing the French ship in Soyo, he sent most of the prisoners to São Tomé but kept the French ship's carpenter in Kongo to fill a vacancy. Yet during his reign, Afonso did oversee the completion of the construction of several churches, a palace, and a walled enclosure around the royal compound, as well as a second enclosure around the Portuguese settlement in Mbanza Kongo. Some of the work completed under his guidance survived into the nineteenth century.[51]

In the end, it seems that stone buildings had limited appeal in Kongo. Afonso's stone palace eventually fell to ruin, and when the seventeenth-century king Garcia II rebuilt the city, he made his own palace of wood and perishable materials. It was a handsome building—Capuchin priests said it was the only two-story building in Kongo—but it was not a stone palace.[52] Abraham Willaerts, a Dutch artist who came to Mbanza Kongo in 1641 to report on the customs and culture of the country, produced an engraving of the city in which Garcia's palace is prominent,

50. See "Letter from António Afonso to António Carneiro," April 3, 1526, in Correspondence.

51. Filippo Pigafetta, *Relatione del Reame de Congo e delle circonvince contrade* (Rome, 1591), p. 40. Although there may have been repairs through the years, there were quite a few ruined walls throughout the town in the late nineteenth century. After the Portuguese takeover of Kongo beginning in 1885, their building projects used up all these stones to build new structures, with the exception of the cathedral of São Salvador (first built in 1549), the only building from the era still standing. The cathedral's ruins were an important part of Angola's petition to have Mbanza Kongo named a World Heritage Site, which UNESCO approved in 2017.

52. Biblioteca Nacional de Madrid, MS 3533, Antonio de Teruel, "Descripción narrativa de la misión seráfica de los Padres Capuchinos y sus progresos en el reyno de Congo," pp. 182–83.

and at the base of the palace in the engraving, one can still see the remains of the wall Afonso built.[53]

While his quarrel with tradesmen was relatively minor, Afonso's view of Portugal and the Portuguese living in his country may well have been sharply altered by João III's maneuvering over the question of the Angola trade in the 1520s and then in 1531–1535 over the question of the diocese of São Tomé. It would be easy to surmise that Portugal aimed at Kongo's sovereignty, given the significant direct meddling with Kongo's vassals and redirecting Kongo's relationship to Rome. Was this spiritual control ultimately to be extended to material authority? Afonso's thinking was clearly noted in Manuel Pacheco's letter of March 28, 1536, when a certain Rui Mendes arrived in the kingdom, "claiming that he was a royal trading agent for the copper mines." While Afonso assisted the efforts, including setting up a foundry in the capital and having a noble accompany Mendes to see mines producing copper and lead, Afonso was "so suspicious" that the arrival of such a factor meant that the "kingdom was going to be taken over along with the mines." He was aware of European conquests elsewhere in the world and that the Portuguese in India "order a fortress built wherever gold and silver are found." Pacheco noted that he "sometimes mentions this fact in response to my requests."[54] While the Portuguese were not well placed to conquer Kongo, the news both from India and the spectacular conquests of the Spanish in America must have given him cause for serious concern.

France and Kongo

Given that so much of Afonso's external diplomacy took place through Portugal, one might expect he would look for some contact with other European powers. However, the only other Europeans to visit Kongo came from France, and they were not interested in engaging in diplomacy. In his letter of December 27, 1525, to the officials of São Tomé—and again in his letter of August 25, 1526, to João III—Afonso announced that he had captured some French sailors who landed in Soyo. The French ship was purchasing copper (in the form of *manilhas*), ivory, and redwood (*takula*). As soon as Afonso learned the ship had landed, he sent Judge Manuel Pacheco, leader of the Portuguese community, to Soyo to see what was happening. Mobilizing a large caravel and another royal vessel, Pacheco led a

53. The engraving was published in Olfert Dapper, *Naukeurige Beschrijvinge der Afrika gewesten* (Amsterdam, 1668).

54. See "Letter from Manuel Pacheco to King Dom João III," March 28, 1536, in Correspondence.

mixed Portuguese and Kongolese force to fight with the well-armed French ship. Faced with a losing battle, the French ship sailed away, stranding the landing party but taking some prisoners. After tricking the landing party into surrendering by offering trade goods, they were taken prisoner, and some later died. Afonso dispatched nine of the surviving captives to São Tomé but retained the ship's pilot, as the man had a good knowledge of Latin, and the carpenter, who Afonso thought could help repair his churches.

Since the late fifteenth century, Portugal claimed a monopoly on trade and navigation in the entire Gulf of Guinea—even if other European powers were reluctant to recognize Portugal's claim and regularly traded there. Private interests in France, however, wished very much to trade there, and in the first quarter of the sixteenth century, France was engaged in a war with Spain. While the fighting was primarily in Italy, French authorities allowed private merchants, the most notable of whom was Jean Ango of Dieppe, to capture Spanish ships and to trade in territory claimed by Portugal in Africa and America. In 1522, French authorities issued privateer Jean Terrien a letter of marque, or permission, to raid shipping and launch attacks on Portuguese possessions.

French privateers were, in general, remarkably successful. In 1524, captains sailing under the flag of Jean Ango, captured the gold that Cortes pillaged from the Aztec Empire. Ango financed and organized many French privateers, sponsored French voyages to Asia, and supported piratical attacks against Portuguese possessions in the South Atlantic, especially in Brazil, where the Portuguese were just beginning to assert themselves. Ango's men founded the first small French colony off the coast of Brazil, a forerunner to "France Antarctique" that would have colonies in the future Rio de Janeiro area as well as at the mouth of the Amazon.[55] Responding to these French attacks on Portuguese concerns, João III issued an order in 1526 for any Portuguese authority or private subject to attack French shipping everywhere in the Atlantic.

In 1539, Gregório Nunes, the Portuguese ambassador to France, submitted to the French court a lengthy dossier of the 300 Portuguese ships captured by French vessels since 1522. Many were in the South Atlantic; none were specifically listed as being around Kongo. The gold trade of Mina, of course, was consistently targeted by pirates; cargoes of gold were infinitely vendible, while other cargoes might not be so easy to dispose of. But this did not mean that ships from São Tomé might not be captured if they carried a cargo of sugar or a cargo of slaves.[56]

---

55. Many of Ango's actions were documented by extensive quotations in Eugène Guénin, *Ango et ses pilotes* (Paris, 1901).

56. Guénin, *Ango*, p. 193.

In fact, France probably had regular commercial contact with independent areas in Africa and America. Though we have few records of French voyages in the region, we know ships had already been conducting both war and trade by the time the French ship appeared in Soyo. The few extant accounts from that time and place usually refer to the action occurring off the coast of Brazil and Guinea, then used as a geographical term including the whole African coast. The French trade in Central Africa probably focused on copper, ivory, and dyewood, not slaves, and the ship that arrived in Soyo was indeed seeking these commodities.

Though indirect, we do have some evidence of fairly regular French commerce with Kongo. In 1527, a group of merchants in Rouen had outfitted a ship, *Marie de Bon Secours* (also known as the *Grand Anglais*), to explore possible routes to India. To keep the true nature and length of the proposed voyage secret from the crew, the master claimed the ship was bound for "Sanct Thome or Mangicongue" and, failing to reach that destination, would travel to Brazil.[57] That a potential crew would not consider unusual a trip to São Tomé or Kongo suggests that French sailors regularly visited those waters.

The French ship that arrived in Soyo probably did not intend to capture Portuguese vessels. But its heavy armament suggested it would be ready to defend itself and, if the circumstances warranted it, to capture Portuguese ships. Though Afonso had no particular reason not to trade with French vessels, he wanted the French to conduct their trade according to the system he had in place. A guide to sailors, probably written in the late 1530s or early 40s by João Afonso—a Portuguese captain who in 1528 deserted to France after long service to Portugal—noted that ships visiting the "River of Congo" should "go up to [the first] village and anchor." There, captains should remain until they were met by "a boat made of one piece" and not "go on without the assurance of the king." The people in that land, he wrote, "are Christians and allies of the King of Portugal."[58] French ships typically traded cloth and clothing goods in exchange for copper, ivory, dyes, and a local pepper.[59]

When he reported to João the details of the action taken against the French ship in Soyo, Afonso noted that many Portuguese vessels in the general vicinity

57. Petition of French crew, 1527 in Sousa Viterbo, *Trabalhos náuticos dos Portugueses*, Part 1 (Lisbon, 1898), p. 84.

58. Jean Alphonse de Saintonge, *Les voyages avantureux* (Paris, 1559), fols. 55–55v.

59. Early trading relationships are described in a plan for a trading voyage to Brazil written by Jean de Dennebault at an unknown date before 1549 (because the ship was to visit and trade in Bahia and makes no mention of the Portuguese presence there), Bibliothèque Nationale de France, Collection Moreau, MS 841, fols. 129–129v.

would not take the French prisoners off, as they "had come to acquire slaves, not Frenchmen."[60] The perceived Portuguese indifference to Afonso's orders and interests lay at the heart of his report on the French. Afonso was clearly not pleased with the behavior of Portuguese, or rather, São Tomé officials. They put to sea without Afonso's permission, so that the captains would not to be denounced in Portugal for misdeeds and disrespected his authority in a variety of other ways.

In his 1529 response to Afonso's 1526 barrage of letters, João III assured the Kongo king that, since he had taken the French prisoners "justly" and needed services, he was free to keep the French captives in Kongo. In his October 1525 letter, Afonso stated his hope that João would respect his promise that Kongo would not mistreat the French captives. João assured Afonso that the Kongo king should not be worried about capturing fellow Christians since, as far as João was concerned, the Frenchmen were just thieves. In that letter, João suggests he would return the prisoners to France to allow the king there to deal with them as he saw fit. This reply was incongruous with the fact that France and Portugal were at the time in the midst of an informal maritime war, one that João III was anxious to end and was likely to turn them politely over to France.

Though Afonso and the Kongolese may have occasionally welcomed the French to their shores, the French were not necessarily anyone's friends. French pirates regularly seized all manner of Portuguese shipping, including ships carrying letters from Afonso. In his letter of December 17, 1540, Afonso worries that João III is not answering his letters and that his letters have not been reaching Portugal. He says, hopefully, that perhaps the French pirates active in the region at the time might have intercepted some of his letters.

Queen Catarina

In his letter of January 18, 1526, Afonso acknowledges receipt of a variety of clothes from Lisbon. Judging by the somber colors of the clothes, it seems possible he was mourning the death of his first wife, whose name is unknown.[61] She had served as his stand-in when he was on campaign against Munzu, the Ambundu ruler, in 1513 and was reputed to be very pious.

---

60. See "Letter from the King of Kongo to King João III," August 25, 1526, in Correspondence.

61. Louis Jadin, in the French translation of this letter, suggested the idea of mourning colors. See Louis Jadin and Mirielle Dicorato, *Correspondance de Dom Afonso, roi du Congo: 1506–1543* (Brussels: Académie royale des sciences colonials, 1974) p. 147, n. 3.

Not long after sending that letter, Afonso was again writing (in an undated summary of 1526–1527) to request Portuguese assistance in securing a papal bull so he could marry one of his cousins. This woman, Catarina, was of third-degree consanguinity with Afonso, too close for a traditional Catholic marriage. But popes often waived issues of consanguinity for closely intermarried elite European families, and Afonso hoped the pope would do the same for him.[62]

The bull proved difficult to obtain. In 1534, João submitted Afonso's request to the Vatican via Martinho de Portugal, the Portuguese ambassador to Rome. He also proposed that the ban on consanguinity be lifted for all of Kongo's citizens. Finally, he asked that Kongo receive this free of the usual charge, citing the incompatibility of currency (*nzimbu* shells being current money in Kongo) as a reason.[63] Ultimately, de Portugal tried to pitch lifting the ban on marriage between cousins as a means of keeping Kongo's new and unsteady Catholicism within the fold of the church. In his two letters to João III dated November 28, 1535 (the letters concerning Master Gil), Afonso anxiously urges the Portuguese ruler to press Rome for permission to wed his cousin.

Another Attempt to Reach Rome

The search for a papal brief to allow Afonso's marriage came with renewed interest in exploring possibilities for diplomatic work with Rome. In 1534, Pope Clement VII died, and as was customary, the Vatican expected Christian countries to declare, via representatives, obeisance to the new pope, Paulo III. Making obeisance to the new pope would, in some ways, allow Afonso to make a statement regarding his independent membership in Christendom and counteract Portugal's claim that Kongo fell under its ecclesiastical authority. Though it is not clear when Afonso decided to send a mission to Rome—his credential documents are undated—a letter introducing some members of the mission was dated February 22, 1539, and it seems logical to assume the credential document was created at the same time.[64]

62. For the legal aspects, François Bontinck, "Du nouveau sur Dom Afonso, roi de Congo," *African Historical Studies* 3 (1970): 154–55.

63. Instructions to D. Martinho de Portugal, May 20, 1532, *MMA* 2:3–5.

64. One of the procuration documents has the date 1532 on its eighteenth-century descriptive cover; the document itself contains the date February 22 but without a year, and the other is completely undated. Brásio dated them to 1535, operating on the assumption that the mission

We have no documents indicating that Afonso intended to send a mission to Rome as soon as the new pope was elected. But in addition to paying the expected obeisance to the pope, such a mission was probably also intended to secure the papal rule granting all Kongolese the same dispensation for consanguinity and allowing Afonso's marriage to Catarina. João III was certainly doing his part to ensure papal support for the dispensation. In August 1539, João III wrote his ambassador to Rome that he, João, would be very happy if the ambassador could secure papal "absolution of the married blacks of Manicongo" for the second degree of consanguinity.[65] The tone of the note suggests this was not the first time he had requested this dispensation for Afonso.

Afonso composed, and had written in a fine hand, a letter of credentials to be delivered by his embassy to the pope. Included in this embassy were Afonso's brother Manuel, a nephew named Afonso, a "nephew further removed" also named Afonso, and yet another nephew named Henrique.[66] The group also included Francisco Muçio Camerte, an Italian doctor, orator, and linguist, who could presumably translate from Portuguese to Italian or Latin and, having lived in Kongo, may have been fluent in Kikongo as well. According to the custom in Kongo, Afonso would simply have been described as "father" (*se*) to all the nephews included in the embassy, and they in turn would have been called his "sons" (*mwana*). But since such terminology would likely have caused confusion in the Vatican, Afonso must have felt the need, in this letter of credentials, to explain in greater detail the relationship between him and his representatives.

The document also lists Afonso's titles in full. This is the only extant document of his to do so. Most of his letters included, at best, some abbreviated form of this list, e.g., "king of Congo and lord of the Ambundos, etc." But in this letter to the pope, Afonso elaborates on that "etc.," listing, for example, the regions of Musulu, Kisama, Angola (or Ndongo), Matamba, Mwilu, Musuku, and the Anzicas (Kingdom of Great Makoko) as being under his rule. Most scholars believe he might have included the same places in earlier lists of his tributaries. But since we don't know much about the wars he fought, we have no way of knowing which of the territories listed in the letter to the pope were long-established titles, which

---

was sent shortly after the accession of Pope Paulo III in 1535. Jadin argues that another dated document from March 25, 1539, includes people who accompanied the mission to Portugal.

65. Manuel Francisco de Barros e Sousa, Visconde de Santarém, and Luiz Augusto Rebello da Silva, eds., *Quadro elementar das relações politicas e diplomaticas de Portugal com as diversas potencias do Mundo* . . ., 12 vols. (Lisbon 1868), 11:247, 344. From the correspondence of Martinho de Portugal.

66. See "Letter of Mandate from the King of Kongo," February [22], 1539, in Correspondence.

were recent acquisitions, or those over which his claims were dubious. The claim to include Angola, was a good example, since even the earliest letters included the more inclusive Ambundu, without the more detailed elaboration.

In any case, the mission got stuck in São Tomé. On July 12, 1540, Afonso's brother Manuel, the leader of the delegation, wrote to João III requesting a well-armed ship to escort the party to Lisbon; the party feared that French pirates, once again active in the region, would capture them. French privateers, operating in the area of Brazil and the Malaguetta Coast (including São Tomé and its region) in defiance of the French government's orders, had caused substantial damage to Portuguese possessions. A 1537 interdict issued against them by King Francis I did not slow the privateers, and complaints about them continued into the 1540s.[67] Indeed, Manuel's own nephew Bastião had been captured and held prisoner by French pirates as he was en route to Lisbon. In his letter of July 12, 1540, Manuel complained of previously having sent "five or six" unanswered letters concerning the transport of the embassy to the Vatican. The king may simply have been ignoring these letters, but it is also entirely possible that French privateers had seized the ships carrying the correspondence.

In his letter of December 17, Afonso also complained that São Tomé ships, responsible for carrying his correspondence to Lisbon, had deliberately left without Afonso's letters to João, and he was certain they'd departed early "to prevent us from sending word to you about the troubles we suffer here." It had been two years since João had replied to one of Afonso's letters. The loss of letters due to the seizure by French pirates of mail-carrying ships certainly did happen, as French pirates took letters from Manuel Pacheco as he was traveling to Portugal on Afonso's behalf. But he also hinted that it might have been malfeasance on the part of the São Tomé authorities. Afonso did "assume that some legitimate reason has prevented you from receiving some of our letters" and aimed his suspicions at "low quality" merchants avoiding control by the crown, which had taken over the Angola trade and excluded São Tomé. Afonso's language is mysterious, however, only alluding to São Tomé traders doing something that the crown, and presumably Afonso, would disapprove of. In any case, these wicked traders were seizing letters because they did not want their misdeeds revealed; or, Afonso added "this is the only explanation we can perceive."[68]

In light of Afonso's disappointment about the creation of the diocese of São Tomé, João may have been reluctant to allow Kongo to send such a mission to Rome. Certainly, this can explain Afonso's letter of December 4, 1540, which he

67. Guénin, *Ango*, pp. 208 (the text of the 1537 interdict and following documents to p. 228).

68. See "Letter from the King of Kongo to João III," December 17, 1540, in Correspondence.

begins by complaining that João III had "forgotten" Kongo and hints that João's failure to respond could not be blamed solely on forgetfulness or French pirates. Afonso then devotes a good portion of the letter to noting that Kongo is, perhaps, Portugal's most lucrative market on the African coast: "Kongo alone brings more revenue than all the other river regions combined"—that is, what was widely called the "Rivers of Guiné" around today's Guinea-Bissau, and the "River of Slaves" in the Niger Delta. In this, he echoed his claims and threats in 1526 concerning the debt Portugal owed to Kongo. It also seemed to Afonso that Portugal was holding the mission back by refusing to help pay its expenses. In the end, Afonso proposes that João make him a grant of 5,000 cruzados against a credit, in Kongo, of 150 *kofu* of *nzimbu* shells to be paid on the price of slaves from a particular market. As an example of the value of this credit, if prices paid for slaves in 1516 are any guide, 150 *kofus* would have purchased 5,000.[69]

Whether this elaborate system of credit was a recent innovation or not is unclear—Afonso makes it appear as a special favor—but certainly, from the beginning of his reign, Afonso had paid expenses by providing slaves, as they were the most readily marketable commodity of his country. This is why in 1514, he arranged to pay some traveling expenses with 50 slaves and a quantity of copper, and when the first group of Kongolese students traveled to Europe, he sent 500 slaves with them to be sold for expenses. We also know that in 1538, the Lóios had a fund of money from Kongo, perhaps from the seized assets of the wayward priests a few years earlier, but also perhaps from Kongo itself. Establishing a line of credit, underwritten by purchasing power in Kongo, would allow a much more flexible way of handling expenses without making one-to-one transfers of goods.

The mission did eventually reach Portugal, but there is no evidence that it made it to Rome—papal records would certainly mention such an event, and they do not. At least some of the mission's members had already returned to Kongo by 1541; Francisco Mucio (Camete), the group's Italian interpreter, signed a petition in Mbanza Kongo on March 20, 1541, though it is possible he left the group earlier for some other reason.

Manuel, however, appears to have made some effort to continue his mission. A Spanish royal diarist noted Manuel's presence in the company of Charles V of Spain while in Aragon on July 24 and November 8, 1542.[70] It is possible that on his way

69. Álvaro Lopes bought slaves at 17 per *lufuku* in 1516, or 34 per *kofu*, so 150 *kofus* would equal 5,100 slaves. Perhaps the price of slaves had lowered since 1516, but it was certainly enough to raise ample money to support the relatively small mission.

70. Jean de Vandenesse, "Journal du voyages de Charles-Quint," in *Collection des voyages des souverains des Pays-Bas*, ed. Louis-Prosper Gachard, 3 vols. (Brussels, 1874–1882), 2:211 and 244.

from Lisbon across Spain, he stopped to see the Black Virgin at Guadaloupe, since Gaspar Barreiros, passing the monastery in 1544, noted that there was a silver lamp there donated by the king of Kongo.[71] The shrine's archives note that a silver lamp along with a permanent fund to support it had been established in 1555 by Diogo I. Barreiros's record suggests that what he saw in 1544 was an earlier and perhaps ad hoc donation made, perhaps, by Manuel on behalf of Afonso.[72]

No doubt that the statue of the Virgin had black skin, as well as the fact that it was, according to legend, based on a painting by the Apostle Luke from life, would surely interest Kongolese Christians. Later, Álvaro I would request that Kongo receive a copy of the "most holy Virgin painted from life [*retratta al naturale*] from one of the four which Saint Luke made . . ." when he sent his ambassador, Duarte Lopes, to Rome in 1583.[73] Perhaps this, like the stories of the Garden of Eden in Central Africa, planted the seeds of Kongo's reconceptualization of the Holy Family as Kongolese that would sprout fully in the preaching of D. Beatriz Kimpa Vita in the early eighteenth century, that the whole of the Nativity had happened in Kongo.[74]

On January 9, 1543, Manuel complained that he had been stuck in Europe for "four or five years" and wanted to return to São Tomé. To fund that voyage, he asked to be given some portion of a fund of 400 cruzados a Portuguese merchant had willed to Afonso. Again, a flexible financial arrangement to handle international expenses.[75]

The End of the Era

Though Afonso's letters of 1540 chiefly focused on international politics and intrigue, domestic politics also came to the fore. In his letter of December 17, 1540, Afonso declared there had been a plot "against our life," masterminded, he claimed, by the "'virtuous' priest Friar Álvaro" Peçanha. Ironically, it "is the payment he gives us for all the favors we conferred on him." Peçanha was charged

71. Gaspar Barreiros, *Corographia de alguns lugares . . .* (Coimbra: João Alvares, 1561), fol. 35v.

72. The monastery's records indicate that it had a silver lamp of twenty-seven marks in weight with an endowment of 155 ducats. See Libro de Bienhechores Antiguos del Monasterio (Códice- 90 A.M:G.), in *Revista Guadalupe*, 16 (1917), p. 88.

73. Instructions to Duarte Lopes, 1583, *MMA* 3:234.

74. John Thornton, *The Kongolese Saint Anthony: Dona Beatriz Kimpa Vita and the Antonian Movement, 1684–1706* (Cambridge: Cambridge University Press, 1998), pp. 113–14.

75. See "Letter from Dom Manuel, the King of Kongo's Brother," January 9, 1543, in Correspondence.

with plotting "to make someone else king." The supreme irony in Afonso's description was that the conspirators carried out their plot at Easter. While the king was hearing mass, "seven or eight white men" pulled out muskets and shot at him. One shot "miraculously" passed through the hem of his garment; unfortunately, the other shots killed a bystander and wounded Afonso's head magistrate and two other people.[76]

Afonso had Peçanha and his brother arrested and expelled from the kingdom to face punishment in Portugal. But even as he recounted all of this in his letter to João, Afonso learned that Peçanha had returned to Kongo, "showing no remorse," to make another attempt on Afonso's life. It was strange, Afonso mused, that someone making a good living in a foreign country would try to kill the king. In any case, Peçanha was not the sole architect of the plot; he had confederates—all of them, like him, white men—who helped him carry it out.

Three months later, Peçanha's Portuguese allies secretly contacted João III. In their letter, they claim Peçanha was framed by another Portuguese officer, Fernão Rodrigues Bulhão. According to the letter, Bulhão had come to Kongo not bringing any goods "other than the concealed greed," apparently to upend the otherwise peaceful and harmonious situation in Kongo where everyone, black or white, lived in perfect harmony.[77] They claim Bulhão was involved in various treasons, of which the most daring and dangerous was to claim that Peçanha, along with some confederates (both white and Kongolese), tried to kill Afonso "and name someone else king." This false accusation against Peçanha was then supported by witnesses who, under threat of torture, lied under oath and confirmed the false charges against him. Bulhão is such an effective dissembler say the authors of the secret letter, that even the king has been fooled into charging Peçanha with the crime and deporting him even though those false witnesses have subsequently admitted to providing coerced testimony.

This letter makes more substantial claims not just against Bulhão and his small cabal of confederates but also against more powerful Kongolese. Having implicated at least some Kongolese in the original plot, the letter goes on to say that Bulhão conducted *nkanus*, a Kikongo word meaning a legal inquest, this time involving Kongolese, "sons, grandsons, and nephews" of the king. These inquests were far-reaching, involving not only royal relatives but "white and mixed-race men as well Beninese, freed slaves, and captives." The malice involved, the writers alleged, was so great that the parties were close to killing each other.

76. See "Letter from the King of Kongo to João III," December 17, 1540, in Correspondence.

77. See "Letter to His Majesty King João III," March 20, 1541, in Correspondence.

Only five Portuguese signed their names to this secret letter. They claimed, however, that some sixty other Portuguese would have signed but feared reprisal from Bulhão and his men. The authors noted that Diogo Botelho Pereira, the new captain of São Tomé, had arrived in Kongo, traveled to the capital, and become so disgusted with the situation he found there that he left. The authors believed Pereira was on their side, suggesting that they represented a faction close to São Tomé.[78] The political landscape had clearly shifted, becoming more complicated, since the early years of Afonso's reign; allegiances were changing, and the battles over power were no longer fought between the king of Kongo's supporters and the Portuguese living on São Tomé.

Gonçalo Nunes Coelho, one of the signatories to the secret letter, had written his own letter to Portugal a year before. He alluded mysteriously to an earlier report he had made on "the country's secular and religious situation," and added that Álvaro Peçanha had concurred in his report and that "Your Highness should address these problems by implementing the measures I propose."[79] Apparently, he now saw the situation as more urgent and "truthfully" felt that João III should "expel all the white men from this kingdom, both clerics and laymen, and replace them with new and good people." While it is not clear exactly where Coelho thought he stood on the question, he was perhaps foreshadowing the situation where the Portuguese would be implicated in a plot against Afonso's life.

Partisan as it might be, the letter did confirm what many suspected: that Afonso was old and would need to name a successor before his imminent death. The Portuguese would have no say in choosing Afonso's successor; this was a matter for the Kongolese to decide. More specifically, it was a matter to be decided by the Kongolese elite, the real political players—exactly the same people who might stand to benefit from Bulhão's alleged investigations (and accusations) of the king's sons, grandsons, and nephews. The elite all had their preferred candidates for succession. It is not hard to imagine them welcoming the opportunity, with the king's death, to force the electors to accept their chosen candidate. It would be even more convenient to have some whites kill the king and take the blame for the assassination.

---

78. Diogo Botelho Pereira was appointed captain of São Tomé in 1540, ANTT Chancelaria de João III, livro 31, fol. 109, August 2, 1540. Born in India to at least one Portuguese parent, Botelho Pereira made himself famous by piloting a tiny sailing ship (*fusta*) all the way from India to Portugal and was given the captaincy of São Tomé, before returning to a post in India Diogo do Couto, *Da Ásia*, Decade 5, Book 1, chap. 2 (Coimbra: Biblioteca da Universidade, 1937).

79. See "Letter from Gonçalo Nunes Coelho to King João III," April 4, 1539, in Correspondence.

By 1540, Afonso had ruled for thirty-four years. His rise to power involved a civil war and was followed by years of political tensions and plots. No election had been held during that time. Kongo was a centralized government; holding on to a position at the top was the best way to survive, and since no one had a strong regional base from which to operate, holding the capital was crucial. Unlike the Portuguese signatories to the letter, we know what happened after Afonso finally died in 1542. While we have few records describing the events, we know that Afonso's son Pedro Nkanga a Mvemba quickly seized the throne, possibly defeating another partisan named Fernando in order to do so. But Afonso's grandson Diogo ultimately won the contest and seized the throne in 1545.

Though Diogo held the throne, Pedro—who was granted asylum in a Mbanza Kongo church—was still strong enough that Diogo did not dare attempt to seize him. Five years later, Diogo would conduct an investigation, not unlike Bulhão's, into allegations that Pedro was organizing, with a group of traitors, a plot to break him out of the church and claim the throne.[80] The results of the investigation, concluded in 1550, presented a great deal of compelling evidence. But Diogo still did not feel strong enough to act. It was not until 1554—nine years after he had first taken the throne—that Diogo finally cleaned house and rounded up all his enemies.[81] Bulhão's investigations of sons, grandsons, and nephews had clearly come close to the mark in identifying the players in the struggle for Kongo's throne.

The plot against Afonso failed, and he lived to the age of about eighty-five. News of Afonso's death reached Europe via a letter dated July 15, 1543, written by his brother Manuel who was still stuck in Lisbon and seeking funds for a return trip to Kongo.

---

80. John Thornton and Linda Heywood, "Treason of Dom Pedro Nkanga a Mvemba against Dom Diogo, King of Kongo, 1550," in *Afro-Latino Voices: Narratives from the Early Modern Ibero-Atlantic World, 1550–1812*, ed. Kathryn Joy McKnight and Leo J. Garofalo (Indianapolis: Hackett Publishing Company, 2009).

81. Cornélio Gomes to Diego Mirón, April 10, 1554, *MMA* 15:190.

EPILOGUE

AFONSO'S LEGACY

Afonso ruled Kongo for thirty-six years, the longest reign in the country's history. Though the historical record does not tell us much about what, if any, lasting impact he had on the political organization of the country, we can confidently say he firmly established the Catholic church there, which lasted for the rest of the kingdom's existence. Moreover, he established an internal and independent religious infrastructure that sustained both basic Christian knowledge and elite literacy. Despite the successful creation of an autonomous literate educational establishment that assured that Christianity would remain a viable religious institution, he was unable to create a Catholic church with its own royally appointed bishop or bishops. Given all he accomplished on behalf of the church, his title "Apostle of Kongo" seems appropriate.

A corollary of the Christianization of Kongo was the creation of a literate elite and, thus, a steady corpus of Kongolese-authored documents recording the history of the country. This literary and epistolary tradition continued after his reign; most subsequent Kongo kings left at least a letter or two behind.

Afonso designed the seal, based on Kongo's coat of arms, which was affixed to the official correspondence of the Kingdom of Kongo. (Because they exist only as certified true copies made for the archives, none of his extant letters bear the seal.) The seal first appears on King Álvaro I's letters, written in 1580 and found in Inquisitorial documents related to the case of a wayward priest.[1]

The establishment of July 25 as Saint James the Greater's Day in Kongo's church calendar is another part of Afonso's legacy. Celebrated with a formal ceremony and an elaborate dance (a *nsanga*, called a *sangamento* in Portuguese-language documents), Saint James the Greater's Day commemorates Afonso's victory over his

1. Arquivo Nacional da Torre do Tombo [ANTT], Inquisisão Lisboa, Processo 2938, fol. 109, Álvaro I to the Inquisition, January 14, 1580. Pigafetta also printed a copy of the seal on the map accompanying *Relatione*.

brother.[2] In Afonso's time, it was also the day on which provincial rulers paid their taxes. Though Afonso does not refer to the celebration in his own correspondence, it was observed by Carmelite missionaries when they visited Kongo in 1584.[3] Citizens of Mbanza Kongo continue to celebrate this day with a five-day-long, largely secular event called "Cultural Days" (Dias Culturais), ending on July 25. I witnessed this event myself in 2011, and at the invitation of His Excellency Vicente Carlos Kiaziku, the bishop of Mbanza Kongo, made a presentation on Afonso, his miraculous victory over this brother, and tax collection day.

Beyond the documents he left behind and the ceremonies celebrating his life, Afonso's legacy lived on through oral tradition. In the 1620s, candidates for the throne of Kongo claimed their rights through descent from one or another of Afonso's daughters. While early seventeenth-century oral tradition referred to Lukeni lua Nimi as the founder, historical accounts from the eighteenth century assigned that role only to Afonso. In the localized clan histories that emerged in the nineteenth century, Afonso is the only recognizable historical king noted in their praise names but was no longer associated with the foundation of the country.

As Afonso's role as genealogical founder emerged, another legend about him appeared in the 1670s: that he had been such a fervent Christian that he became a warrior against traditional religion. Though we know from his own testimony that Afonso worked to combat traditional religion in his time, the new legend added more dramatic elements to the tale. According to these stories, Afonso's mother wore a small "idol" around her neck in defiance of her son's wishes. Even though he pleaded with her to remove it, she was adamant, and he eventually had her buried alive as an example to all who would insist on following the traditional religion.

The story of Afonso's mother was first recorded around 1680 on the occasion of a *sangamento* held in Soyo. The people of Soyo claimed that the first Christian baptisms occurred in their territory and took great pride in the fact. According to local legend, Afonso, hearing of the baptisms conducted in the area, came to see the "Spaniards"—that is, the Portuguese when they visited—from his post as the Duke of Nsundi. Having converted but still in Soyo, Afonso tried to persuade his father to be baptized as well. When his father refused, Afonso marched on

2. Cécile Fromont, "Dance, Image, Myth and Conversion in the Kingdom of Kongo, 1500–1800," *African Arts* (Winter, 2011): 52–63.

3. Text attributed to Diego de la Encarnación, "Relatione de quello occorse . . . ," *MMA* 4:407. This text has errors in it; a better copy (possibly the original) is in Archivio dei Carmelitani descalci, Rome, 430b, "Segue una vera relatione delle speranze che vi sono dell'augmente della fede nostra nelli regni di Congo et Angola et altri circumvincini," fol. 64v, which correctly reads the arrival of the governors of "Bamba e Pango."

the capital with his army. Yet his father still refused, became enraged, and threatened his son. Crying out, "Saint James, help me!" Afonso received a sword from heaven with which he beheaded his father; he was then immediately proclaimed king. But his mother continued to reject Christianity, and Afonso found her supplicating an "idol which her husband had recommended." When he begged her to become a Christian, she retorted, "I was born a pagan and I will die a pagan." Hearing this, and without hesitation, Afonso "dropped her head to his feet."[4]

The story had been embellished even further by the beginning of the eighteenth century. In 1706, the Capuchin priest Lorenzo da Lucca, berating followers of the Antonian movement—led by Beatriz Kimpa Vita, a mystic who claimed possession by Saint Anthony—referred to the legend when he cried out, "Where are you Afonso the First, who for the love of the Faith buried your own mother alive?"[5] According to one lengthy telling set down in 1710 by the Capuchin missionary Bernardo da Gallo, neither Afonso's father nor the Mwene Soyo wished to be baptized; the first to volunteer was Afonso, then the Duke of Nsundi. After becoming king upon his father's death, Afonso persuaded his mother to renounce all but one of her idols, and as in earlier versions, she refused, and he buried her alive. This enraged his brother, ruler of Mpangu, who then made war on Afonso, attacking the king with a mighty army. When, in the heat of battle, Afonso cried out to heaven, Saint James appeared on horseback and routed his foes.[6]

The story was given an even fuller treatment in an anonymous text written in 1782 by someone in the court of José I. This version, called "How the Christian Faith Came to Congo," departs even further from the truth, as described in the documentary sources, than the seventeenth-century versions did. In this version, the sons of the Count of Soyo returned from a visit to Lisbon accompanied by a couple of priests. Uncertain about the prospect of being baptized, the king sent the priests to Nsundi to first baptize his own son. According to the story, Afonso, then the Duke of Nsundi, tested the powers of baptism by having an old man baptized; the man's youth was instantly restored. And as if restoring youth were not enough, anyone else who was baptized could immediately understand and speak Portuguese and Latin. As the king prepared for his own baptism, a cross miraculously fell from heaven.

---

4. Andrea da Pavia, "Viaggio al Congo," fols. 92–92v, in *"Viaggio Apostolico" in Africa di Andrea da Pavia*, ed. Carlo Toso (Rome: Italia Francescana, 2000).

5. Archivio dei Cappuccini di Toscana (Florence), Lettere di Lorenzo da Lucca, p. 296.

6. Bernardo da Gallo, "Conto delle villacazione . . ." fols. 330–330v, in *Una pagina poco nota di storia Congolese*, ed. Carlo Toso (Rome: Italia Francescana, 1999), marking original foliation.

As in the earlier version of this story, this one has his mother refusing to remove her idol in defiance of her son's orders, now the king. Afonso then arranges for his mother to attend an elaborate ceremony held at the church of S. Miguel and digs a pit, hidden by a mat, under her seat in the church. She falls into the hole and is buried alive. When this happens, Afonso draws his sword and denounces his mother as a traitor to the faith, and a cross immediately appears in the sky. This cross became the emblem of Kongo's Order of Christ. Following the death of his mother, Afonso's brother—"Mane-Panzum-a-ginga," the Duke of Mbamba—was defeated in battle with Afonso.[7]

This version of the story, or one close to it, remained popular; both Rafael Castello de Vide and Raimondo da Dicomano relate it in 1785 and 1794, respectively. In a letter of 1814, Kongo's king, Garcia V, refers to a variant of this story, noting, in this case, that the Count of Soyo refused to be baptized before the king. When Afonso ordered his mother to be killed for refusing to give up her idol, her brothers sought to avenge her. But as they approached Mbanza "with great power," five angels from heaven killed them all "without one escaping."[8]

The story of Afonso's mother lives on, even to this day. Jean Cuvelier, the Redemptorist missionary and eventual bishop of Matadi (Belgian Congo), assiduously collected oral traditions as a part of his evangelization efforts. Many Kongolese clans who preserve sometimes-ancient traditions adopt mottos of historical vintage. One clan, for example, called Vuzi dia Nimi, had as its motto in the late 1920s "Don Funsu Mvemba Nzinga wazikidi ngw'andi a kimoyo kakwikila nkanka a Ntinu Nkangi" or "Dom Afonso Mvemba Nzinga buried his mother alive through belief in the faith of the Savior King."[9] In a more current version of the story, which I heard in Mbanza Kongo in 2002, very similar to one also recorded in 2017 by Brazilian researcher Thiago Sapede—Afonso had fallen ill with convulsions, and his grandmother healed him with medicinal plants. Having recovered and realizing that his grandmother had relied on non-Christian practices

7. This document was printed in the *Boletim Oficial da Província de Angola*, nos. 642 and 643, 1858. The original is apparently lost. A close variant was reported by Rafael Castello de Vide in about 1785, Academia das Ciências de Lisboa, MS Vermelho (published on the web, at https://arlindo-correia.com/161007.html) and by Raimondo da Dicomano in about 1795 (on the web, at http://arlindo-correia.com/121208.html).

8. AHU, Angola, cx. 128, doc. 5, Garcia V to Prince Regent of Portugal, March 20, 1814.

9. Jean Cuvelier, *Nkutama a mvila za makanda* (Tumba [Congo], 1934), p. 70. In this motto, Nkangi drives from the verb *-kanga* consistently used in the seventeenth-century catechism to mean "to save," although its primary meaning in Kikongo is "to tie or bind."

to help him, Afonso tricked her into attending a festival and buried her alive in a hidden pit, just as the 1782 account described.[10]

It should be clear that none of these stories are true.[11] In his 1624 history of Kongo—based partly on oral tradition and partly on documentary evidence—Jesuit priest Mateus Cardoso notes in passing that when João Nzinga a Nkuwu died, he was buried in the church of Nossa Senhora along with his wife, Leonor, Afonso's mother. Ironically, this was the same woman who, according to Rui de Pina's contemporary account, asked the priests many questions about the faith and even developed a memory device with pebbles to remember what she was taught. She also provided the early missionaries ample support from her own income. It was she who sent Afonso messages and supported his coming to Mbanza Kongo when he was taking the throne. Though there is no mention of her being buried alive, it is interesting to note that, according to Afonso's letter of 1514, the church of Nossa Senhora was built on the old royal graveyard; thus, his mother was actually buried beneath the church. Afonso himself was eventually buried there, as was his grandson Pedro.[12] In 1548, Jesuit priests also noted that the church, nicknamed "ambiro" (*mbila*, Kikongo for "grave"), was built on the cemetery that Afonso had destroyed to build the church and that he was buried there. Diogo I, the king ruling at that time, planned to be buried there as well.[13]

The emergence of this strange tale is not entirely inexplicable. The idea of burying one's mother, or rather one's maternal lineage, is a widespread trope throughout matrilineal Central Africa. Therefore, the burial is not simply a gruesome deed but a symbol of a change in the political order.[14] Kongo traditions of origin recorded in the early seventeenth century gave a certain Nimi a Lukeni (or variants) credit with founding the kingdom, and sometimes killing a female relative. But that story disappeared from the traditions at the turn of the eighteenth century, just as a new story which traced all the lineages contesting power to the descendants of Afonso,

---

10. I was told this story at the shrine dedicated to "Dona Mpola" the name by which Afonso's mother is now known, by a conclave of elders during my visit with Linda M. Heywood to Mbanza Kongo, September 26, 2002. Sapede's visit is cited in his PhD thesis, "Le roi et le temps, le Kongo et le monde: une histoire globale des transformations politiques du royaume du Kongo (1780–1860)" (PhD Diss., University of Paris, 2020), pp. 172–74.

11. Jean Cuvelier, *L'ancien royaume de Congo* (Bruges, 1946), pp. 288–89, provides some documentation and comparative examples.

12. Mateus Cardoso, *História do Reino de Congo, 1624*, ed. António Brásio (Lisbon, 1969), fol. 33 of the original MS, marked in the edition.

13. Cristovão Ribeiro, August 1, 1548, *MMA* 15:16.

14. Wyatt MacGaffey, *Religion and Society in Central Africa: The BaKongo of Lower Zaire* (Chicago: University of Chicago Press, 1986), pp. 194–95.

a manipulation that occurred first in the 1620s and coexisted with the Nimi a Lukeni story.[15] If Afonso figuratively buried his mother by conversion to Christianity, the struggle that enveloped and destroyed Kongo arose from the claims of the descendants of Afonso.

The fate of Afonso's mother is typical of the changes that take place in oral tradition and its reworking over time. Origin stories in oral tradition are actually more constitutional documents than attempts at rendering history, and so, Afonso's mother reshapes as times change. They are also subject to "feedback" when written history becomes available; for example, the mentioning of convulsions in the twenty-first-century account probably refers to similar origin traditions reported by Jean Cuvelier in his writing on Kongo, not for Afonso's mother but for the founding king.[16]

Kongo's oral tradition is only one part of Afonso's legacy. We have already noted that the story of Afonso's victory over his brother was published variously in Europe from the sixteenth century onward. This was his primary legacy outside of Kikongo-speaking areas until well into the twentieth century. But with the discovery of his letters in the 1870s and the interest that professional historians took in them over the next eighty years, Afonso's contentious relationship with Portugal came to form an important part of his legacy beyond Africa. Especially as framed by Basil Davidson from the early 1960s, the question of the early slave trade has perhaps become his current best-known legacy, with Afonso variously playing the role of naïve Christian convert or abolitionist overcome by European greed.

15. John Thornton, "Origin Traditions and History in Central Africa," *African Arts* (Spring, 2004): 33–35.

16. Cuvelier's account is most accessible in his publication of the original tradition in "Traditions congolaises," p. 199, but it was also presented in Kikongo in the missionary journal *Kukiele*.

TRANSLATOR'S NOTE

Translation is hardly ever a straightforward activity. One-to-one correspondences between words and expressions in the translating and translated languages are only infrequently available. This is especially true when hundreds of years separate the original from its translation. Inevitably, the social and cultural situations in which translations are produced shape both their content and form, sometimes in fundamental ways. For instance, in attempting to make a phrase or even a passage more intelligible to a present-day audience, a translator may end up removing or "domesticating" elements that, though incomprehensible to today's reader, held profound meanings and cultural resonances in their own time and place. What the translation thus gains in readability for a contemporary public, it loses in "fidelity" or faithfulness to the singularities and specificities of the original's sociocultural context. For these reasons, translations are indelibly marked by contingency and indeterminacy. They are inherently fraught with time-bound pitfalls. By the same token, they also betray what I might call—only half in jest and no doubt immodestly—a creative, transformative potential. All this is inevitably true of this translation of the Portuguese-language correspondence of King Afonso I Mvemba a Nzinga, a sixteenth-century African monarch who, in a sense, was himself a translated man.

In a political critique of the act of translation that resonates especially with the present work, Lawrence Venuti extrapolates on the nature of what he considers translation's "ethnocentric violence" (16). He maintains that translation is not only embedded in the specific political and historical situations in which it is produced but implicated in the unequal exchanges that often underpin the relations between "hegemonic English-language nations [and] their global others" (16). To be sure, my own translation likewise "domesticates" the linguistic and cultural differences of a foreign or "other" text to convert it into recognizable and accessible form (Venuti 14). It exemplifies in this fashion a mode of cultural "imperialism" that sustains prevailing hierarchies of margin and center (Venuti 16, 14). As the protagonist of David Diop's recent award-winning novel remarks about an interpreter who relentlessly smooths away the granular edges of his own "foreign" speech, "to translate is to betray at the borders, it . . . compels us to lie about the details to convey the truth in broad strokes [*le vrai en gros*] . . . to risk understanding . . . that the truth of a word is not single but double, even triple, quadruple, quintuple" (Diop 135–136). Diop's protagonist, a Wolof-speaking World War I Senegalese *tirailleur* named Alfa Ndiaye, alludes implicitly here to the "violence" arguably intrinsic to the act of translating, to "the reconstitution of a foreign text [according to] values, beliefs, and representations that pre-exist it in the translating language and culture" (Venuti 14).

At the same time, and as I intimate above, the forcible domestication that Venuti underscores is already intrinsic to the foreign text that I have endeavored to "reconstitute." Afonso's letters reveal a remarkable conversancy both with the rhetorical protocols of sixteenth-century diplomatic communication as well as an idiomatically fluent grasp of Renaissance Portuguese. As John Thornton suggests, this heightened proficiency is almost certainly attributable to the skill and experience of Afonso's long-time secretary, João Teixeira, who was probably among the first group of young scions of noble Kongolese families to have traveled to Portugal to pursue their studies, and who subsequently achieved not just native fluency in Portuguese but a sophisticated level of literacy. Needless to say, then, I fundamentally disagree with the late T. Bentley Duncan, the English-language translator of King Afonso's October 5, 1514 letter to Portugal's King Manuel I, who claims that the proof of the letter's authenticity resides essentially in its bad grammar: "No punctuation . . . monotonous repetition, a limited vocabulary, strangled syntax, and strange errors (particularly in verb forms)" ("Letter" 44 n1). I found few, if any, errors (either strange or common) in verb forms. And most of the characteristics Duncan ascribes to Afonso's letter could easily pertain to any of the early sixteenth-century Portuguese documents I have translated for this collection (including, notably, Portuguese royal correspondence). Tellingly, Duncan fails to recognize a key idiomatic expression in the letter: "[de] candeias às avessas" (literally, "with upside down oil lamps"), which means roughly, "to be at odds with" or "up in arms against" someone. He renders the phrase as "with candles as well" (67) and adduces a footnote explaining how the use of such (metaphoric) "candles" is supposedly customary in "solemn ceremonies"[1] (67 n53). Misrecognizing this and similar vernacular expressions might easily lead one to judge them as instances of "strangled syntax" or even "strange errors." In the end, Duncan's association of an African king's "authenticity" with a lack of fluency in a European language may reveal more about his cultural assumptions than the original text.

---

1. Probably because a crucial tilde over the *a* in the word *ca[n]de[i]as* is omitted in Father António Brásio's transcription, Louis Jadin and Mireille Dicorato, the French language translators of Afonso's correspondence, translate the expression as "avec des chaînes mises à l'envers" ("with chains [*cadeias*] the wrong way around") (97).

The fluency of his correspondence indicates, then, that both Afonso and his letters come to us already in translation, a translation, moreover, wholly invested in erasing any trace of religious and cultural difference. One of Afonso's principal aims is, after all, to persuade his Portuguese counterparts of his fulsome acceptance of Catholic orthodoxy, of the radical removal of any vestigial "pagan idolatry" both from his person and his realms. As several of the letters collected in this volume disclose, the violence this work of assimilation entails is not merely linguistic but quite often devastatingly real. Ultimately, the feudal Catholic culture into which Afonso is vying to assimilate is as unfamiliar to contemporary U.S. culture—whose values of transparency and smooth readability inform my own endeavor to render Afonso's correspondence intelligible—as were the politics and cultural practices of the Kongo people to sixteenth-century Portuguese. Ironically, the arguably violent process of "assimilation" that defines Afonso's fluent prose resembles my own act of translation. In modernizing or making these letters accessible to a contemporary U.S. audience, I, too, have had to chisel away several layers of linguistic, cultural, and "temporal" foreignness.[2] It is such foreign material that I have had to "barter" away, in the manner of Alfa Ndiaye's unreliable interpreter, in the interest of conveying a broader "truth."

It is somewhat incongruous, no doubt, to introduce a translation by highlighting what it loses. Yet it is critical to acknowledge the irreducible polysemy of (foreign) words, to concede that my effort to do right at home may have resulted in doing wrong abroad.[3] As the translator of these documents, it behooves me to provide at least an inkling of the distance that separates my own modernized version from the archaic lexicon of the originals, the formulaic pleonasms and often-labyrinthine turns of phrase that are the indelible marks of their historical and cultural remoteness from us, just as the fluency and readability of my translations are products of my contemporaneity. What I hope these invaluable documents have

2. This translation owes much of its fluency to Elana Rosenthal's patient editing of my sometimes meandering and long-winded sentences and her skillful suppression of occasional linguistic quirks and lexical oddities. I am very grateful for her rigorous editorial work. I must also thank John Thornton for his scrupulous readings of multiple drafts and, last but not least, Rick Todhunter for his guidance, encouragement, and kind and unwavering support throughout this process.

3. In the main, my translation does not follow Venuti's recommendation to produce "foreignizing translations [that signify] the differences of foreign texts [by] disrupting the cultural codes that prevail in the translating language" (15). Venuti contends that "in its effort to do right abroad, this translation practice must do wrong at home" (16). My sentence is a chiasmus of Venuti's; i.e., it repeats its terms in reverse order.

gained with the transparency and readability of my rendition is, of course, their enhanced appeal to a broad and diverse audience.

While a "foreignizing" translation, one that would more closely or perhaps more strategically express the "otherness" of the original, would certainly be of great benefit to a specialized readership, I hope that my sustained attempt to render key "details" accurately compensates for my burnishing the linguistic and cultural distinctiveness of the original letters. I have sought to foreground the wayward indices of original, even suppressed difference that erupt sporadically beneath the "domesticated" surface of Afonso's voluble prose, a bit like the rebellions that flared up persistently across the expanse of his dominions. These traces emerge in the form of Kikongo proper and place names (despite their mangled transcriptions into Portuguese), frequent allusions to the prized *nzimbu* shells that served as currency throughout the Kingdom of Kongo, and the odd Kikongo term that Father António Brásio, the editor of the multi-volume collection of documents pertaining to West and Central Africa (including Afonso's correspondence), either identifies as "terms whose meaning is unknown" or defines inaccurately in his footnotes. John Thornton's knowledge of Kikongo has been of inestimable value to my reconstruction and accurate rendition of these local terms. Although my knowledge of fifteenth- and sixteenth-century Portuguese paleography is elementary, I have on occasion carefully pored over the manuscripts of the letters to decipher several (though not all) of the words Brásio classifies as "unknown." My direct consultation of the manuscript proved especially effective, I believe, in resolving the inexplicable presence of an enigmatic "Lady Ana" (Dona Ana) in Afonso's letter of October 5, 1514 to Manuel I.[4] Just as the venerable patriarch Lusus (the supposed son of the Roman God Bacchus) owes his appearance in Luís de Camões's famed epic about the 1497–1498 voyage of Vasco da Gama to India (*The Lusiads*, 1572) to a reiterated mistranslation, "Dona Ana," too, may be the result of a transcription error.[5]

---

4. See n. 19 for a detailed explanation of my alternate reading of this passage.

5. I am alluding to a well-known passage in the epic's third canto in which Vasco da Gama, proudly extolling his "beloved homeland" to the king of Malindi, refers to Portugal as Lusitania (the ancient Roman province whose area overlapped with Portugal's present-day territory south of the Douro River). Da Gama claims that the toponym derives "from Lusus or Lysa . . . the sons or companions of [the Roman God] Bacchus" and legendary early settlers of the future Iberian kingdom (III. 21). In *The Lusiads*, Bacchus's son Lusus (Luso) not only assumes pride of place in the gallery of national heroes emblazoned on the standards that decorate da Gama's fleet (VII. 74) but emerges as a synecdoche of the people whose expansionist feats the epic memorializes. The source of this curious genealogy is probably the following footnote from Pliny the Elder's *Natural History*: "Lusum enim Liberi patris aut lyssam cum eo bacchantium nomen dedisse Lusitaniae" (Book III, chapter 3) (Luso or Lyssa, companion of Father Liber [Bacchus], gave

As I explain in more detail in a footnote to this specific passage from Afonso's letter, the lexical unit usually decoded as "Lady Ana" (the implausible wife of King Afonso's cousin Dom Pedro who was unlawfully detained along with her husband by an unscrupulous Portuguese sea captain) may in fact denote "leg irons." As conjectural as my rendition of the passage in question may be, it has the dubious merit of not requiring "the invention of Ana" quite possibly from a copier's jumbled graphemes. Rather than reproducing mistakes like this or simply glossing over obscure words and passages, as previous translators of Afonso's letters have done, I have tried to attend closely to these recalcitrant details. In so doing, I hope I was able to convey some modest, local truths as well as a broader, more assimilable one. I hope, in other words, that I have managed to do right abroad.

Luís Madureira

List of Works Cited

Camões, Luís Vaz de. *Os Lusíadas*. Edited by Álvaro Júlio da Costa Pimpão. Introduction by Aníbal Pinto de Castro. Lisbon: Ministério dos Negócios Estrangeiros: Instituto de Camões, 2000.

Correspondence de Dom Afonso, roi du Congo. 1506–1543. Edited and translated by Louis Jadin and Mireille Dicorato. Brussels: Kloninklijke Academie voor Overzeese Wetenschappen, 1974.

Diop, David. *Frère d'âme.* Paris: Éditions du Seuil, 2018.

---

his name to Lusitania). Camões might have come across a key gloss of Pliny's note in the hagiographical poem *Vincentius, Levita et Martyr* (1545) about Saint Vincent of Saragossa (known in Portugal as São Vicente de Fora), written by the Portuguese Dominican friar, theologian, and classical archaeologist André de Resende (c. 1498–1573). In his commentary of Pliny's note, Resende revises the standard translation cited above to read: "Lusus was *the son* of Father Liber, not his partner or companion" (fl. 39, my italics). Whether or not Camões read it firsthand in Resende's hagiography, the friar's "contrarian" translation of Pliny's note likely spawned the ancestral demigod who plays such a prominent symbolic role in the epic. The problem with this mythic forebear of the Portuguese nation is that he owes his existence exclusively to Resende's inaccurate translation of that brief note from the *Natural History*. According to Pliny, the word *lusus* from which *Lusitania* derives is not a proper noun. It does not signify "Lusus, the son [or even "companion"] of Father Bacchus," but rather "the games [*lusum*] of Father Bacchus." The ascription of a mythological forefather to the seafaring "Lusitanians" is, therefore, entirely predicated on the repetition (with a crucial difference) of a mistranslated passage from a classical text.

Gentzler, Edwin. *Contemporary Translation Theories*. 2nd rev. ed. Clevendon: Multilingual Matters Ltd., 2001.

"Letter from Dom Afonso I, King of the Congo, to Dom Manuel I, King of Portugal, 15 October 1514." [Translation and notes by T. Bentley Duncan.] In *Modern Asia and Africa Reading in World History*, Vol. 9 of *Readings in World History*, edited by William H. McNeill and Mitsuko Iriye, 44–71. New York: Oxford University Press, 1971.

Monumenta Missionaria Africana. África occidental (1471–1531). Vol. 1. Edited by Padre António Brásio. Lisbon: Agência Geral do Ultramar, 1952.

Monumenta Missionaria Africana. África occidental (1532–1569). Vol. 2. Edited by Padre António Brásio. Lisbon: Agência Geral do Ultramar, 1953.

Pliny the Elder. *The Natural History.* Edited by John Bostock. Perseus Digital Library. Accessed August 8, 2022. http://www.perseus.tufts.edu/hopper/text?doc=Perseus%3Atext%3A1999.02.0137%3Abook%3D3%3Achapter%3D3.

Pseudo-Plutarch. *De fluviis.* Edited by William W. Goodwin. Perseus Digital Library. Accessed June 16, 2022. http://www.perseus.tufts.edu/hopper/text?doc=Perseus%3Atext%3A2008.01.0400%3Achapter%3D16.

Resende, André de. *Vincentius, Levita et Martyr*. Lisbon: Ludovicum Rhotorigium Typographum, 1545.

Venuti, Lawrence. *The Translator's Invisibility: A History of Translation*. 2nd ed. London: Routledge, 2002.

The Correspondence of

AFONSO I MVEMBA A NZINGA

King of Kongo

Dom Manuel Sends Scholars and Clerics to Kongo (1504)

His Majesty King Manuel was a religious man by nature. During his reign, his prime concern was to serve God and the doctrine of his holy faith. In the year 1504, inspired by his faith, he decided to send scholars of sacred theology to the Kingdom of Kongo. He also sent reading and writing instructors as well as instructors who could teach the church's Gregorian chants. He sent several manuals of Christian doctrine, silk and brocade vestments for the church, silver crosses, chalices, censers, and many other items needed for divine service, all under the supervision of trusted servants. He also covered their wages, clothing, and the cost of the ship's passage entirely with his own royal income.

The efforts of these missionaries and teachers bore much fruit upon their arrival in Kongo. They converted many of the inhabitants to the faith of our Lord Jesus Christ. In addition, His Majesty asked the kings and lords of that barbarous country to send their sons and young relatives to Portugal, so that they could learn the ways of the faith, philosophy, and proper arts and customs. He ordered all this to be done at his own expense, placing these youths in monasteries and the homes of religious and learned families who could instruct them. Several of these youths became well-educated and went on to bear much fruit in their own lands, where they preached the Catholic faith. These achievements merit much praise. In accomplishing these and similar works, and in all the affairs he conducted in his lifetime, His Majesty was always guided by God, who granted him prosperity until the hour of his death, when His Majesty left a good place for a better one.

DAMIÃO DE GÓIS—*Chronica do Feliçissimo Rei Dom Emanuel*.[1]

1. The first edition of the *Chronicle of the Most Fortunate King Dom Manuel* was published in Lisbon in 1566. Its author, Damião de Góis (1502–1574), was a prominent Portuguese humanist philosopher, who was repeatedly accused by the Inquisition and the Jesuit Order of being a practicing Lutheran and a disciple of Erasmus (de Góis's teacher and close friend). De Góis was named High Keeper of the Royal Archives (Guarda-mor da Torre do Tombo) in 1548 and was subsequently entrusted with producing the chronicle of King Manuel I's reign. Although widely regarded as his major work, the *Chronica* was broadly condemned, like many of de Góis's previous works, and several sections of his history were either purged or extensively censored.

Departure of the First "Blue Missionaries" to Kongo (December 1508)

At the end of 1508, His Majesty the King sent to Kongo a cleric by the name of João de Santa Maria[2] from the order of the apostle Saint John the Evangelist,[3] commonly called the "Blue Canons."[4] He traveled with twelve priests of the order to the Kingdom of Kongo, where a church was to be built, and they were to teach and preach the faith of our Lord Jesus Christ. His Majesty also sent craftsmen to build the church and ornaments to adorn it. In addition, he paid salaries to all those who accompanied these clerics so they could live honorably while there. His Majesty always conducted the affairs of our holy faith with such generosity. Indeed, of all the kings who ruled these kingdoms prior to his reign, he was one of the most zealous defenders of the faith.

DAMIÃO DE GÓIS—*Chronica*, Part II, chapter 30.

---

2. The conduct of João de Santa Maria described in King Afonso's letter of October 10, 1514, to King Manuel I and in chap. 8 of Jorge de São Paulo's history of the order (both translated below) contrasts starkly with Damião de Góis's portrayal of his purportedly selfless evangelizing efforts in this brief chapter.

3. John the Evangelist is the name ordinarily attributed to the author of the Gospel of John. Although he has been traditionally identified with John the Apostle, most modern scholars have disputed this identification.

4. The *Congregação dos Cónegos Seculares de São João Evangelista* (Congregation of the Secular Canons of Saint John the Evangelist)—also known as the *Cónegos Azuis* ("Blue Canons," because of the color of their habits), *Congregação dos Lóios* (The Eligius Congregation, after the Church of Santo Elói [Saint Eligius], which was granted to the order in 1440), or *Cónegos de São Salvador de Vilar* (Canons of São Salvador de Vilar, the location of their principal monastic house)—were a Catholic religious congregation founded by Mestre João Vicente around 1420. The order possessed fourteen monastic houses located throughout Portugal. In the sixteenth century, King João III placed all of the kingdom's royal hospitals under their supervision. Many of the canons traveled as missionaries to Africa and India, and several of them became reputable scholars and theologians.

The Fleet of Gonçalo Rodrigues Bound for Kongo (1506)

SUMMARY—*He is ordered to sail a fleet of six ships with 180 men and their respective weapons to wage war against those who rebelled against the Mwene Kongo—Conditions are stipulated for him*

Gonçalo Rodrigues's[5] orders binding him to his contract as stipulated by our lord the king:

1. He will outfit six 30-ton ships and sail them to the City of Kongo, four of his own ships and two old caravels that His Majesty the King will loan him if they have been decommissioned and warehoused.

He will be required to take on board:

12 master gunners

6 caulkers[6]

3 carpenters

6 pilots.

Including these officers, the crew for all six ships should total 180 men, 30 per ship.

2. He should take 12 rowboats, 6 assigned to each ship and 6 to use in the war efforts.

3. His Highness orders 40 small cannons to be loaned to him. As well as:

2 half-caliber cannons with wooden supports

1,200 pounds of gunpowder

1,000 cannonballs for this artillery

50 crossbows

300 halberds

30,000 pounds of biscuits

5. A formal inquest into his crimes gave his official name as Gonçalo Rodrigues Ribeiro, although in most references to him in texts, he is called Gonçalo Ruiz (which is also a surname, but here an abbreviation). He was accused of throwing infants overboard, abandoning passengers, and stealing from others.

6. A person whose work is to caulk the seams of ships.

100 old casks to be used for repairs, if any are found in the warehouse that are no longer in use

150 coats of mail and suits of armor.

4. Besides these items, His Highness will give him 100,000 *reis* in money. And he is duty-bound to sail in the ships with the men.

From all the fortunes our Lord may grant him in Kongo, as a result of the war he will wage against the Blacks from the islands who have rebelled against the Mwene Kongo,[7] including favors the king may grant him, slaves and war loot he may acquire during this campaign, as well as any other benefit God may give him, he, Gonçalo Rodrigues, will first reimburse himself for all the expenses of this expedition and pay his soldiers, in accordance with what is recorded in the account book of all his expenses, which he will leave at the *Casa da Mina*[8] signed by him and the *Casa da Mina*'s officers.

Once he has paid the soldiers and accounted for his costs and any additional expenses related to this expedition, His Highness shall be pleased to grant him the favor of keeping the remainder, excluding one-twentieth in royal tax.

In case the expedition suffers a loss, God forbid, or if he loses some of the items that he borrowed due to negligence, and if he obtains no revenue to defray his costs and wages, he will not be obligated to pay His Majesty the King for any of these items.

5. He will wage the war according to the orders of His Majesty, the Mwene Kongo.

---

7. Large islands near the mouth of the Congo River, inhabited by the Mpanzu a Lumbu, who often carried out rebellions against Afonso's rule (see Chapter 3 for additional information).

8. Originally located in Lagos, Portugal, and subsequently transferred to Lisbon in 1463, the *Casa da Mina* (House of Mina, also known as *Casa da Guiné* and after 1503, as *Casa da Índia*) was a royal commercial institution tasked with keeping inventory over and tightly managing all products coming from Africa that were under the crown's monopoly.

Letter from D. Manuel to the King of Kongo (1512)

SUMMARY—*In this credential letter to the king of Kongo, D. Manuel introduces Ambassador Simão da Silva to him, requesting that the king extend him the same respect he would D. Manuel himself*

Most powerful and excellent king of Kongo, we, Dom Manuel, by the grace of God, king of Portugal and Guinea, send you many salutations as someone we dearly love and cherish and to whom we wish God will grant as long a life and good health as you desire.

We are sending you Simão da Silva, a noble of our house whom we greatly trust and have much goodwill for since he has served us very well and faithfully. We chose to send him to you because we know him to be devoted and loyal and because he will acquit himself well. When we and other Christian princes and kings send such people, it is customary for them to carry our letters of credentials. Those who receive these letters know that they can trust the bearers to convey everything we command them to say on our behalf. Following this custom, we have communicated to Simão da Silva our wishes concerning his mission to your kingdom and what we desire him to do during his stay there with respect to your affairs of peace and war, of justice, and of the governance of your kingdoms and domains. This is why you had requested that we send you an envoy.

We request that you listen to him and place your whole faith in all that he conveys to you on our behalf, just as you would if it were spoken and expressed by us. It will please us greatly to receive your response to this message. We hope, with our Lord, that Simão da Silva's visit will bring you great joy and happiness and that you will find him as good and true in your service as we have found him in ours. It was for this reason that we chose to send him to you. Since it pleased our Lord in his mercy to shine his light upon you and make his holy faith known to you, we hope you find joy in leading your kingdom in the service of his faith, as Christian princes and we ourselves do. Simão da Silva will inform you at length about these matters, and if you act in accordance with the faith, we shall receive great joy and contentment.

DAMIÃO DE GÓIS—*Chronica do Feliçissimo Rei Dom Emanuel* [Chronicle of the Most Fortunate King Dom Manuel]—Lisboa, 1566. 1st edition, Part III, chapter 37.

Letter from the King of Kongo to All His Subjects (1512)

We, Dom Afonso, by the grace of God, king of Kongo and of all its lands and dominions, declare to all who see this letter that, Lord —— was one of the thirty-seven nobles and knights who fought with us at the battle we waged against our brother, who had risen against us to claim our kingdom when our father the king perished. Our brother had gathered a great number of men against us, but we were aided by our Lord Jesus Christ, who never forsakes those who call upon him and who, in his mercy, made Christ's cross appear in the heavens to all our enemies, along with the apostle Saint James and many knights in armor. Because of their appearance and assistance in this battle, we were victorious over our enemies, routing and killing many of them. With God's favor, our kingdoms became peaceful and remain so, praise be to him.

Because Lord —— was one of those who served us in this great victory and risked his life as our loyal servant; and so that his service worthy of immortal reward may always be remembered; and so that not only he but his children and their descendants may forevermore enjoy the honor and acclaim he earned in this battle at the service of our God we fight for, we, who by God's mercy were brought to his faith and delivered from the devil's bondage, shall do as Christian kings and princes customarily do and bestow honor and thanks to those who serve them loyally and well, putting their lives at risk in their good service, as Lord —— did for us. We only wish we had one hundred more men like him to bestow this honor upon. Because he served his lord and king loyally and well, it pleases us to honor and promote him by granting him this coat of arms.

Letter from the King of Kongo to the Lords of the Kingdom (1512)

SUMMARY—*The king of Kongo tells his people how Christianity was introduced into his kingdom—He describes the battle waged against his adversaries—[and] gives a heraldic description of his coat of arms and its historical significance*

I, Dom Afonso, king of Kongo and its lands and dominions, by the grace and mercy of our Lord God, make it known to all the faithful and unfaithful alike that I was once faithless and a servant and worshipper of idols, as were our ancestors and the peoples of our kingdom as well of the dominions of all Ethiopia.[9] I never received the good news of the faith of our Lord Jesus Christ. Through his infinite pity and compassion, he, who has never forsaken those who desired to know him, willed and consented that King John of Portugal, the second of his name, send to my father and me persons who taught us and strove to instill in us the desire to know the faith of Jesus Christ, though [King John] had no evidence whatsoever that our country was well disposed toward accepting the seeds of the Christian faith. This [action] pleased our person very much. Recognizing the error and blindness in which we had hitherto existed, we received the water of holy baptism after my father, the king. A few lords and nobles of our country likewise received it, giving many thanks to our Lord for the great and inestimable mercy he bestowed upon us by delivering us from our subjugation and bondage to the devil. [We thanked him] not only for being willing to bring us into his fold, but also for being willing to adopt us as his children.

Afterward, King Manuel—the successor to the aforementioned King John of Portugal—sent us religious priests from time to time, which was of great help in spreading and increasing the faith of our Lord in our kingdom and dominions. As we were thus striving and seeking with all our strength and desire to increase his holy Catholic faith, my father perished from this world. When we became certain of his death, we departed forthwith from the land where we were staying to the city of Kongo, where I was to take possession of the kingdom, according to our ancient customs. The way was long, the Christians still few, and we could not suffer to have any heathens in our company. Thus, there were only thirty-seven persons in our party (nobles as well as other good attendants and servants of ours) when we arrived in our city.

My brother, who refused to convert to the faith of our Lord, was residing in the city. For that reason, the people, who were nearly all heathen and worshipped idols, wanted to crown him king. My brother came against us with a mighty army of people from within the city, which was large, as well as from the outskirts. Despite having no more than the above-mentioned thirty-seven Christians with our person, we determined to wait for and do battle with them, recalling that the strength of our Lord God does not require great numbers but only his good will. We put our trust in him, who had revealed his faith to us and would help us against those who were his enemies and refused to accept the faith they had been offered. When a countless number of arrows had already been shot at us, and we wanted to move close enough to them to put our assegais and swords to use, our party and

9. Ethiopia was the term commonly used by the Portuguese in the sixteenth century to refer to Africa's western seaboard reaching as far south as the Cape of Good Hope.

we cried out the name of the blessed apostle Saint James. Thereupon we saw all our enemies miraculously turn their backs on us and flee as fast as their strength could carry them. We chased after them, not knowing the cause of their disarray. During our pursuit, a great number of people perished, but we counted no one in our party among the dead.

Upon the consummation of this victory, we learned from those who had come through the struggle unscathed that the reason for the enemy's flight had been our battle cry for the apostle Saint James. They saw a white cross in the sky and a great number of armed men riding on horseback, and this vision frightened them so much that they could not bear to look upon it and thus fled forthwith. This seemed to us of divine cause, and we gave many thanks and praise to our Lord for the favor and compassion he had bestowed upon us. In memory and remembrance of such a clear and evident miracle and so great a victory, we added it to our coat of arms so that the kings who follow us in the kingdom and dominions of Kongo will never forget this great mercy and benefit which was so wondrously done on behalf of the king, the kingdom, and its people. The coat of arms is as follows.

The field is crimson, and the chief of the shield is blue. On the chief of the shield, there is a flory silver cross. In each field of the chief, there are two golden scallop shells and a silver stem, along with one of the five escutcheons of Portugal, which is in blue, with five silver plates disposed in saltire. On each part of said shield, there is a broken, upside-down black idol. On the crimson field, there are five [embowed] arms holding swords pointing upward by the hilt. The golden helmet has its visor up and is surmounted by a royal crown. On the timbre, the five embowed arms with their swords issue from the crown, and [the helmet's] gold and crimson plumes.

The crimson field signifies the great amount of blood spilled in the battle we waged. The chief of the blue shield with the silver cross signifies the white cross that, in the course of this battle, appeared in the sky, which is blue. The flory cross signals our victory against both the enemy and the devil. The scallop shells are the emblem of Saint James, whom we summoned and who came to our rescue. The escutcheon of Portugal signals that Portugal is the foundation of the faith we have in our Lord, and it is the source of our salvation. The two broken black idols next to the said escutcheon of Portugal mean that Portugal was the cause of their being smashed and destroyed. The five embowed arms signal the armed men who appeared in the sky, who were angels riding to our rescue. There are five arms in honor of the five wounds of our Lord Jesus Christ by which we are healed.

Letter from the Mwene Kongo to the Lords of the Kingdom (1512)

SUMMARY—*He relates the history of Kongo's evangelization—The War of Succession and the Christians' victory—He acknowledges receipt of the letter with his coat of arms from Simão da Silva and Dom Pedro, his cousin*

To ensure that the blessings our Almighty God has bestowed upon us shall be known from now until the end of the world, we, Dom Afonso, by His Grace, Mwene Kongo and lord of the Ambundus,[10] proclaim to all who are living and all who will come after us, to our vassals and the inhabitants of our kingdoms as well as all the kings, princes, lords, and peoples from neighboring territories, that our kingdoms were discovered by the kings of Portugal. This occurred during the reign of João II of Portugal, and especially now during the reign of the most high and powerful king and Lord Dom Manuel, king and lord of the kingdoms and dominions of Portugal. Both of these kings, moved by their piety and divine inspiration to increase their holy Catholic faith, established clerics, friars, and religious persons in this country, who revealed to my father the king the path to salvation and brought him knowledge of their holy Catholic faith, which these kings and the inhabitants of Portugal follow. Since they carried out this God-ordained task in keeping with God's mercy, and since they fulfilled his commands as true and faithful Catholics, my father the king received the Christian doctrine. Although he showed good promise as a Christian in the beginning, God did not bestow his grace on him in his lifetime because the devil, envious and ever an enemy of the cross, led him astray.

When these events occurred, we were a young man. Enlightened by the grace of the Holy Spirit, by an extraordinary favor granted to us by the Most Holy Trinity—the Father, the Son, and the Holy Ghost, three persons in a single God, in which we firmly believe—we began to receive the Christian doctrine. By God's mercy alone, it began, day by day and hour by hour, to take root in our heart where it now remains firm. Delivered from all the errors and idol worship that our predecessors lived with before, we discovered true knowledge of our Lord Jesus Christ, God and man, who descended from heaven to earth and became flesh in the virginal womb of the glorious Virgin Mary, his mother, for the salvation of the

10. The Ambundu lived in the north and center of present-day Angola in the sixteenth century. (See Chapter 4 for additional information.)

whole of humankind, which had been under the sway of the devil since our forefather Adam's sin. He died upon the wood of the cross in the city of Jerusalem, was entombed, and on the third day, resurrected from the dead so that his prophecy was fulfilled. By his death, we are redeemed and saved.

Since we were in possession of this true knowledge and continued our studies with religious persons and faithful Christians, we fell into great disfavor with our father, the king, as well as with the highest nobles and the peoples of his kingdoms. With great contempt for us, and much to our misery, he exiled us to lands in the farthest reaches of the kingdom, where we languished for a long time, away from his eyes and bereft of his good graces, but not without feeling glad to suffer for the faith of our Lord.

Nevertheless, as we endured our exile, with the great perseverance that in his mercy God has always granted us—which would enable us to suffer much more if we needed to—with the firm hope that he would come to our assistance, that he would bestow his grace upon us and, at the very least, save our soul, and that our toil and our unwavering faith would not be for nothing, we received word that the king *my* father[11] was passing from this life, and that a brother of ours was taking possession of the kingdom, which by right did not belong to him but to us as the eldest and firstborn. He achieved this with the backing of the kingdom's highest nobles and lords and their peoples, who despised us for having converted to the faith of our Lord Jesus Christ. Since he has never forsaken and will never forsake those who serve and call upon him, he emboldened us to go where our father was. Accompanied by only thirty-six men[12] we had in our service, we reached the place where our father was. When we arrived, he was already dead.

When we saw that our brother was unjustly occupying the throne and that he had shored himself up with a countless number of men and seized our whole kingdom and dominions, we pretended to be ill just to stay alive. While we were in this situation, divine inspiration emboldened us to summon our thirty-six men and prepare ourselves for battle. We marched with them to the main square of the city where our father had died and where an infinite number of people had gathered with our brother. Once there, we cried out for our Lord Jesus Christ and began the battle with our enemies. Inspired by God's grace and with his assistance, our thirty-six men began to call out, "They're fleeing, they're fleeing," and drove our enemies into retreat. Our own enemies testified that a white cross appeared in the heavens and the blessed apostle Saint James, along with many armed knights

11. Although Afonso has thus far consistently referred to himself in the first-person plural (the "royal we"), here he reverts to the first-person singular: *meu padre*.

12. In the two previous letters, Afonso speaks of thirty-seven men.

in white garments, fought against them and cut them down. It was a marvel to behold the overwhelming slaughter.

After his defeat, our brother was arrested, sentenced to death, and executed for rising up against us. Our kingdoms and dominions were finally at peace, as they are to this day, by the grace of God. We told the Lord King Dom Manuel of Portugal about this success and the miracle accomplished by God since King Dom Manuel began the good works that rewarded us, by the grace of God, with so many benefits. It was our cousin Dom Pedro, who was among the thirty-six men who fought with us, that carried word of all this to the king. Both Dom Pedro and the lord king, in the letters we received from him, informed us of the many praises given to Almighty God in his kingdoms for the benefits of his mighty and infinite power.

Recognizing that this was an event worthy of being remembered and that the example it set could be followed anywhere, the king of Portugal sent us this illustration of a coat of arms to bolster our faith and also to celebrate us, along with many other gifts sent with our cousin Dom Pedro and Simão da Silva, a nobleman of his house, who traveled to our land. These arms will be displayed on our shields as crests, as the Christian kings and princes customarily do to signify who they are, where they came from, and make themselves known to others.

The coat of arms that His Majesty sent us represents the cross that was seen in the heavens as well as the apostle Saint James, who battled on our side with all the other saints. With their help and the help of God, our Lord granted us victory. Moreover, to signal that the crest the lord king sent us is part of Portugal's coat of arms, our own coat of arms incorporates the shield of Portugal. This shield represents the victory that the Angel of our Lord granted to the first king of Portugal against several Moorish kings, enemies of his holy faith, whom he defeated in battle.[13] We received the coat of arms the lord king Portugal sent us with great reverence and devotion to our Lord God. We recognized it as a very special favor the lord king of Portugal granted us and we held and continue to hold it in high esteem. The arms are a token of our obligation to our true and faithful brother in Jesus Christ, our most loyal friend, whom we will forever recognize and thank. We shall comply with whatever he commands us and our kingdoms and dominions to do. We shall die defending his cause because our debt to him is infinite, not only in this world but also in the spiritual realm. Thanks to him, our own soul and the

---

13. Afonso alludes here to the Battle of Ourique, the first victory of Portugal's first king, Afonso Henriques, over the Almoravids (or "Moors") waged on July 25, 1139. Most historians attribute little significance to what was probably no more than a skirmish between the then Count of Portucale and the Almoravids. Around two centuries later, however, accounts of the battle were embellished with the legend of Christ's appearance to the future king, supposedly foretelling the transformation of the County of Portucale into the independent Kingdom of Portugal in 1143.

souls of so many people have been saved, and we hope many more will be saved and will learn of and convert to Christ's faith, on whose path the king has led us with great effort and expense. Our Lord in his mercy shall reward him in all his endeavors because everything he has done has been in his service.

We request, recommend, and command that our sons and all their descendants will, until the end of the world and with our blessing, always bear this coat of arms. In every battle they wage, they should be reminded of what it symbolizes, how we earned it, and how the lord king of Portugal sent it to us. This crest affirms our trust in the mercy of God. He will always give my successors victory and will preserve their kingdom until the end of the world. It is also just that those who serve their lord king loyally should be rewarded for their service and have honors and favors bestowed upon them so that their renown and successes may never be forgotten. As the lord king of Portugal has informed us, Christian kings and princes customarily offer these coats of arms to noblemen and knights who serve their kings and lords loyally. He has therefore sent us twenty additional shields to give to the thirty-six who joined us in battle so that they become even nobler and their blood purer and so that their renown and their service to us on the battlefield will be remembered forever. They will make every nobleman strive and inspire one another with a virtuous desire to serve his king loyally and thus live on in perpetual memory. We beseech our Lord Jesus Christ, who in his mercy suffered and died for our sins, to remember and have mercy on us, to preserve us, all our children, and all our peoples in his holy Catholic faith, as we desire.

Written, etc.

DAMIÃO DE GÓIS—*Chronica*, Part III, chapter 38.

Damião de Góis, *Chronicle of Dom Manuel I*

Part 3, Chapter 39

After Dom Pedro arrived in Portugal, His Majesty King Manuel ordered preparations made for Dom Pedro and Dom Henrique to journey to Rome on their mission to the pope

After Dom Pedro arrived in Portugal, His Majesty Dom Manuel ordered all the necessary arrangements to be made for the journey to Rome of Dom Henrique, the son of His Majesty Dom Afonso Mwene Kongo, as well as Dom Pedro and their whole retinue. He directed that they be provided with everything they needed for the journey, from draft animals to people to attend to them. In 1513, they were solemnly received by Pope Leo X because Julius II had died.[14] He gave thanks to God that such barbarous and remote peoples with customs so different from Europe's had converted to the faith of our Lord Jesus Christ. In their second meeting with the pope, these ambassadors offered the pope the letter of faith and obedience they were bringing from His Majesty King Dom Afonso Mwene Kongo. The translation of this letter from the original Latin into our Portuguese tongue follows below:

Letter from the King of Kongo to the Pope (1512)

SUMMARY—*He kisses the pontiff's feet as a sign of obedience—Gives a history of the kingdom's conversion to Christianity—Conveys to His Holiness the names of his ambassadors*

Most holy father, in Christ, most blessed Lord Julius II, supreme pontiff by divine providence.

Your most devout son Dom Afonso by the grace of God, king of Kongo and lord of the Ambundus, kisses your most blessed feet with the greatest devotion. We trust that Your Holiness has heard how King John II of Portugal and his successor, the Catholic king Dom Manuel, sent priests to this land at great effort, diligence, and expense. Thanks to their teachings, we, who had been deceived by the devil and had worshipped idols, were, by divine intervention, delivered from this great error and bondage. After we were introduced to the faith of our Lord and Savior Jesus Christ, we received the water of holy baptism, which cleansed us from the leprosy that afflicted us, saved us from our heathen errors, and delivered us from all of Satan's diabolic superstitions and deceptions. We miraculously received with all our heart and free will the faith of our Lord Jesus Christ.

After we received the faith, we learned that it is customary for Christian kings to send their obedience to Your Blessed Holiness as the true vicar of Christ and shepherd of his flock, and we wished to follow them in this divine and sacred custom. Since the almighty and merciful God has included us among the Christian kings so that we could follow Catholic customs in their holy company, we therefore send

14. Julius II served as pope (and ruler of the Papal States) from 1503 until his death in 1513.

Your Holiness our ambassadors to give you our due and customary obedience, as other Christian kings have done.

One of these ambassadors is my greatly beloved and cherished son Dom Henrique, whom king Dom Manuel of Portugal, my much-beloved brother, ordered to be taught the Holy Scriptures and customs of the Catholic faith. The other is Dom Pedro de Sousa, my greatly beloved cousin. In addition to having them give you our obedience, we have informed them of some matters that they will convey to Your Blessed Holiness on our behalf. We very humbly beseech you to listen and accept the things they say and lend them as much faith as if these things were conveyed by us before Your Blessed Holiness. May God, in his mercy, preserve you in his holy service.

Given in our City of Kongo in the year of Lord Jesus Christ 1512.

A few days later, the pope and the college of cardinals read this letter of accreditation and obedience and gave their reply to the ambassadors, who took their leave from the pope, very pleased at the warm reception, and returned to Portugal. From there, they traveled to Kongo, where His Majesty Dom Afonso was very glad to learn of the favorable outcome of their journey.

DAMIÃO DE GÓIS—*Chronica*, Part III, chapter 39.

Letter from Dom Pedro de Sousa to King Dom Manuel I (1513)

SUMMARY—*He requests that Luís Serrão and the traders in São Tomé be ordered to give him back a slave and a half* [sic]

Sire:

I, Dom Pedro de Sousa, ambassador of His Majesty the King of Kongo, write to inform Your Highness that, when I arrived at the island of São Tomé as head of the mission from His Majesty my lord, I encountered the trading agent Luís Serrão, who seized as royal duty eight and a half slaves[15] that I was bringing to pay for my own and my people's expenses. Sire, His Majesty my lord does not charge royal taxes on any of the goods that white men trade in Kongo. He does not do the same with

15. The Portuguese referred to slaves as *peças* (literally, pieces) in the sixteenth century. A *meia peça* (half a piece or half a slave) designated a child, eight years old or younger.

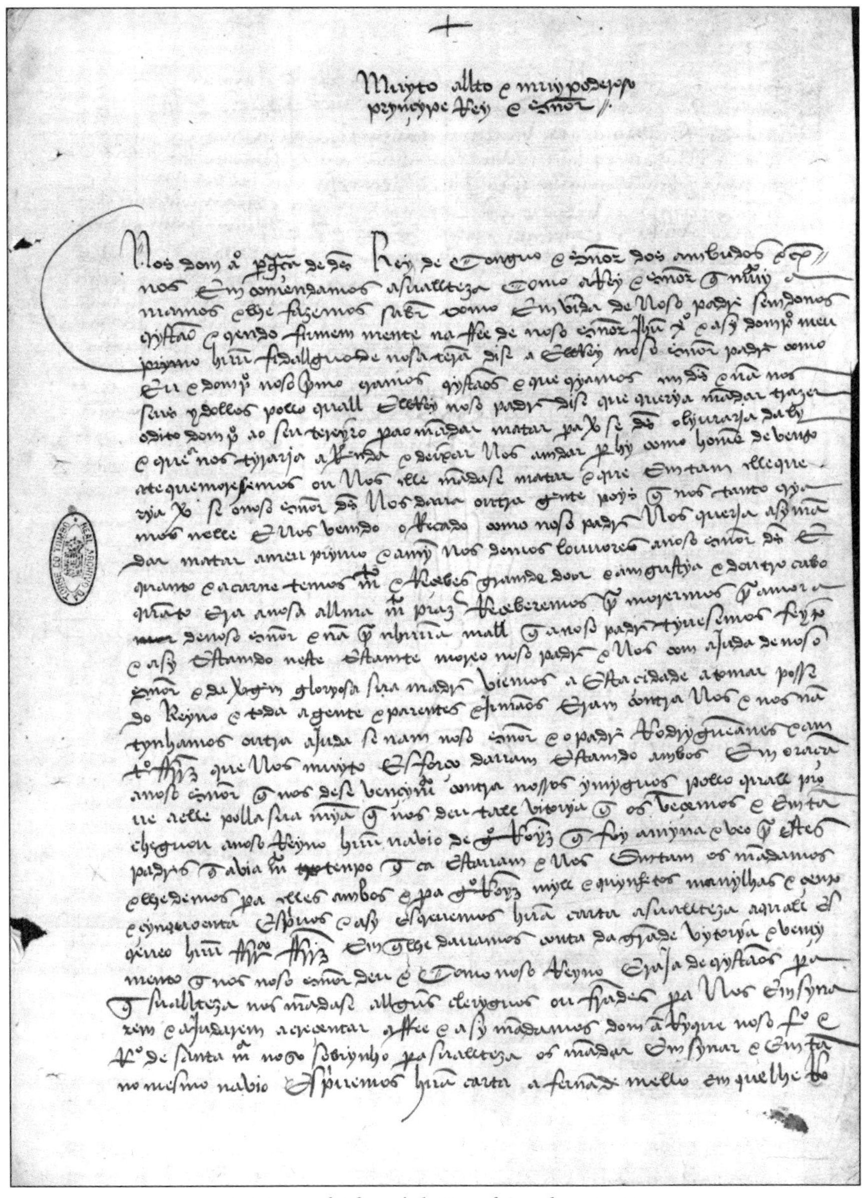
Muyto alto e muy poderoso
principe Rey e Senor

First page of Afonso's letter of October 5, 1514.

his own subjects because they all must pay tax according to the royal instructions. Since they charge no tax in Kongo to traders from this kingdom, it seems to me, Sire, that it is unjust to charge His Majesty my lord taxes on what he ships because seven of the slaves who were seized belonged to His Majesty and only one and a half were mine. I implore Your Highness to order Luís Serrão, or the merchants he works for, to return my slaves to me. I would be grateful to Your Highness.

Letter from the King of Kongo to D. Manuel I (October 5, 1514)

SUMMARY—*Recounts at length his difficulties with Portuguese officers, above all with Fernão de Melo, and the misunderstandings that occurred between them—Relates the sermon he gave his people upon the arrival of the canons of Saint Eligius—He orders an enclosure with high walls to be built for the 400 youths and boys he entrusted to the missionaries—The latter immediately break up the community and resume private lives—He complains about the craftsmen—Refers to the transportation of 22 Blacks, especially in the ship* O Gaio *[*The Jay*]—Requests the donation of S. Tomé in order to have a school for boys and girls from Kongo built there*

Most high and most powerful prince, king and lord.

We, D. Afonso, by the grace of God, king of Kongo and lord of the Ambundus, etc. We commend ourselves to Your Beloved Highness. When our father was still alive, shortly after we had become a Christian and believed firmly in the faith of our Lord Jesus Christ as did D. Pedro, my cousin, a nobleman of our country, told the king our lord that I and D. Pedro, our cousin, were Christians and believed in God, not in his idols. The king, our father, replied that he wanted D. Pedro brought to his palace square and killed to see if God would deliver him and that he would take away the revenue [*renda*] assigned to us and would let us roam about like a wayward man until we either died or he had us killed. He wanted to see if our God would give us other people since we believed in him so much. Upon [hearing] the message that our father wished to have us killed, my cousin and I gave praise to God. As to our flesh, we were very fearful of suffering great pain and anguish, but, on the other hand, as to our soul, we rejoiced that we were to die for the love of our Lord and not because of any evil we might have done to our father. We were at this point when our father died. With the help of our Lord and the glorious Virgin, his mother, we traveled to this city to take possession of the kingdom. All the people, [our] relatives, and brothers were against us, and we had no other help than that of our Lord as well as Father Rodrigo Eanes and António Fernandes, who gave us great encouragement.

While we were both praying for our Lord to grant us victory against our enemies, it pleased him, in his mercy, to give us such a victory over them. Soon after, a ship arrived captained by Gonçalo Rodrigues,[16] which had traveled to Elmina to collect

16. See n. 5 above.

the priests who had been in this country for a long time. We then sent [the priests] and gave to both them and Gonçalo Rodrigues 1,500 hoof-shaped ingots [*manilhas*] and 150 slaves. We also composed a letter to Your Highness, written by Francisco Fernandes, in which we informed you of the great victory and rout our Lord granted us, placing our kingdom in the hands of Christians, and asked Your Highness to send us some clerics or friars to teach us and help increase the faith. To that end, we sent D. Henrique, our son, and Rodrigo de Santa Maria, our nephew, to Your Highness so you could oversee their Christian education.

We sent a letter on the same ship to Fernão de Melo, in which we requested that he send some clerics to visit us and teach us the ways of God. When the priests and Gonçalo Rodrigues arrived on the island of São Tomé, and Fernão de Melo saw that they carried so many goods, he was overcome by greed and dispatched a ship here carrying nothing but a bed blanket, a rug, a valance, a glass bottle, and a single cleric. Gonçalo Pires also came as captain and pilot, and João Godinho as the ship's scribe. We were very pleased to receive this ship because we trusted that it came here at the service of God, but it came at the service of greed. We then asked Gonçalo Pires if Fernão de Melo had any ships he could send us with cannons and muskets that would assist us in burning down the great house of idols, for if we were to burn it without the help of the Christians, then our enemies would once again wage war against us and seek to kill us. He told us that he did not have any such ships but that if we sent him some merchandise, he would purchase ships and send us all the help we needed.

Sire, we would rather send everything there was in our kingdom and spend it all rather than lose faith in our Lord. We had presumed that since we, who had been heathens and only recently learned the ways of God, would suffer at the loss of his faith, then Fernão de Melo, who was a Christian and the son of a Christian, would suffer much more. For this reason, we believed that he would suffer for the faith of our Lord and would purchase some ships with the goods we sent him and swiftly send them to us, helping us increase the faith of our Lord Jesus Christ and destroy the devil's work by burning all the idols. We then asked Gonçalo Pires if the priests Rodrigo Eanes and António Fernandes, who delivered one of our letters to Your Highness, were in Portugal. He told us that one died at sea and the other on [one of the] islands of Cabo Verde, which caused us great sorrow, as much for their deaths as for the fact that Your Highness would not see our letter and that there would be nobody to give you an account of the great victory we had won.

After learning this, we decided to write another letter to Your Highness and send it with one of our nephews called Dom Gonçalo and one of our servants called Manuel in the ship of Fernão de Melo. We also sent Fernão de Melo 800 hoof-shaped ingots and fifty slaves for him and his wife, 50 hoof-shaped ingots for his son, 30 for the captain, and 20 for the ship's scribe, so he could obtain the aid we required. We cried many tears, beseeching Fernão de Melo, for the love of our Lord, to come to our assistance because there were no other Christians among us other than Dom Pedro, our cousin. Our servants and the rest of the people still worshipped idols and stood against us. After the ship set sail for Portugal, we, our cousin Dom Pedro, Francisco Fernandes, and the Christians from Nsundi who had helped us win that battle, all awaited a message from Fernão de Melo. We waited a whole year, and no message from him ever arrived. At that time, sire, we decided to set fire to all the idols as secretly as we could, no longer worrying about waiting for the help of Fernão de Melo since heaven's help was greater than that of the earth. Our Lord would come to our aid and if the people of our kingdom once again rose up against us and killed us, we would welcome such a death with forbearance, for our souls would be saved.

After we began to burn the idols, the people called us a very evil man and spread rumors about us to Dom Jorge Mwene Mbata, who was the head of our kingdom, so that he would have us burned and destroyed. However, our Lord inspired him to become a Christian, and he responded to those who maligned us by stating that he wanted to learn the faith of our Lord Jesus Christ and that if he were to destroy us, his uncle, who else might become king who was a closer relation to him. In this way, we preserved our kingdom and the Christian faith.

Shortly afterward, the canons of Saint Eligius[17] that Your Highness had sent us arrived. As soon as we learned of their arrival in our kingdom, we proclaimed that all our noblemen should go welcome their propitious arrival in the city. We came out to the palace square and delivered the following sermon to all our people:

Now, brethren, you should know that our former religion is all fantasy and empty air because the true faith is that of our Lord God, creator of heaven and earth. He created our father and mother, Adam and Eve, placed them in Eden, and forbade them from eating an apple there. Deluded by the devil, our mother Eve ate it, broke God's commandment, and sinned. She then made our father Adam sin, and for that reason, we were all damned. Seeing how these two were lost because they broke that sole commandment, how much more lost would we be since we have ten commandments? But know that our Lord is so merciful that when he saw that a woman was the cause of our perdition, he willed that another woman should save us, who was the glorious Virgin our Lady, in whose precious womb he cast his blessed Son to become human flesh and redeem and save us. His Son suffered death and the passion to save us and left behind twelve apostles to preach the Gospel throughout the whole world and teach his holy faith, declaring that all who believed in it would be saved

17. See n. 4 above.

and gain entrance to heaven. Until now, we have had no means of knowing Christ. Now, brethren, that he has opened the path to our salvation, you may all rejoice that you are Christians and can learn the ways of his faith and follow the example of these priests who are his servants. They live in great chastity and austerity, fast, and lead very saintly lives. As for the stones and sticks you worship, our Lord gave us stones to build houses and sticks for firewood.

At this point, countless men and women converted to Christianity. Once the speech was finished, we gathered all our brothers, sons, and nephews, as well as the sons of our servants, totaling 400 youths and boys. We ordered very high walls topped with a great many thorns to be raised, so they could not jump over them and run away, and we handed them over to the aforesaid priests to be taught. We also ordered another set of walls adjoining these to be built, with four houses inside, where the priests could remain together, as their order prescribed. The priests weren't together longer than three or four days; João de Santa Maria dissolved the community straight away. Two priests then asked our permission to return to Portugal. Your Highness had sent them here to serve God and lead a good example, and since others were dissolving the order, they wished to leave and avoid witnessing such great harm. These priests were António de Santa Cruz and Diogo de Santa Maria. Father Aleixos died of sorrow. Subsequently, other priests requested that we elect Pero Fernandes as their superior. They did not do this in order to remain cloistered but to set a ploy [*laço*] that would allow them to live separately. We told them that we did not have the power to name a cleric to a high office. At this point, they all separated, each to his own house. They each took with them a group of youths that they were teaching, and they came to us every day to importune us and ask us for money. And so we gave them money, and they all began to trade, buying and selling. Seeing their dissipation, we pleaded with them for the love of our Lord Jesus Christ that, if they bought any slaves, they should only buy male slaves and not any women, which would serve as a bad example and contradict what we had already preached to our people. Nonetheless, they began filling their houses with whores, and Father Pero Fernandes even impregnated a woman in his house, who gave birth to a mulatto child. This caused the youths he was teaching to run away from him and go tell their fathers, mothers, and other relatives what was happening. Because of these improprieties, everyone began to mock and scorn us, saying that what we had told them was all a lie and that the white men were deceiving us, which greatly distressed us because we did not know how to respond to them.

Soon afterward, Estevão da Rocha arrived in the kingdom with a ship. He told us he was Your Highness's chamber boy and was coming to arrest Gonçalo Rodrigues at your behest, at which we greatly rejoiced. When we asked him about

Your Highness's order to apprehend the aforesaid Gonçalo Rodrigues, he told us that the order had come to Fernão de Melo to arrest him if he came to the island. Because Fernão de Melo did not know his whereabouts, he was coming after him, and he told us that if we wished to write Your Highness or send you a message, he would carry it. Since we trusted him because he told us that he was your servant, we sent with him Dom Pedro, that former foe of ours who stood with a mighty army to battle against us when a cross appeared to him in the heavens, holding them back so that they lost the heart to fight. Because of the miracle, they had all witnessed, the aforesaid Dom Pedro had become a Christian along with a great many people. We were sending him to Your Highness so he could recount what he himself had seen. We therefore sent Dom Pedro, our cousin, Dom Manuel, our brother, and other nephews of ours. We sent a letter to Your Highness and another to the queen Lady Leonor,[18] and along with these relatives of ours, we sent Your Highness 700 hoof-shaped ingots and many slaves, parrots, as well as beasts and civets. This Estevão da Rocha told us to send the goods ahead of him, which we did. They were loaded onto the ship, and he followed after with our aforesaid relatives. Once he boarded the ship and saw the goods inside it, he took the letters addressed to Your Highness and threw them on the ground. Then, he broke the arm of one of our nephews named Pedro de Castro, who was there because he refused to leave the ship and was clinging to him. He also threw out Dom Pedro, Dom Manuel, and all our relatives and departed with everything we were sending Your Highness. He did this on the advice of Francisco Fernandes, who sent him a letter with one of our schoolboys. For this reason, we ordered Francisco Fernandes to be arrested, and then ordered the schoolboy killed because he was our subject. We eventually ordered Francisco Fernandes to be released and several other things that are too lengthy to recount.

After witnessing these events, our people and noblemen gave little regard to our decrees and derided us. At that time, we were on our way to a forest to have wood cut to build some timber walls to fence in the schoolboys. It was then that Fernão de Melo arrived in our kingdom on a ship captained by Estevão Zuzarte, his nephew, with Lopo Ferreira as the ship's scribe. With them came our nephew Dom Gonçalo and our servant Manuel. And so we asked Estevão Zuzarte if he was bringing back a reply to the letter that we had sent Your Highness with our aforesaid nephew. He told us that when Dom Gonçalo was about to depart, Your Highness had called for him to hand him the reply to our letter, but Dom Gonçalo

18. Lady Leonor (Eleanor) of Avis (1458–1525) was the daughter of Fernando, Duke of Viseu, and Lady Beatriz, the granddaughter of the founder of Portugal's Avis dynasty, King João I (1357–1433). In 1481, she married her cousin, King João II, and became his widow after his death in 1495, four years after the couple had lost their only son and heir to the throne.

had not wished to go to you. For that reason, he was not bringing it. He said that Your Highness had nonetheless written us a letter that was arriving in another ship coming behind this one and that you were sending us many things and clerics for the service of God. We then told him that we would bear all that Your Highness did with patience, even if your delay might sadden us.

Afterward, we invited him to our city, and he gave us twenthy lengths of coarse woolen cloth, which was not fit to dress small mice. These lengths of cloth were all of forty and fifty cubits each. As soon as he arrived in the city, Estevão Zuzarte immediately began conspiring with one Cristovão de Aguiar, a nephew of Gonçalo Rodrigues who had previously arrived in our kingdom. Cristovão de Aguiar gave us a blue bed blanket and fifteen cubits of coarse woolen cloth. He told us that he was giving us these things as gifts and that, once he decided to return to Portugal, we should send him some slaves or money to purchase slaves. We thus gave him enough money to purchase twenty-seven slaves and gave him many other things. Estevão Zuzarte told us that Fernão de Melo was your cousin and that he was Your Highness's nephew.

When we heard this, we were pleased with him, for we imagined he was who he claimed to be. We granted him many favors and dispatched him directly, sending Fernão de Melo 1,000 hoof-shaped ingots and some slaves. To Estevão Zuzarte, we gave twenty slaves and 300 hoof-shaped ingots. Since he told us he was a nephew of Your Highness, we gave him many cloths and some leopard skins, as well as twenty pots of honey and four civets for Fernão de Melo. He told us that if we sent hoof-shaped ingots or slaves to Your Highness, Your Highness would bear these gifts in mind. We then sent João Fernandes with him with 400 hoof-shaped ingots for you and twenty slaves to purchase clothes for us in Portugal, so we would not go on dressing like a savage.

As soon as the ship arrived on the island, Fernão de Melo took half of the hoof-shaped ingots and nine slaves, which left us with eleven. He purchased more slaves with the hoof-shaped ingots, paying thirty hoof-shaped ingots for each slave. Despite all this, João Fernandes took our few remaining slaves to Portugal and bought what we had ordered. He was bringing us a chest full of black satin and velvet, but Fernão de Melo took this chest and opened it. He had João Fernandes arrested, ordered him back to Portugal, and sent us the empty chest.

We have already written Your Highness about the distemper of Gonçalo Rodrigues and his wrongheadedness. However, we wish to recount to Your Highness what occurred with the stonemasons he brought us to build the church so that Your Highness understands how much Fernão de Melo enjoys undoing God's work. God will nonetheless reward him accordingly. Know, Your Highness, that Gonçalo Rodrigues brought eight craftsmen, left them in our kingdom, and departed on his way to the island of São Tomé. As soon as Fernão de Melo heard of his negligence and how the stonemasons had been left here, he sent one of his ships here with a cleric of his named Manuel Gonçalves as well as other servants of his. In this ship, he sent us four basins of lead, twelve glass bottles, a bundle of fiber, a piece of low-quality brocade, and a sword in exchange for another very good one that we had sent him to be fitted into a scabbard. He kept it and sent us one that belonged to one of his servants, which wasn't worth two cents [*ceitis*].

As soon as he arrived, this cleric began to lead the stonemasons astray. They all asked us for permission to leave after purchasing between fifteen and twenty slaves with the money we had paid them despite their not having done any work for us. When we saw this, we became well aware that Fernão de Melo was ordering them to leave in order to dishonor us. We nevertheless consented to suffer this dishonor for the love of our Lord God. The stonemasons left and took all the slaves and goods they had with them and only three remained here. We dispatched the aforesaid ship posthaste and sent Fernão de Melo 200 hoof-shaped ingots and sixty slaves, not counting the ones we gave his servants. We sent our nephew Pedro Afonso on the ship with a letter to Your Highness, in which we gave you an account of things here and sent 200 hoof-shaped ingots to you and several slaves that Pedro Afonso was to take to Portugal to purchase some clothes for us. And this was because Fernão de Melo had sent us a license to send any goods we wished in his ships.

As soon as this ship arrived on the island, Fernão de Melo seized half of the hoof-shaped ingots and slaves from us, despite having granted us the aforementioned license. He did not allow Pedro Afonso to travel to Portugal and kept him on the island for a year, ordering our goods to be sold for the lowest price he could. With the proceeds, he bought a Guinea slave and sent him to us along with another we had sent him in one of his earlier ships, claiming that they were carpenters. He also sent us a cubit and a half of blue cloth all gnawed away by rats, and he returned to us the letter we wrote Your Highness. Aside from robbing what was ours, he called us many injurious names, so vulgar that they cannot be told to Your Highness, which we endured only for the love of our Lord Jesus Christ. Despite all the deceptions and indignities done to us, we will not stop serving and believing in our Lord because we would rather suffer the indignities of this world and gain the next, which lasts forever, than live in this one amidst pleasures and blandishments and lose our soul. For this reason, brother, we have endured as many afflictions, invectives, and aggravations as we receive every worldly day.

So Your Highness may learn how much they deceive us, you should know that we requested the three stonemasons who remained here to build us a house that could shelter us and the queen and protect us if someone set fire to it on some night, as they could do with these straw-made houses. They began construction and spent a year laying the foundation. Each day they would come and set down a stone and then return home. Afterward, they would come asking for money. For each stone, we gave them one or two *lufukus* [10,000 each or 20,000 *nzimbu* shells]. When the time came to make lime, we asked several noblemen to bring stones and timber. They took another year to kiln-burn the stone while beating up and wounding our noblemen so that they made them run from the construction. They would then come to tell us that they had no helpers, and since we gave them money to buy slaves and provisions to feed them, we would ask them why they did not put them to work. They told us they had run away. In addition, they would tell us they had no wine. We then ordered more money be given to them. In this way, they never agreed to do anything except by dint of money.

Thus, they have been working on this house for five years, and they have not yet completed it, nor will they complete it in ten years. For this reason, we ask Your Highness to remedy the situation, for the love of our Lord God, because the deceptions and injuries these men inflict upon us are also inflicted on Your Highness. Not only are they content to take what is ours, but they are such bad examples of Christians in service of God that our noblemen laugh at the deceit they see them practice with us. When we want to punish them, they tell us that they live neither with Your Highness nor with us and that they owe us nothing. When we heard this, we had no heart to punish them and instead chose to keep our grievances to ourselves. We have already given Your Highness an account of the great suffering we endure each day. Yet, let it all be for the love of God.

We now wish to give Your Highness an account of Rui do Rêgo, whom Your Highness sent here to teach and give us good examples. Soon upon arriving here, he made himself out as a noble and refused to teach a single youth. During Lent, he came to ask us for an ox, which we ordered be given to him. He told us he was starving, so we sent him two rams and asked him to eat them in secret so our people would not see. Despite this request, he went ahead and slaughtered the ox in the middle of Lent before all our noblemen and even offered us meat. Seeing this, our people, in particular the youths who had recently converted to Christianity, all fled back to their homelands. The older ones remained with us and said things that are not fit to recount. They said that while we forbade them from eating meat, the white men gorged on it and that we were deceiving them, and thus they wanted to kill us. With great forbearance and many donations, we placated them once again, telling them to save their own souls and pay no heed to what that man was doing, for if he wished to go to hell, they should let him go. This episode dismayed us so much that we could no longer lay eyes on Rui do Rêgo and commanded that if he were to go to Chela, he should leave on any ship that happened to come to port since he was not instructing us as Your Highness had commanded.

Instead, he might even lead those we had converted with such great effort back to idol-worshipping. And so, he went away and stayed in Chela.

At this time, Simão da Silva arrived with two ships and met Rui do Rêgo there. The latter told him countless wicked things and lies and said that da Silva had been duped. Simão da Silva let himself be swayed by Rui do Rêgo's wrongheadedness, and everything Rêgo had told him. Rêgo did not tell him about the wicked deeds and heresies he had committed. Therefore, Simão da Silva decided not to come see us, as Your Highness had commanded, and sent the doctor here with your letters. We gave him as warm a reception as we would for our brother. A vicar who had come here from the island requested that we let the doctor lodge with him in his home. This cleric slandered us and turned the doctor's mind so he would tell Simão da Silva not to come to us. Your Highness should know that all this was ordered by Fernão de Melo so that no factory [trading outpost] of Your Highness would be built here, and he could continue going on his sprees and stealing from us, as always. Despite this, Sire, the doctor became ill with fever and was not able to return to Simão da Silva with an answer. But he wrote da Silva a letter alerting him not to come, telling him we were a Mr. Nobody ["João Pires"] who did not deserve anything Your Highness sent us. He gave this letter to one of our servants, and it came into our hand, and we showed it to all the servants of Your Highness who had arrived with the fleet. When we saw these words, we realized that they were written at Fernão de Melo's behest, and we gave praise to our Lord God that they called us a Nobody ["João Pires"] because we love him. All these things, lord and brother, we suffer with great wisdom and prudence, shedding many tears, not revealing anything to our nobles and our people so they will not plot some betrayal against us.

We then sent a cousin of ours with a young nobleman and wrote Simão da Silva to come and assuage us and punish these people who were here, for the love of God, because we asked no other thing from Your Highness except to bring them to justice. Because of our pleas and those of our cousin Dom João, da Silva came, but in the middle of the journey, he succumbed to a very strong fever and died. Upon receiving this news, it was as if our hands and feet were broken. Our sorrow was so great that we have never, until this day, felt any pleasure, all because of the great disarray and evils that the men who accompanied him would do later. As soon as he perished, they all came galloping at breakneck speed to ask us for the captaincy. And one of the first to reach us was Manuel Cão, who claimed that Your Highness had ordered both him and Simão da Silva to serve as captains, and that if one of them died, the other should take his place, and that since God had taken Simão da Silva, we should make him captain. We answered that he should wait for the rest of the men to come and that the most qualified would be made captain. Two days hence, Lourenço Vaz and Jorge de Lemos arrived and asked us to make them captains. Seeing how much they pestered us and how much they all wanted to be captain, we called all the white men together and asked them which man among them was the most qualified to be captain. They told us that aboard the ship *Gaio* [*Jay*], there was a trading agent of Your Highness who was more qualified than any other. In case this factor died, they said that either Jorge de Lemos or Lourenço Vaz would be next in line. These two immediately began to confer with one of Fernão de Melo's vicars who was here, who began to mislead them and turned their minds, convincing them that Fernão de Melo ordered them to turn back to stop the factory he had here from being destroyed. This vicar forbade us from seeing Your Highness's instructions. And we told him that if we did not see Your Highness's instructions, we could not know what you commanded. For three days, he refused to give them to us. After we saw and learned what Your Highness commanded, we greatly rejoiced. At that time, our nobles arrived with chests loaded with wares, which we ordered to be brought within our walls, assuming that they were the ones Your Highness had sent us. However, no more than three days later, all the men came to us, asking for the chests, claiming that they belonged to them. We then ordered that they be given only the remaining three that belonged to Simão da Silva. What Your Highness had sent us still remained in the ships. We immediately dispatched Lourenço Vaz to the ships so he could send us the things that Your Highness was bringing us. We told him that if the *Gaio* did not come, we would make him captain since he had more votes than any of the others. At that point, Lourenço Vaz departed, and as soon as he reached Chela, the *Gaio* arrived with Dom Pedro and Álvaro Lopes. Álvaro Lopes told Lourenço Vaz not to send us the merchandise until he met us. Lourenço Vaz then let everything remain as it was, and he soon became ill with fever and perished. Álvaro Lopes and Dom Pedro departed posthaste to catch up with a pilot of Fernão de Melo who was coming this way. They were coming to tell us that we should not accord Fernão de Melo any favors and to give us an account of the affronts and indignities to which he had subjected Dom Pedro and ourselves and how he had ordered Pedro put in leg irons.[19] They told us that as soon as Dom Pedro arrived on the island of

19. In the manuscript, the passage appears as, *mãdaua premder adona na e alle* (which Brásio transcribes as *mãdaua premder a DonAna e elle* [ordered him (Dom Pedro) and Lady Ana arrested]). However, since the final "a" in "adona" is not capitalized, to transcribe the passage as "Dona Ana" seems speculative. A thorough review of documents did not reveal any other reference to Dona Ana (tentatively identified by Jadin and Dicorato as "the spouse" of King Afonso's cousin Dom Pedro, whom the monarch appointed as ambassador to Portugal). Given the lack of any other reference to Dona Ana in the extant contemporaneous documents, I am proposing that *premder adona na e alle* is a transcription error for *mãdaua premder* [*na*] *ado*[*u*]*a* [*a*] [*e*]*lle* (i.e., "ordered him to be put in leg irons [*adova*]").

São Tomé, Fernão de Melo had dishonored him and called him a dog who had traveled to misinform Your Highness. Fernão de Melo said that we were not at war with Mpanzu a Lumbu,[20] that we did not deserve any of the things that Your Highness was sending us, that we were an infidel dog and a thousand other affronts that I would be ashamed to tell Your Highness.

Nonetheless, we gave our Lord God one thousand praises because when we were a youth and our father was still alive and we received a thousand million threats and insults for the love of God, we believed ever more firmly in him. We became a Christian and then waged many wars and wearied ourselves burning idols, and never, despite all these things, did we stop serving God. Now that we are old and have Christian sons and grandsons, would we leave him because Fernão de Melo badmouths us? Despite this, he seized all the horses that Your Highness was sending us. Soon after Dom Pedro and Álvaro Lopes finished giving us this report, we requested that Dom Pedro return immediately and have those goods brought to us because Your Highness had sent them to us. He told us that he was tired and would leave in the morning.

However, every morning that followed, he refused to leave. We were angry to see this, not because we weren't able to petition Your Highness but because we couldn't ask you to increase the faith of our Lord God, which was what we most desired. If the merchandise arrived, we would welcome it because Your Highness was sending it. If it didn't arrive, it would not matter to us because we had not ordered it bought. If we had we ordered it bought, we would strive to obtain it.

We then immediately began to dispatch Your Highness's ships and ordered twenty-two youths from our family to accompany them; we immediately sent to the galleon and caravel two nephews of ours with Dom Francisco, our son, along with 500 slaves for both ships and 30 additional slaves, so that if any of those 500 died, they could be replaced from among the 30. We bid Dom Francisco, our son, to kiss the hands of Your Highness and present you with those slaves as the king's son, not as what Fernão de Melo calls us, and bid our aforesaid nephews do the same. Nineteen slaves would travel in the *Gaio* with Dom Pedro. Thus, my lord and brother, we sent our son with our blessing, and he departed. Five days later, we received news that Munza, an Ambundu noble, had declared war on one of our sons whose territory bordered his and wanted to kill him. We therefore had to go to war and left Álvaro Lopes as captain in the city, accompanied by one of our servants. We instructed Álvaro Lopes to guard all the slaves we sent to Your Highness very closely and to justly punish anyone who committed any wrongdoing,

20. See n. 7 above.

as Your Highness commanded, whether the offender was one of our people or a white man.

And so, we left for the war. Of the men Your Highness had sent, three went with us, and the others remained behind with Álvaro Lopes, for none of them ever wanted to come. Aside from those who remained here, the following men accompanied us: Manuel Gonçalves, António Vieira, João de Estremós, João Gomes, Pêro Fernandes, Fernão Vaz, and a mason who was called Diogo Alonso, who told us, when we were halfway there, that he was dying of hunger. We ordered that he be given meat, and as soon as he got it, he returned to Kongo, leaving us in the battlefield. After we had gone into battle, Diogo Belo and Manuel Cão departed for Chela, to board the ship *Gaio.* They took 100 odd slaves and guarded them so poorly that when they stopped by a stream to drink, the slaves seized them, killed Manuel Cão, and badly wounded the vicar, Diogo Belo. When the vicar returned, his slaves ran off into the hills, robbing and stealing from the markets, tearing down our walls, and burning our houses. The destruction looked like the aftermath of a great war. Seeing the damage that the slaves were causing and that the vicar had no wish to punish them, even though he bought them with our money, Álvaro Lopes ordered them arrested and flogged. My wife, the queen, ordered the ones who killed Manuel Cão arrested and brought to the city. Then she commanded Álvaro Lopes to have them killed because our custom was to put murderers to death, and so Álvaro Lopes obeyed her command and had them killed.

While we were at war, the goods Your Highness had sent us arrived, and with them arrived the bachelor and the fleet's scribe, who carried a ledger accounting for all the merchandise he was to hand over to us. Soon after arriving in this city, the scribe headed back straight away, leaving us the account book without giving us an account of anything. For this reason, each person took what he wished, as if they were gifts for orphans. When we came back, we found the chests empty. We made a list of all their contents to send to Your Highness. After all this, Your Highness should know that we ordered our officers to bring 410 slaves from the battlefield to the ship *Gaio*. João de Estremós brought 190 slaves, whom he handed over to Álvaro Lopes in the palace square. From the 410, Lopes picked 320 of the best and left 90 who were thin and old. We never saw a log or account book listing the slaves. Neither do we know how many of them he sent to Your Highness. When we arrived, we found the bachelor Diogo Fernandes here. We were still making our way home and hadn't yet arrived, but this bachelor wouldn't even let us rest and began telling us that Álvaro Lopes wasn't fit to be captain and that we should dismiss Lopes and make him captain instead. We replied that we had already done this and that the captaincy belonged to him because we were told that it was customary that when the captain and trading agent arrived and the captain died [as had happened to Simão da Silva], the trading agent became captain. Since he wanted to be captain and royal magistrate [*corregedor*], then what could be better than for Álvaro Lopes to be captain and he the royal magistrate, we asked, so that they could both oversee and adjudicate matters of justice? But he never agreed to this. When we saw that he did not wish to talk it over with Álvaro Lopes so that they could both dispense justice, we ordered him to return to the ships, and he left. He spent so much time on the road that when he finally arrived, the ship was no longer there, and he refused to leave. After we sent him on his way to the ships, we immediately dispatched Dom Pedro after him. Dom Pedro took 190 slaves with him, that is, 100 for us and 90 for Your Highness, to offset those who remained because they were thin. He also took with him our obedience to the pope and regards to all our nephews. As soon as Fernão de Melo and Rui do Rêgo's clerics found out that Dom Pedro was on his way there, they had the ship depart with all the haste in the world without Dom Pedro and without our message. This was done on Fernão de Melo's orders so he could confound everything and represent his lies as the truth. Therefore, the ship left without a scribe or person who could give Your Highness an account of the slaves we were sending you, nor someone who could watch over them. Each sailor took the slaves he wished. It was enough to call out to God.

And so, brother, when Dom Pedro reached the river, he saw them sail away. He boarded a dugout and rowed after them, crying out for them to wait. They would not. When he saw this, Dom Pedro turned back and brought back the slaves he was bringing, both the 90 intended for Your Highness as well as the 100 that were ours. And the reason why they refused to take Dom Pedro, brother, was that they all had stolen the merchandise we were sending you and wanted to prevent him from telling you about their thieving. For this reason, we ordered this ship outfitted mainly to convey our obedience and so that Dom Pedro could give Your Highness an account of what we were sending you in our ships as well as the good works that the craftsmen Your Highness sent here have performed.

Namely, Your Highness will know first of all that we sent fifty hides to a cobbler who came here so that he could cut them and make us footwear: twenty goat hides, twenty from rams, and twenty from other animals we have here.[21] He either never bothered to cut these hides or didn't know how to. He thus damaged them all, leaving them useless. He made no more than five pairs of leather shoes, although he had many pelts and all the necessary implements. That is all the good he has done here. The tailor made us a robe with velvet sleeves and a few other items that he now and then grudgingly mends. The tile maker never deigned to make tiles or bricks for us. Each day we give him money and order him to go make them, and

21. The total is obviously sixty.

he never ends up going. Seeing how they have scorned us, we no longer wish to have our blood boil. They never taught any of our servants. On the contrary, if our servants went to see them work in order to learn from them, they beat the servants so badly that they ran away and dared not return. It is said that our noblemen who live far away fear us more than the ones who live in the court. This is true, and it is because the noblemen here witness the ill deeds and derision the craftsmen make us suffer and the bad example they set. If our nobles from afar saw them doing the things that those who accompany us see them do, they would be much worse. You can therefore see, lord and brother, the benefits they have given us and Your Highness. Therefore, if you decide they deserve their wages, you can have the wages sent to them, for we no longer feel obliged to do anything but report the truth to Your Highness because we think it unseemly that they should receive your money and wages in vain.

We now wish to give Your Highness an account of how, following these occurrences, one of Fernão de Melo's ships captained by Lopo Ferreira arrived in our kingdom, bringing back our brother Dom Manuel and our nephews. Dom Manuel brought letters from Fernão de Melo to the father, Friar Nuno. In these letters, Fernão de Melo beseeched him for the love of God to look after his things in Kongo, though he owned nothing here. However, he was referring to Your Highness's factory. He promised Friar Nuno that he would soon send a ship to fetch him and all those who assisted him. He pleaded with the friar to bring to his home one of his female slaves that Álvaro Lopes was keeping. And he wrote another letter to Álvaro Lopes informing him that he would soon have Álvaro Lopes arrested. As soon as these letters arrived, they stirred up great discord and greed among the priests as well as the salaried men. They all wanted to kill Álvaro Lopes and immediately began to buy slaves, even though Your Highness forbade it in your royal instructions, as did one of our edicts that we ordered proclaimed, barring everyone except the trading agent from purchasing slaves. Once they read Fernão de Melo's letters, immense greed overcame them. Before this, they had all lived in peace. The priests had lived piously, but they never again lived in peace after those letters arrived. Then father Friar Nuno came to us directly and told us that it would be right to appoint the bachelor as the royal magistrate so he could carry out justice. He brought a completed patent of authorization and had us sign it. After we signed it, he told us to name as scribe Tomé Lopes, a salaried man who accompanied him. We believed that because he was a priest, he would counsel us only to serve God. So we appointed Tomé Lopes as scribe and signed another patent of authorization.

As soon as they obtained the patents of authorization, they began to associate with one another, and they all ate and drank together, both priests and laymen. In this way, brother, they saw to Fernão de Melo's affairs just as he had instructed them to do in his letters. Every day they made inquiries about us and Álvaro Lopes, your trading agent, and they all wished him ill. They acted as though every one of them was witness, royal magistrate, and scribe. At this time, someone happened to steal a goat that we had given to the priests. For the sake of this goat, they all gathered in the church, rang the bells, and pronounced excommunications. After they did this, they were all up in arms. They cut down a green branch, and, uttering many curses, they said that just as the branch would wither, so would those who went against them and spoke ill of them. Moreover, Friar Nuno took the Black woman Álvaro Lopes kept as a concubine to his own house and kept her within his walls. Our nobles grumbled about this all day and about many other immoral things that we dare not describe in writing to Your Highness because of the excommunication proclaimed against us.

In spite of all this, they all banded together against Álvaro Lopes. To abase us even more, one day, when Lopes was kneeling before us asking us for provisions for the slaves he kept in the factory, the royal magistrate came up behind him and, right under our nose, grabbed him by the hair and stomped on him several times. We were very troubled by this because it was an insult committed directly against us. Álvaro Lopes had a dagger at his waist and showed so much restraint that he never pulled it out; instead, Lopes told the magistrate that he was now in our presence but that once they were both outside, he would make him pay for it. And even this was not enough: later, while we were having a chat, we had started to tell the royal magistrate that Your Highness had only sent him here so that he, Jorge Machado, Álvaro Lopes, and all your servants would live with us and teach us how to serve God and not so they would squabble among each other and live with the tailor and not with the mason. He retorted that he would not live with us for all Your Highness's treasure, nor for all the wealth of Portugal, and that it would be an ill-fated day when he would live with a Black man. So, brother, such are the services and teachings they have rendered us, besides a thousand insolences and other things that we are ashamed to recount to Your Highness. We place these matters in Your Highness's hands so that you can judge for yourself and give each one the punishment he deserves. If it is customary to address kings in this manner and wrench the hair of their men, especially those in charge of administering justice, and if Your Highness demands it for your service, then we will suffer it with patience for the love of our Lord God, just as we have suffered many other things for his love in the past.

Brother, after Fernão de Melo's ship had left Dom Manuel and our nephews ashore, it traveled to the Mpanzu a Lumbu coast, where Fernão de Melo was sending many silks and textiles to trade with and befriend the local people, despite knowing that we were at war with them because they are nonbelievers. We have waged many wars against them, in which they have killed many of our nobles, relatives, and white men. Fernão de Melo did this, brother, to harm us and set a bad example for our nobles, so they would say that the reason why the white men sought friendly ties with the Mpanzu a Lumbus was that the whites followed God's true law and we were teaching them falsehoods. In this way, our nobles would rise up against us and return to the idols. When our Lord saw his ill intention, he gave him the reward he gives those who serve the devil. As soon as they arrived in Mpanzu a Lumbu, they went ashore to set up the trade, and the nonbelievers who met them there killed Lopo Ferreira, the captain, and three or four more men. The others escaped to the boat and fled.

Now, Your Highness, consider how many ways Fernão de Melo has sought to destroy us and mislead Your Highness about us to force you to forget to visit us. We request that Your Highness ask Fernão de Melo why he detained our son Dom Francisco and why he did not allow him to sail in Your Highness's ships to where we were sending him out of love, for Your Highness had sent word that we should send twenty or thirty youths from our family. We sent our son so he could present all the slaves and goods we were offering Your Highness. And Fernão de Melo did not let him go and left him wandering around his island with a wooden rod in hand, begging for the love of God, and he did the same to our nephews. This caused us great sorrow, as to the flesh, for Dom Francisco issued from our loins, but as to the soul, it does not enrage us, for we were sending our son to seek after and learn the ways of God. To seek after and learn the faith of our Lord Jesus Christ, we would consider worthwhile all the earthly trials he might endure. We suffer them for the love of our Lord God, and for that he will always remember us.

We now beseech Your Highness, for the love of our Lord Jesus Christ, not to forsake us, nor to let the fruit and Christian religion that have been planted in our kingdom go to waste because we can do no more. We only have one mouth to teach and preach with. We have already wedded [according to church law], as have all our nobles who live near us. Those who live far away refuse to wed [according to church law], given all the bad examples they see every day, and they refuse to obey us. We therefore beseech Your Highness for the love of God to help get them married. Should Your Highness wish to help us in the spiritual realm, we will kiss your royal hands if you send five or six ships to come for us, our children, and our relatives so that we do not have to witness their eternal damnation.

We now ask Your Highness to bring Fernão de Melo to justice for all he has done to defame us and has worked so hard to destroy. Your Highness should order him to pay us for all the goods he has fraudulently taken from us. He has never fulfilled a single promise. And if he does not have the goods to cover his payments to us, then make him give us the island since it belongs to him. That will appease us. Your Highness should not assume that we ask for the island for any reason

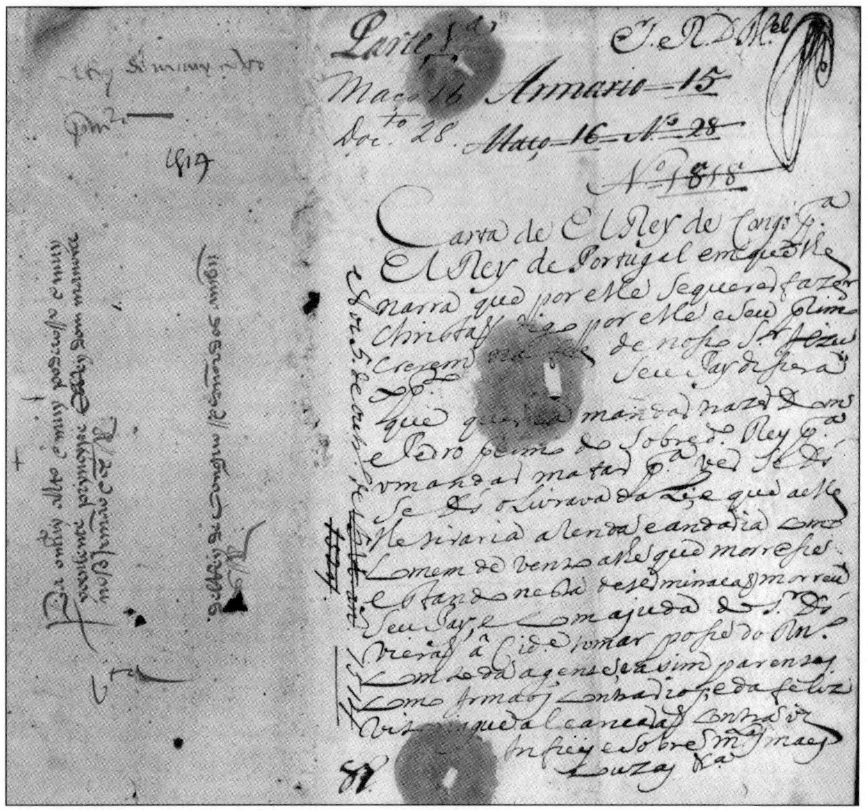
Parte 1.a

Armario 15

Maço 16

Doc.to 28. Maço 16 N.o 28

N.o 1818

Carta de El Rey de Congo p.a

El Rey de Portugal em que lhe

Eighteenth-century summary of Afonso's letter of October 5, 1514; *see p. xvi.*

other than to increase the Christian faith. As Your Highness must know, youths do not learn as well when they live with their mothers and fathers as they do when they live apart from them. For this purpose, we will send one of our relatives, and Your Highness will send a good and virtuous priest so they can attend mainly to spiritual matters but also to practical matters on the island. Since the island is so close to our kingdom, we could send many young men and women there to learn because here, they all run away. One day 200 come, and the next, only 100. They would learn quickly on the island, and we would need priests, wine, and flour for the Holy Sacrament there.

We will not write Your Highness any further because we would need a large ream of paper to recount all the conflicts that have happened here. However, Dom Pedro will give Your Highness a longer account of everything. And if anything in this letter is poorly written, we beg your forgiveness, for we do not know Portugal's writing styles. We write this letter with the assistance of a schoolboy of ours because we do not dare do it with any of the learned men who are here; all the more learned ones are guilty of various sins. We would kiss Your Highness's royal hands if you would write a letter to the Mwene Mbata Dom Jorge and another to Mwene Mpangu, who are the principal lords of our kingdom, in which Your Highness expresses your gratitude to them for being good Christians. You should also send them two priests, besides the ones you would send us, so they could celebrate mass in their churches, confess them, and teach the ways of serving God. Your Highness should know that these two nobles live a good eighty or ninety leagues away from us and that each has his church for the good of God. We have placed two schoolboys with each of them to teach them, their children, and their relatives. We have therefore started and have accomplished a very fruitful endeavor. Your Highness should now consider finishing it because we have reached the limit of our strength and have achieved all we can. Nevertheless, if they had priests to celebrate mass and confess them, it would uphold the firmness of God and will be to his great credit.

May our Lord increase Your Highness's life and royal estate so that you may help us increase his holy faith.

João Teixeira, servant of the most patient and much beleaguered prince king of the Kingdoms of Kongo, in the year 1514, on the fifth day of October.

Signed: King Dom Afonso

Letter from the King of Kongo to Manuel I (May 31, 1515)

SUMMARY—*Where he asks that the king either grant him permission or charge Manuel Vaz with handling his financial affairs in Portugal—He sends his nephews Dom Francisco and Dom Pedro Afonso to Portugal*

Most high and powerful lord:

Inasmuch as we wanted to dispatch some of our merchandise to your kingdoms, as we have previously requested Your Highness in writing, so that we may avail ourselves of sundry goods, and in order to fulfill the doctrines of our faith and the needs of our person, we beseeched Manuel Vaz, your royal servant who has recently come to us, to take charge of our affairs, since we have always found that he was very loyal to us when we have entrusted him with certain matters. And all our people get on well with him, and he has served us very well, both over there, when he handled affairs on our behalf, as well as here. Because we know that nobody attends to our affairs better than he and because he told us that he could not agree to [represent me] without Your Highness's leave, we request that Your Highness command him to take charge of our affairs and serve us in this capacity. For we have no other man but he with whom we could trust our assets in [your] kingdoms. Should he refuse to do this willingly, we would be most grateful if Your Highness compelled him to do it by force. We are again sending our nephews, Dom Francisco and Dom Pedro Afonso [to Portugal], to request, as our envoys and our relatives, this and other favors of Your Highness. May the Lord increase the days and estate of Your Royal Highness in his holy service.

Written in our City of Kongo, on the last day of the month of May of 1515, by João Teixeira.

His Majesty King Afonso

Addressed to: the most high and powerful king of Portugal, lord, etc., our brother

Letter from the King of Kongo to King Manuel I (May 31, 1515)

SUMMARY—*He requests assistance in matters of religion—Condemns the greed of the missionaries—He requests masons and carpenters to build a school where his relatives may learn*

Most high and most powerful lord:

We, King Afonso, by the grace of God, king of the Kongo Kingdom and lord of the Ambundus, etc., with the deference and reverence that kings must accord one another, place ourselves in your protection. Sire, we praise and give many thanks to you and God the Father on high, the Son and the Holy Spirit who must be knocking at the door of your heart for you to write such letters of solace, which have pleased us and soothed our heart for many years.

Nevertheless, Sire, there are things about which I cannot keep silent, even though, despite all my knowledge, all my efforts, and all my discernment, I am not worthy of teaching the doctrine of the Catholic faith without the aid of the most holy and most powerful Lord Jesus Christ, king of kings and lord of the angels, through whom and by the will of God, all good and holy things are done. Without him we can accomplish nothing. Nevertheless, Sire, although we are sinners and such things base and trifling, our holy Catholic faith requires good counsel and good examples [to thrive], for the people in our Kingdom of Kongo lived according to their own will, befouled by women and idolatries. Uprooting these customs requires the help of God and of Your Highness because, Sire, we are but men who do not know the hour and moment when the Lord will ordain our death. For in this kingdom, our faith is as [brittle as] glass because of the bad examples given by the men who came here to teach us. Greed for a few riches ruins the truth, my brother, for it was greed that led the Jews to crucify the Son of God, who continues to this day to be crucified by bad examples and bad deeds. In our days, the passion of the Son of God is greater than in the time of the Jews, for in the time of the Jews, he endured suffering and death to save humankind and for the sake of us, who wander weeping in this vale of misery and tears.

For these days, my brother, the greedy give many bad examples and crucify our Lord anew when they go against his will and befoul again after they are born, for we are all spiritually born through the water of baptism, the precious stone that is eternal life. Because when our Lord suffered [on the cross], he intended to save us and deliver us from thralldom to the devil, from the world and the flesh, so that we may join him in eternal glory.

Nevertheless, my lord and brother, the present time is more mean-spirited than times past, for the very same people who administer the body and blood of our Lord Jesus Christ are the ones who chase away the truth, [and] are enticed by the world, by greed, by the devil, and the temptations of the flesh. They forsake the promise they have made of their own free will to raise [the host] at the altar and preach the [Christian] doctrine and teach the word of eternal life that is the word of our Lord Jesus Christ. He himself taught [his word] through his works, examples, and miracles, having endured so much anguish at the hands of the Jews and suffered so many tribulations for the sake of his love and the salvation of the world.

The greedy evildoers who hold this holiest of sacraments that is the flesh and blood of our Lord Jesus Christ in their hands, only for show, while their heart is full of worldly greed, betray the word of our Lord they teach by setting bad examples. [Instead of] taking the key to the heavenly kingdom that is the doctrine of our holy Catholic faith to open our simple hearts, so we may enter eternal life, they use the infernal key of worldly greed to commit not only their own bodies and souls to hell. Through their bad examples, they also abet those who are blind to enter [hell] along with them. I beseech you, my brother, to come to my aid for the exaltation of our Catholic faith. My brother, it would be better for us not to have come into this world than to be born to witness the perdition of the souls of so many of our innocent relatives, brothers, cousins, nephews, nieces, and grandchildren, for lack of good examples to follow.

Lord, I ask you to send us carpenters and stonemasons to build a school to teach our relatives and our people. Although greedy and envious men set bad examples, and [although] I cannot move their hearts, I can remedy [this ill] with Holy Scripture for the word of the Holy Spirit is as adverse to worldly things, the flesh and the devil as [is] our Lord Jesus Christ. It can grant many days of life and grandeur to your royal estate.

Written in the City of Kongo, today, the thirty-first day of May 1515 by João Teixeira.

[From] King D. Afonso

Addressed to: The most high and powerful lord king of Portugal, etc., our brother

Ambassador of Kongo (1515)

SUMMARY—*He requests that a tamed mule that was taken from him be returned to him in place of another that he had been given, which was a pack mule riddled with saddle sores and unfit to ride*

Sire, I, Dom Pedro de Sousa, ambassador to the king of Kongo, submit this grievance to Your Grace for the great injuries done to me. I beseech Your Grace to come to my aid, as one might expect from Your Grace since I am a foreigner and do not wish to take my complaints to our lord king every single day. Your Grace should know that our lord king gave me a mule to ride as a gift. I had my servants take care of this mule and had it shoed two or three times a month with the money I received as a spending allowance. After I had this mule tamed and accustomed to me, the stable master took it away and gave me another so wild that the twenty Moors from the stables could not control her kicking and biting. Nevertheless, Sire, I worked so hard on her with my servants that I tamed her. And now, after having tamed her, the stable master has sent her to Castille and given me a pack mule riddled with saddle sores, unfit for anyone to ride. It seems to me, Sire, that I'm being mocked. This is not what is done to Your Majesty's servants in my homeland, the kingdom of my lord king when they go visit him. I beseech Your Grace to order the stable master to return my mule to me, for it took me great effort to tame her, or to give me another that would be suitable to my station and not a pack beast fit for some lowly countryman because I am well aware of how nobles are treated in Portugal. For this I shall be much obliged [to Your Grace].

On the reverse: from the ambassador of Kongo

Letter from the Mwene Kongo to Dom Manuel I (March 4, 1516)

SUMMARY—*Grave misunderstandings among the Portuguese authorities in Kongo—Álvaro Lopes kills the royal magistrate—the Mwene Kongo sends him to the island of São Tomé*

Your Highness has already heard that Simão da Silva died when he arrived in this kingdom before I could see him, which caused a great disturbance among the Portuguese people, and nobody could tell me the truth about Your Highness's intentions. Then, my cousin Dom Pedro arrived with Álvaro Lopes and informed me that Your Highness had appointed Álvaro Lopes as trading agent, since he was your servant whom Your Highness trusted. And, Sire, I made him captain and trading agent. When the royal magistrate arrived and found out that Álvaro Lopes was captain, he told me the man was an idiot and unfit to be captain, among many other vile words to me. Sire, I pleaded with him to be Lopes's friend and for them to administer justice together and do as Your Highness commanded. The magistrate never agreed to this and instead asked my permission to go back to Portugal in a ship called *O Gaio*. He pleaded so insistently that I gave him permission to leave. At this time, Sire, I had to go to war with the Ambundus, who had risen up against me, so I left Álvaro Lopes, acting in my stead as captain of Kongo, where my wife, the queen, remained. While I was away, Álvaro Lopes acted with justice in all matters.

When I returned from the war, Sire, I was told that the magistrate was downriver at the port of Mpinda and that he had taken ill and had not left for Portugal because the ship had already departed by the time he arrived. I immediately sent for him and sheltered him within my walls, pleading with him several times to be a friend to Álvaro Lopes so that they would both serve Your Highness and govern the other Portuguese people with justice. However, he never agreed to this. Instead, he began to meet with other Portuguese people who wished Álvaro Lopes ill because Lopes showed them Your Highness's royal instructions and required them to comply with them. For this reason, they all came to resent him so much that everyone—friars, clerics, and laymen—formed a single faction against Álvaro Lopes, with the magistrate at its head. They paid no heed to Álvaro Lopes or to what I commanded, but rather, Sire, they refused to serve me.

When I saw this, I requested the book of royal ordinances that Your Highness had sent me, written in vernacular Portuguese, and the magistrate told me he had it. When I requested it from him again, he told me he had no such book, that all his books were in Latin, and he refused to give it to me. And his young servant took it from him. I beseech Your Highness to do me the kindness of inquiring as to the book's whereabouts and sending it to me because I am very much in need of it. It stands to reason that we cannot apply the new law by relying on the old one.

Several days later, the father Friar Nuno brought me a patent of authorization and asked me to sign it, telling me that if I didn't sign it, I would be excommunicated, and he wouldn't be able to celebrate mass for me or administer any sacrament to me. The patent of authorization granted the royal magistrate the right to bring my people to trial and interrogate them, as was done in Portugal, because this was in the service of God. And, Sire, since this seemed to me to be so, I consented to it and signed the patent. As soon as the magistrate had it in his hands, he began to carry out investigations against Álvaro Lopes with so much arrogance that I did not know what to do other than leave them alone since they were both servants of Your Highness.

A few days afterward, Sire, I gave Álvaro Lopes four *lufuku* [measures of 10,000 *nzimbu* shells each] to purchase slaves for Your Highness. And a few days after this, while the magistrate and Friar Nuno sat with me in a house where I was lodging, Álvaro Lopes came and kneeled before me and said: "Sire, I have purchased twenty-five slaves with the money Your Lordship gave me. There are six and a half *lufuku* measures of *nzimbu* shells left over; please tell me what to do with them." And I told him to spend it on more slaves and add them to the others. At the end of this exchange, the magistrate rose from where he sat with Friar Nuno and said: "Sire, how can this thieving crook not be ashamed to address Your Lordship, since he has robbed you and His Majesty, King D. Manuel I, your brother?" Álvaro Lopes asked: "What have I stolen from His Majesty the King?" And the magistrate answered: "The twenty-five slaves you sent to Portugal." Álvaro Lopes told him: "Ask Your Lordship who gave them to me." And I said that I had awarded him ten slaves upon his arrival and fifteen more afterward because this was the truth, Sire. In the middle of this argument, the magistrate attacked Álvaro Lopes and hit him three or four times with his staff, which shocked me and left me at a loss for words. Álvaro Lopes, who had a sword and a dagger on his belt, rose and said: "Magistrate, you represent justice, and you have insulted me before His Lordship. Why didn't you do this outside? Did our lord, the king, send us here to act this way? What you have done was not done to me but to His Majesty the Mwene Kongo, here before you. Nevertheless, watch out for me because I will kill you." And he left. I was shocked, Sire, and did not know what to do with them since they were both servants of Your Highness.

Later, I was informed one night that Álvaro Lopes had killed the royal magistrate and taken sanctuary in the church. The next day, all the white men petitioned me to remove him from the church and have him beheaded. I refused and instead waited until Manuel Vaz arrived and ordered him to take Lopes to the island of São Tomé and place him inside a church since he had also taken refuge in one here. I report all this to you, Sire, to clear my conscience and to inform Your Highness of the truth.

City of Kongo, on the fourth of March, in the year 1516.

King Dom Afonso, Mwene Kongo

Letter from the Vicar Rui de Aguiar to King Manuel I (May 25, 1516)

SUMMARY—*He relates how D. Afonso evangelizes the kingdom—His knowledge of the prophets, Gospels, and the lives of the saints—How he dispenses justice—Schools for pupils of both sexes—Requests books for school children, above all*

King Dom Afonso's only concern is to follow in the footsteps of our Lord. He has just ordered every subject in the entire kingdom to pay a tithe,[22] declaring that he wants to carry the torch in front of him, not behind him. Your Highness should know about his Christian spirit; he seems to me not a man but an angel whom the Lord has sent to this kingdom in order to convert it, judging by all he says. I assure Your Highness that he not only teaches us but knows more than we do about the prophets, the Gospels of our Lord Jesus Christ, the lives of all the saints, and all that pertains to the holy mother church. If Your Highness saw him, you would be astonished. He expresses himself so well and so reasonably that it seems to me that the Holy Spirit is speaking through him. He does nothing but study, and many times he falls asleep on his books. He often forgets to eat and drink when he discusses the ways of our Lord. He feels so uplifted by the Holy Scripture that he forgets himself. Even when he holds an audience or judges a dispute, he speaks only of God and his saints.

Lord, he studies the Holy Gospel. When the priest finishes giving mass, he asks for his benediction. As soon as he receives it, they both start preaching to the people with great love and compassion, pleading and beseeching them to convert and turn to God. His people are amazed by him, and we are even more astonished at

22. The tithe (*dízima* in Portuguese) was a tax of one-tenth of the annual produce or income which was used to support the church.

his virtue and the faith he shows in our Lord. This is what he does every day, aside from preaching to his people, as I have informed Your Highness.

Moreover, Your Highness should know that he is very just and harshly punishes those who worship idols. He orders them burnt along with their idols. He maintains officers of justice all over his kingdoms, tasked with arresting all those they know keep idols or practice sorcery and any other offense against our holy Catholic faith. In addition, he has already distributed many kingdom-born Christians throughout his kingdoms, who run schools and teach the people our holy faith. There are also schools for young girls. One of his sisters teaches in one of these schools. She is at least sixty years old and can read very well, which she learned to do in her old age. Your Highness would be very pleased to see her. Other women and girls also know how to read. They go to church every weekday. At mass, they entrust themselves to our Lord. Your Highness should also know that these people are greatly enriching their Christian spirit, with great virtue, as they learn the Lord's truth. Your Highness should therefore continue to help these people and rejoice in sending them the remedy for their salvation, in particular, books, because they need them more than anything else for their salvation. Needless to say, the king of Kongo has a great love and fondness for Your Highness. I have heard him say that he begged our Lord not to let him die before meeting Your Highness in person. Likewise, I heard him say that Your Highness was the king of Kongo and that he, the Mwene Kongo, belonged to Portugal. He repeats this to anyone who wishes to listen.

Your Highness should know that all that I declare here is absolutely true. If I lie to Your Highness, may God destroy my body and soul. May Your Highness remember the great blessing that you have begun to perform here. For that, our Lord, in his goodness, will reward you.

The 25th day of the month of May, in the year 1516.

Concerning Some Matters That Touch on the Kingdom of Kongo (1516)

SUMMARY—*His Majesty the King sends Father Rui de Aguiar, Baltasar de Castro, and António Vieira to Kongo—Dom Afonso's reaction upon learning about Portuguese legislation*

In this year of 1516, King Dom Manuel sent a cleric named Rui de Aguiar to Kongo as vicar to attend to matters of religion. Along with him [the king sent]

António Vieira and Baltasar de Castro, his servants, with trading goods and gifts of silver serving sets for the home of His Majesty King Dom Afonso and his wife, the queen. They all arrived safely at the end of their journey in the Congo River, and after anchoring the ship, they carried the goods and merchandise in rowboats and dugouts to the house of a nobleman named Mwene Soyo, who lived three leagues up the river. He was a vassal and relative of His Majesty the King. The king was so pleased with the arrival of these ambassadors that he ordered many games and festivities to be performed according to their African custom and usage. The king sent envoys to meet them and provided them with everything they might need. He told them in writing to remain on the island of Soyo until he returned from a war that he was waging against some neighboring vassal lords who had risen against him. A few days later, he returned victorious from this war, with eighty war captives, who were the sons of prominent men from the provinces that had rebelled, and they were each ordered to pay a tribute in gold and silver each year.

While the king was at war, the vicar Rui de Aguiar had a church built in the town of Soyo and named it after Saint Anthony of blessed memory, which pleased the townspeople very much because the majority of them were Christian.

After the king returned from the war, he sent word to the vicar to come and join him in the City of Kongo, which was located roughly fifty leagues from Soyo. The vicar and his staff were very warmly received and hosted. After a few days, the vicar petitioned the king to send him some talented youths to be taught. The king was so pleased by this that not only did he immediately send him these youths, but he ordered several houses to be built within a great enclosure, in which he placed one thousand such youths, who were all children of noblemen, with instructors to teach them reading, writing, and grammar and school them in matters of our holy faith.

The account I have already written here attests to the virtues of King Dom Afonso and his devoutness as a Catholic Christian, and so do the formal words that this same vicar Rui de Aguiar wrote in a letter addressed to His Majesty King Dom Manuel:

> *Text of May 25, 1516 letter by Father Rui de Aguiar (above) follows here in the original.*

Among the books and other things His Majesty King Dom Manuel sent to His Majesty King Dom Afonso of Kongo, he included the royal ordinances of these kingdoms of Portugal. His Majesty King Dom Afonso read them all, sometimes in the presence of Baltasar de Castro (as Baltasar de Castro told me [de Góis, the chronicler] in person upon his return from Kongo). After carefully considering these ordinances, along with all the details of each law and article, as well as how they were to be enforced, he realized it was impossible to reduce his subjects and vassals to a similarly regulated life. If he were to do this, they would all suffer so many pains each day that he would have a harder time carrying out and enforcing these ordinances than he had in governing his kingdoms and dominions. Speaking of what he had read, he once asked the aforesaid Baltasar de Castro, laughing, "What punishment is given in Portugal to those who place their feet on the ground?" as though saying that there were so many laws, ordinances, articles, clauses, and summaries of them all, together with the exceptions, that it was impossible for anyone to live in full compliance with them and not to do something that would incur a criminal sentence, civil infraction, convict exile, or fines to the crown and officers of the law. There is much to inspire praise in this king, not just for having been enlightened by the grace of our holy faith and having adopted our customs, but for doing all this in a country as barbarous and ignorant of European governance as this one was at the time.

DAMIÃO DE GÓIS—*Chronica,* Part IV, chapter 3.

Report of an Inquiry Ordered by the Mwene Kongo (April 27, 1517)

SUMMARY—*After a record of the gifts sent to him by the king of Portugal is mislaid, Dom Afonso orders a rigorous inquiry to be carried out*

Inquiry ordered by the Christian lord Dom Afonso, Mwene Kongo and lord of the Ambundus, etc., concerning the list that was not found enclosed in his brother's, the king of Portugal's, letter, which mentioned that it included a list of all the things he was sending him.

In the year of our Lord Jesus Christ 1517, on the 27th day of the month of April, in the City of Kongo, inside the walls and royal chambers of the most high and Christian lord Dom Afonso, Mwene Kongo and lord of the Ambundus, etc., the lord informed me, the scribe named below, that his brother the king of Portugal had sent a ship to this kingdom, and that this ship, captained by António Vieira, carried certain items, both clothing and other articles for the church and the exaltation of our holy faith. After arriving in Soyo, the ship's captain wrote him a letter to let him know of his arrival, asking for a noble to come, accompanied by at least 1,000 men, to carry back the clothes and other items, as will be described in more detail below. After writing this letter, he traveled from Soyo to the land of the Ambundus, where His Royal Highness was waging war. Soon after arriving there, António Vieira gave the lord Mwene Kongo four letters from the lord king of Portugal, his brother. In one of these letters, the king stated that he was enclosing the list of all the things he was sending him on the aforementioned ship, but the list was not inside the letter. Since the list was not included in the letter, the lord Mwene Kongo asked António Vieira, as well as Baltasar de Castro, the ship's scribe, about it. They replied that they had no notice of any list other than a letter they brought from the trading agents that recorded everything they were bringing. They didn't know whether this letter had been left in Soyo along with the clothes and other gifts. Two days later, the scribe brought the king the letter from the trading agents and told him that they had brought no other list except that one. The lord Mwene Kongo charged me with examining witnesses to ask them why the list of gifts was not found inside the royal letter as said letter stated, in order to inform the king of Portugal of the truth of the matter and determine whether someone had forgotten to enclose the list with the letter in Portugal, or whether someone had removed it during the journey. At the king's orders, I interviewed the following witnesses. I, Rui Godinho, wrote this.

On the 28th day of April, I, the scribe, examined the following witnesses, whom I had swear upon the Holy Gospels to tell the whole truth and nothing but the truth about what they knew regarding this list, which they pledged to do under oath. I, Rui Godinho, wrote this.

1. Gabriel Martins, a witness whom I, the scribe, had swear upon the Holy Gospels, stated that it was true that the Mwene Kongo had complained that His Majesty the King of Portugal, his brother, had written him a letter in which a list of the gifts was enclosed; however, he found no such list enclosed, nor was one provided to him. Instead, the ship's scribe had given him a list apparently drafted and signed by the trading agents of the *Casa da Mina*[23] (House of Mina) in Lisbon. The witness stated that he had seen the letter from His Majesty the King of Portugal and read the closing lines: "We enclose in this letter the list of all the things that we are sending you." This witness knows nothing more and didn't have anything else to say about this matter. I, Rui Godinho, wrote this.

[signed] Gabriel Martins

23. See n. 8 above.

2. Marcos Fernandes, squire of His Majesty the King of Portugal, a witness whom I, the scribe, had swear upon the Holy Gospels, said that it was true that a ship, reputedly belonging to His Majesty the King of Portugal, captained by António Vieira, had arrived from Portugal in Soyo, a seaport of this kingdom. The witness saw a letter that António Vieira wrote to the lord Mwene Kongo, in which he requested a nobleman to come accompanied by at least 1,000 men to carry all the goods and articles. The witness further stated that he saw António Vieira on the war front, where the king was, and heard the ship's scribe say that the Mwene Kongo had complained to António Vieira in the City of Kongo that he had not found the list of the gifts, which the king of Portugal said he had enclosed in one of the letters he wrote to the Mwene Kongo, and the Mwene Kongo had asked António Vieira about the list. The witness stated that he had read the closing lines of the letter: "We enclose in this letter the list of all the things that we are sending you." The witness also said that he heard the Mwene Kongo state that when he had asked António Vieira and the scribe about the list, they replied that it had been left inside a strongbox down in Soyo and that some days later, the witness couldn't say how many, the scribe had brought the king a list apparently signed by the trading agents of the *Casa da Mina*, but the witness didn't know what this list contained. The witness knows nothing else about this matter. I, Rui Godinho, wrote this.

[signed] Marcos Fernandes

3. Jerónimo de Leão, squire of our lady Queen Leonor,[24] a witness whom I, the scribe, had swear upon the Holy Gospels, said that it was true that the Mwene Kongo had shown him a letter from António Vieira, in which he informed him that he had arrived and was bringing many clothes and items that would greatly please His Royal Lordship, and also that a nobleman should be sent accompanied by 1,000 men to carry all these goods. The witness further stated that he was in the City of Kongo when António Vieira arrived from the war, followed by the lord Mwene Kongo a few days later. He also said that some days later, the lord showed him four letters that his brother, the king of Portugal, had sent him, in one of which he said that he was sending him clothes and other items that he knew he needed and that he was enclosing the list of everything he was sending him. The Mwene Kongo complained to him that he didn't find the list of gifts enclosed in that letter. And the lord king showed the witness a letter that was said to be from the trading agents, which included a list of items that His Majesty sent him. His

24. See n. 18 above.

Majesty the Mwene Kongo told him that he could not believe that this letter was from the trading agents since he had not found the list enclosed in the letter from his brother the king. The witness said he knew nothing else about this matter. I, Rui Godinho, wrote this.

[signed] Jerónimo de Leão

4. Fernão Matela, a witness whom I, the scribe, had swear upon the Holy Gospels, stated that it was true that he saw a letter that António Vieira wrote from Soyo to the lord Mwene Kongo, in which he petitioned His Royal Lordship to send him a nobleman, accompanied by at least 1,000 men, to bring back the clothes and articles. The witness stated that he heard António Vieira say that he had gone to the war front, where His Lordship was, and had given him the four letters he was bringing him from his brother, His Majesty the King of Portugal. The witness also said that upon arriving in the City of Kongo, the lord Mwene Kongo read in one of the letters that the lord King of Portugal told him, "we enclose in this letter the list of all the things that we are sending you." The witness had not seen the list; he had only heard the lord Mwene Kongo complain that he had been given the letter without the enclosed list. When António Vieira and the ship's scribe handed the letters to His Royal Lordship, the witness heard him ask them about the list of gifts and heard them answer that they had no knowledge of such a list but had a list made by the trading agents of the *Casa da Mina*, which they had left in Soyo. The witness added that some days later, he couldn't say how many, the scribe had given the trading agents' list to the lord Mwene Kongo. The witness knows nothing else about this matter. I, Rui Godinho, wrote this.

[signed] Fernão Matela

Having carried out this inquiry, I, scribe, at the orders of the lord Mwene Kongo, closed and sealed it in order to send it to his brother, the king, as he requests, in his letter. Signed here with my customary mark, attesting to its truth. I, Rui Godinho wrote this.

[signed] Rui Godinho

In the verso: Inquiry addressed from His Majesty the Mwene Kongo to his brother, His Majesty the King of Portugal.

Inquiry concerning the list of the items sent by His Majesty the King to His Majesty the Mwene Kongo that was not found inside his chest.

Letter from the King of Kongo to Manuel I (May 26, 1517)

SUMMARY—*He requests permission to buy a ship—In case his request is denied, he asks that slaves be allowed to be loaded on board every ship sailing to Kongo and be exempt from royal duties*

Most powerful and high prince and king, my brother:

Kissing Your Highness's royal hands, I write to inform you of my great need for a ship, which I have already written to you about a few times. I have mentioned what a great favor you would grant me if you allowed me to purchase one. I do not know why Your Highness does not wish to agree to my request; I only want a ship so I will be able to better supply myself with the articles I need to perform the service of God. I would be grateful to Your Highness if you do not object to my nephew Dom Rodrigo buying us a ship, as I have instructed him to do, provided that Your Highness grants him permission. If you say no, I would instead request the favor of a royal license that would allow every ship that comes to my kingdom to be loaded with slaves, for whom I will not be charged royal duties. I have made little money off of all the slaves I have shipped so far because all the profits go to taxes.

May the Lord increase Your Highness's days and royal state as much as I desire.

Written in the City of Kongo, on the 26th day of May by Rui Godinho in the year 1517.

King Dom Afonso

ADDRESSED TO: Most high and powerful prince and King Dom Manuel, my brother

FROM: His Majesty the Mwene Kongo concerning a license to purchase a ship

Letter from the King of Kongo to Manuel I (May 27, 1517)

SUMMARY—*Speaks of the poor performance of his relatives, the students sent to Portugal—Requests that they be redistributed among the religious houses, punished but not returned to the Kingdom of Kongo*

Most powerful and high prince and king, my brother:

I have read a letter from Your Highness informing me that my relatives, whom I sent to your kingdom to gain an education, have done very poorly. I am very sorry to hear this because I only sent them to you to learn of our Lord Jesus Christ, help increase our holy Catholic faith, and light the way for those in my kingdoms who are blind to the faith so that, after my death, they can continue our faith in our Lord Jesus Christ. This is why I sent them to be very well-instructed and disciplined. Therefore, it seems to me that Your Highness's ban on students from Kongo traveling to Portugal will allow the enemies of our holy Catholic faith to take advantage of our weaknesses. It will also be a source of extreme shame to me before my people because I have always told them that I received great assistance from Portugal to aid in the instruction and increase of our holy faith. I consider it better for these students from Kongo to be punished instead of expelled. It is through difficult trials that the kingdom of heaven is gained. Your Highness's solution should be to divide them among religious houses across the kingdom so that they would not be able to see each other. In this way, they would yield good fruit in the service of God. Any student who fails to do what he should after being separated from the others should be thoroughly punished.

Written in Kongo, on the 27th day of May by Rui Godinho in the year 1517.

King Dom Afonso

ADDRESSED TO: Most high and powerful prince and king of Portugal, my brother

FROM: The king of Kongo

Letter from the King of Kongo to Manuel I (June 8, 1517)

SUMMARY—*On behalf of Father Rui de Aguiar, vicar of Kongo, he requests various objects for the church to be delivered on the earliest ship*

Most powerful and high prince and king, my brother:

Kissing Your Highness's royal hands, I write to inform you that my lack of some church items leads me to trouble Your Highness, which I likely would not need to do if I owned a ship. If I possessed a ship, I would have these items shipped to me at my expense, and Your Highness would not be bothered by my requests for so many things. However, I cannot avoid appealing to you now because I don't own a ship.

Father Rui de Aguiar, the vicar that Your Highness has recently sent here, requests from me the following items for the church. I would kiss Your Highness's hands if you could ship to me: a silver cross; a chest for the Holy Sacrament; curtains for the altar; a half-dozen surplices; two books of hymns, one for weekdays and the other for Sundays; a pair of vestments; two pairs of missals; two pairs of breviaries;[25] one pair of altar hangings; half a dozen osculatories;[26] a dozen altarpieces for the churches that already exist in the kingdom; and a quintal[27] of wrought beeswax[28] to celebrate mass. I am in dire need of these things, and I would kiss Your Highness's hands if you were to send them to me on the earliest ship headed to our kingdom. This would be of great service to our Lord.

Written in Kongo, on the 8th day of June, by Rui Godinho in the year 1517.

King Dom Afonso

ADDRESSED TO: Most high and powerful prince and king of Portugal, my brother

FROM: The king of Kongo

25. Prayer books.

26. Religious tablets, usually adorned with the image of Christ or the Virgin Mary, which the priest kisses during mass ("the kiss of peace") and then passes around the congregation so the faithful can kiss it in turn.

27. Hundredweight.

28. Used for candles.

Letter[29] from the King of Kongo to Manuel I (June 13, 1517)

SUMMARY—*He announces that he has begun construction of a residence as well as a church due to the increasing number of Christians—Requests masons and carpenters from His Majesty the King in order to finish construction*

Most powerful and high prince and king, my brother:

Kissing Your Highness's royal hands, I write to inform you that five or six years ago, I began building a house where I might find shelter. Also, I have just begun building a church, which has been greatly needed in the City of Kongo because it has many people and, by the grace of our Lord, more people have become Christians. Neither the house nor the church has been finished, as Your Highness will have learned. I lack the masons to finish them, and I am in great need of them. I would kiss Your Highness's hands if you sent me some masons to complete the construction as well as carpenters to do the woodwork. Your Highness will do me a great favor, and it will be a great honor and service to God.

Written in Kongo, on the 13th day of June, by Rui Godinho in the year 1517.

King Dom Afonso

In the verso: From the Mwene Kongo, masons, etc.

ADDRESSED TO: Most high and powerful prince and king of Portugal, my brother

FROM: The king of Kongo

29. This letter is identical to the next one (they were transcribed in separate documents); only the summary is slightly different.

Letter[30] from the King of Kongo to Manuel I (June 13, 1517)

SUMMARY—*Around five or six years ago he started building a residence—He began building a church in the City of Kongo, which was much needed—He requests masons and carpenters in order to finish both*

Most powerful and high prince and king, my brother:

Kissing Your Highness's royal hands, I write to inform you that a good five or six years ago, I began building a house where I might find shelter. Also, I have just begun building a church, which the City of Kongo greatly needs because it has many people and because, by the grace of our Lord, more of the people have converted to Christianity. Neither the house nor the church has been finished, as Your Highness will have heard. I lack the masons to finish it, and I am in great need of them. I would kiss Your Highness's hands if you sent me some masons to complete them as well as carpenters to do the woodwork. Your Highness will do me a great favor, and it will be a great honor and service to God.

Written in Kongo, on the 13th day of June. Done by Rui Godinho in the year 1517.

Signed: King Dom Afonso

In the verso: From His Majesty the Mwene Kongo, masons, etc.

ADDRESSED TO: Most high and powerful prince and king of Portugal, my brother

FROM: The Mwene Kongo

30. See n. 29 above.

Letter from D. Manuel I to the Mwene Kongo (c. 1517)

SUMMARY—*He charges António Vieira with a mission to the Mwene Kongo—If António Vieira brings slaves from Kongo to São Tomé, they will be charged to António Vieira as revenue*

Noble and honored Mwene Kongo, we, King Dom Manuel, send you many greetings. You will speak to António Vieira about Dom Pedro de Sousa, whom you sent to us and whom we have permitted to remain here, as António Vieira will inform you. We earnestly request you place your entire faith in him, and we would be most grateful to you if you did so.

You, António Vieira, will convey the following to His Majesty the Mwene Kongo regarding Dom Pedro de Sousa:

You will tell him that: because we have been informed that he is not satisfied with Dom Pedro's conduct and that he may prefer if Dom Pedro remained here than if he returned to Kongo; because, moreover, his journey to Rome, where he was to give his obedience to the pope, cannot take place at this time since the pope who was in power when his mission was planned has died;[31] and also due to the Great Wars raging in Italy, we have decided to have Dom Pedro stay here for now. We will take good care of him while he is here, and we will grant him every favor and courtesy as his status merits. We ask that the Mwene Kongo convey to you, António Vieira, his preference for Dom Pedro to either stay in Portugal or return to Kongo. We will gladly and willingly do what he most prefers.

We, the king, inform you, our treasurer or tax collector on the island of São Tomé, that we are dispatching António Vieira to the Kingdom of Kongo. If he leaves any slaves or goods with you upon his return, you and your notary should make note of this and credit the revenue you receive from him to yourself, and you will acknowledge what António Vieira has delivered to you, have your notary set it down in writing as well as what has been charged to António Vieira as revenue, and you should both sign it. You should keep all accounts in good order until we send instructions for handling the goods. If António Vieira leaves slaves with you, you should take very good care of them.

31. Julius II, who died on February 21, 1513. See n. 14 above.

You should not allow these slaves to perish due to your negligence. If by your fault, they die or escape, you will pay us back from your own funds. In addition, we order that you accord António Vieira, both upon his arrival there and upon his return, all the assistance and due diligence that you can, whether that involves the maintenance and repairs of his ship or anything else. You should aim to serve us well and not allow any negligence on your part to act against our interest. If you fail to do this, we will subject you to punishment as we see fit.

Dom Pedro of Kongo at the Caldas Hospital (1519)

SUMMARY—*Black Dom Pedro, the Mwene Kongo's nephew, was administered his last rites at the Caldas Hospital, passed away, and was buried*

On the 29th day of the month of March, 4 *reis* were spent on bread and 2 *reis* on sardines. In addition, 3 *reis* were spent on bread used to administer the last rites to the Black Dom Pedro. Afterward, he passed away in the hospital.

On the 22nd day of March, 20 *reis* were spent on bread and 10 *reis* on fish for the Blacks who came here for the alms offered by our lady the queen.

On the last day of the month of March, 8 *reis* were spent on bread and 10 *reis* on fish for Dom João, the nephew of the Mwene Kongo.

João de Coja spent 300 *reis*, which he gave to the vicar and chaplains for funerals and masses held for [. . .][32] and Dom Pedro, the nephew of the Mwene Kongo, all of whom passed away in this hospital.

At the end of the month of March, Dom João paid 18 *reis* to Pêro Mendes and 20 *reis* for the grave where Dom Pedro, the nephew of His Majesty the Mwene Kongo, was interred.

CITY OF LEIRIA PUBLIC LIBRARY—Caldas Hospital—*Book of Revenue and Expenses*

32. Several names are missing from the manuscript.

Dom António Mwene Soyo's Acknowledgment of Receipt of the Clothes Sent to the King of Kongo (December 1, 1520)

SUMMARY—*The clothes sent to His Majesty King of Kongo by His Majesty King of Portugal*

I, Dom António Mwene Soyo, certify that I have received from Bernardo Corso, the pilot of the ship *Conceição*, these three items of clothing for the king of Kongo:

1. a hemmed open hood of curled velvet
2. a tunic of the same fabric, hemmed in velvet
3. silk-lined sleeves.

In addition, he received:

4. an open, rounded silk cloak with a backstitched hem
5. a cape of curled fabric, hemmed in velvet
6. a trimmed hood, backstitched with silk thread
7. a black-trimmed tunic, all in silk
8. a gray damask jerkin, hemmed in velvet
9. a black jerkin of velveted satin
10. a scarlet-red jerkin of velveted satin
11. two pairs of trousers: one purple and one black
12. crotches for trousers
13. plus, a letter to the king
14. plus, a sealed crate loaded with muskets.

I, the pilot, certify that I received all the goods listed above, and I had the ship's notary, Fernão Vaz, draw up this acknowledgment of receipt, signed by me in the presence of the following witnesses:[33]

Mpinda, on the first day of December of the year 1520.

Fernão Vaz
Dom António Manuel Varela
Rodrigo Alves
Gaspar de Barros

33. The two lines that follow with the witnesses' signatures are illegible.

In the verso: Acknowledgment of receipt from Dom António Mwene Soyo of the clothes that His Majesty the King sent to the king of Kongo.

Gregório da Quadra in the Kingdom of Kongo (1520)

SUMMARY—*Dom Manuel sends Gregório da Quadra to Kongo to discover a route from this kingdom to Ethiopia*

After Gregório da Quadra left Lisbon, his ship sailed to the harbor of the Congo River. This river flows through a good portion of the Kingdom of Kongo and is one of the longest-known rivers in the entire world; it crosses many countries and is so wide at its estuary that you cannot see the opposite shore. After his arrival in this port, Gregório da Quadra journeyed to the court of His Majesty the King of Kongo, sixty miles inland, to deliver the letters he was bringing from His Majesty King Dom Manuel. This king was the first Christian king of Kongo, and I have written extensively about him in this Chronicle. In his own language, he was called Mvemba a Nzinga, which means Mvemba son of Nzinga. It is customary for the kings and lords of Kongo to take the surnames of their fathers and great-grandfathers and great-great-grandfathers on the father's side, which they see as a great honor.

Gregório da Quadra was very warmly received by His Majesty, but the king did not immediately respond on the affairs Gregório da Quadra was sent to discuss with him without first consulting his Portuguese advisors, who were always with him. He trusted them more than his own countrymen. Nevertheless, even though they were Portuguese, they showed little passion for their native king and counseled the king of Kongo not to allow Gregório da Quadra to attempt an inland expedition to Ethiopia[34] under any circumstances. They claimed that His Majesty King Dom Manuel was so eager to befriend the Abyssinian king that, if he discovered the route to Abyssinia, little by little, he would start taking over the Kingdom of Kongo as well as all the other kingdoms that lie between Kongo and Abyssinia and beyond. Swayed by this counsel, the king of Kongo not only refused to allow Gregório da Quadra to leave on his expedition but immediately ordered him to return to Portugal with the king's replies to His Majesty King Manuel's letters. By

34. See n. 9 above.

the time Gregório da Quadra arrived in Portugal, King Dom Manuel had died. Worn down by the travails of this world, Gregório da Quadra took his vows with the Franciscan Order of Friars Minor Capuchin, where he remained until he died a virtuous and Catholic Christian. I knew him to be a good Christian even before he joined this religious order because when His Majesty sent him on this voyage to Kongo, I was in touch with him for a few days. In our conversations, I found him to be a God-fearing man. A clear testament to his Christian virtue was the choice he made to live out his life entirely in the service of God, far from the travails of this world, of which he endured his share while he lived, as I heard him recount to me many times.

Damião de Góis, *Chronica*, Part IV, chapter 54.

Patent of Authorization to the Officers of São Tomé (December 27, 1525)

SUMMARY—*He sends nine Frenchmen to Portugal, including a priest, apprehended in a ship in the port of Soyo. They were neither assaulted nor mistreated.*

We, Dom Afonso, by the grace of God, king of Kongo, etc., inform the royal magistrate, the royal auditor, the judges, officers of justice, trading agent, and other officers of the king, our brother, stationed in the island of São Tomé, that we are sending in this Portuguese trading vessel nine Frenchmen seized from a French ship that arrived in the port of Soyo. Among them are the pilot and a priest. We request that they be taken to the lord king, our brother, accompanied by one of our servants who is carrying letters from us that describe the incident.

We have promised them that their lives are safe and reaffirmed this promise in writing to the king, and we now entrust them to you. On behalf of His Majesty the King, our brother, we advise you not to assault or mistreat these Frenchmen because we have pledged them our protection. You should allow them to board a ship without delay so they can travel directly to Portugal with our servant, whose only task is to introduce them. You should help our servant with anything he needs before he embarks. We thank you very much. If you comply with our request, we shall regard it as a service to our king and our brother.

Written in the City of Kongo, on the 27th day of December 1525 by Gonçalo Nunes, the king's private secretary.

Signed: His Majesty King Dom Afonso

Signed: Nunes

To the royal magistrate, royal auditor, justices, justice officers, officers of the king our brother. In the Island of São Tomé, about the nine Frenchmen he is sending.

In the verso: Presented on the first of April. The royal magistrate stated that this document should be perused in detail.

Letter from the King of Kongo to His Majesty the King of Portugal (1526?)

SUMMARY—*He requests the return from Rome of two of his nephews as ordained bishops—Since the kingdom's territory was too large for a single bishop, it was essential for them to come to Kongo to preach and ordain native-born priests*

Your Highness will do us a great favor and a service to God if you permit our two nephews to travel from Rome after being ordained as bishops. As I have told Your Highness on many occasions, this kingdom of ours is quite large, inhabited by many peoples and divided into vast districts ruled by powerful lords. It is not possible for a single prelate to serve the entire kingdom. Because they are native-born and very close relatives of ours, these two bishops will have the trust of everyone in the lands where they preach the faith of Jesus Christ and teach the Christian religion for the service of God. They will find much success and become worthy of being remembered for increasing our holy Catholic faith. They will be able to pronounce rulings and ordain our native-born priests.

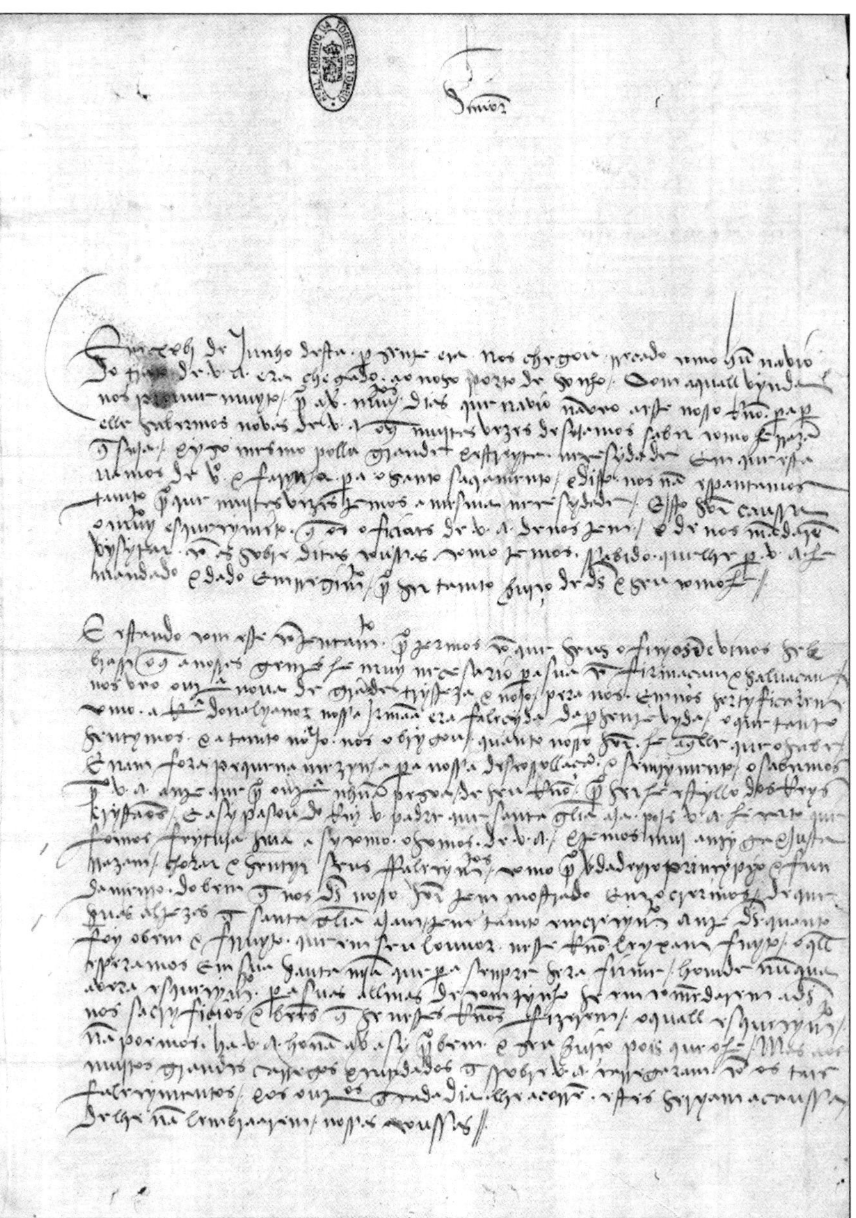

First page of Afonso's undated letter of 1526.

Receipt from the King of Kongo to Manuel Vaz (January 18, 1526)

SUMMARY—*He acknowledges receiving gifts sent to him in a chest by the king of Portugal*

We, Dom Afonso, by the grace of God, king of Kongo, etc., inform you, Manuel Vaz, knight in the royal house of our brother, His Majesty the King of Portugal, and royal trading agent in the island of São Tomé, that we received from Rodrigo Alves the three outfits sent to us from Portugal by the king, which you had Manuel Vaz deliver to us: a black hood of fine fabric from Lille, backstitched with silk thread; an open cloak of hemmed Courtray fabric, trimmed with black velvet; another open cloak of hemmed Courtray fabric, backstitched with silk thread; a tunic of hemmed Courtray fabric, backstitched with velvet, with split sleeves lined with taffeta; another tunic of hemmed Courtray fabric, backstitched with black velvet; another tunic of very fine black fabric with bands of taffeta; a gray damask jerkin, backstitched and trimmed with velvet of the same dark color; a jerkin of black silk velvet; another jerkin of scarlet-red silk velvet; a pair of trousers of purple fabric; another pair of black woolen trousers.[35] These outfits were packed inside a chest along with two pieces of hemp. We are sending you this signed receipt to certify that we have received these items.

Written by Gonçalo Nunes in the City of Kongo, on the 18th of January 1526.

Signed: His Majesty Dom Afonso

Signed: Nunes

Acknowledgment of receipt of three outfits that the trading agent Manuel Vaz sent to His Royal Lordship with Rodrigo Alves, who delivered them.

35. The predominance of the color black in Afonso's imported clothes suggests that these are mourning clothes. It is possible that Afonso was grieving for his recently deceased wife.

Letter from António Afonso to António Carneiro (April 3, 1526)

SUMMARY—*He affirms that the king of Kongo feels vexed because he has no friars, no carpenters, no masons, and no materials for the sacred rites—He gives recommendations for several of the Portuguese residing there*

Sire:

I write you this letter with the deference and obedience I will always give Your Lordship for as long as I live. I intend to give you a necessary account of my mission. Sire, I arrived in the Kingdom of Kongo, where I am now, from the island of São Tomé on a ship under António Pires's command. I came, Sire, to buy slaves and ship them to São Tomé, where they will pay for their sustenance with their labor. As I mentioned to Your Lordship, the ship sailed to the island with the slaves, and I stayed in Kongo to prepare the shipments and make arrangements for when the ship returns. The other shipment was not as well handled as the king of Kongo would have liked. It did not go well because His Royal Highness and his entire council were upset that they didn't have what they needed to perform the sacred rites, that is, priests, as well as carpenters and masons, to build new churches and finish those under construction. The pilot also failed to wait a while longer before he departed. Since the king was taken by surprise by the ship's quick departure, he had no time to collect the goods that he wished to send to Portugal as gifts. These goods are now ready and await the ship's return. As Your Lordship will see below, the king is always gracious toward you, and willing to send you well-provisioned ships from his kingdoms. He will always provide for your men who come to visit him, as he has so liberally provided for me, because I am a servant of Your Lordship. As soon as the ship arrived, the king abundantly supplied it with supplies of food and meat and many other things that were greatly needed.

I tell you, Sire: just as His Royal Highness has shown a generous disposition toward Your Lordship and those servants of yours who come to his kingdoms, so should Your Lordship show the same good disposition in dealing with his affairs in Portugal as he requests Your Lordship to do in the letters he writes you. Indeed, he expects you to respond as you would if he were in your presence. This, my lord, is what I told him and the honorable and virtuous people in this kingdom who desire to serve Your Lordship and do serve you by spending their own treasure. One of these virtuous people, Sire, is Manuel Varela, the bearer of this letter, who handled the successful shipment and ensured that his trading agents would not be remiss in anything. You would do me a great favor, Sire, were you to assist and reward him with all that he is entitled to and provide him with everything His Majesty the King of Kongo requests. He greatly deserves it, Sire. In addition, Sire, António Simões, a nobleman who is here, has proven steadfast in attending to Your Lordship's affairs and has greatly favored me because I'm your servant. He is eager to meet you personally, so he may serve you better than he is able to do here. Believe me, Your Lordship, for what I tell you is the whole truth. I will say no more, Sire, other than to plead with Your Lordship not to forget His Royal Highness the King of Kongo because by assisting him, you are also doing a great service to God.

Written on the third day of April, in the year 1526.

Your Lordship's servant

Signed: António Afonso

TO: the most esteemed Lord António Carneiro, nobleman of the house of His Majesty our King and royal secretary, my lord

Letter from the King of Kongo to King João III (March 18, 1526)

SUMMARY—*He recalls how often he had asked King Dom Manuel to send missionaries—He asks [Dom João III] to send fifty priests and describes how they should be distributed throughout the kingdom. He refers to the request of [his son], the bishop Dom Henrique, to travel to the Kingdom of Kongo on a religious mission—He asks for six priests from the Order of Saint Elói [Eligius] to accompany the bishop Dom Henrique*

Sire,

We, Dom Afonso, by the grace of God, king of Kongo, lord of the Ambundus and the conquered territory of Mpanzu a Lumbu,[36] etc., kiss Your Highness's royal hands with all the respect you deserve. We remind Your Highness that it must have been about forty years ago that our Lord, in his mercy and compassion, showed us the light, saving us from the darkness we were living in. Our Lord granted us

36. See n. 7 above.

this blessing so that his name and faith would be praised in this land of Ethiopia.[37] We hope that this will always be so, for he was served when he showed us the righteous and holy path that leads us to the salvation of our souls. May he bless Your Highness with a long life and increase your royal estate so that you may continue to support this kingdom by sending us the balm needed for our own salvation and the salvation of this kingdom and its peoples, who live in the hope that they will find solace through Your Highness's intervention and will be granted what they need so much.

First, as Your Highness knows, we wrote His Majesty your father, may he rest in holy glory, several times about our need for a large number of priests to travel throughout the great expanse of our kingdom and dominions and cleanse them of the scourge of idolatry that plagues them. Since our land is vast, we cannot cleanse it on our own. We therefore require many priests to be sent throughout our kingdom and dominions to serve our Lord and increase our holy Catholic faith. We would find solace in seeing what we desire so much come to pass because we know the great need our kingdom is experiencing. We see the many souls that are becoming lost but could still be saved and become virtuous in the eyes of our Lord with Your Highness's intervention. We trust that Your Highness will grant this request in full because it is the first we have sent you since you became king. In the name of the death and passion that our Lord suffered for all sinners, we implore Your Highness to send us fifty priests, even though we need many more. Nonetheless, we are not requesting any more [clerics] so as not to trouble Your Highness excessively. We will send them throughout our kingdom and dominions, assigning them to the places where they are most needed and [their efforts] can bear the most fruit. Sire, to give you a sense of how we want to distribute these priests, we will name here some of the dominions within this kingdom. We will focus on the major ones because to name them all would make for long and tedious reading for Your Highness:

1. There is a dominion called Nsundi, where we appointed as lord one of our sons, who is called Francisco. It is a very large territory where we shall station a vicar and six priests, who will be supplied with everything they need.
2. Another dominion is called Mbamba, where we appointed as lord another son of ours called Dom Henrique. This is a vast and populous land, which requires a vicar and six priests. They will be well supplied with all they need and will keep very busy because the territory is large and densely populated.

37. See n. 9 above.

3. There is another dominion called Mbata, which has even more people and needs at least eight priests as well as a vicar. We have appointed as lord of this dominion one of the principal nobles of our kingdom called Dom Jorge, whom we love greatly for his good character.
4. Another dominion is called Wembo, where we appointed as lord one of our brothers called Dom Pedro. It is a vast and populous territory that requires a vicar and six priests.
5. Another dominion is named Mpangu, which we have donated to the bishop and our beloved son so he can cover his expenses. It is a large and bountiful land that needs a vicar and six priests.

We will not list any more of our dominions for Your Highness to keep our letter brief. Sire, we will therefore distribute these priests throughout our kingdom in the way [we describe above]. Others will travel to the places where they are most needed, chastise the people with holy words, and bring them the true knowledge [of God]. Your Highness can surely imagine how much these rustic, simple people, who know only how to live and die, are in need [of guidance]. In order to make them understand the truth of our faith, they must be continuously taught until they come to truly know the path to salvation. In this way, Sire, the priests' efforts will bear fruit and result in the salvation of many souls who are now becoming lost for lack of priests and linger in this [sinful] state. We inform Your Highness of this so you can [ensure] their salvation through holy baptism and the doctrine of our holy faith. We implore you for the love of our Lord to remember us and this kingdom, which awaits the mercy of our Lord and the balms—that is, the many priests that this kingdom so dearly needs for its salvation—that will soothe our wounds. And when these many souls are saved, they will pray to our Lord for Your Highness because they were saved thanks to your intervention. By the wounds of our Lord, we thus implore you, Sire, not to forsake us, but instead send more people to visit us than His Majesty your father did, because now that we are in the last quarter of our life and do not know when God will take us back to him, we require your visits more than ever. It would bring us great joy in our final days if Your Highness sent us these priests so that we would be able to leave this kingdom and dominions in peace, devoted to the love and service of our Lord. For this reason, Sire, you should send us many priests, for they are the balm to the open wounds afflicting the people of this kingdom and [will ensure] that Satan, our enemy, will have no power whatsoever over their souls. The remedy against this lies in the hands of Your Highness, and we hope that the name of Jesus Christ and the example of his death and passion will protect us and lead us to salvation.

Second, our son, the bishop, has asked us several times to allow him to visit this kingdom accompanied by the small group of four clerics he keeps with him. This group is so small that it cannot even officiate a mass, much less serve so vast a kingdom. We do not want to give him permission to leave the capital because this kingdom is so large that if he wanted to travel its full extent, he would need several priests to accompany and assist him. Moreover, we fear that if he traveled far from us, he would be poisoned to death, which would cause us great pain and sorrow. We would not survive his death because we love him deeply, and he is a source of great solace to us and the entire kingdom. This is why we have not allowed him to travel and have forced him to remain here—despite the fact that he dearly wishes to go and has requested to do so several times. It is for this reason that he has not yet done it. Therefore, Sire, we implore Your Highness to come to our aid and give us the means to grant our son's request and grant the other requests listed in this letter.

Third, we implore Your Highness to grant permission for six clerics from the order of Saint Eligius[38] to come here to keep our son the bishop company. He was raised among them, and it would be a great solace to him to be with them. Three companions from the same order traveled with him, and by the time this letter was written, one had returned to Portugal, and the other two will soon go back to Portugal as well. If Your Highness considers what these priests and all the others who travel to our kingdom take back with them, you will see that we do not reward them poorly for their services. We will continue to do this [e.g., reward them handsomely] for as long as God grants us life.

May our Lord increase your life and royal estate and keep you in his holy service. Amen.

Written by the royal scribe João Teixeira in the City of Kongo, on the 18th of March 1526.

Signed: His Majesty King Dom Afonso

38. See n. 4 above.

Letter from the King of Kongo to King João III (July 6, 1526)

SUMMARY—*He gives notice of the arrival of a Portuguese ship in the port of Soyo—He offers his condolences for the death of Queen Leonor—He requests priests, wine, and flour to celebrate mass—He implores the king not to send any more merchants to Kongo*

Sire:

On June 26th of this year, we received word that one of Your Highness's trading ships had arrived in the port of Soyo. The arrival of this ship pleased us greatly because it had been several days since a ship had arrived in our kingdom and because it brought us news of Your Highness. For understandable reasons, we have been longing to hear from you for a long time. We also find ourselves in dire need of wine and flour for the blessed Sacrament. This is no surprise to us since we have found ourselves in similar need so many times. The cause for this, Sire, is the neglect Your Highness's officers show toward us and their failure to bring us these items when they visit us, as we understand Your Highness has commanded them to do in your royal instructions since it is of such great service both to Your Highness and to God.

While we were rejoicing at the prospect of having what we needed to celebrate the divine rites, which our people urgently need for their salvation, we received news that caused us great sorrow. We learned that the queen Lady Leonor, our sister, had passed away.[39] Only our Lord knows the depth of the grief we felt for her. It was only a meager balm to our anguish that Your Highness, following the practice of Christian kings, notified us directly rather than have someone else from your kingdom do it.

That is also how your father, the king, may he rest in holy glory, acted. Surely, Your Highness, we are your father's creation, as we are Your Highness's as well. We therefore have good reason to weep and grieve for the deaths of your father and the queen. Their Royal Highnesses, may they rest in holy glory, were the true beginning of the good that our Lord God has granted us for believing in him. God will exalt them for the good works they have done and the fruit they have sown in this kingdom for his praise. We hope that, with God's mercy, their work here will remain forever secure and that it will not be neglected so their souls can

39. King João II's widow who died on November 17, 1525. See n. 18 above.

continue to be praised to God for the good works they have done in this kingdom. We do not believe you neglect us because Your Highness does not see the benefit of serving God because it is to God's benefit. We believe that it is due to the many burdens and cares that have befallen Your Highness with these deaths in your family and those you confront each day. These are the reasons why Your Highness may not address our concerns.

Sire, Your Highness knows that our kingdom is losing its way, and we must provide the solution that this situation calls for. The cause of our troubles is the excessive permissiveness with which your trading agents and officials allow the men who come to this kingdom to establish shops and sell merchandise. These men engage in practices that we strictly forbid, and they scatter throughout our kingdom and dominions in such large numbers that many of our vassals, who had pledged obedience to us, have now renounced their obedience because they have a greater abundance of goods available to them than we do. Previously, they had been satisfied with the goods we provided them, and they remained subject to our laws and their vassalage to us. This disrupts both God's service and the security and peace of our state and our kingdoms.

However, we do not consider this harm as terrible as what we suffer each day when these traders carry away our native-born countrymen and the children of our nobles and vassals as well as relatives of ours. This continues because thieves and unscrupulous men, driven by their greed for goods from your kingdom, snatch them and sell them to these traders. Sire, this corruption and depravity has reached such a level that our homeland is becoming completely depopulated. Your Highness should not tolerate this situation, nor is it to your benefit. In order to avoid it, we need only priests and a few people to teach in our kingdoms' schools. We have even less need of additional goods, except for wine and flour for the blessed Sacrament, and we request Your Highness's help in this matter. Please instruct your trading agents to send neither traders nor trading goods here because we do not wish to carry out trade and export slaves. Once again, we beg Your Highness to agree to this request. Otherwise, we will not be able to relieve this unmistakable suffering. May our Lord protect and hold Your Highness in his mercy and guide you to do his holy service. I kiss Your Highness's hands many times over.

From the City of Kongo, written on the 6th day of July, in the year 1526 by João Teixeira

Signed: His Majesty King Dom Afonso

TO: The most powerful and excellent Prince Dom João, our brother

FROM: His Majesty the Mwene Kongo

Letter from the King of Kongo to King João III (August 25, 1526)

SUMMARY—*He acknowledges receipt of two letters concerning the Frenchmen who traveled to Soyo—There was a priest among the Frenchmen who had been detained—He complains about the Portuguese pilots—As a remedy for the ills afflicting the kingdom, he requests several priests to be sent there—He demands three or four good grammar instructors, five or six masons, and ten carpenters to finish construction on the churches, especially the Church of Our Lady of Victory*

Sire:

We have been given two letters from Your Highness that arrived in two of your trading vessels. Both addressed the same subject: the Frenchmen who arrived in the port of Soyo in this kingdom. We have provided Your Highness with extensive information about them in previous letters, and we will do so here once again. As soon as we were notified of their arrival at the port of Soyo, we immediately sent down Manuel Pacheco, a servant of Your Highness's, who was serving as our royal magistrate and had arrived in Afonso de Torres's ship. We ordered one of your trading ships, with all your men and ours, to do their utmost to seize the French vessel. But the French ship was very well equipped with firearms and artillery, and the crew was warned of our attack by the people they had on land, so we were not able to seize it. Seeing that we were setting traps to harm them, they set sail after seizing a dugout with some of our people who had been spying on them. We seized the Frenchmen who remained on land, along with their rowboat, through deception: we showed them large quantities of ivory, redwood, and hoof-shaped ingots [*manilhas*] and told them it was all for them. These facts are well known, and your countrymen who were present will confirm what I've written unless they wish to hide the truth.

Several of these Frenchmen who remained on land have died, Sire, and only twelve survive. We have sent them down several times to be handed over to the pilots of Your Highness's trading vessels. The majority of these pilots would not take them on board because they were loading up slaves, saying that they had come to acquire slaves, not Frenchmen. Others refused to wait for the Frenchmen or for our message and departed with neither. This is why the Frenchmen have remained in our kingdom until now. They have been given only the privileges that evildoers who harm Your Highness deserve, as your countrymen have witnessed with their own eyes.

As soon as we read Your Highness's letters and learned of your wishes, we ordered the Frenchmen to be put in prison. They were taken down in irons to be handed over to the pilot and taken to Portugal. They were placed under the charge of a servant of ours on the island of Continao[40] so he could hand them over to Your Highness. We had made these arrangements several days in advance, so they could have been taken on board if the pilots had allowed them to. In total, there were ten prisoners, one of whom claims to be a priest who celebrates mass. Two remain in this kingdom: One is a carpenter, whom we cannot spare because we have no one else in this kingdom who can build a roof over our churches. The other, who is said to be a pilot, remained because he is well-versed in grammar and can open a school to teach our relatives who already know a little Latin so they do not lose what they have learned. If Your Highness has better use for these two than the good services for which we have kept them, we will release them immediately.

We have not written Your Highness more often about the service of God and the things we need to sustain his holy faith because the Portuguese pilots have no respect for our person and our requests. Whenever we plead with them not to depart without a message or shipment from us, they leave as soon as they have the slaves they want. They never wait to load our own slaves and often leave them on land.

We often go five or six months without celebrating mass or the Sacrament because that is what Your Highness's officers wish. This is a poor way of serving God, and it greatly distresses our people. They whisper that Your Highness has forgotten about us and about the Christian spirit that His Royal Majesty, your father, may he rest in holy glory, had kept up for so many years in this kingdom by sending us missions, provisions, and aid through great effort and perseverance on his part, and to our great solace. All this effort has been cast in doubt by the neglect Your Highness appears to have shown us and the lack of regard the pilots have displayed by leaving without taking our messages, claiming that they have been ordered to do this by Your Highness's officers. Whenever we send down our letters, they have already departed, and then they claim that they informed us of their departure and that we did not wish to send you anything. This is how they cover up their faults and cause Your Highness to hate and completely forget about us. We implore Your Highness to pay no attention to slanderers, nor to people whose only concern is to conduct trade, sell their ill-gotten goods, and harm and corrupt our kingdom and Christianity with the unregulated trade they have been carrying on for so many years in this region. Your predecessors, Christian

40. The location of this island is unclear. It may have been one of the large islands near the debouchure of the Congo River.

and Catholic kings and princes just as Your Highness is, have paid a great cost and their precious treasure in order to toil, in God's service, to introduce to new peoples the holy Catholic faith and preserve it, the faith that we have all pledged to uphold. It is hardly possible to undertake this work with so much trading and such depravity. These practices have a powerful influence on the simple-minded and ignorant people who abandon their belief in God to follow them instead. This would not happen if the cause of this situation were removed. This is how the devil lays his snare and leads both parties to damnation. Here, Sire, greed attains colossal dimensions; our countrymen go so far as to seize our own Christian relatives and sell them as slaves. This degradation has grown so much that we do not have the strength to fix it, short of executing our people in great numbers. In this way, the just will suffer with the unjust.

None of this would continue, Sire, if you were to support us as His Royal Majesty, your father, did with spiritual remedies by sending us many more priests, who are direly needed to perform holy rites and confessions and to preach and teach Christian doctrine. They could divide themselves into groups of two and travel throughout our kingdom, which is very large and populated by a great many peoples. In this way, they would spread the word of God to the hearts of the people so that even if they were offered some diabolic poison, the virtue of this balm would heal and save them from damnation.

Sire, you should also stop sending merchants who ply their evil trade, which prevents the salvation of souls and harms the works of honest labor. The same goes for the mulatto [biracial] seamen go-betweens[41] from the Cacheu region [in Guinea-Bissau] and the Beninese, who are spreading through our kingdom and do no service to God. Instead, they pass on their customs, which are vile and sinful. Yet we are unable to banish them from our kingdoms.

In addition, Sire, we are in dire need of three or four good grammar instructors so that our people who have begun learning Portuguese can become proficient in the language. We have several of our countrymen and yours here who know how to teach reading and writing. However, for the most part, these men don't know how to explain the ways of the faith or settle theological doubts, which is very necessary.

41. The original Portuguese term that I have translated as "seaman go-between" is *grumete*. Its literal meaning is "cabin boy" or "apprentice seaman." Many of these mariners came from Senegambia and the Upper Guinea Coast (i.e., Guinea-Bissau) and were hired by Portuguese and Luso-African traders. They served an essential function not only as guides, helping these merchants navigate rivers and sail along the West African coast, but also as traders themselves or go-betweens. See José da Silva Horta, "Evidence for a Luso-African Identity in 'Portuguese' Account on 'Guinea of Cape Verde' (Sixteenth-Seventeenth Centuries)," *History in Africa* 27 (2000): 104–5.

In addition, Sire, we need five or six masons and carpenters to finish the churches that are under construction in the service and praise of our Lord God, especially a church called Our Lady of Victory, which we started building in a very thick forest where kings were formerly buried, in keeping with their ancient idolatry. We cleared and cut down this forest, which was very difficult, both because of the roughness of the terrain and because we weren't sure if the kingdom's notables would be willing to allow it. Yet they were so diligent that they chopped down the thick trees with their own hands and carried the stones for the church on their backs. This seemed to happen by divine grace. We therefore give much praise to the Lord God for the miracle of making their hearts willingly comply with our purpose. We have no need for lime makers because we have many countrymen who know how to make lime in our kingdom.

We plead with Your Highness, for the love of Jesus Christ, to agree to help and support us in all that we mention here, and which we have requested so many times, because it is all in the service of God as well as your own. It all rests on your conscience because we do not have the strength to do any more. We have strived to accomplish everything we are able to without additional assistance. We beg for you to solve these problems that we cannot remedy without the help and favor of Your Highness; we plead for your aid since it is your duty. It is not the place of the king of Castille or France, and we will not request any other Christian king to do it because of the high respect we have for you. Such consideration is not expected of these kings because they have little stake in this kingdom. This kingdom is as loyal and willing to serve you as Portugal, the one that has by right been bequeathed to you. Second, there is no place for ingratitude in our heart because we will always remember the many spiritual and material gifts we have received. It would be thoughtless of us not to value the injuries that the Kingdom of Portugal, our own and true mother, does to us more than the feigned and counterfeit blandishments offered by a deceitful stepmother, even if we all hold the same law and faith in common. I will say no more about this matter because Your Highness knows how we feel about you and that our kingdom and dominions will always be committed to serving you. We implore Your Highness to respond to this letter with real actions. Please answer the other letters that Manuel Varela is carrying with him, which address this matter as well as others that are for the true service of God. This will relieve your conscience. May our Lord, in his holy mercy and compassion, always hold Your Highness in his protection. May he grant you a long life, increase your royal estate, and keep it in his blessed service.

From the City of Kongo, written on the 25th day of August 1526 by João Teixeira.

Signed: His Majesty King Dom Afonso

TO: The most excellent and powerful king and lord, His Majesty the King of Portugal

FROM: His Majesty the Mwene Kongo

> *[António Brásio, the editor of the Portuguese edition of Afonso's correspondence, adds the following sixteenth-century note, which he found in the Torre do Tombo National Archives and appears to summarize the above letter and the document that follows.]*

Memorandum regarding the affairs of His Majesty the King of Kongo:

1. Asks Your Highness to answer his letters.
2. Clerics, apothecaries, masons, and carpenters.
3. The papal bull that granted his marriage to his first wife, given that the letter mentions a remote ancestor.
4. Through this man, His Majesty requests burlap, pitch, and a caulker to build two brigs to be used to travel upriver and declares that he will pay for all the master craftsmen's wages.
5. That Your Highness should remember to send Dom Afonso articles to celebrate mass with.
6. That Your Highness should send one of your vessels in which he can load his merchandise, as he mentions in his letter.
7. That Your Highness should grant him the favor of naming his son bishop of Kongo.
8. Luís Eanes, who is bringing these letters from His Majesty the King of Kongo, claims that ten years ago, twenty-one slaves that belonged to him were seized in the name of Duarte Belo and Pedro Álvares Gentil, who alleged that His Majesty the King of Kongo owed them some goods. Eanes asks Your Highness to order his slaves to be released and the security deposit he made to be reimbursed as well. He declares that Belo and Gentil should demand payment from His Majesty the King of Kongo, if he indeed owes them anything since the slaves are his [Eanes's], and because they were his property, he had given half of them as payment to the two ship operators. He requests Your Highness to grant him justice in this matter.
9. Since His Majesty the King of Kongo often sends Luís Eanes and Pero Fernandes to the island of São Tomé with his merchandise, and since they sometimes bring back goods of their own, they further ask Your Highness to order that his ships stop requiring half of their merchandise as payment, and charge them less than that, given that they serve Your Highness and the

king of Kongo. They will be grateful to Your Highness for addressing this matter.

10. They ask Your Highness to please give them clothes.
11. They request Your Highness to send them back to Kongo early before winter comes.

In the verso: matters concerning the Blacks who arrived from Kongo.

Letter from the King of Kongo to King Dom João III (August 25, 1526)

SUMMARY—*The bishop Dom Henrique's illness—He requests that Dom Afonso be ordained in order to become bishop of Kongo—Dom Afonso I intends to send ivory to pay for expenses incurred by the Kongo students in Portugal*

Sire:

Since a few matters slipped our mind, we are writing again to add them here because they are for the service of God.

Your Highness knows that our son, the bishop, has constantly been ill since he arrived in this kingdom. Without him, we have no other prominent mainstay here to help us sustain the holy Christianity that God in his mercy has bestowed upon us. He is the only torch before our eyes. We would fall into darkness if it were put out. May God not permit this to happen in our lifetime. We implore Your Highness to establish a bishop in this kingdom. He very much deserves this, both because he is our son and because of the reasons that we describe in a letter we sent with Manuel Varela.

We thus implore you, for your benefit and service, to help us appoint Dom Afonso, a nephew of ours who has been studying in Portugal for many years, as bishop to serve God.[42] We would like him to be ordained as a cleric to reap the fruit of his knowledge by serving God in these kingdoms. Once he arrives here, we will do our utmost to ensure that he is nominated bishop, if Your Highness agrees that this would be in your service and God's. Nobody wishes to serve Your

42. Dom Afonso, King Afonso I's nephew and namesake, never returned to the Kingdom of Kongo. He went on to become a professor of Latin studies in Lisbon.

Highness, nor desires your honor and salvation more fervently than we do. If Your Highness sends Dom Afonso to us, we believe that he will perform well since he has been well-schooled and conducts himself well. For this, we give many thanks and much praise to our Lord God. All our relatives that His Majesty, your father, ordered António Vieira to take to Portugal to receive the same instruction have given us nothing but sorrow since they have died. Only this one has remained for our solace, and receiving news about him has given us further consolation.

Note: Sire, each day we get large quantities of ivory, which we wish to send in your ships to your kingdoms so that it can be used to cover the expenses that Your Highness has incurred in conducting our affairs. Although we keep sending ivory down to the port of Soyo, your pilots keep refusing to load it. As a result, it is as good as lost. We implore Your Highness to order it to be loaded in your ships because it is all in the service of God and Your Highness. May God grant Your Highness a long life in his holy service.

Written in the City of Kongo, on the 25th day of August 1526, by Gonçalo Eanes.

TO: The most excellent and powerful king and lord, His Majesty the king of Portugal, etc.

FROM: The Mwene Kongo

Letter from Baltasar de Castro to King Dom João III (October 15, 1526)

SUMMARY—*He writes that the king of Kongo freed him from captivity at the hands of King Ngola—He expresses his desire to explore all territories up the Congo River*

Sire,

I, Baltasar de Castro, a former valet of His Majesty, your father, may he rest in holy glory, inform Your Highness that the king of Kongo freed me from captivity at the hands of the Ngola. I arrived at this city on the last day of the month of September 1526, and His Majesty gave me clothes because I was naked when I arrived. I learned here that Your Highness had seized our goods. If this is so, it was a result of false information because I served His Majesty, your father, truly and faithfully in all that he ordered me to do. I expected to be amply rewarded for my services because I deserved and still deserve it, and I will make certain that this happens.

The Ngola killed the ambassador who was sent to Your Highness. In due time, Your Highness will learn how and why this happened. The reason I'm being detained in Kongo is that His Majesty the King of Kongo sent an emissary to get the Ngola to release me along with a cleric to convert the Ngola to Christianity. The Ngola did convert, but then certain things happened that led him to abandon Christianity, which Your Highness will learn soon. This emissary that the king of Kongo sent brought ruin to everything. He returned to Kongo, leaving me in captivity, so I wrote to His Majesty the King of Kongo, telling him what was happening and telling him to hold this man until I arrived. And His Majesty did so. I managed to get away, and when I arrived in this city, I learned that this man had defamed me as a nonbeliever[43] and claimed that he had seen mountains of silver, precious stones, and other things in the lands of the Ngola. After spending six years in the Ngola's lands, I never saw any of these things. I wrote down what I learned of the Ngola's country and its resources and sent my report with Manuel Pacheco when he left me there. These and other matters will now need to be investigated in Portugal, and I have initiated legal proceedings so that such an inquiry may be started. When this process is completed, and everything has been cleared up, I believe His Majesty the King of Kongo will allow me to leave to inform Your Highness of the truth about all these matters.

I believe the king of Kongo wants to explore the territory that lies farther up the Congo River. He is certain that it's possible to navigate upriver. His Majesty has written Your Highness with additional details about an expedition. I request that Your Highness write His Majesty the King of Kongo and ask him to put me in charge of this exploration. As Your Highness will see, if it falls into my hands, I believe I will finally be able to ascertain whether this river is navigable after being so many years in the dark about it. By granting me this request, Your Highness would do me a great favor.

The Ngola complains a lot about the baron and Dom Pedro de Castro. When he feels so inclined, he also says of . . .[44]

Written on the 15th of October of 1526. May our Lord increase Your Highness's royal estate.

Signed: Baltasar de Castro

TO: His Majesty our Lord the King

FROM: Sir Baltasar de Castro, from Kongo, 1526

---

43. *Mouro* in the original, literally "Moor" or Muslim.

44. The name and the rest of the sentence are missing.

Letter from the King of Kongo to King Dom João III (October 18, 1526)

SUMMARY—*He asks for physicians, surgeons, and apothecaries with effective medicines—He establishes regulations for the slave trade in the kingdom to prevent the sale of free men*

Sire:

Your Highness has favored us by writing that we may request by letter anything we need, and you will send it. After God, the peace and well-being of our kingdoms depend on our own longevity. Yet, because of our old age, we continually suffer many illnesses that debilitate us to such an extent that they have brought us to the verge of death. Our children, relatives, and countrymen also suffer from these illnesses due to the lack of physicians and surgeons with the knowledge to administer true remedies to these ailments and the lack of medicines and potions to treat them more effectively. Because of this, many of those who have already learned the ways of our Lord Jesus Christ have perished. The rest of the people, for the most part, treat themselves with herbs and twigs and other ancient methods, and if they survive, they place their whole faith in these plants and ceremonies. If they die, they consider themselves saved, which is of little service to God.

This great tragedy should be prevented. It would be wrong not to help because, after God, all the good we possess, as well as the medicine to heal us, have come from Your Highness. We beg Your Highness to grace us with the favor of sending us two physicians, two apothecaries, and a surgeon with their medicines and tools because we are in dire need of every single one of them. We will treat them well and favor them so that their long journey to travel to us will be rewarded. We implore Your Highness to grant us our request because, in addition to helping us, it is very much in the service of God.

In addition, Sire, our kingdom faces another obstacle, which is of very little service to God. Many of our countrymen capture and sell many of our free people to satisfy their immense greed for the goods that your subjects bring from your kingdom. They often abduct noblemen and their children as well as relatives of ours and sell them to the white men in our kingdoms. As soon as the white men buy these captives, they brand them with hot irons, and our guards find them while they are waiting to be shipped out. The white men claim they purchased them but cannot say from whom. We must do justice by those who were free persons and restore their freedom, for that's what they cry out for.

In order to put a stop to this great scourge, we decreed by law that every white man staying in our kingdoms who purchases slaves by any means must first notify three noble officials from our royal court whom we trust: Dom Pedro Mwene Mpunzu; Dom Manuel Mwene Saba, our royal magistrate; and Gonçalo Pires, our chief vessel operator. They will determine whether these slaves are indeed captives or free persons. Therefore, there will be no doubt about whether these slaves should be traded, and they may be taken away by ship. If the slaves are not captives, the traders will forfeit them. We grant the favor of continuing the slave trade to Your Highness because of your stake in this trade and because you earn a lot of profit from the slaves shipped from our kingdom. Otherwise, for the above-mentioned reasons, we would not authorize it. We are informing Your Highness of all this so that you know the truth when you are told lies that persuade you from giving us the care that we need for the service of God. We would be grateful to hear from you about this by letter.

Sire, we profusely kiss Your Highness's hands.

In the City of Kongo, written by João Teixeira on the 18th day of October of the year 1426.

Signed: His Majesty King Dom Afonso

TO: Our brother, the most high and powerful prince and king of Portugal

FROM: His Majesty the Mwene Kongo

Letter from Dom João III to the King of Kongo (End of 1529)

SUMMARY—*He establishes the regulations for the clergy and craftsmen—Plans to send Bishop Henrique to Rome—Slavery—Royal succession—Economic organization—Relations with Angola—Organization of schools—Letters to lords and noblemen of Kongo—Regulations concerning the vicar*

Noble and powerful king of Kongo:

I have read the letters[45] you sent with your servant Luís Eanes. Regarding the Frenchmen, I know only too well that it was my countrymen's fault that they

45. The two letters above, dated August 25, 1526.

were not seized and that you earnestly wished to capture them. The two you have kept should remain with you since you justly captured them, and you need them so much. I will release the ones you sent to me and allow them to travel to their homeland as a token of my deep affection for you. You shouldn't regard these men as Frenchmen or Christians, for they are thieves, and when the king of France gets a hold of them, they will be harshly punished. You can therefore release the two you have kept when you grow tired of them or have them write home and ask for goods to ransom themselves since, by right, they are your captives.

I was very sorry to read what you told me about the priests and the ongoing animosity between you and them. As your son the bishop can tell you, when His Majesty and my lord Manuel I had to send clerics to your kingdom, he selected from the best. According to what I'm told, the ones you mention were presented as such. At this point, as you reach old age, I want to do my utmost to put your mind at rest concerning this matter because it is what you strive the hardest to achieve in this world. This is what I will do. I will appoint the chaplains from my own royal chapel to serve you. Just as their parents were servants of His Majesty my lord and father, may he rest in holy glory, so are they mine. If they do what they should, I will reward them when they return to me, and if they do the opposite, I will punish them. The other priests who were sent before had nothing to fear for their excesses. I believe that if the measures I propose below are followed, our Lord will be served, and both you and I will be happy.

1. This is how I believe we should proceed: My chaplains will travel with their vicar, and you will give them joint lodgings and board. The favors you grant them will also be shared among all of them. That is, according to the royal instructions they will be given here, they and the vicar will agree to divide your gifts and favors, as well as tithes, alms, and mass offerings, among themselves like brothers. It will please me very much if you avoid giving anything to any of them individually, instead only giving them shared gifts, and if you provide well for them, especially food. I know they will not go without good favors since you have always granted them.

I request therefore that you allow these priests to purchase slaves securely if they have collected enough money and wish to do so. You should allow any white man they request a contract with to assist them with these purchases. Likewise, you should provide them with enough servants of yours to carry their goods safely.

This is how you should act if you need anything from a particular priest: You will not ask the specific priest but only the vicar, who will send you the priest you need to perform the specific task you require from him, even if you order him to leave the city during Lent. You will follow this same process for everything pertaining to the chaplains. If you have draft animals available and they ask for them, you should let them have them because they are men who aren't used to moving on foot.

And this is how you should deal with the craftsmen: They will have a master craftsman whose orders the others will obey. When giving out favors and food, you will proceed in the same manner as I suggest with the priests. Once again, I recommend that you not give anything to any single individual but to all of them together to avoid generating resentment. If they all stay together, they will stay happy and remain in your good graces and service.

As for the physicians and apothecaries, let's first see if their potions get spoiled when they prepare them in your land and if their remedies remain effective there. If their remedies do prove effective, I will send you additional physicians and apothecaries immediately. You will treat them the same way, as I describe above.

Since these men often ask you for local fabrics to make clothes, I would be greatly pleased if you distribute the fabrics in this way: You will give the vicar the goods for the priests and give the master craftsman the goods for the other craftsmen, and they can distribute them among themselves as needed. The same goes for cats, wooden beds,[46] and antelopes,[47] as well as any other great and small gifts you may offer them. They should be given to the persons I mention above so they can be equally distributed among them. In this way, they will all be satisfied with your gifts and will not resent you for giving everything to some and nothing to others.

2. I believe four schoolmasters will be enough for you. I am told that there are men in your kingdom who have the skill to teach. Nevertheless, I implore you to make these four follow the same procedure as the others. If they refuse, send them back to us, and I will send you others.

---

46. The term for "wooden bed" is *challo* in the original. Brásio lists the word as "unknown," while Jadin and Dicorato simply omit the term in their translation of this letter (173). The word *chalo* remains current in contemporary Brazilian Portuguese. The Florentine relation, Biblioteca Nazionale Centrale, Firenze, Panciatichiano 200, fol. 171 describes it as "a bed made on four stakes covered with a mat which they call chaló," which probably derives from the Kikongo word for bed, *nzalu*. See John K. Thornton, "The Florentine Relation: A Newly Discovered Sixteenth-Century Description of the Kingdom of Kongo," *History in Africa* 50 (2023).

47. The word that I translate as "antelopes" is *cheues*. It is also flagged by Brásio as "unknown." Jadin and Dicorato pass over the term in their translation, as they do *challos*. I am surmising that *cheues* means antelopes because the modern Portuguese term for a young gazelle is *quevel*. While the transposition of the dyad *ch* for *qu* is common in sixteenth-century Portuguese, I have not been able to establish whether some variant of the word existed in the sixteenth century. My translation of the term is therefore speculative and might well be incorrect.

As for the other Portuguese, it is up to you to decide how many people remain in your kingdom. The reason why your sons have Portuguese attendants is that they are great lords. These Portuguese men should know how to read and write and will therefore always do some service to God. Your sons should reward them with what they deserve, so that they have no reason to ask favors from you. Men do not leave their homelands without expecting to gain some profit for their efforts.

Also, some men will need to remain there to purchase slaves for the priests, craftsmen, and schoolmasters.

The men that you hire and that remain in your kingdom will be required to follow your orders while there. However, you should treat them as servants of yours and mine. I am told that the number of disturbances and unpleasant encounters they have had along the roads of your kingdom has greatly increased. I have no doubt that they are to blame for some of the mistreatment they receive. But at other times, the people's lawlessness could be the cause. You must be sure that no Portuguese man travels through your kingdom unless he's accompanied by a trusted servant of yours. You should order them to be sheltered in houses and not left to sleep outside, as they say happens now. I hope Kongo returns to what it was so that my goodwill and affection for it remain strong.

I read another letter from you in which you ask me to appoint your son as the bishop of Kongo.[48] Certainly, this was the main reason why I recalled him to Portugal because His Majesty and my lord Dom Manuel I had strongly recommended that I do so. Indeed, I would like him to travel to Rome to give the pope your obedience. All Christian kings have recently been ordered to send their prelates to Rome for a Vatican Council, and I recalled your son in order to send him there in that capacity.[49]

Due to a dispute between Pope Clement VII and my cousin Emperor Charles V, the pope was detained—rather, besieged in a city on the outskirts of Rome. He is now back in Rome.[50] As a result of this situation, all of us Christian kings have been ordered to send the highest-ranked prelates in our kingdoms to pay a visit to

48. The letter dated August 25, 1526 above.

49. This passage probably refers to early attempts to convene what became known as the Council of Trent, which would not begin until 1545. Pope Clement VII (1523–1534) delayed calling the Council in the wake of the violent events that came to be known as the Sack of Rome (1527–1528).

50. King João III is referring here to the Sack of Rome, carried out by the mutinous forces of João III's "cousin," the Holy Roman Emperor Charles V (I of Spain). Rioting over unpaid wages, Charles V's largely mercenary army stormed Rome in May 1527, killing around 1,000 Swiss Guards, slaughtering as many as 25,000 civilians, and laying waste to the city. Pope Clement VII managed to escape and take refuge in the Castel Sant'Angelo near the Vatican. Besieged by

the pope. As the bishop of your kingdom, your son will therefore need to travel to Rome. It will be a great honor to you, and I would value it above all else in this world because if my brother Cardinal D. Afonso goes to Rome, he and your son would travel together. If your son has not yet left by the time you receive this letter, since it might not be possible for him to make everything ready in time to board the ship that I have sent for him, I will wait until he arrives. I am sending a ship for him to travel in directly if he hasn't yet departed. This ship would take him to the island of São Tomé, and then two or three other ships would travel from there along with his.

You write in your letters that you do not want slaves to be traded in your kingdom because the trade is depopulating the land. I believe that you only say this because of the troubles the Portuguese traders have caused you, because I have been told that Kongo is very large and that it's so densely peopled that it seems as though no slaves have left at all. I am also told that you have slaves purchased outside the kingdom's borders and that you have them marry each other and convert to Christianity. For these reasons, the land remains heavily populated, and all this seems good to me. Moreover, with the new instructions that my people will now follow, combined with your own about having slaves purchased in the *pumbos,* or slave markets in the interior, I believe there will be plenty of slaves.

As for the slaves sold in Mbanza Kongo, there should be an area of the market designated for trading slaves in order to determine whether they are Kongo natives or outsiders. In this area, you should place two of your servants who would be able to recognize the slaves. No household should be allowed to sell any slaves if these two men aren't present for the sale. It would be difficult to have the royal officers you mention perform this task since they perform other more important duties for you. These two men will purchase slaves for the priests one day, and the next for the craftsmen, and the day after that for the schoolmasters. Each will pay their assigned share, as is the custom, and, this way, everything will come to a good end.

I can tell you now that, like you, I would like the slave trade in your kingdom to end and provide you with only the flour and wine to celebrate mass, if that seems suitable to you. For that I would need to send you only one lateen caravel per year. However, I don't believe it does you or your kingdom any honor because it is more impressive to export 10,000 slaves, 10,000 *manilhas*, or hoof-shaped ingots, and as many ivory tusks per year than to declare that there is no more trade in Kongo, or that only a single ship will travel there each year. With respect to this matter, as with the rest, it will be done as you wish.

Charles's riotous troops, Clement was eventually forced to surrender. He agreed to pay a vast ransom and cede considerable territory to Charles V.

You also ask me for a ship, which astonishes me because all my ships are yours. You must remember how João de Melo deceitfully sold you a ship. Even now, the 2,000 *reais* in expenses that he incurred remain outstanding, in addition to the aggravation it has caused you. Do not think that my predecessors and I have paid the costs of sending ships to sea in order to acquire profit and riches. Our only goal is to ensure the safety of the navigation and sea routes for our seafarers whose livelihoods depend on them. They are the ones who profit, not kings, as you know from your experience in your own kingdom.

You remember the fleet His Majesty and Lord Dom Manuel I sent at your request, commanded by Gonçalo Rodrigues, and how many losses it suffered there. The same goes for the fleet commanded by Simão da Silva, who died there. All royal affairs are like this; they are for the sake of honor, not profit. You might believe that the ships that travel there bring in enough money to pay for the crew's salary. Many times, however, they don't even make enough for that. So you may use my ships as if they belonged to you and do with them as you wish.

The fact that you don't want goods to be shipped to Kongo goes against the practice of every nation. Goods come to Portugal from every part of the world, and everyone who wishes to buy and sell merchandise can do so at will. In this way, countries are kept well-supplied with every good. Goods are also shipped from Portugal to every part of the world. Why would your noblemen rise up against you if they receive merchandise from Portugal? Do your power and greatness count for nothing? I am quite familiar with your type of warfare and how much you are feared by everyone.

It seems to me that at the very least you should allow *nzimbu* shells to circulate in the country because it is almost the same as your currency. It wouldn't be so bad if there were three or four stores in Mbanza Kongo where your subjects could buy and sell goods like every Christian kingdom.

Merchants would rush to your kingdom from every part of the world, which would glorify it and show that you are the greatest lord in Ethiopia [Africa].

3. I genuinely wish to put all these things and many others into practice with you. This letter does not include everything I would like you to do for the growth and greatness of your kingdom. Consider how long it's been since God bestowed the royal scepter upon you. You must have succeeded in gaining as much as twice your original territory, and I heard that you have fathered noble sons.

I was astonished to learn that when you march to war, you still raise banners made of animal hides and other materials from ancient times. This is not right. Your royal banner should be made of silk, like those of Christian kings and other lords and commanders, which is appropriate for royalty. If you haven't been able to make such banners because you lack silk, let me know.

I have learned that three of your sons are brave knights and great lords and that none of them has taken the oath as prince yet. I believe that it is very bad that you haven't considered what will happen after your passing. I therefore implore you to gather all your sons and brothers and the lords of your kingdom in a council as soon as you receive this letter, so you can decide together who will inherit your kingdom. After you have considered their good counsel, you should put your decision into effect by naming the one you agreed upon as the best suited for the role of prince and heir. You should choose the one who is the most Catholic and closest to God. This good beginning cannot lead to a bad result.

Nevertheless, I would like to discuss all this with you as someone I hold very dear. I am told that Dom Henrique Mwene Mbamba is your eldest son, a great lord in your kingdom, and beloved by all. It would be a grave mistake and sin to deprive someone of what rightfully belongs to him. Unless there are justifiable reasons why he does not deserve the position, I remind you that if this son of yours is as good and virtuous as they say, and since he is the eldest, you should not deny him what divine right grants to Christian princes.

After the prince has taken the oath for the security and tranquility of your kingdom, I recommend that from now on, you rest from the toils of this world to ensure your peaceful old age, that you seek rest for your body and glory for your soul. You will accomplish this by adorning the temple of God and leaving it to your son to take up arms and wage war. The most important knowledge a man can have in this world is the knowledge of how to save himself. For the sake of my deep affection for you, I implore you not to burden your days with more physical labor nor to leave your city. With the help of the craftsmen I send, for the praise of God and the forgiveness of your sins, you should quickly build the cathedral you told me about and place your tomb inside it. Judging by your great power to accomplish virtuous deeds, I'm confident that the cathedral will soon be completed, which will do so much service to God, and that he will allow you to build many others in your lifetime.

They tell me that you have well-built stone walls surrounding excellent lime-painted masonry houses. For the sake of your affection for me, please have the wall enclosure completed as soon as possible. You should have land cleared to build all the necessary houses in the style of the land. For your safety, you should move your quarters inside the walls. According to what I'm told, if you remain outside the walls, you face grave danger from fires.

I am astounded at how your kingdom and your nobility can preserve the way you receive payments. Since people know how to read and write in your kingdom, you should adopt the method that all of us Christian kings have: keeping revenue books for your kingdom where you record the names of all your nobles. Each noble should be ordered to pay a certain amount per year, and you should establish conditions of mutual obligation. They should agree to pay you, and you should agree not to seize their lands as long as they comply with the conditions of the contract. This way, they will remain secure and run your kingdom's trading posts, and you will ensure a steady stream of revenue and collect it more easily. They should make these payments annually, not every three years, as I am told they pay you now. Also, you should be sure that the most powerful men in your kingdom do not mistreat the common people.

In addition, I learned that you requested pitch and burlap from my trading agent on the island of São Tomé. It is being shipped to you. If, as I am told, you want them for ships to explore the source of the Congo River, I would be delighted if you carried this out since you have the power to do it. I will make one condition. You should not lead this exploration yourself; instead, you should stay behind and order your captains to do it. I grant you permission to use as many Portuguese men as you need for this expedition.

4. I'm told that you have some unicorn horns but that you're not sure if that's what they are. I would be grateful if you could send me a pair of them. If they are authentic, I will send you a letter about how you can take advantage of their healing properties.

I believe that you can do without a Portuguese magistrate with jurisdiction rights as well as a Portuguese notary, as has been the practice so far. You only need a notary from your country who can acknowledge receipt of the Portuguese contracts. You will need to have the Portuguese comply with these contracts since you know how differently they behave in your country. If it seems appropriate to you, you could have a Portuguese notary record your treasure; it is always better to have people who are not your countrymen looking after it. I'm told that Marcos Fernandes, a squire of mine, is currently in charge of this task for the entire country. I am very pleased that he can serve you this way. In order to avoid having multiple servants, you could place the notary in charge of providing you with wine and make him your cupbearer as well.

Please do me the great favor of not writing me with concerns about the goods the Portuguese traders bring to your kingdom. As soon as they take their goods into the interior and the people have gathered to buy them, you can order whatever you wish to be seized away from them or order it to be brought before you and then decree what seems best to you.

I'm told that you are very unhappy that we trade with the Ngola's kingdom. I don't know why since trading with him brings us more honor and profit. I've been informed that the Ngola was once a Christian and that you had him baptized. As you will know better than I, he had the church torn down because the Portuguese came to fight with swords inside the church. Now we need to find out whether he wants to reconcile himself with the church. If he doesn't, we can, by right, order him to do so. If he refuses to return to God, we will need to wage war against him. If he chooses the righteous path, then all of us Christian kings must supply him with the means for living according to our holy faith. I implore you not to be upset if I send a ship there for this purpose. I promise you that if he offends you in any way and refuses to become a Christian, I will give you all the help you need to avenge yourself against him. Since this is a matter of conscience and God commands it, I wish to put it into practice.

As you know, it would be very difficult for a priest to travel inland, and we lack the necessary supplies, so I think it's preferable to attempt to reach the Ngola's kingdom by sea, even if it's more expensive. If you are adamant about not trading with the Ngola and not providing him with articles for the church, I will clear my conscience and put it on yours because I am determined not to offend you. Nevertheless, look into your conscience, and consider that the Ngola's soul can be saved. That is worth more than the whole world, and we are obligated to devote our lives and money to saving the souls of our fellow people. If you believe that I'm driven by another motive, you may ask me directly. Don't stand against such a great service to God as bringing a soul to the knowledge of our holy faith. Don't trouble yourself about anything because our Lord has miraculously blessed you, Lord Afonso, king of Kongo, granting you so much honor and power, a reign that has lasted so long and earned so much admiration that no other kingdom in Ethiopia comes close to it. If you decide not to serve God in the Ngola's kingdom, then you should find a way to bring back Álvaro Eanes, the cleric you sent there, because it will be very risky and difficult for him to travel back by land.

The method of instruction you use in your schools has been highly praised. However, you should have the queen, your wife, take charge of the girls' instruction at home, separate from the boys, so they can learn without any impropriety. I recommend this because the queen is a literate and godly woman, and I'm told that you chose her as a companion because of those gifts and virtues. Nothing should stand in the way of good learning. To enable the schoolmaster to work better and give each student time to learn, you should not allow so many students together in the same classroom, as I'm told is the case, because they will not be able to receive as good an education as they would if there were fewer students. You can also feed a smaller number of students better than a larger number because no bodily need should keep any student from learning. These students should be chosen from your grandchildren, nephews, nieces, and the children of your nobles since I'm told that, among the many favors God has granted you, you have been blessed with more than 300 grandchildren and great-grandchildren. I can have someone bring up to 12 of them to Portugal, if you would like to send them. Here they can receive an education that will allow them to successfully take over and better govern their fathers' dominions. You will see how well I will care and provide for them. I'm informed that you have complained about the one or two who passed away here. God knows how much His Majesty, my lord, may he rest in holy glory, mourned their deaths. They did not die for lack of anything but by the will of God, which none of us can escape. This shouldn't cause you anguish or anxiety about sending others to Portugal; I assure you that under my power, they will be well treated and instructed. If it pleases God, they will return to Kongo, and God will grant you a long enough life to witness it and greatly rejoice.

If the vicar asks you to arrest a priest, you should do it and send him to the vicar in irons, so he can do with him what he deems best. If the vicar wants to send him in irons to Portugal, you should bring him to the ship under close watch. You should do the same with the master craftsman so that the priests and craftsmen fear the vicar as well as the master craftsman and will not violate their instructions.

5. Please let me know if you need anything from my kingdoms, and I will be as ready and willing to supply it as you will be to receive it. You may discuss all your affairs and desires with me because, as you can see from my letters, I share all of mine with you.

I address the following letters to your sons and nobles, so they will be certain that if they stray from what you have decreed either during your lifetime or after your death, they will have me as their enemy, just as I will be their friend if they comply with your decrees.

LETTERS TO THE NOBLES

1. Letter to Dom Henrique Mwene Mbamba, the king's eldest son and a high lord of the land.
2. Another letter to Mwene Nsundi, a son of the king and a great lord.
3. Letter to Mwene Wandu, also a son of His Majesty, a great lord and a very good Christian, and the bishop's brother on his mother's side.
4. Letter to Dom Pedro Mwene Swana, the king's younger son and a great lord.
5. Letter to a daughter of the king, who, in keeping with the custom of the land, is regarded as both the daughter and the mother of a king, and ruler of the entire Kongo.

6. Letter to Dom Jorge Mwene Mbata, who is the leading voice in Kongo and without whom, according to the custom of the land, no king may be elected.
7. Letter to João Álvares, commander of Kongo, a very literate man and a very good Christian, who is in charge of maintaining a secure entry into Kongo.
8. Letter to Dom Manuel, the king's brother and a great lord, one of the most devout Christians in Kongo.
9. Letter to Dom Rodrigo, the king's nephew, who has already been to Portugal, a very good man who rules over a great expanse of land and many people.
10. Letter to Dom Afonso, the king's brother, a youth and very good Christian, who serves as judge over the Portuguese.
11. A letter to His Majesty requesting that he send draft animals and all the necessary supplies for the journey from the port [of Mpinda] to the city [of Kongo].

ROYAL INSTRUCTIONS FOR THE VICAR OF KONGO

This is how you (insert name here) should proceed on this voyage for God's service and mine.

1. After embarking, you will travel to the island of São Tomé, where you will be provided with refreshments. Taking the necessary provisions, depart for Kongo. While you stop over on the island, follow the orders that (insert name here), who is serving as captain of the ship, will give you because he is an experienced man who knows how you should proceed.
2. Set up your purveyor on this island, who will be in charge of the goods you ship from Kongo.
3. When you arrive in the port of Kongo, do not stray from the captain's orders since he knows how to keep you and your shipmates safe and healthy.
4. As soon as you receive word from His Majesty, the Mwene Kongo, asking you to come, you should head out together. Do as the captain orders, rest and sleep where he tells you to, and never stray from his orders because that is what is advisable for your health and safety.
5. After you travel to the city and have an audience with His Majesty, I command you to stay together in your lodgings, just as you have traveled together, and to eat and sleep together. If there aren't enough houses available, His Majesty the Mwene Kongo will order any more you need to be built, according to your instructions.

6. I command you to place all the gifts from His Majesty the Mwene Kongo in strongboxes and make a complete list of everything. Give this list to a person that you designate for the task. Order another priest to record all your expenses and income with everyone's approval, that is, from the purchase and sale of slaves and other goods that bring you profit as well as any trading you engage in. Record all these transactions as carefully as you can.

When you send a priest outside the city to hear confessions, administer sacraments, or heal souls during Lent, I command you to have him take an oath to give you every item he acquires outside the city so that you can place it with the rest of the items you may have collected. If you discover that the priest you sent out of the city conceals something, no matter how small, I consider it just that he lose everything he has acquired up to that point and that you have him shipped back to me in irons.

As soon as you have gathered your money together, ask His Majesty the Mwene Kongo to provide you with men to purchase slaves for you. A few Portuguese should go with them, so they can spend your money most profitably. The characteristics of each land will determine what you need to do in order to conduct the most profitable trade. Once again, I command you to carry out your trade as peacefully and honestly as you can.

If you or another priest happen to acquire more goods than the others, I order you to appraise it among yourselves as you see fit. Once you have established the value of the goods, they will be sold in a brotherly fashion. Once you receive the proceeds, each one of you will gain a *soldo* per *libra* of what he contributed.[51] You should keep the money from the sale of the goods separate from the gifts and money you may receive from masses and alms. This way you will have fewer difficulties.

I order you not to distribute a single slave among yourselves in Kongo but instead send them all together to the island of São Tomé. If you sell any slave in Kongo, you can divide the proceeds there. By keeping and shipping all the slaves together, everyone will incur the same risk jointly as well. This way, when God brings you to the island of São Tomé, every one of you will have the same as everyone else. Therefore, you will all look after your earnings without quarreling with each other, and that is the greatest treasure in the world.

51. The *libra* (literally, "pound") was the unit of account (*moeda de conta*, in Portuguese) in sixteenth-century Portugal, i.e., the standard monetary unit of measurement for goods and other transactions. The *soldo* was a Portuguese tin coin minted in Asia (Malacca) of relatively low value. One *libra* was typically subdivided into twenty *soldos*.

If God takes any of you, you will make sure to record his passing and have your notary draw up an inventory of everything he earned before his death. If you have purchased any slaves that the deceased holds a share in, you will take his share of slaves and do your best to sell them along with the remainder of his goods. Once everything has been converted into currency, and you have it in hand, you will bring it to his heirs and not give it to any other person unless you receive instructions from me issued after the drafting of this document, granting you permission to distribute the money in a manner different from that which these instructions stipulate.

I decree that none of you should keep fabrics, wooden beds, monkeys, and parrots, acquired by any means, nor anything else worth money, unless you grant one another permission to do so. This condition will apply if any of you want to wear a tunic made of Kongo fabric or keep a parrot in your house. Whether it is slaves or any other article of value, you should under no circumstances claim sole ownership of anything, but instead, you will all share ownership.

If a priest is sent back to Portugal for just cause, you should give him all the goods that he has acquired up to the time of his departure or return and order him to leave the portion allotted to him on the island of São Tomé.

If he leaves without your permission, he will incur the penalty stated above, namely, he will forfeit his goods.

If, for example, a convict is removed from a church where he has sought sanctuary or something similar happens that makes excommunication necessary, before you take any action, you should consult with His Majesty the Mwene Kongo and ask him to restore the right of sanctuary to the church. You should proceed in this manner in every instance, as peacefully as you can and without conflict. If in the course of attending to church business, you decide not to celebrate mass on a certain day, I order the priests in your company not to depart from your command. If they celebrate mass secretly, they will face the penalty of losing all their goods, as described above. The same should be done any time they disobey you.

Your Lordship may add what you see fit to what I have noted down here and delete what you consider unnecessary.

In the verso: The letter delivered by Manuel de Castro to the Mwene Kongo.

Letter from the King of Kongo to João III (January 1, 1530)

SUMMARY—*He sends his notes about the actions of the Portuguese in Kongo—He also sends two hoof-shaped silver ingots [*manilhas*], a gift from a nobleman from Matamba*

Sire:

I order the men who carry this letter, Jerónimo de Leão and my nephew Dom Simão, to kiss Your Highness's hands. This letter contains my notes on everything that your countrymen have done to me in this kingdom. I ask Your Highness to closely consider these notes because I unburden my conscience in them. Please grant me the favor of a prompt response carried by Jerónimo de Leão. It is a great consolation to have him by my side because Queen Dona Leonor,[52] may she rest in holy glory, sent him to this kingdom to serve me. He also brings you two hoof-shaped silver ingots [*manilhas*], which a nobleman who is from a part of my country called Matamba sent me.

Written in Kongo on the 28th day of January of 1530 by Dom João Teixeira.

Signed: His Majesty Dom Afonso

TO: The most high and powerful prince king and lord, His Majesty the King of Portugal

Letter from the King of Kongo to João III (February 9, 1530)

SUMMARY—*He announces the departure of Jerónimo de Leão for Portugal—He gives him the strongest recommendation and asks that he be sent back*

Jerónimo de Leão, a squire and a servant in the house of Queen Leonor,[53] may she rest in holy glory, is leaving our kingdom now. The queen sent him to serve us, carrying a letter from her. He has been living with us for seven years and has never done anything

52. See n. 18 above.

53. See n. 18 above.

wrong or anything to cause my displeasure, nor has he done any disservice to us. In everything he has done, he has demonstrated the good breeding, Christian doctrine, and many virtues he acquired during the many years he spent in the queen's great royal house. Because we are so pleased with the respect he has shown us and his good services, we granted him permission to travel and visit his noble house on the condition that, once he has shown the reverence he owes Your Highness as his king and lord by kissing your royal hands, he returns to us to continue serving us, to our great solace. I implore Your Highness to listen to his account of the affairs of Kongo and the region of Ethiopia because he can inform you better and more truthfully than anyone else who has observed them. His long-standing experience in this country as well as his knowledge and discretion, make him capable of this task. Your Highness should listen to and have faith in him. What I tell you about him is sure to be helpful to you.

We therefore implore Your Highness to please send Jerónimo de Leão back to this kingdom if you must send word to us by someone or order a servant to carry out duties in your service. Given the services he has done for us, and since he belongs to your royal house, we will place more faith in him than anyone else you may send to our kingdom. His visit would also bring us great joy and pleasure, and we would be very grateful to Your Highness to welcome him.

Written in the City of Kongo, on the 9th day of February of 1530 by João Teixeira

Signed: His Majesty Dom Afonso

TO: The most high and powerful prince king Dom João

Letter from the King of Kongo to Pope Paul III (February 21, 1535)

SUMMARY—*He offers his obedience as a Christian king to the pope—He nominates his ambassadors—He requests the favors that the pope usually confers*

Most blessed holiness father and lord Paul III by God's mercy supreme pontiff of the holy mother church. I, Dom Afonso, by the grace of God, king of Kongo, Vungu, Kakongo, Ngoyo, of the lands up to and beyond [the river] Nzari, lord of the Ambundus and the Ngola, Kisama, Musulu, Matamba, Muyllu, Musuku, of the Anzicos and the conquered territory of Mbanza Loango, etc. As a faithful Christian king and an obedient son of the holy mother church, I humbly kiss Your Holiness's feet.

I write to inform you that, by the boundless mercy of Lord God, I and most of the peoples in my kingdoms and dominions have come to know the holy Catholic faith, the law of our Savior Jesus Christ. We have received the sacrament of holy baptism, which our Lord, in his most holy mercy, willed us to receive. After we received the word of God, we have done as much as possible through every means we could muster to perform divine offices and observe ecclesiastical ceremonies, as well as perform God's service and increase our holy faith. For this reason, most blessed and holy father, as I am a faithful Christian king, an obedient son of our holy mother church, and a firm believer in the ways of our most holy faith, I and my successors, as well as the subjects in my kingdoms and dominions, have long desired to be received under the grace, favor, and assistance of Your Holiness and the Holy Apostolic See. We seek to obtain from you the spiritual favors that other Christian kings and princes receive for the wellbeing of our souls and the growth of our holy faith. I and the other Christians in Kongo desire your spiritual favor and assistance and wish to be guided by the sacrifices of the holy mother church, so that the faith of Jesus Christ our Savior may continue to grow in every part of our kingdom.

I am sending Dom Manuel, my brother, a member of my royal council and our principal representative; Dom Afonso, our nephew on my brother's side once removed; Dr. Francisco Múcio Camerte, my spokesperson and interpreter; Dom Afonso, my nephew further removed; and Dom Henrique, my nephew on one of my brothers' side, all people I trust. Empowered by me, their superior, and acting in my name and that of my successors, they will offer Your Holiness and the Holy Apostolic See the obedience we owe you as a Catholic and Christian king and people.

I implore Your Holiness to kindly receive and graciously hear our ambassadors and believe them when they speak on my behalf. I ask Your Holiness to grant them, with the generosity you usually give other Christian kings and princes, all the graces, indulgences, freedoms, and privileges that they justly request for myself, my successors, and the clergy, churches, monasteries, and people of these kingdoms and dominions. May our true Lord God preserve you, most holy and blessed father, and your state in his service for many years.

Written in the City of Kongo on the 21st of February in the year of our Lord 15[35] by Dom João Teixeira.

Signed: His Majesty Dom Afonso

TO: The most holy and blessed father, Lord Paul III and his successors[54] [Holy] Apostolic [See]

54. Words missing from the manuscript.

Letter from the King of Kongo to King Dom João III (December 28, 1535)

SUMMARY—*He requests His Majesty to admit António, a nephew of the novice master Gil, as a student in the Collège de Sainte-Barbe in Paris because he hopes to make him a great man of letters and provide instruction in the Kongo language*

Sire:

Since Your Highness fondly embraces any matters that are of service to God, we bring the present one to your attention. When Your Highness sent novice master Gil to this kingdom to serve us, he brought his nine-year-old nephew with him. We took the boy as our valet so he could learn to speak our country's language as a native of these kingdoms. For God's sake and our own, we implore Your Highness to include him among the Portuguese students you have sent to pursue their studies in Paris.[55] We hope in God that when he finishes his studies, his learning will allow him to do a great service to God by preaching the Christian doctrine to our peoples in their native language and ensuring the salvation of their souls. Novice master Gil, who is completing the term of service Your Highness assigned him, will be traveling back with his nephew António, our valet, in order to introduce him to Your Highness and remind you of our request. We would be most grateful if Your Highness granted us this favor.

Written in the City of Kongo by João Teixeira on the 28th of December of the year 1535.

Signed: His Majesty Dom Afonso

TO: The most high and powerful prince Dom João of Portugal

---

55. According to Father António Brásio (1906–1985), editor of the *Monumenta Missionaria Africana*, King Afonso I alludes here to the renowned Collège Sainte-Barbe, founded in 1460 (and until its closure in 1999, the oldest college in Paris), where many Portuguese pupils pursued their studies at the time.

The King of Kongo to King Dom João III (December 28, 1535)

SUMMARY—*He announces the departure for Portugal of novice master Gil, his preacher—He asks the king to send him back as soon as possible with the papal bulls absolving his marriage and legitimizing his children, so he may live as a good Christian*

Sire:

We detained our preacher, the novice master Gil here and did not allow him to leave before we recovered from our illness, which, by God's mercy, has not killed us. We therefore beg Your Highness to listen to him with compassion and send him back to us so that we may hear the word of God from his lips for our solace and the salvation of our people. This is why we have written to summon him back from the island of São Tomé. He is returning to Portugal to comply with Your Highness's order but will bring us back the papal bulls absolving our marriage and legitimizing our sons,[56] which we urgently need in order to live without sin and for the salvation of our soul. We would be most grateful if Your Highness granted us this favor.

Written in the City of Kongo by João Teixeira, on the 28th day of December in the year 1535.

Signed: His Majesty Dom Afonso

TO: The most high and powerful prince Dom João of Portugal

56. Contemporaneous documents, including letters by King João III and the papal nuncio, suggest that King Afonso I may have been requesting dispensation to marry a woman who was related to him by a third degree of consanguinity (i.e., a first cousin or great niece). As indicated by Afonso I's letter of January 18, 1526, acknowledging receipt of a gift of mourning clothes from the Portuguese monarch, the king of Kongo may have recently become a widower.

Letter from Manuel Pacheco to King Dom João III (March 28, 1536)

SUMMARY—*The state of the clergy—The king of Kongo's plan to discover the lake—The king of Kongo's qualms about the mines and smelting factories*

Sire:

While in the kingdom of Kongo, I was given one letter from you to the king of Kongo and another to me. In the latter, you remind me to send back a few priests whose guilty consciences prevented them from leaving because they were here without permission from the bishop of São Tomé, in particular a certain novice master Gil. After His Majesty the King of Kongo read this letter, he conveyed Your Highness's instructions to master Gil and the others. Everyone obeyed, except master Gil, who made every effort to avoid leaving. Since Your Highness ordered his departure, I had to compel him to leave against his will. He is now heading back to Portugal, Sire. Since the way he lived while he was here confirms that he fears little for his conscience, I worry about what he will say to Your Highness and the bishop to attack my honor. I am letting Your Highness know this since I will not be there to defend myself.

Regarding the creation of a new Christian society here, as well as the way of life of the priests who are here now and those you will send here in the future: Your Highness urgently needs to instruct the bishop to find a way to ensure that they remain celibate and trade fairly. Their indulgences cause much trouble here.

1. Sire, I have already informed Your Highness in previous letters that one of the main reasons why His Majesty the King of Kongo has kept me here and not granted me permission to return to Portugal is that he wanted me to sail two ships he had built upriver to the [Yellala] falls and try to explore the river and discover the lake that is its source.[57] Since I had to extend my stay due to the delayed arrival of equipment for this expedition that the king of Kongo had requested from Your Highness, he appointed me magistrate in the jurisdiction Your Highness gave to him. I accepted this duty because I considered it to be in the service of God and Your Highness. I have done this by upholding the law here and performing other services every day, as Afonso de Torres, as well as the trading agent and other

57. Cartography of the time proposed the origin of the Congo River as well as the Nile and Zambezi as a Central African lake.

officers, will inform Your Highness. I have therefore kept the men who are here within the bounds of the law, enforced good trading practices, and ensured that the ships are fully loaded. There aren't enough ships arriving here to prevent cargo from being left on the dock. During the five years I have been here, never have fewer than four to five thousand slaves been shipped per year, not including the countless number who die because of the lack of ships. I have therefore ordered the goods belonging to those who have passed away here to be warehoused, shipped to the island of São Tomé, and then handed over to Your Highness's officers of justice so they can be delivered to their rightful owners. I have acted in a similar way with affairs of war, for which His Majesty sometimes requests my assistance. For the past five years, I have helped him fortify his kingdom in the face of the many wars that heathens wage against him without receiving any reward, which I don't want anyway, since my only reward is that Your Highness knows that I serve you and your royal estate as I should.

2. I also inform Your Highness that a man named Rui Mendes arrived in this kingdom accompanied by some smelters, claiming that he was a royal trading agent for the copper mines. Because His Majesty the King of Kongo is so suspicious, when he heard that a trading agent was arriving with smelters, he believed his kingdom was going to be taken over along with the mines. He was therefore sorry to hear that the trading agent was coming, saying that Your Highness would need no other trading agent except him. Nevertheless, the king had forges made and shelters set up in his royal court and inside his palace. It was there that he had the ore smelted, a sample of which he sent you when he wrote to tell you about the mines and which I believe is steel. Afterward, I reminded him of the true reasons behind Your Highness's decisions so often that he agreed to allow the smelters to go to the copper mines and inspect a lead mine accompanied by one of his nobles. I don't know what news they'll bring. He only wants the satisfaction of serving Your Highness. However, he was concerned when he heard that Your Highness rules over India and that you order a fortress built wherever gold and silver are found. He sometimes mentions this fact in response to my requests.

3. At this point, I have nothing more to report to Your Highness since every year I write in detail to Afonso de Torres, to the trading agent and the officers responsible for overseeing the slave trade. I tell them to send many ships here crewed by pilots and sailors who are not traders. His Majesty the King of Kongo already had enough carved wood to make two ships, and this fills me with hope that the exploration of the source lake can be done this year. I don't know what outcome it will bring. I can only hope, Sire, that he will do it this year because if he doesn't do it

now, he will never do it. I beseech God to bring prosperity to Your Highness and your royal estate and keep you in his blessed service.

Written March 28, 1536.

A servant of Your Highness.

Signed: Manuel Pacheco

TO: His Majesty our lord

FROM: The kingdom of Kongo / matters related to his service

Letter of Mandate from the King of Kongo (February [22], 1539)

SUMMARY—*He nominates representatives to travel to Rome and declare their obedience to Pope Paul III in his name—He grants them the power to request all the favors and privileges for the sake of spreading the faith in the kingdom's provinces*

I, Dom Afonso, by the grace of God, king of Kongo, Vungu, Kakongo, Ngoyo, of the lands up to and beyond Nzari, lord of the Ambundus and the Ngola, Kisama, Musulu, Matamba, Muyllu, Musuku, of the Anzicos and the conquered territory of Mpanzulumbu, etc., declare to all those with the authority and responsibility to read this letter that, as a Christian king and obedient son of the holy mother church, I grant, in my name and in the name of my successors, the obedience I owe to the current head of the Catholic church, the most holy and blessed Pope Paul III, as well as to his successors elected to the Holy See. I therefore nominate as my delegates, ambassadors, and authorized representatives Dom Manuel, my dear brother and main representative in my royal council; Dom Afonso, my nephew on my brother's side; Dr. Francisco Múcio Camerte, my spokesperson and interpreter; Dom Afonso,[58] my nephew further removed; and Dom Henrique, my nephew on one of my brothers' side, all men whom I greatly trust.

58. The name is illegible in this manuscript. The name I have included appears in Afonso's February 21, 1535, letter to the pope.

I grant special powers and permission[59] to all of them, the head of the mission as well as each one of its members, to make all the truthful oaths that the ambassadors and authorized representatives of Christian kings are required by custom to make in these circumstances.

As a Christian king and obedient son of the Holy See, I pledge to abide by the obedience promised by each one of these representatives, as specified above. I pledge to fulfill these promises and seek to protect and grow the holy Catholic faith and uphold it with all my might. I also pledge to obey and lend all the assistance I can to Your Holiness and your successors elected to the Holy See, as is my right and obligation as a faithful Christian king.

I therefore grant authority to each and every one of my delegates and ambassadors, since they are all equally empowered, to request, in my name, from Your Holiness and the Apostolic See all the favors, indulgences, privileges, and freedoms that their royal instructions specify as well as others they may consider appropriate. To the best of my ability and as is my duty, I grant them the power to carry out all these tasks since it is right and necessary. To show that everything I have written here is true, I have ordered this letter of mandate to be drafted and signed with my signature and stamped with my seal.

Written in the City of Kongo by Dom João Teixeira on the 22nd day of February of the year of our Lord Jesus Christ 1539.

Signed: His Majesty King Dom Afonso

Letter from the King of Kongo to King Dom João III (March 25, 1539)

SUMMARY—*He recommends a grandson and five nephews he is sending to Portugal; two will pursue their education, two will travel on a mission to Rome, and two will take minor orders—He refers to others sent to Portugal in the time of King Dom Manuel*

Sire:

I am sending six of our relatives to accompany our brother Dom Manuel, whom we are sending to Rome to pledge our obedience to the pope, as we inform Your

59. Several words were erased from the manuscript, so I have had to reconstruct a substantial portion of this sentence.

Highness in the letter he is carrying. We write to let Your Highness know how they are related to us, so they can be granted the favors to which they are entitled. Dom Manuel is our grandson, the son of our daughter, a nobleman with many lands and vassals, and a member of our royal court's twelve peers. Dom Pedro de Castro is our nephew on the side of both parents since he is the son of first cousins.[60] Dom Pedro has already been to the Kingdom of Portugal with our son the bishop Dom Henrique, may he rest in holy glory. These two will stay in the Kingdom of Portugal to learn to read and write and study the ways of the Lord God. Dom Mateus and Dom Henrique are also our nephews, and we have ordered them to accompany our brother, the ambassador we have sent to Rome, so they can study and report on the good and holy things they witness in Rome to those who have not seen them. Dom Gonçalo and Dom Francisco de Meneses are our nephews as well and quite close to us. From a very young age, they were raised in the church and our chapel. They will be receiving minor orders and the learning they require to be eligible for other orders when the time comes.

We beg Your Highness the favor of agreeing to welcome them, provide for them, and treat them as our blood relatives. By doing so, Your Highness will ensure that they follow the instructions we gave them when they left this kingdom. We send Your Highness this reminder and ask you this favor because when your father the king was alive, may God keep him in his glory, we sent, at his request, twenty-odd youths, grandsons, nephews, and relatives of ours with António Vieira to be educated for the service of God, for that was the intention of the lord king. António Vieira left some of these youths in the land of Mpanzu a Lumbu, who are our enemies. We were able to rescue them later with great difficulty. Vieira left a few others on the island of São Tomé, and they came back to us later. Vieira took only ten youths to your kingdom. To this day, we don't know what has happened to them, if they are dead or alive. We have no news to give their fathers and mothers. Since no one knew or remembered that they were relatives of ours, we presume that they all died in neglect. We expect the ones we're sending now will have a different fate and earn Your Highness's favor and kindness. May the Lord God most high protect your life and royal estate in his service.

60. Afonso was clearly aware of the distinction between how kinship was calculated in Kongo versus Portugal. In seventeenth-century Kikongo (we have no sixteenth-century texts), there is no special designation for nephew; it would be *mwana*, which also means "son" and extends to "nephew" in that generation. See Giacinto Brugiotti da Vetralla, *Regvlae quaedam pro dificillimi Congensium idiomatis faciliori captu ad Gramatacae norman redactae* (Rome: Propaganda Fide, 1659), p. 98.

Written in the City of Kongo by Dom João Teixeira on the 25th day of March of the year 1539.

Signed: His Majesty King Dom Afonso

TO: The most high and powerful king, his lord and majesty, the king of Portugal, our brother

FROM: His Majesty the King of Kongo on the 25th of March

Letter from Gonçalo Nunes Coelho to King João III (April 20, 1539)

SUMMARY—*He mentions communication difficulties with Lisbon—On behalf of Gimdarlache, he tells about the discovery of copper, lead, and silver mines—He asks for radical secular and ecclesiastical reforms and the expulsion of all the whites from the kingdom.*

Sire:

Before such a great and powerful king, a ruler so virtuous and enlightened that he outshines Alexander the Great, one should use few and succinct words. I have been in the Kingdom of Kongo for more than fourteen years. I came here to escape miserable poverty that I could not bear. I was able to overcome my poverty through the honest work I have done in this country as the magistrate and notary of His Royal Lordship the Mwene Kongo. I am nearly seventy years old and have witnessed many things which, by right, Your Highness should know. I believe Rui Mendes, the royal minerals agent, has delivered some of this information to you in his letter. If I have failed to let Your Highness know the information that I provide here sooner, it is because in this country, it is considered to be a greater flaw to write to Your Highness than to commit a serious crime. For example, guards have been placed at ports and at the crossing points from here to Soyo, forty leagues from here. All the letters sent to or from the Kingdom of Portugal and the island of São Tomé are seized and brought to His Royal Lordship the Mwene Kongo. May God forgive whoever advised him so poorly. Whoever this person may be, he is not the first to advise him to do this. It is widely believed that people who feared receiving orders for their punishment from the Kingdom of Portugal considered it safer to have all correspondence go to His Royal Lordship the Mwene Kongo. That way, if there are letters about the preservation of justice, they can never be read. This allows the men involved to find out if someone has written Your Highness to condemn their offenses by imposing new laws that would harm these men and limit trade.

Gimdarlache, a German smelter who stayed in Kongo after Rui Mendes left with several craftsmen, has asked me a few times to write Your Highness about the mines he discovered. Because it is in the service of Your Highness, I will do so despite any danger or suffering this may cause me. Since I do this for the sake of justice, my suffering would be justified.

Gimdarlache has written to the royal chaplain and asked him to present his letter to Your Highness. In this letter, he confirms that he has experienced the mines firsthand and seen huge amounts of wealth and riches with his own eyes. This seemed so unlikely to me that I told him I would only write what he reported if he took an oath that it is all true. He assured me that the yield from copper, lead, and silver was greater than the revenue of all of Spain. Because he assured me that all of this was true and because it was in the service of Your Highness, I wrote about it here so that you may do with this information what is best for you.

I have described the country's secular and religious situation in my letters to the royal chaplain so he could keep Your Highness fully apprised of the situation. As I believe Álvaro Peçanha has written Your Highness, Your Highness should address these problems by implementing the measures I propose. Things are going from bad to worse, depending on the part of the country. If you delay too much, you will not be able to repair the damage we can expect. Truthfully, I tell Your Highness that it would be a great help to the human and divine realms to expel all the white men from this kingdom, both clerics and laymen, and replace them with new and good people. Envy and greed rule the world, and they have made their home in the kingdom where we currently live.

Written in the City of Kongo on April 20 of the year 1539.

Signed: Gonçalo Nunes Coelho

TO: His Majesty our Lord

FROM: Kongo

Letter from the King of Kongo to King João III (December 4, 1540)

SUMMARY—*He mentions the advantages that Portugal could gain from Kongo—He requests a loan of 5,000 cruzados for expenses related to the mission he sent to Rome*

Sire:

It is needless to point out the reasons why Your Highness should not forget us since they are so obvious. However, in case you have forgotten them, we will still mention some here so you can commit them to memory.

One of the titles of Your Highness, among several that so properly belong to you, is lord of Guinea. This is not a small dominion since I rule only over Kongo. The remaining territory is vast, and Your Highness should be duty-bound to God and to us to look after it well since you are our lord and brother, and we are bound together by God. Given our spiritual alliance, we owe God nothing less. Thanks to the efforts of your ancestors, we came to know the holy Catholic faith. With the help of our Redeemer and Your Highness's goodwill, we remain faithful to him to this day. While we owe this to Your Highness, you are no less obligated to us to honor the spiritual benefits that have resulted from our conversion. Because Christian princes have their foremost obligation to Christ, we implore Your Highness[61] to please do as we request. The whole world, especially Christendom, would praise you highly for it. More than anyone else in the world, Your Highness should clearly be the foundation of the holy Catholic faith in this land of Ethiopia since it is under your instruction and influence, and you would be greatly honored by this crowning achievement. For our part, we can only do our best to earn Your Highness's favor and goodwill by ensuring that you maintain this honor by not turning away from us. We have not chosen the earthly path over the eternal as is commonly done nowadays.

Let us place all of Guinea on one side and Kongo on the other and then consider which side gives you the greatest profit in trade. We will see that Kongo alone brings more revenue than all the other river regions combined. If Your Highness has the revenue and expense books from your trade examined, you will clearly see that no other king from this part of the world takes better care of Your Highness, grants you more favors, and holds your affairs in higher regard than we do. We

61. The end of the sentence is disturbed by a hole in the manuscript, so I have had to reconstruct it.

have opened markets, roadways, and waterways; we have opened *pumbus* [inland slave markets] even though all this has earned little praise from Your Highness. What seems worst to us is that Your Highness has not moved our alliance forward. This should not be the case since you should support and assist us with our needs, not as you do with the other kings of Ethiopia but in proportion to our merit. Just as we soar higher than the others with respect to divine favor, so should Your Highness consider our affairs more valuable than theirs.

It should therefore be considered appropriate in your kingdom if we are given help and support in the form of proportionate revenue for our legitimate needs, such as the one we are currently experiencing. It is draining much of our income, and no one but Your Highness can come to our aid. In honor of the passion of our Lord Jesus Christ, we beg Your Highness the favor of loaning us 5,000 cruzados in exchange for 150 *lufukus* [measures of 20,000 *nzimbu* shells], which is the currency used to purchase slaves in our kingdom, to cover the expense of sending our brother, the ambassador Dom Manuel, to pledge obedience to the pope. For this financial aid, we will set up a *pumbu* [inland slave market], where enough slaves will be sold to reimburse in Portuguese coin the amount Your Highness would graciously lend us.

Since we, most excellent and powerful prince, are well aware of your greatness, we trust that our eminently reasonable request will not be denied. If the benefits to Your Highness[62] and to the noble knights of your house would justify giving us aid, how much more justifiable would it be when you consider the benefits it will bring to our royal person?

Most high, excellent and powerful prince, my lord and brother, may our Lord God protect your person and royal estate.

Written by Dom João in the City of Kongo, on the 4th of December of the year 1540.

Signed: His Majesty King Dom Afonso

TO: The most high, excellent and powerful prince Dom João, my lord and brother, King of Portugal, by the grace of God

FROM: His Majesty the King of Kongo, ~~March~~ (*sic*) [December] 4, 1540

62. This phrase is also my own reconstruction since this section of the sentence is missing in the manuscript. The original manscript (ANTT CC I-68-92) has a hole with about enough space for three or four words.

Letter from the King of Kongo to João III (December 17, 1540)

SUMMARY—He gives a positive account of Manuel Pacheco—He complains about the insolence of the ship captains and pilots—He accuses Friar Álvaro of plotting to kill him and Álvaro Peçanha of betraying him, which was the reason why he expelled the latter from the kingdom

Sire:

Most high and powerful Lord and Prince, as your loyal brother, we write to Your Highness with an account of the affairs of our kingdom, as we usually do in our letters to you. For a long time, we have waited expectantly for your responses about important issues. Because two years have passed and we have yet to receive an answer from Your Highness about these issues, we assume that some legitimate reason has prevented you from receiving some of our letters, such as those we sent with your good servant Manuel Pacheco, in which we gave a detailed account of these issues. Anything we did not include in the letters, we asked Manuel Pacheco to tell Your Highness in person, requesting Your Highness to trust everything he told you since we have the utmost confidence in him. As we learned later, the French seized some of these letters from Manuel Pacheco. Others were taken from him on the island of São Tomé to punish him [for his loyalty to us] and prevent Your Highness from seeing them. This is the only explanation we can perceive.

We have written Your Highness many times requesting you to allow the ships that arrive here to take the letters we have written you, which detail everything that has happened here. Whenever we want to send a servant of ours to deliver the letters, we are told that there is neither a ship available nor someone who can carry the letters. There was a time when the ship captains and pilots who arrived at the port of Mpinda in our kingdom behaved considerately toward us. As soon as the ship docked, they would send word to us if they carried anything we needed. Nowadays, they do this neither when they arrive nor when they depart, which pains us greatly. I do not know[63] if the reason why this happens is that Your Highness granted rights to the trade and the low quality of the people who carry out the trade. We implore Your Highness to make changes to be sure that your interests will be served. Even now, after preparing for our brother and ambassador's departure [to Portugal], we have been informed that the ship he was supposed to travel

63. Afonso uses "I" here instead of his customary royal "we."

on had left port without him. The only reason why this happened was to prevent us from sending word to you about the troubles we suffer here.

We have told Your Highness before about how the "virtuous"[64] priest Friar Álvaro plotted against our life by ordering seven or eight white men to fire their muskets at us while we attended mass one Easter Sunday and kill us in front of the true Savior of the world, who condescended to save us and miraculously deliver us from this great danger. The musket ball grazed the hem of our shirt, struck our head magistrate, and then continued its trajectory by killing one man and wounding two others. The reason for this attack can only be that they want to make someone else king. God has delivered us from this trial and commanded that we be granted the life we have devoted to serving him.

Álvaro Peçanha, a native of your kingdom, plotted to kill us. As became clear to us, this is the payment he gives us for all the favors we conferred on him. Consider, Your Highness, how these foreigners schemed to kill the king of the country where they came to earn their living. We merely ordered Peçanha and his brother to leave our kingdom as a [light] punishment for these faults and the disservice they did to God. Showing no remorse, Peçanha traveled to the port of Mpinda and from there to Portugal. We truly believe that he wished us dead. But he instead seems to seek death for himself since he has sailed back to our kingdom, even after we expelled him to be punished in Portugal for treason, for trying to overthrow us by force. Your Highness should deal with these and [related] issues as seems reasonable to God and in his service and yours.

Most high, excellent, and powerful prince and brother: may the Lord God always preserve your royal person and state.

Written by Dom João in the City of Kongo, on the 17th of December of the year 1540.

Signed: His Majesty King Dom Afonso

TO: The most high and powerful prince, king of Portugal

FROM: His Majesty the King of Kongo, December 17, 1540

64. Quotation marks added to underscore Afonso's ironic use of the term.

Letter to His Majesty King João III (March 20, 1541)

SUMMARY—*Several Portuguese subjects complain about Fernão Rodrigues Bulhão's misconduct in Kongo*

Sire:

So many wrongs have been committed in Kongo that it would be a greater evil to silence them, so we are writing about them here since we are Your Highness's servants, and so that you may set right any wrongs that are possible to fix and would be to your benefit. As for those that are impossible to repair, only God can remedy them.

After the departure of one of your vassals—who had carried out many disruptive actions that were of little service to God, Your Highness, this country, and its native peoples as well as foreigners—Kongo was left in such a state of peace that everyone seemed to share the same tranquil nature, both in religious and secular affairs. It seemed to us that so much mutual understanding could only come from our Lord God, who had decided that it was in his service to put an end to past disputes. We lived in happiness and in hope of greater well-being under this harmony until the evil adversary who is against all peace sent a Portuguese man named Fernão Rodrigues Bulhão, who claims to be a resident of Vila Franca de Xira on the banks of the great Tagus River. It would have been better if God had never allowed him to be born. As everyone saw, this man did not bring any resources or goods to the kingdom other than the concealed greed that his actions soon revealed.

In this way, he hatched a scheme and claimed that Álvaro Peçanha, a Portuguese nobleman, as well as other white and local men, were planning to kill the king of Kongo and name someone else king. To support his lie, he found and bribed both Black and white witnesses, who testified according to statements that he prepared himself. These witnesses testified without being sworn in, and Bulhão was both the questioner and a party to the process. In some cases, he was also the notary and supplemented the witnesses' recollections with details they knew nothing about. He questioned witnesses both day and night, wherever he liked, and by instilling the fear of death into these witnesses, he defrauded both the king of Kongo and Your Highness's vassals, as did the witnesses, who said whatever he wanted them to. He had others arrested and tortured in prison and would not release them until they testified as he wanted. In this way, he had Álvaro Peçanha banished from the kingdom under the accusation of treason. He confiscated Peçanha's property, leaving him ruined and destitute, the victim of this terrible lie and unimaginable betrayal. Indeed, the witnesses themselves are recanting their testimony, admitting it was false, both under oath and not. They wish to clear their consciences, and some have confessed in front of the king of Kongo and all of his people.

Not satisfied with all these offenses, Fernão Rodrigues plotted and ordered other *nkanus*[65] or judicial inquiries in which he involved His Majesty's sons, grandsons, and nephews, white and mixed-race men as well Beninese, freed slaves, and captives. The wickedness of this weaver of plots had become so rampant that everyone came very close to killing each another. If God forbid this had happened, not a single white man would have been left alive. The local people have already begun to call for their deaths since so much evil comes from white men. There is no doubt that the white men would have been killed if His Majesty had not managed to prevent it with his great wisdom and devout Catholicism, insisting on investigating the truth of the situation. In order to carry out these abuses with greater impunity, Fernão Rodrigues worked with those who had benefitted from his actions to become the magistrate, even though there was a magistrate already in place who has always used the authority of his title to perform great service to God and Your Highness.

With the title of magistrate, Fernão Rodrigues has even greater power to commit the above-mentioned wrongdoings. He has stolen the goods of the orphans and dead men and traded them with impunity. He gifts these stolen goods to undeserving people against Your Highness's orders so they can trade them on his behalf and theirs. He also oppresses the people with his unjust verdicts, abusing the power of his position as magistrate, which would not be tolerated in any other country because here, no one wishes to do Your Highness a disservice and pave the way for other, greater evils. For these reasons, most of the white men are leaving this kingdom.

Your Highness should understand that if we do not expel this plague of a man from this kingdom, he will bring it to ruin all by himself, both in the spiritual and worldly senses. Since his accursed disease spreads over everything, it requires a punishment that matches the extent of his blame. This punishment will serve as a true remedy for the people of this country and a cure for their distrust. It will also set a strong example for the white men who remain here. The truthfulness of everything we are reporting to Your Highness can be confirmed by the sixty or seventy

65. *Mocanos* in the original, which Brásio incorrectly describes in a footnote as synonymous with *mocambos*, a word he defines as revolts by runaway slaves. Jadin and Dicorato translate the word similarly as *révoltes de noirs dans la brousse* (revolts by blacks in the bush) (220). The correct Kikongo term is *nkanu* (plural, *mikanu*), which means judicial inquiry.

Portuguese men in this kingdom, if Your Highness thinks it is necessary to question them. If they have not signed this letter, it is because there are many here who would reveal that they had done so. Diogo Botelho, a noble knight in your royal house, can inform Your Highness of all this. He headed back to Portugal soon after arriving in this kingdom because he could not tolerate the evils that he saw during his short time here and which do great disservice to God and Your Highness.

May our Lord God most high preserve the life of Your Highness and the greatness of your royal state. We kiss your royal hands most humbly, as our lord and king.

City of Kongo, March 20, 1541

Signed:
Gaspar Lopes Martim Varela
Master Francisco Mutius, notary
Gonçalo Nunes Coelho
António Calado

TO: His Majesty our Lord, [from those] in his service

Letter from Dom Manuel, the King of Kongo's Brother (January 9, 1543)

SUMMARY—*Having been ill and away from his family for many years, he wishes to board a ship to Kongo as soon as possible—In the meantime, he requests His Majesty give him the necessary provisions—He requests the return of 400 cruzados belonging to his brother*

Sire:

I have sent my son Dom João Manuel, the bearer of this letter, to ask Your Highness[66] for the favor of responding quickly to the letters that my brother His Majesty the King of Kongo has written to Your Highness. I have been away from my kingdom for four or five years and have spent all the money I brought with me. I am now a man of advanced years and so ill that I do not dare travel from here to Almeirim, where Your Highness is now staying. Moreover, my brother the

66. This section of the manuscript is partly gnawed, so what follows is a reconstruction.

king is so old that I fear I will not find him alive when I travel to Kongo, may God not permit it. In addition, I have not received a single cent of allowance from Your Highness because Fernão,[67] whom Your Highness charged with delivering it to us, did not take care to send it to us. For the sake of the passion of Jesus Christ, I request Your Highness to grant me permission to return to my wife at the beginning of this summer, which is coming up quickly. Or Your Highness could provide me with everything I need until I am able to return to my kingdom.

I therefore ask Your Highness to deliver to me, as a loyal trustee, the 400 cruzados that the deceased Diogo de Campos acknowledged in his will that he owed my brother the king. I have explained this at length to Your Highness in a petition that Dr. Cristovão Esteves submitted on my behalf. Because I'm closely related to my brother, it is fitting that I request this favor from Your Highness.

May the lord God on high increase Your Highness's days and royal estate and keep you in his service, as we all desire.

Written in Lisbon today, the 9th of January 1543

This unworthy servant and vassal of Your Highness

Signed: Dom Manuel

TO: His Majesty, my lord

The Reign of D. Afonso I of Kongo (1493?–1543)

SUMMARY—*D. Afonso, Prince of Kongo, is baptized—Struggle for the succession of the kingdom—Death of D. Afonso*

Rui de Sousa returned to this Kingdom of Portugal. The prince, son of King John of Kongo, returned from his station along the border with the enemy. Once the church was completed, he was baptized along with several of the noblemen who followed him and many of those who attended the ceremony. The prince took the baptismal name Afonso as a token of his affection for Prince Afonso, the son of King John II of Portugal. As more and more people were baptized, the devil lost more and more of his jurisdiction; in order to recover some of what he had lost,

67. Last name missing.

he now labored to bring a royal person under his power. The devil took for himself a son of the king called Panso Aquitimo, who refused to receive the water of baptism. Panso Aquitimo distanced himself from interactions with his father and gathered into his fold some of those who shared his purpose.

Along with the son's hard-heartedness, the devil used the priests to provoke the king. The church decreed that the king must choose only a single wife and must dissociate himself from the many other wives he kept. As a result of the priests' pronouncement, the wives would lose their status as royal spouses. But the royal wives persuaded the wives of the king's confidants to manipulate their husbands into advising the king to reject this pronouncement. The king, an old man already inclined to maintain his past ways of living, was swayed by the advice of his own people. The religious fervor he'd felt at first began to chill, and he began to return to the old ways and customs.

Prince Afonso, who held on to his Christian faith more firmly, was unhappy with these developments and defended his faith with all his might. The men admonished by the prince began to turn the king against him until they'd forced him out of the king's grace; these men convinced the king to instead admit his heathen son Panso Aquitimo into his favor. They reasoned that if the Panso were chosen as king, they could once again live according to their past customs. Ethiopians [i.e., Africans] are easily swayed by fetishes and put all their credence and faith in them. So, as part of their evil work, the devil's ministers convinced the king that the Christians had taught his son, Dom Afonso, how to fly, and that every night he flew eighty leagues away from the kingdom to visit and couple with those of the king's wives who were trying to hinder the king; Prince Afonso then returned home on the same night. The devil's ministers also told the king that Prince Afonso knew how to dry up rivers. Moreover, they said Prince Afonso prevented good news from becoming known, which meant that the king would not receive as much tribute from the rest of the kingdom as usual and would thus not have enough to reward those who served him faithfully. As a result, they said, Prince Afonso would rise up with the rest of the kingdom against him.

Outraged at his son because of these and other falsehoods, the king cut off Prince Afonso's tax assignments. But some noblemen who were friendly with the prince reproached the king for his actions, telling him the accusations were lies and that his son was seen, both day and night, in the lands where he was living. To learn the truth about his son, the king ordered the use of a common fetish. He had a youth take this fetish, tied up in a piece of fabric, to Cufua Coanfulo, one of the wives he suspected. The youth told Cufua Coanfulo that the fetish was sent by Prince Afonso to protect her from the death sentence the king had imposed on her and all his other wives. But, since she was innocent of the crime that the gift being sent to her was [meant to protect her from]; she told the youth to leave the piece of fabric on the ground. She then notified the king of his son's offering, saying a number of things that proved her innocence and confirmed that everything he had been told about the prince was false. A few days later, without giving any advance notice, the king sent for the prince and reinstated and increased his tax assignments and land holdings. The public address he then delivered was attended by those who sowed suspicion about the prince. Having caught them off guard, the king had them immediately put to death.

But it did not take long for the devil to find another path. As the prince was returning to his lands, enlightened by God and having earned his father's favor, he issued a proclamation declaring that any person found with an idol in his home would be put to death. The prince's opponents notified the king as soon as this happened. They exaggerated the gravity of the situation, leading the king to believe that the people were sufficiently inflamed to rise up against his royal person if he did not deal with this matter.

Summoned to the court to address this issue, the prince declared that he would sooner lose his life than obey his father; he did not waver from his commitment to this task in praise of God. Among the prince's followers, there was a certain D. Gonçalo, a prudent man who professed the Christian faith and zeal for the honor of God, who endeavored to bring the king to his side. D. Gonçalo's prudence, the prince's words, and God's governance all influenced the prince's decision to delay his journey to the court. He stalled, using one pretext after another, all related to his service to the king, the rule and management of the land, and the collection of the money sent to him. In the end, because God wished to end the prince's persecution, he afflicted the king with an illness so serious that he died of it.

The king's death also eased the minds of our men, many of whom—given the kind of life the king led and the scant yield of their efforts with him—had separated from him and allied with the prince. With the aid of the clergy, the prince converted and baptized the greater part of his dominions, which were called Isundi. This displeased the king and all those who had returned to their earlier way of life. The prince was aware of his father's displeasure. While the king was sick, some noblemen summoned the prince and informed him that his father was on the verge of death. They also told him that his brother Panso was advancing toward the city with a group of his armed followers and that Panso intended to take the city for himself. But the prince never put faith in these reports. He believed that his father feigned his illness in order to lure him into the city. However, once the king's death was confirmed, he made his way to the city in only three days since he had already begun his journey there before the news of his [father's death] reached him. Before he entered [the city], his mother, the queen, sent word that he should come in secretly by night without a raucous group of men. She advised him to send in his men a few at a time, carrying baskets on their heads with their weapons inside, which they should say were provisions they were bringing for her.

After entering the city in this way, the prince came out to a great square in front of the royal palaces, where he ordered the country's notables to gather and gave a well-reasoned speech. At the end [of his speech], before leaving [the city], the [nobles] proclaimed him king according to their custom, with a great celebration, loud cheers, and music. This clamor was heard in the city's outskirts, where [the prince's] brother was awaiting more men to make himself king by force.

When he [Panso] discovered the cause of the uproar and how few men his brother had with him, he attacked the city without waiting for any more of his men to arrive. At that time, King Afonso only had thirty-seven Christians with him. As a man skilled in the craft of war and better ruled by God, he ordered his men not to worry about him but instead await his brother's invasion in the great courtyard, for he trusted in God's pity and believed that he would grant him victory over his enemies. His hope held true: his brother's force was the first to enter the courtyard, raining arrows, and it was a miracle to behold how the few men who fought with the king called out to the apostle Saint James, and [the king called] upon the name of Jesus for help, and he kept invoking him until his brother's men turned their backs on him and ran into [the king's] second company, which crushed them.

In order to grant this Catholic king complete victory, God [ordained] that as his brother was fleeing through a forest, he fell into a hunting trap set for some wild beast, where he was caught, along with one of his chief commanders, by those in pursuit. This commander, having no faith that his life would be spared once he arrived before the king, sent a plea to him, in the name of the God he believed in, to allow him to be baptized before being put to death, for he did not want to lose his soul, even if his body was already lost. [This commander] believed that this was the one true God that men must worship because during the battle he had seen a great number of armed men on horseback following a sign just like one the Christians worshipped, and they fled from the battle because they saw this fearful vision of their enemies. Seeing this man's penitence, not only did the king have him baptized, but he pardoned the man as well. To atone for his role in the attempted coup, this man, along with his entire family, was charged with sweeping and cleaning the church and bringing water to baptize all the heathens. This was the penitence imposed on this honorable and Catholic man, D. Gonçalo, who greatly assisted the king with matters of faith. When this commander was baptized and took his given name, D. Gonçalo, the king appointed him commander of a portion of his dominions and [put him in charge] of the collection of his revenues.

Panso Aquitimo, the king's brother, perished in resentment, as much from the wounds he sustained when he fell into the hunting trap as from his sorrow at his circumstance.

Once these matters were settled, the king maintained peace in his kingdom, despite several rebellious noblemen in several regions who fought for their idolatry. Yet God always gave him victory over them. God granted him so much life that he reigned for fifty-odd years and died when he was eighty-five years old. From the time he received the faith until the last day of his life, not only did he embody all the virtues of a true Christian prince, but he even served as an apostle by preaching and converting on his own a great part of his people, devoting most of his life to safeguarding the honor of God. In order to become a better preacher, he learned how to read in our language, and he studied the life of Christ and the Gospels, the lives of the saints, and other Catholic doctrines, which he was able to understand after some instruction from our priests, [and then] proclaim it all to his barbarous people. He also sent his sons, grandsons, and nephews, as well as some noble youths to the Kingdom of Portugal to study letters, not just ours but also Latin and sacred. In this way, there have already been two bishops in his kingdom, who served God by exercising their office and gladdened the kings of Portugal, at whose expense all these deeds were carried out.

In memory of this miraculous victory that our Lord conferred upon King Afonso, in which his enemies saw the sign of the cross and the celestial cavalry of angels accompanied by the apostle Saint James; and because his father was baptized on the day of the Invention of the Cross [May 3]; and also because, by means of the [royal] seal King John [II of Portugal] had sent him (as mentioned above) [in *Décadas*, Book 3, Chapter 9], he obtained great victories over the Mundequete [Bateke] peoples, he took as his coat of arms a flowery white cross in a red field with a blue chief of the shield. In each corner of the chief there are two golden scallop shells, in memory of the apostle Saint James, and a silver stem along with one of the five escutcheons of Portugal, which is in blue, with five silver bezants in saltire, etc.

João de Barros, *Ásia,* Década I, Book 3, cap. 10.[68]

68. João de Barros (1496–1570) is considered one of the greatest Portuguese historians of the country's overseas expansion. He was appointed *feitor* or trading agent of the *Casa da Índia e da Mina* in 1532 and about a decade later offered the king (João III) to write a history of the Portuguese in India, Asia, and Africa entitled *Décadas da Ásia (Decades of Asia)*, three volumes of which were published in his lifetime between 1552 and 1563.

ADDITIONAL TRANSLATIONS

Pope Paul III's Brief to the King of Kongo (March 17, 1535)

SUMMARY—*He recalls the creation of the diocese of São Tomé, to which the Kingdom of Kongo belonged—He recommends Dom Diogo Ortiz de Vilhegas, the first bishop of that church*

Dearest son in Christ, illustrious king of Kongo, salutations in Christ:

It is worthy of praise and divine recognition when secular princes support and honor church dioceses, and above all, the prelates nominated by the pope's authority.

Our predecessor, Pope Clement VII, of glorious memory, founded the diocese of São Tomé and elevated the existing parish church on the island of São Tomé to the rank of cathedral, calling upon Saint Thomas. He received the consent of his brothers the cardinals, myself among them. He founded the diocese of São Tomé by his papal authority and gave it the territory spanning from the fortress of São Jorge da Mina on the African mainland and the diocese of the Island of Santiago to the Cape of Good Hope. Your Kingdom of Kongo is located within this territory, as well as the islands you mentioned. With the consent of the cardinals, Pope Clement VII placed our son Dom Diogo at the head of this new diocese, as you will read in the relevant papal briefs.

Before these briefs could be written, our predecessor passed away. We have continued to grant our goodwill upon the elected bishop Dom Diogo. In recognition of his merits, we wish him to take charge of this diocese. May God support his ministers. In the name of your faith to God and the Holy See, we urge Your Majesty to support him in this office and provide him with all the assistance you can. With God's help and your support, Dom Diogo will succeed in discharging his apostolic duties.

Written in Rome, on the 17th of March 1535.

Confirmation of letters sent about a bishopric that cannot be granted (not from the Auditor Jerome Bios).

In the verso: March 17, 1535 Anno Domini. Concerning the elected bishop of São Tomé and adjoining parts of Africa and the Atlantic Ocean.

Received from the king of Kongo, which is close to the Cape of Good Hope [sic].

Note from the Secretary:[69] Concerning the affairs of the Black King that we call the king of Congro (sic), though if we restrict ourselves to the Congro (sic), one could call him emperor, king, or duke, depending on the territory in question.

Pope Paul III's Brief to the King of Kongo (May 5, 1535)

SUMMARY—*He is very pleased to learn of the progress in spreading the faith—He urges him to continue with these goals*

Pope Paul III sends his papal greetings and blessings to his dearest son Afonso, the illustrious King of Kongo.

We were very pleased to learn that you have accomplished the work not only of a good king but also of a shepherd of souls since you have been moved by great piety to convert all your own people as well as your neighbors', continuously preaching and urging them to follow the faith. You have ensured that our holy religion will spread in those regions by admonishing, cautioning, and even, whenever necessary, converting other heathen kings by force.

May Almighty God bless you, my son, and may he protect your religious passion by granting his bliss and good fortune upon you. May his infinite goodness, which has given such a sublime example of piety in our times, grant you and your loved ones a long life. Although it is unnecessary to ask you this, dearest son, we urge you to maintain your righteous principles and to guide your children to behave as piously as you have. Leave them your virtues along with your kingdom as your legacy. We have no doubt that this is what you have done and will continue to do.

69. In Italian in the original.

Even though God will grant you greater eternal rewards, we send you the Holy See's goodwill, and in the future, we will not hesitate to comply with all your pious desires. You will see this when the occasion presents itself.

Rome, May 5, 1535. The 5th year of our Pontificate.

Odorico Raynaldi, *Ecclesiastic Annals* from the year 1535, no. 59.

Epílogo e Compêndio da Origem da Congregação de São João Evangelista (1658)

By Jorge de São Paulo[70]

CHAPTER 8

Concerning two clerics who took up trading in the Kingdom of Kongo and their successors

The most refined cunning disguises itself in the clothes of false virtue. A vice that shows itself is evil, but one that conceals itself is twice as evil since it cloaks itself with piety in order to sin. What does the conquering of the world or the circumnavigation of the earth matter when our deeds contradict our public goal of uprooting idol-worshipping and introducing the Catholic faith, and greed becomes insatiable? And when the way we carry out our goal is used to gain riches? A deed that is intended to be virtuous usually becomes wicked because of our weakness. When, even as religious passion brings about a holy conquest, it is soon corrupted by the selfishness of greedy souls, the great curse of humankind? When greed is more powerful than religious observance? Our order expected our mission to Kongo to bring us great recognition and one of our greatest glories by saving those heathen souls through the great spiritual passion of the missionaries and without causing any scandal to the bishop Dom Henrique. Nevertheless, in an unexpected turn of events, one bad servant of this secular order, by masking his greed for earthly goods

70. Jorge de São Paulo, author of this *Epilogue and Compendium of the Origin of the Congregation of Saint John the Evangelist*, was himself a member of the order. Although not widely known among historians, this unpublished history of the congregation, currently housed in the Library and District Archive of the city of Braga (Biblioteca e Arquivo Distrital de Braga), remains a key source of information about this influential secular religious order.

with zeal to spread the light of the Gospel among the heathens, gave a bad account of his character.

Like the twelve apostles of our Lord Jesus Christ, the thirteen clerics of our order who traveled to Kongo in 1508 to continue the conversion of the idol-worshippers all strove to accomplish the service of God and bring spiritual healing to the heathens. They desired to convert them to the faith far more than to trade earthly goods. Yet there was one perverse Judas among them called Fernão de São João. He returned to Kongo with the bishop Dom Henrique and had permission from the order only to acquire goods to support his sisters with alms obtained from preaching and celebrating mass. Driven by selfishness, which is the main agent that corrupts the hearts of men, he went against the rules of the order and took up trading and trafficking. He set up a trading post in São Tomé and hired a commercial agent in Lisbon. Even though his true trade should have been with heaven by preaching the Gospels, and even though he was often warned by the bishop and reprimanded by the Priors General of the Congregation, he never complied with their orders. Instead, he continued to carry out his trade with merchants while wearing the habit, which greatly scandalized His Majesty Dom Afonso and the people that he had been sent to set a good example for. For thirteen days,[71] he continued unrepentant, despite the warnings he received to stop these commercial activities and return to his convent. He never did, and he revealed himself to be ungrateful to the religion in which he was raised. No amount of reasoning ever convinced him to stop because he was caught in the grip of avarice, which turns gold into a weapon against religious obedience and chains stronger than iron. Greed tears open the doors of the heart to force out the virtue of poverty. It closed his heart to his superiors' saintly warnings. He was accompanied in these trading activities by Father António de São João, but the latter obeyed the order and returned to the Portuguese kingdom to hand over everything he had acquired to the Convent of São João de Xabregas, as is recorded in the complaint that the Prior General submitted to His Majesty Dom João III.

Father Fernão de São João continued unrepentantly in his activities. He compelled the Priors General Diogo de Santa Maria and Simão de São Miguel to order all the merchandise that he had acquired while wearing his habit, which he had stored in *Casa da Índia* in Lisbon[72] and in the island of São Tomé's trading post, to be confiscated and handed over to the Congregation's prosecutors. In 1532 and 1535, His Majesty issued decrees for the seizure of his goods. Because the congregation foresaw that Fernão de São João might abandon the habit of the order and

71. Section partially erased in the manuscript and reconstructed here.

72. See n. 8 above.

appeal to Rome to keep the large quantity of goods he had acquired, the order informed the pope of Fernão's disobedience and his illicit trading while wearing the order's habit, to everyone's outrage, and requested His Holiness Pope Paul III to refrain from accepting any appeal on his part that he should recover his merchandise because he was no longer a cleric.

Once his goods were brought to this kingdom, the congregation sold them all and locked away the money in a strong box in São Bento, along with the money from the Kingdom of Kongo. All the proceeds were distributed between the Church of Saint Elói [Eligius] in Lisbon and the Loios Convent in Arraiolos to be put toward their good works. Fernão de São João was issued an order of detention and was punished for his transgressions and other offenses related to his illicit trading activities, which so scandalized His Majesty Dom Afonso Mwene Kongo and his vassals as well as His Majesty the King of Portugal Dom João III and his ministers, who had received the Mwene Kongo's complaints about this insubordinate trader. Fernão de São João was harshly punished and transferred to the newly founded Convent of Arraiolos. The construction costs for the convent reached 300,000,[73] of which more than 100 came from the sale of the confiscated goods. Because this money was spent on the convent's construction, the Captain General of the order directed an annual requiem mass with three biblical lessons and evensong to be celebrated in this convent for the soul of Father Fernão de São João.

Everything contained in this chapter refers to the Convent of Saint Eligius.

---

73. No currency or coin is specified. We may plausibly surmise that the chronicler is referring to the *real*, the unit of currency in Portugal and its colonial possessions until the fall of the Portuguese monarchy in the early twentieth century (c. 1911), when it was replaced by the *escudo*.

Index

Bold page numbers indicate an image or image caption.